THE INTER-AMERICAN HUMAN RIGHTS SYSTEM

To Olivia

The Inter-American Human Rights System

SCOTT DAVIDSON

Associate Professor of Law, University of Canterbury

Dartmouth

Aldershot • Brookfield USA • Singapore • Sydney

Published by
Dartmouth Publishing Company Limited
Gower House
Croft Road
Aldershot
Hants GU11 3HR
England

Dartmouth Publishing Company
Old Post Road
Brookfield
Vermont 05036
USA

British Library Cataloguing in Publication Data
Davidson, J. S. (J. Scott), 1954-
    The inter-American human rights system
    1.Human rights - America
    I.Title
    323'.097

Library of Congress Cataloging-in-Publication Data
Davidson, J. Scott, 1963-
    The Inter-American human rights system / J. Scott Davidson.
        p.   cm.
    Includes bibliographical references and index.
    ISBN 1-85521-776-7 (hardbound)
    1. Inter-American Commission on Human Rights. 2. Inter-American
Court of Human Rights. 3. Human rights -- America. I. Title.
    KDZ578.I5D38 1996
    341.4'81--dc20   96-36538
                                                                    CIP

ISBN 1 85521 776 7

Printed in Great Britain by Antony Rowe Ltd, Chippenham, Wiltshire

Contents

Preface

From the Arctic wastes of Canada to the hostile coast of Tierra del Fuego the Western Hemisphere embraces a wide diversity of political, economic, social and cultural systems. These range from the affluent stable democracies of the north to the often precarious political systems and economies of the Caribbean and Central and Latin America. While it has often been assumed that the shared geography of the region implies a common political and economic destiny for all American states, the expression of regional solidarity and cooperation has often been fitful, if not dysfunctional. The swings between dictatorship and democracy in much of the Southern Cone, the more or less constant irritant of the Castro government in Cuba and the waxing and waning of the United States interventionist adventures in the region have all tended to render the idea and fact of cooperation elusive. The main vehicle for cooperation has been the Organization of American States (OAS), but this has often been perceived as an instrument of, and a mouthpiece for, United States hegemony in the region. Despite this, the OAS has spawned a sophisticated human rights system in the post World War Two period which has demonstrated the capacity to evolve to meet the changing circumstances of the hemisphere. From its inauspicious beginnings as an 'autonomous entity' of the OAS, the Inter-American Commission on Human Rights has developed into a fully fledged organ of the Organization with extensive powers under both the OAS Charter and the American Convention on Human Rights and its related instruments. Its powers to conduct investigations into the state of first and second generation human rights in all states of the hemisphere, to conduct on-site investigations and to receive petitions from individuals in all OAS Member States bears witness not only to its continual development within the framework of institutional evolution, but also to its tenacity. While the jurisprudence of the Commission may not always please the purist, it nonetheless serves as a useful reminder to lawyers that much may be accomplished by legal creativity tempered by a sense of political realism.

Like the Commission, the Inter-American Court of Human Rights began its activities in a low key. Unlike the Commission, however, this was not because the Court had to struggle to establish its institutional identity and competence, but because states were unwilling to accede to its contentious jurisdiction and the Commission was reticent in exercising its discretion to remit cases to the Court. Despite these unpromising beginnings, the Court's work has increased steadily in both its advisory and contentious jurisdictions. It may be no coincidence that the expansion of work under its contentious jurisdiction reflects a decade-long trend in favour of democratic politics in some of the states of the Southern Cone. Certainly present and future judges will not, unlike their predecessor Judge Maximo Cisneros, be able to bewail the lack of opportunity to hear a contentious case during their term of office.[1] The future of the inter-American human rights system seems, at the time of writing, to be assured. While it is probably too early and too unwise to suggest that the struggle to establish the system and its credibility is over, there is no doubt that the prognosis is better now than it was in earlier decades.

This is not my first foray into publishing on human rights in the Americas, but it is my first attempt to provide a narrative account of the system and the jurisprudence which has emerged from its institutions. While it would be impossible to better Lawrence LeBlanc's pioneering work on the early development of the Commission or to compete with Cecilia Medina's matchless account of the Commission's work in the area of gross and systematic violations of human rights, I hope that this book will provide an introductory and reasonably readable account of the institutions, processes and jurisprudence of the inter-American human rights system in a single volume. There has, to my knowledge, been no previous attempt to analyze the jurisprudence of the Commission and the Court to any great extent, so I hope that my efforts here will provide a small basis for future research. Coverage of the structure and work of the Inter-American Court of Human Rights in this book draws liberally from my previous book of the same name which was published by Dartmouth in 1992. It has, of course, been necessary to take account of the manifold developments which have affected that institution in the intervening four years.

It is customary in a book of this kind to thank those people without whose aid and assistance it would have been difficult to accomplish the task of creation. In this instance it is more a case of rounding up the usual suspects. I should like to thank Margaret Greville and her unfailingly helpful and cheerful staff in the University of Canterbury Law Library for tolerating my frequent requests for difficult to obtain OAS materials. To my colleague David

Rowe I wish to offer my sincere thanks for giving so freely of his time in preparing the page proofs of this book. I must also express my gratitude to Philippa Le Couteur who undertook some valuable research for chapter 7 and who also proof read and prepared the index to this work. Without her help the publisher's deadline would not have been met. Finally, I should like to thank my wife Olivia and my son Paul for their support during the time that this book was being researched and written. The cheerfulness and wit with which they punctuate every day provided the necessary leaven for an enterprise such as this. As usual, all sins of commission and omission remain mine alone.

Note

[1] Declaration by Judge Maximo Cisneros, Advisory Opinion OC-5/85 of November 13, 1985, *Compulsory Membership in an Association Prescribed by Law for the Practice of Journalism,* Series A, No. 5. See infra, p. 192.

Table of Cases

Table of Treaties

1 The Inter-American System and Human Rights

Introduction

In order to appreciate fully the way in which the inter-American human rights system now functions, it is necessary to understand its present structure and the way in which this has developed. The protection of human rights has always been an integral part of the principles upon which the Organization of American States (OAS) has been based and a number of organs have, within the framework of the OAS, developed their competences in this field in an evolutionary and incremental way. The first part of this work is therefore devoted to a brief description of the development of the inter-American system in general in order to place the system's concern with human rights in context.[1]

Origins and Development of the System

The origins of the modern inter-American system may be located in the creation of the International Union of American Republics at the First International Conference of American States which took place in Washington DC between 2 October 1889 and 9 April 1890.[2] The International Union was not an international organization in the now accepted sense of the term, but rather a system of conferences the objectives of which were to facilitate the exchange of commercial information and to settle disputes peacefully among the Member States.[3] The International Union was assisted in its activities by the Commercial Bureau of the American Republics which was established at the same time.[4] The Bureau, which was based in Washington DC and which was supervised by the Secretary of State of the United States of America, operated as the Union's secretariat and provided a clearing house for commercial information.[5] This initial approach to inter-American relations reflected the United States' desire for hegemony in the hemisphere which had been articulated as early as 1823 by President Monroe.[6] The Monroe Doctrine was premised upon non-intervention by the European powers in the Americas and the establishment of the United States of America as the region's leading power.[7] By sponsoring and underwriting the creation of a system which was essentially commercially orientated the United States consolidated and ensured its economic and political dominance in the Western Hemisphere. Whatever the motivation for the creation and development of the Union, however, the United States was instrumental in forging a regional organization which was largely free from European interference and influence, and which was able to speak for the hemisphere as a whole, albeit with a strong North American accent. At the Fourth Conference which took place in Buenos Aires in 1910, it was decided that the International Union and its Commercial Bureau should be endowed with broader functions and renamed the Pan-American Union.[8] The revised mandate of the new Union again reflected US hegemony and its functions thus remained broadly economic and essentially non-political and non-military. The conferences continued under the auspices of the Union until 1938.[9]

At the Inter-American Conference for the maintenance of Peace in Buenos Aires in 1936 a new system of cooperation called 'consultation' was developed in order to provide a mechanism under which the American s could respond to urgent events affecting the hemisphere.[10] A number of consultations dealing with questions of war, peace and security took place both prior to and during the Second World War. Before the end of the war in 1945 a special conference was called in Mexico City on the problems of war and peace.[11] The major concern of the Latin American States at this conference was the increasingly powerful position assumed by the United States following its pivotal role in the success of the Allies against the Axis Powers. They were also particularly concerned that they might be relegated to a position of secondary importance both in terms of the post-war international order, especially in the creation of the new international organizations designed to keep the peace and to reorder the chaotic economic situation, and in terms of a reduction in economic assistance from the United States to facilitate domestic restructuring. The Latin American States considered that the most effective way to counter these concerns was to strengthen the institutional character of the Pan-American Union by endowing it with permanent organs with which to carry out its functions and pursue its objectives. One of the most important outcomes of the 1945 Mexico conference, however, was the adoption of the Act of Chapultepec.[12] This non-binding conference declaration reaffirmed the concept of solidarity, security and collective self-defence among the American States and was subsequently transformed into the Inter-American Treaty of Reciprocal Assistance 1947[13] or, as it is more commonly known, the Rio Treaty. This treaty transformed the political commitments contained in the Act of Chapultepec into legally binding obligations and provided for a consultative organ of foreign ministers which would meet whenever the peace and security of the region was threatened by an armed attack.[14] The Rio Treaty also proved to be the forerunner to the OAS whose Charter was adopted in 1948 at the Ninth International Conference of American States which was held in Bogota, Colombia.[15] The Charter, which is also sometimes known as the Pact of Bogota, entered into force on 13 December 1951.[16]

Since its entry into force in 1951 the OAS Charter has been amended four times. On each occasion amendments have sought to give effect to perceived weaknesses in both the Organization's structure and its articulation of the primary principles of regional solidarity, collective security, non-intervention, democracy and human rights. Following President Kennedy's announcement of the Alliance for Progress in 1964 the Member States of the OAS decided to place greater emphasis upon economic and social development within the region. It was thus at the Second Special Inter-American Conference which was held in Rio de Janeiro, Brazil in 1965 to discuss how progress might best be made in these areas that it was recognized by the Member States that the structure of the Charter was inadequate to pursue any new social and developmental goals which the Organization might set itself. Progress on institutional amendment and development to facilitate coordination and cooperation in the economic and social field was not made until the convening of the Third Special Inter-American Conference in Buenos Aires in 1967.[17] The Protocol of Buenos Aires, which was adopted at the 1967 conference but which did not enter into force until 1970, established the basic institutional structure of the OAS which is still in existence today. The General Assembly replaced the Inter-American Conference as the plenary organ of the Organization, and three Councils with broad executive powers were created. These were the Permanent Council, the Inter-American Economic and Social Council and the Inter-American Council for Education.

The second amendment to the Charter took place in 1985 at a Special General Assembly held at Cartagena de Indias, Colombia.[18] This meeting took place at a crucial period in the political development of Latin America. While totalitarian regimes of left and right were still in power in Latin and Central America, the fall of the military junta in Argentina seemed to herald a trend towards democratization in the region. The Protocol of Cartagena de Indias therefore integrated the concepts of representative democracy and non-intervention as 'essential purposes'[19] of the OAS and set in train certain further institutional amendments. In particular, the post of Secretary-General of the OAS was established which gave the holder of this office powers similar to those of the Secretary-General of the United Nations under Article 99 of the United Nations Charter.[20] Further concern with poor economic development and the threat to democracy within the region became evident during the late 1980s and early 1990s and in 1992 the Special Council convened a meeting to consider these questions. Following this meeting the Protocol of Washington was adopted on 14 December 1992.[21] This protocol not only provides for the circumstances in which, following the overthrow of a democratically elected government in one of the Member States, the Member State in question might be suspended from participating in the OAS, but it also strengthens the cooperative and collaborative procedures for dealing with extreme poverty in the hemisphere. Here Article 33 of the amended Charter lays down the economic and social goals to which Member States agree 'to devote their utmost efforts' and a number of other provisions deal with the institutional amendments appropriate to pursuing such goals.

The fourth and latest amendment to the OAS Charter was brought about by much the same imperatives which have beset the Organization since its inception. These are the broad variety of problems confronting the OAS today: the lack of institutional coherence and cohesion, duplication of effort by its organs in certain areas and decreasing resources. In order to deal with these issues, the OAS General Assembly held its Nineteenth Special Session on 10 June 1993 in the Nicaraguan capital city of Managua. The Protocol which was adopted at this session made a significant institutional amendment to the Charter.[22] By bringing together the Inter-American Economic and Social Council and the Inter-American Council for Education, Science and Culture it created a new organ: the Inter-American Council for Integral Development.[23] This organ is entrusted with the functions of supporting the General Assembly in pursuit of the Organization of American States' development goals and policies, and promoting and coordinating activities in this broad area.

The Organization of American States

The OAS, membership of which is open to all American states which ratify the OAS Charter,[24] is a regional arrangement or agency within the meaning of Article 52 of the United Nations Charter.[25] The many purposes and principles of the Organization are set out in Articles 2 and 3 of the Charter, while the rights and duties of states and procedures for peaceful settlement of disputes are contained in Chapters IV and V respectively. Chapter VI elaborates the system of collective security, largely by reference to, and incorporation of, the 1947 Rio Treaty, while Chapter VII deals in a detailed and comprehensive fashion with the question of integral development. The remainder of the Charter is mainly concerned with the institutional structure of the OAS.

The Institutional Structure of the Organization of American States

This section is designed to give an overview of the main organs of the OAS and their general functions. This is of importance from the point of view of human rights since the various organs of the OAS have greater or lesser degrees of responsibility for their promotion, implementation and protection in the Americas. Chapter VIII, which consists of a single provision, Article 52, states that 'the [OAS] accomplishes its purposes by means of the following organs:
a) The General Assembly;
b) The Meeting of Consultation of Ministers of Foreign Affairs;
c) The Councils;
d) The Inter-American Juridical Committee;
e) The Inter-American Commission on Human Rights;
f) The General Secretariat;
g) The Specialized Conferences; and
h) The Specialized Organs.'

Each of these organs or category of organs will be examined in turn below.

The General Assembly. The General Assembly is the plenary body of the OAS and is defined in Article 53 as the 'supreme organ of the Organization of American States'. It is composed of all the Member States of the Organization[26] and has an exceptionally broad mandate to oversee the totality of activities of the OAS.[27] The General Assembly meets once a year in a short session,[28] although it may be called into special session with the approval of two thirds of the Member States if circumstances are deemed to warrant this.[29] By virtue of Article 53(a) the competence of the General Assembly in the field of human rights would appear to be all-embracing.[30]

The Meeting of Consultation of Ministers of Foreign Affairs. This body is designed to meet at short notice when 'problems of an urgent nature and of common interest to the American states' arise.[31] A meeting of the Foreign Ministers may also be convened by the Permanent Council at the request of any Member State of the OAS,[32] but it must meet without delay when the security of the region is threatened by an armed attack.[33]

The Permanent Council. Although there are three Councils of the Organization,[34] it is the Permanent Council which exercises the most important functions in terms of the operation of the OAS. Although subsidiary to the

General Assembly and Consultation of Foreign Ministers, the Permanent Council is nevertheless a high-ranking body composed of persons of ambassadorial status[35] which acts as the preparatory body for the General Assembly.[36] Under Article 81 it is the function of the Chairman of the Permanent Council to call a meeting of the Consultation of Foreign Ministers whenever the circumstances envisaged by Article 64 arise, and the Council itself must exercise the duties of the Foreign Ministers as the Organ of Consultation under the Charter and the Rio Treaty until the Foreign Ministers are able to act themselves. In addition, the Permanent Council exercises broad functions in relation to the maintenance of peace and security and facilitating the peaceful settlement of disputes among the Organization's Member States.[37] It is also the executive organ of the General Assembly and of the Meeting of Consultation of Ministers of Foreign Affairs in that it is entrusted with carrying out and implementing the decisions of those bodies.

The Inter-American Economic and Social Council. The purpose of the Economic and Social Council, which is composed of 'one principal representative of the highest rank of each Member State',[38] is to promote cooperation among the American states in order to accelerate economic and social development in accordance with the standards set forth in Chapter VII of the Charter.[39] While this may appear to have little concern with human rights at first sight, it should be noted that the Charter,[40] the American Declaration of the Rights and Duties of Man[41] (which has been held to be an authoritative interpretation of the Charter by the Inter-American Court of Human Rights),[42] the American Convention on Human Rights[43] and its Additional Protocol on economic, social and cultural rights[44] all refer both directly and indirectly to economic, social and cultural rights as enforceable human rights.[45]

The Inter-American Council for Education, Science and Culture. The purposes of this body, which is again composed of one representative of the highest rank appointed by each of the Member States,[46] are expressed in Article 99. Not only is the Council required to 'promote friendly relations and mutual understanding between the peoples of the Americas through educational, scientific and cultural cooperation and exchange' but it must also have regard to the object of these activities which is to 'raise the cultural level of the peoples [of the Americas], reaffirm their dignity as individuals, prepare them fully for the tasks of progress, and strengthen their devotion to peace, democracy and social justice ...' From this it is clear that the Council's activities are intimately connected with the broad sweep of human rights, ranging from the civil and political to the economic, social and cultural. It is apparent therefore that the Council may on occasion well have need to request the Court to interpret certain instruments relating to its widely stated competences.

The Inter-American Commission on Human Rights.[47] The Commission only became an organ of the OAS following the amendment of the Charter by the Protocol of Buenos Aires in 1967.[48] Prior to that it was simply an 'autonomous entity' of the Organization which had been created by a resolution of the Fifth Meeting of Consultation of the Ministers of Foreign Affairs at Santiago in 1959. Although the Commission at that time was clearly not an organ of the OAS it achieved substantial progress in executing its mandate within a short period of time despite its indefinite legal status.[49] Chapter XVI of the amended Charter comprises only one relatively exiguous provision, Article 111, which provides that the principal function of the Commission is 'to promote the observance and protection of human rights and to serve as a consultative organ of the Organization in these matters'. This is a broad mandate which is further amplified by the Commission's Statute and Rules of Procedure.[50] It should also be noted at this point that the Commission serves not only as a Charter organ but also as an organ of the American Convention on Human Rights.[51]

The General Secretariat. This body, whose seat is in Washington DC,[52] is the central and permanent organ of the OAS.[53] It performs all the functions assigned to it under the Charter and those entrusted to it by the General Assembly and the Meeting of Consultation of Foreign Ministers.[54] The Secretariat is headed by the Secretary-General of the OAS who is elected for a five year period and who may not serve more than two periods of office.[55] The Secretary-General may participate in all meetings of the OAS, but may not vote.[56]

The Specialized Conferences. Article 128 of the Charter provides that the Specialized Conferences are inter-governmental meetings designed to deal with special technical matters or to develop particular aspects of inter-American cooperation. These conferences, which have dealt with a wide range of subject matter,[57] may be convened by the General Assembly, the Meeting of Consultation of Foreign Ministers, at the request of one of the Councils or Specialized Organizations or on its own initiative.

The Specialized Organs. These bodies are inter-governmental organizations established by multilateral treaty, but brought within the framework of the OAS by incorporation through the medium of Article 130. Their function is to consider technical[58] matters of common interest to the American states.

The organizations now having direct relationship with the OAS are the Inter-American Commission of Women,[59] the Inter-American Children's Institute, the Inter-American Indian Institute, the Pan-American Institute of Geography and History, the Inter-American Institute of Agricultural Sciences, the Pan-American Health Organization and the Pan-American Sanitary Bureau. From the point of view of human rights, it is significant that these organizations are incorporated into the OAS structure since, being organs of the Organization in a broad sense, they too possess the right to seek advisory opinions from the Court on human rights matters within their spheres of competence under Article 64(1).

The Regional System for Protecting Human Rights

The inter-American system for the protection of human rights possesses a distinctive dual structure. All American states which are members of the OAS have human rights obligations under the Charter,[60] while some states voluntarily assume obligations by becoming party to the American Convention on Human Rights and its associated additional protocol. The two strands of protection do not, however, stand alone, but interact and may, at certain points, be regarded as symbiotic. They share a common institution in the Inter-American Commission on Human Rights, which discharges different functions with respect to both the Charter and the Convention. Similarly, while the Court is a creature of the Convention, it also has certain jurisdictional competences regarding the Charter by virtue of the exercise of its exceptionally broad advisory jurisdiction under Article 64 of the Convention.[61] In order to understand the functional relationship between the two elements of the system it is necessary to examine the evolution of the present structure.

The OAS Charter and the American Declaration of the Rights and Duties of Man

As noted above, the OAS is based on certain primary or fundamental principles including those of regional solidarity, collective security, non-intervention, democracy and human rights. The *travaux préparatoires* of the Charter indicate that there was a divergence of opinion among the states' representatives about the precise legal status which was to be accorded to each of the principles enunciated. Some states argued that the principles ought to be legally binding whereas others took the view that they should simply be the tenets which guided Member States' conduct. To some extent, the problem of the hierarchy of these principles seems to have been solved by placing those principles which were simply to be guides to conduct in Chapter II of the Charter, while those which were to be legally binding were placed in Chapter III. While Chapter II of the Charter is simply entitled 'Principles', Chapter III is entitled 'Fundamental Rights and Duties of States' thus implying that the latter has a clear mandatory quality attached to it.

As far as the protection of democracy and fundamental rights is concerned, there are a number of direct and indirect but exiguous references to these principles in various parts of the Charter. The Preamble states:[62]

> Convinced that the historic mission of America is to offer to man a land of liberty and a favorable environment for the development of his personality and the realisation of his just aspirations ...
>
> Confident that the true significance of American solidarity and good neighborliness can only mean the consolidation on this continent, with the framework of democratic institutions, of a system of individual liberty and social justice based on respect for the essential rights of man.

Chapter II of the Charter then goes on to 'reaffirm' human rights as one of the principles of the OAS. As LeBlanc observes, the use of the word 'reaffirm' in this context was intended by the drafters of the Charter to emphasize that they were simply reiterating principles which had already been affirmed in various resolutions adopted at previous inter-American conferences and meetings.[63] Article 3(k)[64] of the Charter thus provides:

> The American States proclaim the fundamental rights of the individual without distinction as to race, nationality, creed or sex.

A further reference to human rights is also included in Article 16. As noted above, this falls within Chapter III of the Charter and may therefore be presumed, *prima facie,* to be legally binding. It provides:

> Each State has the right to develop its cultural, political, and economic life freely and naturally. In this free development, the State shall respect the rights of the individual and the principles of universal morality.

Despite the initial observations about the legally binding quality of the Charter provisions relating to human rights, the matter has been the subject of some debate. Thomas and Thomas,[65] for example, take the view that, although the Charter is a legal instrument, the nature and scope of the obligations created varies according to wording used in the individual provisions. They therefore argue that, while Article 3(k) is simply declaratory, Article 16[66] creates legally binding obligations. Fenwick,[67] on the other hand, argues that, although Chapter I deals with broader aspects of the conduct of American States and Chapter II deals with the specific juridical relations between these States, taken together they create rules of conduct binding on all Member States.[68] Another commentator, Kunz, takes a more robust view.[69] He argues that the principles in question amount only to an expression of policy and a programme of action and do not create legal norms.[70] The Inter-American Juridical Committee adopts a contrary position, arguing that the Chapter on principles, being contained in a legally binding instrument, created legal obligations for Member States.[71]

It is certainly difficult to disagree with the position taken by Thomas and Thomas[72] that the use of the word 'shall' in Article 16 is imperative and imposes a legal duty upon the Member States to respect the rights of individuals. Furthermore, it may be argued that Article 5 creates, to use the words of the International Law Commission, obligations of conduct rather than obligations of result. That is, Member States are legally obliged to comport themselves in such a way as to give effect to the principles to which they have reaffirmed their commitment in the pursuit of the purposes of the Organization as expressed in Article 2 of the Charter. This view is also taken by Cecilia Medina who, after reviewing the *travaux préparatoires* of the Charter (which she describes as 'confusing on this point') states that 'it is an undeniable fact that the principles of the Organization became Article 5 of the Charter and that the Charter was signed and ratified and thereby acquired the legal force of an international treaty'. [73]

If one accepts that the Charter created a clear and unequivocal obligation for Member States to respect the fundamental rights of the individual, two major issues remained unaddressed by the original instrument. First, although the Charter refers to the fundamental rights of the individual, it does not reveal the identity of these rights. It contains no catalogue of protectable rights, nor does it indicate the method by which such rights might be identified. The second issue relates to the enforcement or supervision of the rights to which reference is made. Within the original Charter there was no specific reference to the competence of any of the OAS institutions to take measures to promote or protect respect for fundamental rights of the individual.

The first problem concerning the absence of an appropriate catalogue of the fundamental rights of the individual which were worthy of protection by the Member States of the OAS was partially remedied by the adoption at the same Bogota Conference of the American Declaration of the Rights and Duties of Man.[74]

In 1945 the Inter-American Conference on Problems of War and Peace held at Chapultepec in Mexico had mandated the Inter-American Juridical Committee to prepare a draft declaration on the rights of man in order to secure such rights in accordance with international law.[75] The method by which this was to be achieved was not entirely clear from the mandate provided to the Committee. Resolution XL indicated that the draft declaration was ultimately intended for adoption by the American states as a legally binding treaty[76] whereas Resolution IX suggested that the Declaration should be drafted as an annex to the OAS Charter, so it could be amended from time to time without revision of the Charter.[77] In the face of such ambiguity, the approach adopted by the Committee was to suggest that the Declaration should constitute a legally binding commitment for all Member States of the Organization, although enforcement of the rights should be left to the legislation and organs of 'each separate state acting in pursuance of its own constitution'.[78] The Committee therefore proposed that Article XX of the Declaration should read:[79]

> The provisions of this Declaration shall be a part of the law of each individual state to be respected and enforced by the administrative and judicial authorities in the same manner as all other laws of the state.
> The provisions of this Declaration shall not be abrogated or modified except in accordance with the terms of an inter-American agreement or an agreement of the United Nations binding upon the American states.

The Committee also suggested that an inter-American Consultative Commission on Human Rights might be created in order to advise Member States on how fundamental rights might be protected within their territory.[80] Clearly, had the Declaration been adopted as a treaty, a significant number of its provisions would have had self-executing effect within the jurisdiction of those Member States possessing monist constitutions.[81] Despite this, the Committee argued that it was a general principle of international law that states must take the necessary measures to adjust their domestic law so as to bring it into conformity with their international legal obligations: they could not avoid such obligations by arguing that they were inconsistent with their existing municipal law.[82] This was not a position with which a majority of the American states were prepared to agree, and the offending article was excised from the draft Declaration.[83] The Committee's second draft of the Declaration was remitted to a working group of the Bogota Conference and thence to a sub-commission of the Sixth Commission of the Conference.[84] Within the Sixth Commission, there was a general lack of support for the adoption of the

Declaration as a legally binding convention, and the ultimate recommendation of the Commission was that the Declaration should be adopted as a simple resolution of the Conference.

The adoption of the American Declaration of the Rights and Duties of Man as Resolution XXX, an ordinary resolution of the Bogota Conference, demonstrated conclusively that the instrument was devoid of legally binding effect. This view was further reinforced by the use of language in the Declaration which indicated that the protection of fundamental rights in the Americas was essentially a function of the Member States, and was likely to be programmatic and developmental in nature. The Preamble to the Declaration stated:[85]

> The international protection of the rights of man should be the principal *guide* of an *evolving* American law;
> The affirmation of essential human rights by the American states together with the guarantees given by the internal regimes of the states establish the initial system of protection considered by the American states as being suited to the present social and juridical conditions not without a recognition on their part that they should *increasingly strengthen* the system in the international field as conditions become more favorable.

As LeBlanc writes, the Conference also ensured that no case could be made for arguing that the Declaration constituted or was intended to constitute an authoritative list of the 'fundamental rights of the individual' referred to in Article 5(j) (now 5(k)) of the Charter.[86] The United States of America went even further, placing on the record of the Conference that it did not consider Article 5(j) to refer to any other specific document on the subject of fundamental rights.[87]

The likely reason for the shift in attitudes among the American states to the question of human rights during the period 1945 to 1948 is best explained by reference to the changing political context in that era. The Mexico Conference of 1945 had taken place against the backdrop of the end of the Second World War and a general attitude in international society that the conflict had, to a large degree, been brought about by the large scale denial of human rights. It was argued that human rights violations had led to instability in international relations and had resulted in threats to peace.[88] This indeed was one of the very premises upon which the United Nations itself had been founded, with the Charter clearly linking respect for human rights and self-determination of peoples with international peace and security.[89] By 1948, however, the political context had changed dramatically with the emergence of the Cold War and the re-emergence of the interventionist impulse of the United States in the Western Hemisphere. Indeed, it may be argued that it was the desire on the part of the American states to limit US opportunities for intervention in the affairs of other states of the hemisphere that formed the major rationale for the adoption of the Declaration as a non-binding resolution.[90]

Whatever the original legal status of the Declaration, there is no doubt that with the passage of time that status has changed. Through a process of incorporation by institutional change within the framework of the inter-American system in general, the Declaration has acquired the status of an authoritative interpretation of the reference to 'fundamental rights of the individual' in Article 5(k) of the Charter.[91] While this is clearly contrary to the original intentions of the OAS Member States, it nonetheless evinces a decisive shift in their attitude towards the supervision and enforceability of the rights listed in the Declaration. The way in which the legal status of the Declaration has changed over the years can only be understood by examining the way in which the Inter-American Commission has emerged as a fully fledged institution of the Organization of American States. This is a matter which will be considered in some detail below.[92] Before engaging in this task, however, an examination of the contents of the Declaration is warranted.

The American Declaration on the Rights and Duties of Man is comprised of two chapters. Chapter One deals with rights and Chapter Two sets out the duties which individuals owe to society. The Declaration contains some twenty eight rights which are a mixture of civil and political or first generation rights and economic, social and cultural or second generation rights.[93] All the rights are expressed in an exiguous and direct fashion and are subject only to a general limitation provision, Article XXVIII, which provides:

> The rights of man are limited by the rights of others, by the security of all, and by the just demands of the general welfare and the advancement of democracy.

Unlike the rights protected by the American Convention, the rights referred to in the Declaration are not subject to any individual and specific 'clawback' clauses.[94] The rights and duties contained in the American Declaration are: the right to life, liberty and personal security (Article I), the right to equality before the law (Article II), the right to religious freedom and worship (Article III), the right to freedom of investigation, opinion, expression and dissemination (Article IV), the right to protection of honour, personal reputation and private and family life (Article V), the right to a family and to the protection thereof (Article VI), the right to protection for mothers and children (Article VII), the right to residence and movement (Article VIII), the right to inviolability of the home (Article IX), the right to the inviolability and transmission of correspondence (Article X), the right to the preservation of health and to well-being (Article XI), the right to education (Article XII), the right to the benefits of culture (Article XIII), the right to work and fair remuneration (Article XIV), the right to leisure time and to the use thereof (Article XV), the right to social security (Article XVI), the right to recognition of juridical personality and of civil rights (Article XVII), the right to a fair trial (Article XVIII), the right to a nationality (Article XIX), the right to vote and to participate in government (Article XX), the right of assembly (Article XXI), the right of association (Article XXII), the right to property (Article XXIII), the right to petition (Article XXIV), the right to protection from arbitrary arrest (Article XXV), the right to due process of law (Article XXVI), the right of asylum (Article XXVII), the scope of the right of man (Article XXVIII), duties to society (Article XXIX), duties towards children and parents (Article XXX), duty to receive instruction (Article XXXI), duty to vote (Article XXXII), duty to obey the law (Article XXXIII), duty to serve the community and the nation (Article XXXIV), duties with respect to social security and welfare (Article XXXV), duty to pay taxes (Article XXXVI), duty to work (Article XXXVII), duty to refrain from political activity in a foreign country (Article XXXVIII).

Although the Declaration took the form of a simple list of rights and duties, this was not the approach which the Inter-American Juridical Committee adopted when it prepared its drafts of the instrument. In its initial draft the IAJC not only enumerated the rights which were to be protected by the American states, but also indicated the limitations upon those rights by the application of 'clawback' clauses. A number of governments objected to the specificity of this approach, and in its second draft of the Declaration, the IAJC restricted itself to adopting the approach of simply providing a list of agreed rights.[95] Despite this modification, the Member States attending the Bogota Conference in 1948 further reduced the detail of the protected rights and included a separate chapter on the duties of man which had appeared in neither of the two original IAJC drafts of the Declaration.[96] This approach by the Member States had a significant impact upon the position of second generation rights which the IAJC had included in the initial drafts, arguably reducing the effectiveness of the rights stated.[97] As the Committee itself noted:[98]

> The simple enunciation of very general standards, which are unanimously accepted in theory without being actually put into practice, would not respond to the generous aspiration of the Pan American Assemblies to guarantee in this

Hemisphere the rights and freedoms of the human individual, which are today the true expression of a representative system.

It cannot be said that the early life of the American Declaration was particularly auspicious. It was marked by caution and timidity which arose largely from the fear by Latin American states that acceptance of a more robust instrument would lead to incursions into their sovereignty and threats to their independence; hence the Declaration began as a non-legal document containing a list of broadly stated rights. Nonetheless, with the institutional development of the inter-American system, the Declaration acquired an increasingly important role until it eventually assumed the status of an authoritative interpretation of the references to human rights within the Charter. How this occurred can only be understood by examining the development of the Inter-American Commission on Human Rights.

Evolution and Development of the Inter-American Commission on Human Rights

Although the IAJC had mooted the creation of a Consultative Commission on Human Rights with advisory powers at the time of drafting the American Declaration, and had also subsequently mooted the creation of an inter-American court on human rights, no action was taken by the OAS to develop an institution with competence to supervise or enforce human rights until 1959.[99] At the Fifth Meeting of Consultation of Ministers of Foreign Affairs at Santiago in 1959, however, conditions were rather more propitious for progress in this area. Political instability and the clear relationship between effective human rights protection and the maintenance of democracy created a climate in which the Venezuelan President Betancourt was able to propose that human rights protection should not be regarded as intervention in the internal affairs of American states.[100] While this proposal was not accepted by the majority of Member States' representatives, they nonetheless adopted a two part resolution.[101] The first part of Resolution VIII called upon the IAJC to draft a convention on human rights and a convention for the creation of an Inter-American Court of Human Rights or other organizations 'appropriate for the protection and observance of those rights'. This part of the resolution was adopted unanimously. The second part of the resolution called upon the Permanent Council of the OAS:

> To create an Inter-American Commission on Human Rights composed of seven members elected, as individuals, by the Council of the Organization of American States from panels of three presented by the governments. The Commission,

which shall be organized by the Council of the Organization and have the specific functions that the Council assigns to it, shall be charged with furthering respect for such rights.

This part of the resolution did not fare as well as the first part. Although fifteen Member States voted in favour of Resolution VIII, Brazil, the Dominican Republic, Mexico and Uruguay voted against it, while Bolivia and the US abstained. Once again, the main reason for opposing the creation of an Inter-American Commission was the fear on the part of some states that it would have the power to intervene in their internal affairs.[102] Nonetheless, in accordance with the mandate of the Consultation of Ministers of Foreign Affairs, the Council established a committee to draft a statute for the proposed Inter-American Commission on Human Rights.[103] After the submission of a number of drafts to the Member States, the Council finally adopted the Statute of the Commission after excising a right of individual petition to the Commission which had been included in the Committee's final draft.[104]

The Commission was established in 1960 when the Council adopted its Statute. In this instrument the Commission was described as an 'autonomous entity' of the OAS and was charged with the function of promoting and protecting human rights.[105] Clearly the creation of the Commission by a conference resolution as an autonomous entity of the OAS was designed to preserve its political neutrality and general autonomy. Had it been established as a subsidiary organ of the OAS Council it would have lacked the independence and impartiality necessary to fulfil its functions.[106] The human rights referred to in Article 1 of the 1960 Statute were further elaborated by Article 2 of the same instrument. Here it was declared:

> For the purposes of the present Statute, human rights are understood to be the rights set forth in the American Declaration of the Rights and Duties of Man.

The new Commission's powers were heavily circumscribed. Under Article 9 of the 1960 Statute it was assigned largely advisory and recommendatory functions. Article 9 endowed the Commission with the following functions and powers:

> a) To develop awareness of human rights among the peoples of the Americas;
> b) To make recommendations to the Governments of the Member States in general, if it considers such action advisable, for the adoption of progressive measures in favor of human rights within the framework of their domestic legislation and, in accordance with their constitutional precepts, appropriate measures to further the faithful observance of those rights;

c) To prepare such studies or reports as it considers advisable in the performance of its duties;
d) To urge the Governments of the Member States to supply it with information on the measures adopted by them in matters of human rights;
e) To serve the Organization of American States as an advisory body in respect of human rights.

Despite the apparently limited scope of the Commission's competence as expressed in Article 9 of the Statute, it nonetheless concluded at its first session that it had power to make specific joint and individual recommendations on human rights violations to Member States of the OAS, and to undertake studies and make reports on human rights situations in states where large-scale violations were alleged to have taken place.[107] Despite the receipt of a large number of communications from individuals, however, the Commission decided that it did not have the competence to make individual decisions in relation to such petitions.[108] It did agree, however, that the existence of individual petitions could be used as evidence in fulfilling its functions under Articles 9(b) and (c) of its Statute.[109]

The Commission's lack of competence to accept and act upon individual communications was remedied at the Second Special Inter-American Conference which was held in Rio de Janeiro in 1965. This conference had been convened at the request of Guatemala in order to discuss, *inter alia*, the strengthening of democracy and the better protection of human rights in the Americas.[110] At the conference the Member States adopted resolution XXII which resolved as follows:[111]

1. To request the Inter-American Commission on Human Rights to conduct a continuing survey of the observance of fundamental human rights in each of the Member States of the Organization.
2. To request the Commission to give particular attention in this survey to observance of the human rights referred to in Articles I, II, III, IV, XVIII, XXV and XXVI of the American Declaration of the Rights and Duties of Man.
3. To authorize the Commission to examine communications submitted to it and any other available information, to address to the government of any American state a request for information deemed pertinent by the Commission.
4. To request the Commission to submit a report annually to the Inter-American Conference or Meeting of Consultation of Ministers of Foreign Affairs. This report should include a statement of progress achieved in realization of the goals set forth in the American Declaration.
5. In exercising the functions set forth in paragraphs 2 and 3 of this resolution the Commission shall first ascertain whether the domestic legal procedures and remedies of a Member State have been duly pursued and exhausted.

Paragraphs 6 and 7 of the resolution simply dealt with a number of administrative arrangements affecting the operation of the Commission, but paragraph 8 resolved 'that the Statute of the Inter-American Commission on Human Rights shall be amended in accordance with the provisions of this resolution'. The adoption of this resolution by the majority of OAS Member States, including the United States of America, signified a marked change in their attitude towards endowing the Commission with power to receive and investigate individual communications. LeBlanc suggests that the reason for this was because the majority of American states had formed a favourable impression of the Commission during the period 1960-65 and that it had become clear that the Commission was able to perform a valuable role in protecting human rights in the region.[112]

At its Thirteenth Session held in Mexico City from 18 to 28 April 1966, the Commission executed the amendments to its Statute as required by Resolution XXII by adding Article 9(bis).[113] This new Article provided:

The Commission shall have the following additional functions and powers:

a) To give particular attention to observance of the human rights referred to in Articles I, II, III, IV, XVIII, XXV, and XXVI of the American Declaration of the Rights and Duties of Man;

b) To examine communications submitted to it and any other available information; to address to the government of any American state a request for information deemed pertinent by the Commission; and to make recommendations, when it deems this appropriate, with the objective of bringing about more effective observance of fundamental human rights;

c) To submit a report annually to the Inter-American Conference or to the Meeting of the Consultation of Ministers of Foreign Affairs, which should include: (i) a statement of progress achieved in realisation of the goals set forth in the American Declaration; (ii) a statement of areas in which further steps are needed to give effect to the human rights set forth in the American Declaration; and (iii) such observations as the Commission may deem appropriate on matters covered in the communications submitted to it and in other information available to the Commission;

d) To ascertain as a condition precedent to the exercise of the powers set forth in paragraphs b) and c) of the present Article, whether the internal legal procedure and remedies of a Member State have been duly pursued and exhausted.

In adopting Article 9(bis) it is noticeable that the Commission did not include the first paragraph of Resolution XXII which, in effect, provided the general context for the amendment. The result of this was that the Commission appeared to provide itself with two procedures: a new procedure relating to the management of the individual petition mechanism and the old procedure in which 'cognizance' was taken of petitions as part of the Commission's general supervisory function under the Charter. It is doubtful whether this was the intended effect of Resolution XXII, but the Commission consolidated the approach implied in its revised Statute through the adoption of specific Regulations governing its procedures in this area. The Commission thus effectively endowed itself with two procedures: the first was that which it had always followed in taking cognizance of individual petitions in conducting its general supervisory functions under Article 9 of its original Statute which related to all rights set forth in the American Declaration, and the second was the individual petition procedure under which only the specific rights mentioned in Article 9(bis) were to be the subject of the new individual petition procedure.[114] Although this result may not have been intended by the American states, it nonetheless had certain advantages of a pragmatic nature. It may be argued that, had the Commission been obliged to comply with the requirement to exhaust local remedies before the compilation and adoption of reports under its general supervisory competence, this would have retarded the process immeasurably.[115] As it was, the 'dual' procedure permitted the Commission to draw a distinction between 'general cases' and 'individual cases' in its inquiries into the human rights situations in the OAS Member States. While this distinction has not been expressly articulated in the Commission's practice on many occasions, it did assume critical importance in a number of cases involving Brazil.

In *Case 1684 (Brazil)*,[116] a number of denunciations alleging violations of a number of the favoured rights contained in Article 9(bis) were levelled against the government of Brazil. In accordance with the individual petition procedure,[117] the government was provided with the pertinent parts of the denunciations and a request to conduct *in loco* observation was made by the Commission. Brazil not only refused to allow the Commission to conduct an on-site investigation but also argued that it had not conducted an investigation into whether or not there had been prior exhaustion of domestic remedies. The Rapporteurs appointed in this case, Drs Durward Sandifer and Jimenez de Arechaga, argued that, since this was a general case which revealed a widespread pattern of human rights violations, there was no need to examine each individual denunciation in order to determine whether domestic remedies had been exhausted in each case.[118] The rationale for this was explained by Dr Sandifer. He said:[119]

Resolution XXII ... by which the powers of the Commission had been expanded, resulted in the creation of a new type of case - the 'individual case' - for which a condition precedent to its creation was established in that the Commission should verify the exhaustion of the internal legal remedies which resulted in article 9(bis)(d) of the Statute, and that this Resolution did not affect the powers of the Commission in the examination of 'general cases' as this authority was already embodied in article 9 of the Statute approved in 1960. Therefore, exhaustion of legal remedies should not be considered a requirement applicable to general cases.

The majority of the Commission[120] held that *Case 1684 (Brazil)* was indeed a general case for which it was not necessary to satisfy the condition requiring the exhaustion of domestic legal remedies contained in Article 9(bis)(d) of the Commission's amended Statute.[121] The effect of this was to establish in the Commission's jurisprudence a distinction between individual cases in which domestic remedies had to be shown to be exhausted as a condition precedent to admissibility of the case before the Commission and general cases where the satisfaction of such a condition precedent was unnecessary.[122]

Despite the advances made by the Commission in enhancing its supervisory and protective functions under the OAS Charter it was, as Buergenthal rightly notes, based upon very weak constitutional foundations.[123] The Commission had been founded upon a simple resolution of an OAS conference, and the inclusion of the American Declaration, itself the product of a resolution of a meeting of the Consultation of Ministers of Foreign Affairs, had been incorporated into the Commission's Statute by a resolution of another meeting of the same body. In addition to this, the competence of the Commission to entertain individual petitions under its Statute had been effected by another conference resolution. Given this, it is perhaps surprising that the Commission was able to achieve so much during the period from its foundation until its incorporation proper into the OAS Charter as a fully fledged institution of the OAS in 1970. Indeed, as Buergenthal also notes:[124]

> The pre-1970 practice and achievements of the Commission gain in significance once it is remembered that prior to the revision of the Charter the inter-American human rights system ... owed its existence not to a treaty or other legally binding instrument but to OAS resolutions and pronouncements of uncertain authority.

Although there had been a proposal to amend the OAS Charter as early as 1965,[125] no action was taken on this issue until the convocation of a Third Special Inter-American Conference at Buenos Aires between 15 and 27 February 1967. As indicated above, the impetus for the calling of the conference was the result of some regional dissatisfaction with the capacity of the Organization of American States' institutions to deal with the economic and political problems affecting the region.[126] While the conference was not entirely successful in confronting the issues which had led to its calling, it nonetheless succeeded in providing the OAS with a more effective institutional structure by way of a number of amendments effected by the resulting Protocol of Buenos Aires.[127] In addition to the creation of a General Assembly, which was to be the supreme plenary organ of the Organization, the protocol also enhanced the mechanisms for cooperation in defence and security matters and established three new Councils with discrete responsibilities. The major modification made to the Charter system by the Protocol of Buenos Aires which was to have a profound effect on the promotion and protection of human rights was the transformation of the Inter-American Commission on Human Rights from an 'autonomous entity' of the OAS by Article 51 into an expressly designated organ of the OAS. This placed the Commission on a sound legal footing and gave it a precise constitutional status within the framework of the Organization. Of greater significance, however, was the fact that not only was the Commission incorporated into the Charter, but so too was its Statute. This had the effect of further institutionalizing the American Declaration which was specifically referred to in Article 2 of the Commission's Statute. This clearly conferred some kind of normative status on the American Declaration, but whether this took effect in the form of a treaty or simply as an authoritative interpretation of the Charter remained unclear for some time.[128]

In addition to the designation of the Inter-American Commission on Human Rights as an organ of the OAS by Article 51[129] of the amended Charter, a new Article 112[130] further provided:

> There shall be an Inter-American Commission on Human Rights, whose principal function shall be to promote the observance and protection of human rights and to serve as a consultative organ of the Organization in these matters. An inter-American convention on human rights shall determine the structure, competence and procedure of this Commission, as well as those of other organs responsible for these matters.

The language used in Article 112, following as it did upon Article 51 which designated the Commission as a Charter organ, seemed to suggest that after the entry into force of the protocol amending the Charter, which did not occur until some three years later in 1970, a 'new' Commission would come into existence.[131] Notwithstanding this use of mandatory language in Article

112, the Commission appeared to have no difficulty in maintaining continuity between its existence as an 'autonomous entity' and as an 'organ' of the OAS. In addition to Article 112, however, the drafters of the protocol also inserted Article 150 into the Charter. This provision, which foreshadowed the drafting and entry into force of an American convention on human rights, provided that, until such a convention came into force, 'the present Inter-American Commission on Human Rights shall keep vigilance over the observance of human rights'. This led some commentators to question whether there would be two Commissions - one for the Charter system and one for the Convention - or one Commission applying different procedures for the different instruments under which it was operating. The question was resolved in favour of the latter view when the American Convention entered into force in 1978. The Commission's new Statute[132] made it clear in Article 1 that the Commission would be a single body with separate procedures for the Charter and the Convention.[133] Article 1(2) provided:

> For the purpose of the present Statute, human rights are understood to be:
> a) The rights set forth in the American Convention on Human Rights in relation to the States Parties thereto;
> b) The rights set forth in the American Declaration of the Rights and Duties of Man.

Another question raised by Article 150 was, what was meant by the use of the term 'present Commission'? Buergenthal took the view that this reference was to the Commission as constituted by its Statute at that time which in turn was incorporated into the Charter system as an organ of the OAS. He analyzed the overall effects of the Charter amendment by the Protocol of Buenos Aires thus:[134]

> First, Article 51 of the Charter supersedes Article 1 of the Statute and transforms the Commission from an 'autonomous entity' of the OAS into one of its principal organs. Second, the Commission now derives its existence as well as its powers from a duly ratified multilateral treaty. It cannot consequently be abolished nor divested of its powers without an amendment of the OAS Charter. Since the powers of the Commission, particularly those set out in Article 9 and 9(bis) of the Statute, now have a treaty basis, they need no longer to be legitimated by reference to controversial theories regarding the legal effect of OAS conference resolutions. Finally, by transforming the legal status of the Commission and its Statute, the revised OAS Charter has also significantly strengthened the normative character of the American Declaration of the Rights and Duties of Man.

As Buergenthal rightly observes, the transformation of the Commission into an organ of the OAS through incorporation into the Charter system provided it with a clear treaty-based legal foundation and also, by implication, transformed the status of the American Declaration. While the Declaration had, before the entry into force of the Protocol of Buenos Aires, simply enjoyed the status of a conference resolution, it was now a constituent part of the OAS constitutional system. There had been some doubt expressed about the precise normative status of the Declaration prior to this time,[135] but following the 1970 amendment of the Charter, its legal position was manifestly clearer. While the juridical status of the American Declaration has been considered in a number of cases before the Commission and the Inter-American Court of Human Rights in the post-1970 amendment period, it has been analyzed most effectively by the Commission in the *'Baby Boy' Case*[136] in 1981 and by the Court in its *Tenth Advisory Opinion: Interpretation of the American Declaration*.[137]

The *Baby Boy Case* resulted from a petition lodged by Catholics for Christian Political Action, a non-governmental organization based in the United States of America, against the United States and the State of Massachusetts on behalf of an aborted male foetus - the 'Baby Boy' of the case. The foetus had been aborted at the request of his mother by a doctor who had subsequently been charged and convicted of manslaughter. Since the case arose some three years after the Supreme Court had delivered two judgments liberalizing the law on abortion[138] the conviction was overturned on appeal by the Supreme Judicial Court of Massachusetts because, in accordance with these decisions, there was no evidence of recklessness on the part of the doctor or evidence of viability of the life of the foetus outside the mother's womb. The petitioners claimed that United States' law, in permitting abortion, violated, *inter alia*, the right to life guaranteed by Article I of the American Declaration. The first question which the Commission was obliged to consider was the admissibility of the case. This in turn depended upon whether the American Declaration created binding obligations for the United States. The Commission had little difficulty in holding that it did. It held:

15. The international obligation of the United States of America, as a member of the Organization of American States (OAS), under the jurisdiction of the Inter-American Commission on Human Rights (IACHR) is governed by the Charter of OAS (Bogota, 1948) as Amended by the Protocol of Buenos Aires on February 27, 1967, ratified by United States on April 23, 1968.
16. As a consequence of articles 3j, 16, 51e, 112 and 150 of this Treaty, the provisions of other instruments and resolutions of the OAS on human rights,

acquired *binding force*. Those instruments and resolutions approved with the vote of U.S. Government, are the following:
American Declaration of the Rights and Duties of Man (Bogota, 1948)
Statute and Regulations of the IACHR 1960, as amended by resolution XXII of the Second Special Inter-American Conference (Rio de Janeiro, 1965)
Statute and Regulations of IACHR of 1979-80.[139]

The difficulty with the wording used by the Commission is that it does not make clear what exactly 'binding force' means. In the context it would seem to suggest that, through the process of incorporation, the American Declaration had either become a treaty or had taken on a treaty-like quality. This was a matter with which the United States took issue in a subsequent case before the Commission concerning the imposition of the death penalty on juveniles.[140] In this case the petitioners had argued that 'the United States is legally bound by the American Declaration' and that it should therefore be interpreted according to the canons of treaty interpretation contained in the Vienna Convention on the Law of Treaties 1969.[141] While not expressly asserting that the Declaration was a treaty, this was nonetheless the implication of the petitioners' approach. This position was countered strongly by the United States Government which argued that 'the Declaration is not a treaty and it is not binding on the United States'.[142] In addition to this, the United States expressed its clear disagreement with the finding of the Commission in the *Baby Boy Case* that the 'Declaration had acquired binding force with the adoption of the revised OAS Charter'.[143] In the United States' view 'the Declaration was not drafted with the intent to create legal obligations'.[144] In dealing with the United States' argument here, the Commission simply reiterated its conclusion in paragraph 16 of the *Baby Boy Case* stating that, as a consequence of the relevant provisions of the Charter, to which the United States was party, the American Declaration had 'acquired binding force'.[145] It is also interesting to note that, in this case, the Commission referred to Buergenthal's article on the revised OAS Charter[146] in which he had stated:[147]

> The OAS Charter does not define 'human rights'. Therefore, since Article 150 incorporates the provisions of the Statute [of the Commission] by reference, 'human rights' within the meaning of Article 150 are those 'set forth' in the American Declaration. The human rights provisions of the American Declaration can today consequently be deemed to derive their normative character from the OAS Charter itself.

It would seem therefore that the Commission's reference to 'binding force' in the *Baby Boy Case* and in the *Juvenile Death Penalty Case*, supported as it is by reference to Buergenthal's argument, means that the American Declaration enjoys the status of a legally binding treaty by reason of its incorporation into the Charter system. This, however, was a position which the United States was not prepared to accept. In a *Request for Reconsideration of Resolution 3/87, Case 9647 (United States)*[148] the United States, while not challenging the Commission's decision that the juvenile death penalty did not violate the right to life in Article I of the American Declaration, nevertheless contested the way in which the Commission had used the petition to discuss the juvenile justice system in the United States as well as the formation of customary international law and *ius cogens*. As an aside to the main object of the request, however, the US asserted:[149]

> The US also notes that the Commission in reiterating ... its erroneous conclusion that the Declaration acquired binding force with the adoption of the Protocol in Buenos Aires, makes no effort to respond to the arguments to the contrary made by the US in its submission of July 15, 1986. Further evidence that the character of the Declaration did not change with the entry into force of the revised Charter in 1970 is given by the fact that the terms of the Commission's competence over individual communications contained in Article 20 of its Statute have not changed since its adoption in 1965.

Thus, whatever the Commission's view of the legal status of the American Declaration, it was abundantly clear that it was not shared by the United States of America. In 1989, however, the Inter-American Court was presented with the opportunity by way of the exercise of its advisory jurisdiction under Article 64(1) of the American Convention to give a declaratory ruling on this controversial matter.[150] Under Article 64(1) the Court has competence to render advisory opinions at the request of OAS Member States and certain organs of the OAS 'regarding the interpretation of this Convention or of other treaties concerning the protection of human rights in the American states'. Colombia, acting under this provision, put the following question to the Court:[151]

> Does Article 64 authorize the Inter-American Court of Human Rights to render advisory opinions at the request of a Member State or of one of the organs of the OAS, regarding the interpretation of the American Declaration on the Rights and Duties of Man ...

While Colombia acknowledged that the Declaration was not a treaty, it nonetheless pointed out that this did not automatically answer the question posed. It argued:[152]

It is perfectly reasonable to assume that the interpretation of the human rights provisions contained in the Charter of the OAS, as revised by the Protocol of Buenos Aires involves, in principle, an analysis of the rights and duties of man proclaimed by the Declaration, and thus requires the determination of the normative *status* of the Declaration within the legal framework of the inter-American system for the protection of human rights.

In accordance with Article 52 of the Court's Rules of Procedure,[153] the Secretariat wrote to the OAS Member States and organs requesting written observations on this case. Of the intervening states, only Uruguay took the view that the Declaration was a treaty. It said, 'the juridical nature of the Declaration is that of a binding, multilateral instrument that enunciates, defines and specifies fundamental principles recognized by the American states and which crystallizes norms of customary international law generally accepted by those states'.[154] Peru was rather more cautious, saying that the Declaration had 'a hierarchy similar to that of the Convention', but it appeared to limit this statement to the States Parties to the Convention and curiously did not seek either explicitly or implicitly to extend it to OAS Member States which were not party to the Convention.[155] This was clearly a highly erroneous view which the Court simply ignored. Costa Rica[156] and Colombia[157] were content to regard the Declaration as an authoritative interpretation of the Charter, while Venezuela[158] and the United States[159] shared the view that the Declaration contained only basic moral principles and broad political statements which were not legally binding The United States at the public hearing adopted the position that 'the American Declaration is not a treaty, and that therefore the Court does not have jurisdiction under Article 64 to interpret it or determine its normative status within the inter-American human rights system'.[160] The United States further argued that 'it would seriously undermine the established international law of treaties to say that the Declaration is legally binding'.[161]

In dealing with the question of admissibility the Court held that Colombia, as a Member State of the OAS, was competent to request a ruling under Article 64(1). The fact that the Declaration was not a treaty did not, in the Court's view, mean that it was not appropriate subject matter for an advisory opinion. By interpreting the question put by Colombia, the Court was able to draw a distinction between the interpretation of the Declaration and an interpretation of Article 64(1) itself. Here the Court admitted that in dealing with the request for an advisory opinion it 'might have to pass on the legal status of the Declaration'.[162] Despite this, the Court held that 'the mere fact ... that the interpretation of the Convention or other treaties concerning human rights might require the Court to analyze international instruments which may or may not be treaties *stricto sensu* does not mean that the request for an advisory opinion is inadmissible, provided that the context is the interpretation of the instruments mentioned in Article 64(1) of the Convention'.[163] It would thus seem that, as long as a request is framed in terms of an interpretation of Article 64, or indeed any other article of the Convention, that request will be admissible, even though it may involve the interpretation of some other instrument. The Court then went on to observe that the question concerning the legal status of the Declaration bore on the merits of the request and not on the question of admissibility; thus, 'even if the Court were to conclude that the Declaration has no normative force within the inter-American system, that decision would not make the request inadmissible because it would have been reached in the context of an interpretation of Article 64(1)'.[164] The Court therefore saw no reason to exercise its discretion not to admit the request.[165]

In determining the legal status of the Declaration the Court began by analyzing whether or not it was a treaty within the definitions provided by the Vienna Convention on the Law of Treaties 1969 and the Vienna Convention on the Law of Treaties among States and International Organizations or among International Organizations 1986.[166] Here it found that the Declaration did not fall within the Vienna Conventions' definitions since, by reference to its drafting history, it was neither conceived of nor approved as a treaty.[167] In the Court's view this did not, however, lead to the conclusion that the Court lacked jurisdiction to render an advisory opinion concerning an interpretation of the Declaration.[168] As the Court observed, the American Convention itself mentioned the Declaration in both its preamble and in Article 29 and said that as a consequence of this, 'in interpreting the Convention in the exercise of its advisory jurisdiction, the Court may have to interpret the Declaration'.[169]

The Court then turned its attention to the way in which the inter-American human rights system had evolved since its inception.[170] In so doing, the Court adopted the same inter-temporal law techniques as those applied by the ICJ[171] and the European Court of Human Rights,[172] both of which have interpreted legal instruments as 'living documents' having a scope and validity determined by present legal conditions and not those extant at the time the instruments were drafted. In this way, interpretation keeps pace with legal and social developments. Using this methodology, the Court then proceeded to examine the way in which the Declaration had been transformed from a non-binding resolution to an authoritative interpretation of the Charter. Before charting the Declaration's evolutionary course, however, the Court sought to set the inter-American developments in a broader context. It found that such regional developments, of which the Declaration was part, reflected advances in international human rights law in which, over the period in question, 'certain essential human rights'[173] had assumed the status of *erga omnes* obligations.[174] Thus, by implication, the Court appeared to be saying that the Declaration had itself become a statement of *ius cogens* which, by definition, was binding on all OAS Member States. Unfortunately, the Court did not take this rather controversial observation to its logical conclusion, but simply moved on to consider the institutional development which had led to the incorporation of the Declaration into the Charter.[175]

The reasoning used by the Court in its analysis of the incorporation of the Declaration into the Charter more or less confirms the position taken by the Commission in the *'Baby Boy'* and *Juvenile Death Penalty Cases*[176] and the thesis advanced by Buergenthal in his 1971 article.[177] The Court first examined the provisions of the Charter which referred to the fundamental rights of man.[178] It then noted that the Commission was, by Articles 112 and 150, an organ of the OAS whose function it was to promote the observance and protection of human rights. The Court then noted that Article 1 of the Commission's Statute defined human rights as the rights set forth in the American Convention for the States Parties to that instrument and the rights set forth in the American Declaration in relation to all other OAS Member States.[179] The Court also observed that the supreme organ of the OAS, the General Assembly, had on a number of occasions and in a number of resolutions 'repeatedly recognized that the American Declaration is a source of international obligations' for the Member States of the OAS'.[180] These resolutions had predated the entry into force of the American Convention and the implication in their being cited was clearly that the standards set forth in the Declaration were those to be applied as a matter of international obligation when promoting and protecting human rights in respect of all OAS Member States both prior to and after the entry into force of the American Convention. In support of its reasoning the Court also curiously cited the Preamble to the American Convention to Prevent and Punish Torture 1985[181] which had entered into force *after* the American Convention on Human Rights and which provides:

> All acts of torture or any other cruel, inhuman or degrading treatment or punishment constitute an offence against human dignity and a denial of the principles set forth in the Charter of the Organization of American States and in the Charter of the United Nations and are violations of the Declaration of the Rights and Duties of Man and the Universal Declaration of Human Rights.

Given the developments in human rights law over the period in question and given the institutional incorporation of the Declaration into the Charter system, the Court concluded:[182]

> [I]t may be said that by means of an authoritative interpretation, the Member States of the Organization have signalled their agreement that the Declaration contains and defines the fundamental human rights referred to in the Charter. Thus the Charter of the Organization cannot be interpreted and applied as far as human rights are concerned without relating its norms, consistent with the practice of the organs of the OAS, to the corresponding provision of the Declaration.[183]

The Court went on to say that 'the Declaration is the text that defines the human rights referred to in the Charter and that as a consequence of this it constitutes a source of obligation for OAS Member States'.[184] Furthermore, while the American Convention on Human Rights provides the specific source of obligations with respect to the protection of human rights for States Parties to that instrument, it must nevertheless 'be remembered that, given the provisions of Article 29(d), these states cannot escape the obligations they have as members of the OAS under the Declaration'.[185] The Court thus concluded that, although the Declaration is not a treaty, this does not 'lead to the conclusion that it does not have legal effect, nor that the Court lacks the power to interpret it ...'.[186] The Court's answer to the question posed by Colombia was therefore:[187]

> Article 64(1) of the American Convention authorizes the Court, at the request of the Member States of the OAS or any duly qualified OAS organ to render advisory opinions interpreting the American Declaration of the Rights and Duties of Man, provided that in doing so the Court is acting within the scope and framework of its jurisdiction in relation to the Charter and the Convention or other treaties concerning the protection of human rights in the American states.

It is not easy to draw definitive conclusions from the Court's *Tenth Advisory Opinion,* since much of the language used is oracular and the reasoning not entirely clear. It is possible to state conclusively, however, that the American Declaration is not a treaty. It is also possible to say with certainty that the Declaration creates legally binding obligations for all OAS Member States. What it is not possible to state is the precise nature of these legally binding obligations. It may be that, as a matter of inference, the obligations derive from customary international law or from regional inter-American customary law which has through the process of treaty amendment been incorporated into the Charter system.[188] If this is a correct interpretation, then the Court was less than exact in its analysis, and certainly did not review any of the doctrinal arguments which favour or disfavour its incorporationist approach.[189] As the United States of America protested in its written submission to the Court:[190]

> The United States recognizes the good intentions of those who would transform the American Declaration from a statement of principles into a binding legal instrument. But good intentions do not make law. It would seriously undermine the process of international law making - by which sovereign states voluntarily undertake specified legal obligations - to impose legal obligations on states through a process of 'reinterpretation' or 'inference' from a non-binding statement of principles.

The approach adopted by the Court undoubtedly raises a number of problems, to which the US and other states alluded in their preliminary objections to a potential finding that the Declaration might create legal obligations. First, as the US pointed, out the Declaration was not drafted as a legal instrument and it therefore 'lacks the precision necessary to resolve complex legal questions'.[191] A glance at the Declaration will confirm this opinion. It comprehends both a wide range of civil, political, economic, social and cultural rights, some of which lack the necessary specificity for direct application. Second, although the Court found that states had 'signaled their agreement' to the binding quality of the Declaration, this view was, as we have seen above, vigorously contested by Venezuela and the United States of America. The first argument adduced above is not, however, insuperable and may be countered by the assertion that human rights standards by their very nature lack precision and as a consequence demand interpretation by a competent judicial or quasi-judicial organ. Such an argument would surely not be lost upon the United States whose own Supreme Court is regularly called upon to interpret Bill of Rights provisions which are no clearer than many of the rights contained in the American Declaration. It may also be argued that the Inter-American Commission is such an organ. Certainly, it is possible to point to the fact that a number of cases which have been dealt with by the Commission have involved significant conventional legal analysis based upon interpretation of the American Declaration.

The American Convention on Human Rights

The American Convention on Human Rights (the Pact of San José) and its Protocols on Economic, Social and Cultural Rights (the Protocol of San Salvador) and the abolition of the death penalty comprise the second major limb of the inter-American system of human rights protection.[192] It may be recalled that the suggestion of drafting an American convention on human rights had been raised as early as 1945 with the adoption of Resolution XL at the Inter-American Conference on the Problems of War and Peace in Mexico City.[193] Given the absence of political will, however, no further action was taken on drafting a regional human rights convention until the Fifth Meeting of Consultation of Ministers of Foreign Affairs in 1959. By Resolution VII of that meeting, not only was the Inter-American Commission created,[194] but the Inter-American Juridical Committee was also instructed to prepare a draft convention.[195] The draft was completed by the IAJC in 1965, and was submitted for consideration at the Second Special Inter-American Conference held in Rio de Janeiro in November 1965.[196] The Conference finally resolved to send the draft convention to the Inter-American Commission for study. Following a number of delays, one of which was occasioned by the question of whether it was necessary for the Americas to have a regional convention following adoption by the United Nations of the International Covenant on Civil and Political Rights,[197] the American Convention on Human Rights was eventually adopted at a special inter-governmental conference at San José, Costa Rica in 1969. It entered into force in July 1978 following the deposit of the eleventh instrument of ratification in accordance with Article 74(2) of the Convention.

The format of the Convention and its institutional structure is similar to that of the European Convention on Human Rights and Fundamental Freedoms of 1950, but it is plain that the drafters of the American Convention drew on the experiences of its European counterpart and thereby avoided some of the less satisfactory aspects of the former.[198] The European Convention was not, however, the only source of inspiration for the American Convention. It also drew on the United Nations International Covenant on Civil and Political Rights and, more particularly on the American Declaration.[199] Indeed, as noted above, Article 29 of the Convention, under the rubric of 'Restrictions Regarding Interpretation', specifically provides that it shall not be interpreted as excluding or limiting the effect of the American Declaration or 'other international acts of the same nature'. It would thus seem that, where the rights contained in the other instruments are wider in their application than those contained in the American Convention, they are to be given full effect.[200] The rights contained in the American Convention, which are primarily civil and political or first generation rights, are: the right to juridical personality (Article 3); the right to life (Article 4); the right to humane treatment (Article 5); freedom from slavery (Article 6); the right to personal liberty (Article 7); the right to a fair trial (Article 8); freedom from ex post facto laws (Article

9); the right to compensation for miscarriage of justice (Article 10); the right to privacy (Article 11); freedom of conscience and religion (Article 12); freedom of thought and expression (Article 13); the right of reply (Article 14); the right of assembly (Article 15); freedom of association (Article 16); the rights of the family (Article 17); the right to a name (Article 18); the rights of the child (Article 19); the right to a nationality (Article 20); the right to property (Article 21); freedom of movement and residence (Article 22); the right to participate in government (Article 23); the right to equal protection before the law (Article 24); and the right to judicial protection (Article 25). As Buergenthal observes, 'the catalog of rights which the American Convention proclaims is longer than that of the European Convention, and many of its provisions establish more advanced and enlightened guarantees than does its European counterpart, or for that matter, the Political Covenant'. He here cites Article 4 (right to life), Article 5 (right to humane treatment), Article 17(5) (non-discrimination on basis of birth) and Article 23 (right to participate in government).[201] This aspect of the American Convention will be analyzed in greater detail below.[202]

Under the heading of 'progressive development', Article 26 further provides that State Parties undertake to adopt measures with a view to achieving the economic, social, educational, scientific and cultural standards set forth in the OAS Charter 'as amended by the Protocol of Buenos Aires'. Since the Charter has been amended twice since the adoption of the Protocol of Buenos Aires, this provision now appears somewhat dated. As noted above,[203] consequent amendments to the Charter have reinforced the areas dealing with economic and social issues and have both widened and subsumed most references to these matters under a new Chapter VII which is entitled 'Integral Development'. Logically, Article 26 might be read down simply to refer to the Charter in its current amended form, and should not be restricted to prior amendments alone. It may also be argued that this provision has also been rendered partially redundant by the adoption of a protocol to the American Convention on economic, social and cultural rights which was adopted in 1988.

The Additional Protocol to the American Convention on Human Rights on Economic Social and Cultural Rights (The Protocol of San Salvador)

Article 77 of the American Convention provides that any State Party and the Commission may submit proposed protocols to the Convention for consideration by the General Assembly with a view to gradually including other rights and freedoms within the Convention's system of protection. In order to promote the development of economic, social and cultural right, the Commission submitted a draft protocol to the General Assembly in 1986. This draft was transmitted to the Member States of the Organization for their observations,[204] following receipt of which the Permanent Council was to prepare a final draft which was to be approved by the States Parties to the American Convention at the eighteenth regular session of the General Assembly.[205] After refinement of the draft Protocol by a working group,[206] the Additional Protocol to the American Convention on Human Rights in the area of Economic, Social and Cultural Rights was approved at the eighteenth regular session of the General Assembly on 14 November 1988. As the General Assembly session was held in the capital city of El Salvador, the Protocol is sometimes referred to as the Protocol of San Salvador.

Like the American Convention the Additional Protocol draws upon both the American Declaration, the Universal Declaration and the UN International Covenant on Cultural, Economic and Social Rights for its inspiration,[207] but has novel elements both in the rights recognized[208] and in the mechanisms for supervising and enforcing those rights.[209] The rights recognized in the Protocol are: the right to work (Article 6); just, equitable and satisfactory conditions of work (Article 7); trade union rights (Article 8); the right to social security (Article 9); the right to health (Article 10); the right to a healthy environment (Article 11); the right to food (Article 12); the right to education (Article 13); the right to the benefits of culture (Article 14); the right to the formation and protection of families (Article 15); the rights of children (Article 16); protection of the elderly (Article 17) and protection of the handicapped (Article 18). The Protocol also incorporates a particularly novel element in that it makes Articles 8 and 13 subject to the individual petition procedure contained in Article 44 of the American Convention. The individual petition procedure of the Convention will be considered in detail below.[210]

Additional Protocol to the American Convention on Human Rights on the Abolition of the Death Penalty

For many years the Inter-American Commission had been concerned about the widespread and general application of the death penalty in a large number of American states. Despite a number of resolutions on the subject,[211] no attempt was made to secure the abolition of the death penalty in the original American Convention on Human Rights, largely because the climate was not propitious for such a radical move at that time, and it was felt that by omitting such an obligation the Convention would attract a greater number of signatories.[212] It is clear nonetheless that the drafters of the Convention were much occupied by the question of the death penalty because five out of the six paragraphs of Article 4 concerning the right to life deal with limitations on the application of capital punishment. In particular, Article 4(4) provides that once the death penalty has been abolished by a State Party, it may not be re-established.[213] In its 1986-87 Annual Report, the Commission suggested, in accordance with Article 77 of the American Convention, that the time was ripe for the adoption of an additional protocol to the Convention outlawing the use of capital punishment.[214] Its justification for making this proposal was the abolitionist tendency which was manifest in a number of domestic jurisdictions and in a number of international instruments.[215] It therefore approved a draft protocol consisting of three articles, the material part of which provided:

> Article 1
> The States Parties to this Protocol shall not impose the death penalty on any person under their jurisdiction. Accordingly, no one may be punished by the death penalty nor executed.

In 1987 the General Assembly mandated the Commission to study the draft protocol,[216] and in the following year it confirmed that the Permanent Council should submit the text proposed by the Commission for approval by the General Assembly.[217] The Permanent Council prepared a report recommending the Commission's text[218] and the Protocol was adopted by Resolution 1042 of the General Assembly on 8 June 1990. The Protocol consists of four Articles, the majority of which deal with the procedural issues: its substantive part differs little from the Commission's proposed draft. This provides:

> Article 1
> The States Parties to this Protocol shall not apply the death penalty in their territory to any person subject to their jurisdiction.

It is noteworthy that the Protocol, despite the abolitionist intent evinced in its title, does not require States Parties to abolish the death penalty, but simply instructs them not to apply it. This might be compared with the Sixth Protocol to the European Convention on Human Rights and the Second Optional Protocol to the International Covenant on Civil and Political Rights which requires parties to take steps to abolish the death penalty prior to ratification or accession. Thus an American state which has legislation permitting the application of the death penalty, but which does not apply that law, may still become party to this Protocol to the American Convention.[219] The abolitionist intent of the Protocol is also impaired by Article 2 which permits States Parties to reserve the right 'to apply the death penalty in wartime in accordance with international law, for extremely serious crimes of a military nature'. As Schabas points out,[220] the reference to international law in Article 2 incorporates the death penalty provisions of the Geneva Conventions III and IV and their Additional Protocols.[221]

The rationale for the adoption of the Protocol is expressed in its Preamble. It begins by recognizing the restriction of the application of the death penalty by Article 4 of the Convention, but continues to suggest that, despite the recognition of the permissibility of applying the death penalty in this provision, it is in fact contrary to the substantive content of the right to life by stating that 'everyone has the inalienable right to respect for his life, *a right that cannot be suspended for any reason*'.[222] The view that the right to life might be evolving in this way is also supported by paragraphs 6 and 7 of the Preamble which state that 'an international agreement must be arrived at that will entail a progressive development of the American Convention on Human Rights' and that the States Parties to the Convention 'have expressed their intention to adopt an international agreement with a view to consolidating the practice of not applying the death penalty in the Americas'. The Preamble also manifests a pragmatic basis for eliminating the death penalty by providing that 'application of the death penalty has irrevocable consequences, forecloses the correction of judicial error, and precludes any possibility of changing or rehabilitating those convicted'.[223]

Despite the evident support for the Protocol at the time of its adoption in 1990, few states have actually become party to it. As of 1994, six states had signed the Protocol,[224] but of those six only Panama, Uruguay and Venezuela have actually ratified it.[225] By Article 4 the Protocol will enter into force among the states that ratify or accede to it when they deposit their instruments of ratification or accession with the General Secretariat of the OAS. Schabas suggests, presumably by implication from the language used, that the Protocol will enter into force upon ratification by two states.[226] While this appears to be the correct interpretation of Article 4, it is nonetheless strange that an additional commitment of a unilateral nature made within the framework of an already extant treaty should require an additional element of reciprocity, especially given the Inter-American Court's view on the *sui generis* nature of human rights treaties.[227]

State Obligations under the American Convention and its Protocols

Chapter I of the American Convention establishes the general obligations for States Parties to that instrument. Article 1(1) provides:

> The States Parties to this convention undertake to respect the rights and freedoms recognized herein and to ensure to all persons subject to their jurisdiction the free and full exercise of those rights and freedoms, without any discrimination for reason of race, color, sex, language, religion, political or other opinion national or social origin, economic status, birth, or any other social condition.

There are a number of features in this provision which are worthy of general comment. First, when read in conjunction with Article 26, which relates to economic, social and cultural rights, it is apparent that the rights and freedoms which are referred to in Article 1(1) are simply those civil and political rights which are expressly mentioned in Chapter II of the Convention. An examination of Article 26, which is contained within its own chapter entitled 'Economic, Social and Cultural Rights',[228] indicates that the nature of the States Parties' obligations with respect to that class of rights is of a different order. Article 26 itself is headed 'Progressive Development' and this is the quality which is clearly manifest in the provision itself. It provides that 'the States Parties undertake to adopt measures ... with a view to achieving progressively ... the full realization of the rights implicit in the economic, social, education, scientific, and cultural standards set forth in the Charter of the Organization of American States as amended by the Protocol of Buenos Aires'. Thus, while the civil and political rights contained in the Convention are to be respected and ensured immediately and without qualification, the unspecified economic, social and cultural rights are, as is common in most other instruments recognizing this category of second generation rights, to be implemented progressively.[229] Nonetheless, it still remains incumbent upon States Parties to 'adopt measures' in the economic, social and cultural rights area. This is clearly an obligation of conduct to take the necessary steps to give concrete effect to progressive measures of implementation. The fact that there is no comprehensive catalogue of second generation rights contained in the Convention is not decisive in defeating the obligations established by Article 26 for, following the Inter-American Court's *Tenth Advisory Opinion: Interpretation of the American Declaration,* the economic, social and cultural rights specified in the American Declaration amount to an authoritative interpretation of the references to human rights in the OAS Charter, and that instrument is itself specifically referred to in Article 26. Where difficulty does arise, however, is in determining what the content of each of the second generation rights referred to in the American Declaration actually is, since there is no guidance within that instrument. This objection can be countered not only by an examination of the jurisprudence of the Inter-American Commission which has pronounced on economic, social and cultural rights on numerous occasions, but also by reference to Article 29(d) of the Convention which says that 'no provision of this Convention shall be interpreted as ... excluding or limiting the effect that the American Declaration of the Rights and Duties of Man and other international instruments of the same nature may have'. This suggests that the United Nations International Covenant on Economic, Social and Cultural Rights is a source from which States Parties may draw in determining what the precise nature of their obligations might be in relation to the second generation rights referred to in Article 26.

The second aspect of Article 1(1) which requires some comment is the twofold obligation to 'respect' and 'ensure the free and full exercise' of the civil and political rights recognized by the Convention. A State Party therefore has both positive and negative obligations under Article 1(1). Since the rights referred to are predominantly first generation rights or 'freedoms from', the primary obligation is negative and requires states to refrain from interfering with those rights. Thus, for example, States Parties are under an obligation not to interfere with an individual's right to privacy under Article 11 of the Convention. As the Court said in the *Honduran Disappearance Cases*:[230]

> According to Article 1(1), any exercise of public power that violates the rights recognized by the Convention is illegal. Whenever a state organ, official or public entity violates one of those rights, this constitutes a failure of the duty to respect the rights and freedoms set forth in the Convention.

It further noted that the notion of protecting human rights 'must necessarily comprise the concept of the restriction of the exercise of state power'.[231] Furthermore, the adoption of laws which are in direct contravention of the Convention's provisions will also result in a breach of that instrument and the engagement of international responsibility on the part of the delinquent state. As the Court ruled in its *Fourteenth Advisory Opinion: State and Individual Responsibility,*[232]

> There can be no doubt that ... the obligation to adopt all necessary measures to give effect to the rights and freedoms guaranteed by the Convention includes

the commitment not to adopt those that would result in the violation of those very rights and freedoms.

The obligation to 'ensure' the free and full exercise of the rights in the Convention raises rather more difficult issues of a technical nature. While the word 'ensure' undoubtedly implies that there is an obligation upon States Parties to create the institutional mechanisms through which the recognized rights are capable of vindication, it is questionable whether or not this relates solely to the vertical relationship between States Parties to the Convention and the persons to whom it applies, or whether it also refers to the general conditions governing horizontal relations between private individuals. If, for example, lawless groups are permitted to terrorize the civilian population of a State Party and the government of that State is unwilling or perhaps unable to take the necessary measures to put an end to such activities, will it be in breach of its obligation to 'ensure' the free and full exercise of the protected rights? Both the Commission and the Court have answered this question affirmatively.[233] In its Country report on Guatemala in 1981 the Commission observed:[234]

> The Commission has repeatedly stressed the obligation the governments have of maintaining public order and the personal safety of the country's inhabitants. For that purpose, the governments must prevent and suppress acts of violence, even forcefully, whether committed by public officials or private individuals, whether their motives are political or otherwise.

The Court has also concurred with this view, and may even be said to have taken the concept further. In the *Honduran Disappearance Cases*, it held:[235]

> This obligation implies the duty of the States Parties to organize the governmental apparatus and, in general, all the structures through which public power is exercised, so that they are capable of juridically ensuring the free and full enjoyment of human rights. As a consequence of this obligation, the states must prevent, investigate and punish any violation of the rights recognized by the Convention and, moreover, if possible attempt to restore the right violated and provide compensation as warranted for damages resulting from the violation.

This is a far-reaching holding by the Court with clear implications not only for the formal organization of the justice system within a State Party, but also for its actual operation. As the Court observed, the free and full exercise of human rights is not ensured simply by the existence of a formal legal system, 'it also requires the government to conduct itself so as to effectively ensure the free and full exercise of human rights'.[236] As a consequence of this, States Parties to the Convention are under a legal duty to take 'reasonable steps' to prevent human rights violations and to use all the means at their disposal to carry out investigations of violations, to identify those responsible, to punish them and to ensure that the victim is provided with adequate compensation.[237] Thus the duty under Article 1(1) subsumes two discrete obligations: the duty to prevent breaches of the rights protected by the Convention and the duty to investigate such breaches where they might have occurred.[238] In the Court's view it matters not that violations of the rights protected by the Convention have been breached by governmental agents or private individuals. If the State Party fails to prevent the violation or to prosecute it with due diligence, it will be responsible for breaching its obligations under Article 1(1).[239] As the Court noted, however, the duty to investigate is not breached merely because the investigation does not produce a satisfactory result, but 'it must be undertaken in a serious manner and not as a mere formality preordained to be ineffective'.[240]

The view that States Parties must possess formal legal systems capable of providing real remedies in cases of violations of human rights where such violations might be the result of governmental or private conduct was also considered in the Court's *Fifth Advisory Opinion: Compulsory Membership*.[241] The question which had arisen here was whether a Costa Rican law which required journalists to join a statutory organization for the regulation and licensing of the profession was consistent with, *inter alia*, Article 13 of the Convention (freedom of thought and expression). In analyzing this question, however, the Court was required to comment upon Article 13(3) which provides:

> The right of expression may not be restricted by indirect methods or means, such as the abuse of government or private controls over newsprint, radio broadcasting frequencies, or equipment used in the dissemination of information or by any other means tending to impede the communication and circulation of ideas and opinions.

It will be noted here that the provision in question refers explicitly to 'private controls' over the media which might have a tendency to interfere with the right to freedom of expression, thus indicating that States Parties are under an obligation to regulate such controls. The Court, however, stated that Article 13(3) must be read in conjunction with Article 1(1) and that as a consequence of this States Parties must 'ensure' that the private controls referred Article 13(3) do not result in a violation of freedom of expression.[242] While the Court did not make an express ruling on this point, the implication here is that, if a State Party does not take the necessary measures both to prevent and control 'private' violations of Article 13, it will be in breach of its general obligations under Article 1(1). Since the Court was of the view that privately owned media monopolies and oligopolies might impede the communication and circulation of ideas and opinions,[243] it seems reasonably clear that, in order to avoid a violation of both Article 13 and hence Article 1(1), States Parties must be in possession of laws or have institutional mechanisms in place which are directed towards either preventing the emergence of media monopolies or oligopolies or controlling the way in which such undertakings might behave.

Further examination of Article 1(1) reveals that the States Parties are to respect and ensure the free and full exercise of the rights recognized to all persons subject to their jurisdiction. Article 1(2) continues to state that 'for the purposes of this Convention, "person" means every human being'. This signifies that the application *ratione personae* of the Convention is simply to natural persons: entities such as corporations and other associations enjoying legal personality are not *per se* protected. As Buergenthal points out, however, despite the fact that legal persons do not, as such, fall within the protective ambit of the Convention, nevertheless, in certain circumstances, State Party action against a legal entity may violate individual human rights.[244] As an example of this he suggests that the outlawing of a labour union may amount to a denial of the right to freedom of association enjoyed by the individual members, but the union, as an independent entity, does not enjoy the protection of the Convention.[245] The definition of 'person' as a human being also has direct implications in analyzing the right to life under Article 4. Article 4(1) provides:

> Every person has the right to have his life respected. This right shall be protected by law and, in general, from the moment of conception. No one shall be arbitrarily deprived of his life.

Since the right to life of every person is to be respected, in general, from the moment of conception, it would seem to follow from this, and the definition of person in Article 1(2) that the unborn foetus is a human being who is in possession of such a right. This would appear to make abortion *prima facie* unlawful. This was a matter which was discussed at some length in the *'Baby Boy' Case*.[246] The substantive merits of the decision in that case will be analyzed below.[247]

It will also be noted that it is persons who are 'subject' to the States Parties' jurisdiction whose rights are to be respected and ensured. The clear implication of this is that it matters not whether the person whose rights have been violated within the territory of a State Party is a national of that state or whether he or she is an alien. El Salvador, for example, is under as much of an obligation to respect and ensure the rights of a visiting United States citizen as it is to respect the rights of its own citizens. The question, however, is whether jurisdiction is limited solely to territorial jurisdiction or whether its ambit extends beyond that to embrace issues of personal jurisdiction. If, for instance, assassins were despatched from one State Party to murder a political dissident of that state's nationality who was a political refugee living elsewhere would the Convention still apply even though offending the act took place outside the State Party's jurisdiction? If the practice of the Human Rights Committee under the Optional Protocol to the International Covenant on Civil and Political Rights is followed, the answer to this question should be in the affirmative. In *Celiberti v Uruguay*[248] the Human Rights Committee was required to determine the admissibility of an application lodged under the First Optional Protocol to the International Covenant on Civil and Political Rights. In this case a Uruguayan citizen living in Italy and visiting Brazil had been abducted by agents of the Uruguayan state and was returned to Uruguay where she was arbitrarily imprisoned and tortured. Uruguay, contesting the admissibility of the application, claimed that the act complained of had not taken place within the jurisdiction of Uruguay by virtue of Articles 1 and 2(1) of the Protocol.[249] The Committee rejected this contention, expressing the view that the reference to jurisdiction in Article 1 of the Protocol was 'not to the place where the violation occurred, but rather to the relationship between the individual and the state in relation to the rights set forth in the Covenant wherever they occurred'.[250] The Committee also went on to say that 'it would be unconscionable to so interpret the responsibility under Article 2 of the Covenant as to permit a State Party to perpetrate a violation of the Covenant on the territory of another state, which violation it could not perpetrate on its own territory'.[251] Given the similarity of the wording in Article 1(1) of the American Convention with that in Article 1 of the First Optional Protocol, it seems that, should a similar situation arise, the supervisory institutions under the American Convention should come to the same conclusions as those of the Human Rights Committee and ground jurisdiction not only on a territorial basis, but also on the basis of the link of nationality between a state and the victim of a violation.

Obligations of Federal States

Article 28 of the American Convention, which is sometimes referred to as the 'federal clause', provides:

> 1. Where a State Party is constituted as a federal state, the national government of such State Party shall implement all the provisions of the Convention over whose subject matter it exercises legislative and judicial jurisdiction.
>
> 2. With respect to the provisions over whose subject matter the constituent units of the federal state have jurisdiction, the national government shall immediately take suitable measures, in accordance with its constitution and its laws, to the end that the competent authorities of the constituent units may adopt appropriate provisions for the fulfilment of this Convention.

As Buergenthal notes,[252] the federal clause is an anachronism which was included in the American Convention at the insistence of the United States of America. Its *raison d'être* was to ensure that federal governments assumed international obligations relating only to their own spheres of jurisdictional competence and not those which fell outside their purview and within the competence of their federal constituents. Other human rights instruments do not possess such a clause, and Article 50 of the International Covenant on Civil and Political Rights specifies the converse by providing that 'the provisions of the present Covenant shall extend to all parts of federal states without any limitations or exceptions'.

The effect of Article 28 was considered by the Commission in *Case 10.180 (Mexico)*.[253] In this case the petitioners complained that the electoral law of the state of Nueva Leon violated Article 23 of the American Convention in that it left control of the electoral process, including grounds for review, entirely within the hands of the state government. Mexico argued that it had no constitutional right to intervene in the affairs of one of its constituent states in this matter, and that Article 28(2) of the American Convention provided justification for this view. The Commission rejected this argument. While the Commission recognized that Article 28(2) protected the relationship between central government and constituent states within a federal constitution, it also noted that, if the central government took the view that rights guaranteed by the Convention only became legally valid when the necessary steps were taken by states within a federation, this would relieve the central government of its obligations under the Convention and would 'leave people without international protection'.[254] Such an interpretation would, in the Commission's view, be incompatible with Article 29(a) of the

Convention.[255] The Commission went on to say that the Mexican government's interpretation of Article 28(2) was:[256]

> ... utterly inconsistent with the responsibility assumed by the Mexican State in ratifying the American Convention on Human Rights, in light of which these matters should have been considered before the instrument was signed and ratified. If before such signature it was felt that the National Government was constitutionally powerless to secure compliance with the provisions of the American Convention from the constituent entities of the Federation, the Mexican State should not have taken on commitments it would be unable to meet.

In the light of this it might be queried whether Article 28 serves any practical purpose or whether it is entirely redundant. Indeed, Buergenthal's original observation that this provision is an anachronism would appear to be valid.

Obligations of States Parties under the Protocol of San Salvador

In contradistinction to the immediate and unconditional obligations imposed upon States Parties to the Convention under Article 1(1), the obligations for parties to the Additional Protocol are progressive and programmatic. This is consistent not only with the approach adopted in Article 26 of the Convention,[257] but also with the statement of state obligations in other cognate instruments such as the International Covenant on Economic, Social and Cultural Rights.[258] Article 1 of the Additional Protocol provides:

> The States Parties to this Additional Protocol to the American Convention on Human Rights undertake to adopt the necessary measures, both domestically and through cooperation among the states, especially economic and technical, to the extent allowed by their available resources, and taking into account their degree of development, for the purpose of achieving progressively and pursuant to their internal legislation, the full observance of the rights recognized in this Protocol.

A number of comments may be made about this provision. First, it imposes a clear obligation of conduct upon States Parties to adopt measures in order to make progress towards the objective of full observance of the rights contained in the protocol. This is an unqualified obligation, and states are clearly bound to take appropriate measures immediately upon becoming party to the Additional Protocol. A State Party which fails to initiate a programme for giving progressive effect to the rights recognized will be in breach of its obligation. Second, the measures must be taken both domestically and in cooperation with other states. Normally, domestic legislation will be the favoured route to realization of the Additional Protocol's rights, but cooperation within the framework of a regional organization, such as the OAS itself, might be necessary for the economic expansion required for the realization of a range of social welfare rights. The third point to note is that the obligation in Article 1 is differentiated. Not only is the obligation of conduct to adopt the necessary measures conditioned by the resources available to States Parties, it is also placed within the context of the current level of development of the individual State Party in question. Thus although a State with low GDP and a low level of economic development will be required to show some evidence of progress towards full observance of the rights protected by the Additional Protocol, the degree of progress required will not be as substantial in absolute terms as that required from a State Party with a greater resource base.

Article 1 cannot, however, be read in isolation. Article 19, which deals with the means of protection under the Additional Protocol, requires the States Parties to 'submit periodic reports on the measures they have taken to *ensure* due respect for the rights set forth'.[259] If the word 'ensure' in Article 19 is attributed the same meaning as that given to it by the Court in the *Honduran Disappearance Cases,* this would imply that States Parties are not only under a duty to give maximum effect to economic, social and cultural rights, but that they are also required to put in place institutional legal structures which permit their vindication. It might be argued that the nature of second generation rights is such that they are not automatically justiciable. Although this argument may have some force, it does not reckon with the fact that the Additional Protocol also extends the individual petition mechanism contained within the American Convention[260] to Article 8(1)(a) (Trade union rights) and Article 13 (Right to education). An individual who alleges that a State Party has violated these rights may, upon satisfaction of the Convention's normal procedural requirements, seek vindication of his or her rights before the Commission and, perhaps, the Court. Furthermore, Article 3 provides that the rights set forth in Additional Protocol must be accorded to individuals 'without discrimination of any kind for reasons related to race, color, sex, language, religion, political or other opinions, national or social origin, economic status, birth or any other social condition'. It is clear, therefore, that once any of the rights in the Protocol are accorded to one individual, then they must be accorded to all, save in circumstances where persons may be distinguished by objectively justifiable criteria.[261]

Domestic Effects of the American Convention

While Article 1 of the American Convention imposes both positive and negative duties upon States Parties to respect and ensure the rights recognized therein, these are supported by Article 2 which deals with the Convention's domestic legal effects. This provides:

> Where the exercise of any of the rights or freedoms referred to in Article 1 is not already ensured by legislative or other provisions, the States Parties undertake to adopt, in accordance with their constitutional processes and the provisions of this Convention, such legislative or other measures as may be necessary to give effect to those rights or freedoms.

While Article 2 appears to be self-explanatory, and, perhaps, redundant, in the light of the fact that all parties to a treaty are under a duty at international law to make the necessary adjustments to their municipal law in order to comply with their international obligations, it may nevertheless have important consequences for States Parties in which the provisions of treaties may be self-executing. The legislative history of the Convention suggests that this provision was adopted for mixed motives. A preliminary study by Carlos A Dunshee Abranches took the view that the incorporation of a provision such as article 2 in the Convention was unnecessary, arguing that 'under the constitutional system prevailing among the American states, the provisions of treaties are incorporated into municipal law through ratification , that is prior enactment of the competent legislative organs, without the need for a special law'.[262] He further suggested that a State Party could defend its failure to protect a Convention right on the grounds that it was in the process of adopting an appropriate law to ensure that right's full protection.[263] The Chilean delegation, however, argued that there was a clear need for the adoption of such a provision requiring States Parties to take appropriate domestic legislative action because of the obscurity of some of the Convention's provisions.[264] The United States delegation was motivated by different considerations. While agreeing with the introduction of the Article by Chile, they argued that it was necessary to allow states to implement the Convention in a manner consistent with their own domestic practices.[265] This would allow states 'to make the articles of the treaty effective *ipso facto* as domestic law' while 'other states may prefer to rely solely on domestic law to implement the articles of the treaty'.[266] It was clearly the United States' preferred strategy to ensure that, as far as it was concerned, the substantive provisions of the Convention should be non-self-executing.[267] As the United States delegation observed in its analysis of Article 2, it would:[268]

... permit us to apply, where appropriate, our Constitution, our domestic legislation already in existence, our court decisions and our administrative practice in carrying out the obligations of the Convention. It will also mean that we will be able to draft any new legislation that is needed in terms that can be readily and clearly assimilated into our domestic codes. In other words, it is not the intention of the US to interpret the articles of the treaty in Part I as being self-executing.

While the United States delegation might have wished to place its view on the conference record that it did not regard the American Convention as being capable of producing self-executing effects, this is by no means conclusive. In the final analysis it will be open to the competent courts of the States Parties to determine whether or not any of the substantive provisions of the Convention possess the qualities necessary for direct municipal application. As Buergenthal suggests, this observation applies as much to the courts of the United States as it does to the courts of other States Parties.[269]

Although in many ways an unsatisfactory case, some insight into the meaning and effect of Article 2 can be gleaned from the Inter-American Court's *Seventh Advisory Opinion: Right to Reply*.[270] In this case Costa Rica requested the Court to rule on whether it could be assumed that 'the full and free exercise of the right protected by Article 14 ... is already guaranteed to all persons under the jurisdiction of the State of Costa Rica by virtue of the obligations assumed by our country under Article 1 of [the] Convention'.[271] If the answer to this question was in the negative, Costa Rica then asked whether it was obliged to adopt the 'legislative or other measures' necessary to give effect to the right under Article 2 of the Convention.[272] If this were the case, what should the nature of these 'legislative or other measures' be?[273]

Before analyzing the nature of these questions and the ruling in the case, it should be noted that the Court decided to take jurisdiction in this request for an advisory opinion only by the narrowest of margins. Three of the seven judges in the case[274] held the view that the Court did not have jurisdiction in this matter since they considered that Costa Rica's request concerned the interpretation of its municipal law and not an interpretation of the American Convention or related instruments. Despite this, the dissenting judges participated in the substantive phase of the opinion, as required by the Courts Rules of Procedure.[275] In order to minimize the area of disagreement between the judges, the Court reformulated the questions posed by Costa Rica to bring them within the ambit of the Court's competence.[276] By doing this the Court was able to render an opinion which Judge Buergenthal described as 'unobjectionable'.[277] It may be remarked that it also produced an opinion possessing a particularly anodyne and opaque quality.

The American Convention on Human Rights differs from its European and international counterparts by providing in Article 14 a right to reply for persons injured by inaccurate or offensive statements or ideas[278] disseminated to the public using legally regulated media. The existence of this provision would seem to be inspired by two related concerns: first, that it is the function of government to create appropriate mechanisms for the resolution of human rights violations occasioned by private actions,[279] and second, the fact that Article 14 is intimately connected with the fundamental right of freedom of thought and expression which is guaranteed by Article 13 of the American Convention,[280] in particular, the limitations which are imposed upon that right by Article 13(2).[281] The Court also noted other provisions of the Convention which impacted directly on the symbiotic relationship between rights and duties. These were Article 32(2), the application of which in the area of freedom of expression was examined in *Compulsory Membership* and Articles 11(1) and 11(3) which state:

> 1. Everyone has the right to have his honour respected and his dignity recognized.
> 2. ....
> 3. Everyone has the right to the protection of the law against such interference or attacks.

These obligations to respect the rights of others are, indeed, reinforced within Article 14(1) itself which provides that injured persons have the right to reply or correction using the same medium 'under such conditions as the law may establish'. This suggests that the right to reply or correction is optional since it is phrased in permissive fashion. The Court, however, rejected this contention. First, it stated that States Parties are under an obligation to take the necessary measures under Article 1(1) and Article 2 to ensure the rights guaranteed by the Convention and to give effect to them within their domestic law. Further, the purpose of the Convention 'is to recognize individual rights and freedoms and not simply to empower the states to do so'.[282] Thus, regardless of state action, the right to reply was guaranteed by the Convention.[283] Nonetheless, the question remained as to the precise extent of the right to reply and the degree of discretion allowed to the state in order to give full force to the right under its domestic law. Here, the Court noted that the detailed conditions governing the right to reply were not contained in Article 14(1). While, for example, the provision referred to the fact that the right should be exercisable using the same means of communication as that in which the original defamation was uttered, it did not indicate whether beneficiaries of the right were entitled to the same amount of space, the period of time within which the right was to be exercised, what language was admissible and so on.[284] The Court nonetheless ruled that Article 14 required the 'establishment of the conditions for exercising the right to reply of correction by "law"' but that in guaranteeing the right the contents of the appropriate domestic laws might vary from state to state 'within certain reasonable limits and within the framework of the concepts stated by the Court'.[285]

Despite the permissive nature of the language used in Article 14(1) and the vagueness of the guide-lines established by the Court, it nonetheless took the view that this did not impair the duty of States Parties under Article 2 of the Convention to give effect to the obligations contained in Article 14.[286] It is suggested that this is likely to create problems for States Parties which will perhaps be unsure exactly to what extent they must modify their domestic laws to ensure that the conditions of Article 14 are met. The lack of precision in the drafting of Article 14 would certainly not render it self-executing in those states with monist constitutions, and it is therefore unreasonable to impose the burden of implementation upon the state without being more specific as to the precise extent of the obligations in question. This objection would not apply, however, to more clearly drafted provisions of the American Convention which may be capable of possessing self-executing effect.

It will be noted also that the conditions governing the right to reply or correction must be established by 'law'. The meaning of this particular word has been considered in the context of Article 30, where the Court has noted[287] that the word did not necessarily have the same meaning throughout the Convention and must therefore be determined on a case by case basis.[288] In this case the Court took the view that, since the conditions governing the right to reply had to be established by the States Parties in accordance with their obligations under Article 2 of the Convention, it was necessary, in order to comply with that provision 'to adopt ... such legislative or other measures as may be necessary to give effect to [the] rights and freedoms'. This, the Court concluded, included 'all those measures designed to regulate the exercise of the right to reply or correction'.[289] An interpretation of the Court's conclusion would therefore seem to suggest that the right to reply might be guaranteed by measures less than legislation. This would include, for example, any rights derived from common law in States Parties possessing this system of municipal law, and, perhaps, executive action short of formal law.[290] The extent to which the meaning of Article 2 can be extrapolated from this advisory opinion is unclear, but it does seem to suggest that the methods by which States Parties might give effect to the rights protected by the American Convention are manifold, and that as long as they bear the hallmark of legal certainty within the State Party in question, that State will have fulfilled its obligation under the Convention.

Restrictions to and Derogations from the Rights Protected by the American Convention

Like all human rights instruments, the American Convention contains provisions which permit restrictions upon the exercise of certain rights where their full, unbridled enjoyment would lead to the denial of the rights of others.[291] While such permissible restrictions are referred to explicitly in the provisions protecting specific rights, Article 30 of the Convention provides a statement of principles which must be applied in every case where a State Party seeks to curtail the enjoyment of a particular right. Article 30 provides:

> The restrictions that, pursuant to this Convention, may be placed on the enjoyment or exercise of the rights or freedoms recognized herein may not be applied except in accordance with laws enacted for reasons of general interest and in accordance with the purpose for which such restrictions have been established.

The American Convention also contains a further provision, Article 27, which permits states to suspend the enjoyment of certain rights under well-defined conditions. This provides:

> In time of war, public danger or other emergency that threatens the independence or security of a State Party, it may take measures derogating from its obligations under the present Convention to the extent and for the period of time strictly required by the exigencies of the situation, provided that such measures are not inconsistent with its other obligations under international law and do not involve discrimination of the ground of race, color, sex, language, religion or social origin.

It should be noted that there is a clear conceptual difference between restrictions on the enjoyment of rights under Article 30 and the suspension of those rights under Article 27. This distinction has been explained neatly by the Court in its *Sixth Advisory Opinion: The Word 'Laws'*.[292] Here, the Court noted that restrictions on rights referred to in Article 30 are authorized by the Convention itself, whereas the suppression of rights is in general impermissible under Article 29(a).[293] Only 'in exceptional cases and under conditions precisely spelled out' in Article 27 will the *temporary* suppression of rights be legitimate.[294] The Court also ruled, however, that Article 30 could not be regarded as an authorization to establish new restrictions to rights protected by the Convention additional to those allowed under the rules governing each of the rights in question.[295]

Before examining the jurisprudence of the Court on Articles 27 and 30, a cursory examination of the contents of these provisions is necessary. The terms of Article 30 make it clear that certain criteria must be evident in any attempt by a State Party to restrict the enjoyment of any of the rights protected by the Convention. First, the restriction must be one which is recognized by the provisions of the Convention themselves. Certain rights such as the right to life (Article 4), the right to humane treatment (Article 5) and freedom from slavery (Article 6) are not subject to the possibility of restriction, and may not therefore be 'clawed back' by the state. Second, rights which are capable of being restricted may only be so by the application of laws 'enacted for reasons of general interest and in accordance with the purpose for which such restrictions have been established'. This makes it clear that restrictions may not be imposed arbitrarily but must be justified by reference to the public good and effected by laws which have been properly adopted. This conclusion is supported by the jurisprudence of the Court.[296] Third, the grounds upon which the restrictions are established must be in accordance with the criteria stipulated in the Convention. These are the interests of national security, public safety or public order, or to protect public health or morals or the rights or freedoms of others.[297] Finally, some provisions require specifically that the restrictions imposed may only be those which are 'necessary in a democratic society'[298] although it may be argued that by virtue of Article 29(c) any restrictions to the rights recognized by the Convention may only be effected having proper regard to the requirements of representative democracy.[299]

While Article 30 deals with restrictions to certain rights within the terms of the Convention itself, Article 27 comprehends the circumstances in which States Parties may actually suspend the operation of certain of the protected rights. The importance of this particular provision to the inter-American human rights system cannot be exaggerated given the willingness of non-democratic regimes within the Western Hemisphere to resort to states of emergency or states of siege in order to buttress their totalitarian rule.[300] While the provision is clearly designed to give a margin of appreciation to States Parties in determining whether or not the conditions for the suspension of rights exist, it is similarly clear that certain concrete criteria must be satisfied and that, ultimately, the Convention institutions are the final arbiters in determining whether or not a State Party is acting within the bounds of its margin of appreciation.[301] The first criterion which a state must show when seeking to derogate from the protection of certain rights under the Convention is that there exists a state of war, public danger or other emergency which threatens its independence or security. While each of these is a flexible concept, it is apparent that the threat perceived by the State Party might be either external or internal. Although external threats are possibly easier to prove than internal threats, a state must still demonstrate that such a threat exists: a mere allegation of an internal threat to security will be insufficient to meet the standard required by the Convention. Second, the derogation from the rights protected must be strictly limited both in temporal terms and in terms of the exigencies of the situation. This latter is a rule of proportionality indicating that the measures taken by a State Party must not exceed the purposes for which they were adopted. It is also noteworthy that the State Party must also impose a definite time limit upon the measures of suspension which it has taken. This is not simply a matter of inference from Article 27(1), but Article 27(3) makes clear that this is a matter of obligation. Third, such measures must not be inconsistent with a State Party's other obligations under international law nor must they discriminate on grounds of race, colour, sex, language, religion or social origin although it would seem that discrimination on grounds of national origin might still be permissible.[302] Despite the existence of these safeguards with which States Parties must comply in derogating from the rights protected by the Convention, certain rights remain incapable of suspension. Article 27(2) stipulates that the application of Article 27(1) 'does not authorize the suspension of the following Articles: Article 3 (Right to Juridical Personality), Article 4 (Right to Life), Article 5 (Right to Humane Treatment), Article 6 (Freedom from Slavery), Article 9 (Freedom from *Ex Post Facto* Laws), Article 12 (Freedom of Conscience and Religion), Article 17 (Rights of the Family), Article 18 (Right to a Name), Article 19 (Rights of the Child), Article 20 (Right to Nationality), and Article 23 (Right to Participate in Government)'. Article 27(2) also provides that the judicial guarantees essential for the protection of the rights mentioned may also not be suspended. This latter has been the subject of comment by the Court in three advisory opinions which will be considered in detail immediately below.

A State Party which wishes to suspend any of the rights not referred to in Article 27(2) must comply with certain procedural requirements established by Article 27(3). This provides that a state availing itself of the right of suspension must immediately inform the other States Parties to the Convention through the Secretary General of the OAS. It must indicate which rights it has suspended, the reasons which gave rise to the suspension and the date set for the termination of such suspension.

Although the majority of the requirements contained in Articles 30 and 27 may seem self-evident, certain aspects of these provisions have been the subject of requests for advisory opinions. These advisory opinions handed down by the Court have done much to clarify not only the specific characteristics of those parts of the provisions under consideration, but also their wider relationship to certain fundamental principles which underpin the inter-American human rights system as a whole. In *The Word 'Laws'*, the Court was requested by Uruguay to rule on the meaning of the word 'laws' within the context of Article 30. Although the question put to the Court was restricted to the meaning of the word 'laws', the Court nonetheless took the opportunity to rule upon the criteria necessary for a legitimate application of restrictions under Article 30. It identified three criteria which must be applied concurrently if the restrictions were to be lawful. These were:[303]

> a) that the restriction in question be expressly authorized by the Convention and meet the special conditions for such authorization;
> b) that the ends for which the restriction has been established be legitimate, that is, that they pursue 'reasons of general interest' and do not stray from the 'purpose for which [they] have been established' ...
> c) that such restrictions be established by laws and applied pursuant to them.

The Court indicated, however, that word 'laws' was to be interpreted as a term used in an international treaty and the meaning could not be dictated by municipal law definitions of that term.[304] It nevertheless observed that the concept of laws could not be interpreted in the abstract and must not therefore be divorced from the context of the legal system giving meaning to the term.[305] Furthermore, the meaning of 'laws' was also conditioned by the nature and origin of the system established for the protection of human rights.[306] Here, the principle of legality demanded that restrictions to human rights may only be established in accordance with a law passed by the legislature in accordance with constitutional requirements.[307] In this regard the Court said:[308]

> Although it is true that this procedure does not always prevent a law passed by the Legislature from being in violation of human rights - a possibility that underlines the need for some system of subsequent control - there can be no doubt that it is an important obstacle to the arbitrary exercise of power.

In making this ruling the Court was clearly drawing upon certain conceptions of the nature of human rights and their relationship to the democratic process and the rule of law. While the underlying philosophy of each of these concepts remained largely unarticulated, it is nonetheless clear that the Court regarded each of these as being interlinked and mutually supporting. Thus, by implication, it seems that the Court was making an assertion that the democratic process and human rights are inextricably linked, and the whole structure is encompassed by the rule of law. This thinking by the Court in *The Word 'Laws'* has been more fully explored by it in subsequent cases regarding suspension of rights contained in the Convention and will be considered in further detail below.[309] Given this particular perspective, however, the Court concluded: [310]

> ... the word 'laws', used in Article 30, can have no other meaning than that of formal law, that is, a legal norm passed by the legislature and promulgated by the Executive branch, pursuant to the procedure set out in the domestic law of each state.

Despite reaching this clear conclusion, the Court nonetheless considered it necessary to deal with the additional requirements imposed by Article 30 in order to render legitimate restrictions imposed in accordance with the definition of 'laws' described above. In particular, the concepts of general welfare and public order were necessary prerequisites to the exercise of legitimate restrictions on rights guaranteed by the Convention. Once again, the Court held that these were terms which must be interpreted within the context of the Convention 'which had its own philosophy under which the American states "require the political organization of these States on the basis of the effective exercise of representative democracy" (Charter of the OAS, Art. 3(d)); and the rights of man, which "are based upon attributes of his human personality"'. Here the Court recalled its judgment in *Compulsory Membership,* where it had considered these concepts in detail, and reaffirmed the meanings which it had given to them there.[311] From this it concluded:[312]

> The 'laws' referred to in Article 30 are, therefore, normative acts directed towards the general welfare, passed by a democratically elected legislature and promulgated by the Executive Branch. This meaning is fully consistent with the general context of the Convention, in line with the philosophy of the inter-American system. Only formal law, as the Court understands that term, can restrict the enjoyment and exercise of the rights recognized by the Convention.

The principles of representative democracy, legality and the rule of law which inspired the Court's decision in *The Word 'Laws'* were also at the root of its decisions in two cases involving derogations from, or suspension of, rights protected by the Convention. In the first of these cases, *Habeas Corpus in Emergency Situations,*[313] the Court was requested by the Commission to interpret Articles 7(6), 25(1), and 27(2) of the Convention in order to determine, as was the Commission's belief, that these provisions, when read in conjunction, prevented States Parties from suspending the remedy of *habeas corpus* during situations of emergency, although this was not directly referred to in Article 27(2). The Commission's reason for seeking the opinion lay in the fact that, while a number of States Parties believed that they were entitled to make such a suspension, the Commission was of the opinion that in so doing further serious human rights abuses, such as disappearances, were masked.[314] In a similar request, Uruguay asked the Court to offer an advisory opinion interpreting the scope of the Convention's prohibition of the suspension of the judicial guarantees essential for the protection of the rights referred to in Article 27(2).[315] In particular, Uruguay asked the Court to rule on which of the judicial guarantees were 'essential' and the relationship between Article 27(2) and Articles 25 and 8 of the Convention.

In both these cases the Court, in interpreting Article 27, placed considerable weight on the principles upon which the inter-American system was founded. It noted, in particular, the 'inseparable bond between the principle of legality, democratic institutions and the rule of law'.[316] In this context therefore, the Court ruled:[317]

> The concept of rights and freedoms as well as that of their guarantees cannot be divorced from the system of values and principles that inspire it. In a democratic society, the rights and freedoms inherent in the human person, the guarantees applicable to them and the rule of law form a triad. Each component thereof defines itself, complements and depends on the others for its meaning.

Relying on these principles, therefore, the Court took the view that temporary suspension of guarantees did not give states a *carte blanche* in the degree of suppression in which it was entitled to engage. Certain minimum standards must be observed. As the Court said, 'this does not mean ... that the suspension of guarantees implies a temporary suspension of the rule of law, nor does it authorize those in power to act in disregard of the principle of legality by which they are bound all times'.[318] What then were the appropriate limitations upon state action in derogating from protected rights in times of emergency? The first limitation arose from the fact that Article 27(1) itself makes clear that it is a provision designed to deal with exceptional situations only. It operates only 'in time of war, public danger or other emergency that threatens the independence or security of a State Party'.[319] Further the derogation must only be 'to the extent and for the period of time strictly required by the exigencies of the situation' and must not involve 'discrimination on the ground of race, color, sex, language, religion or social origin'.[320] The first point arising from this particular provision is that Article 27(1) implies a rule of proportionality: the measures taken must be appropriate to meet the needs of the situation. As the Court observed, this will vary from situation to situation, and what might be permissible in one set of circumstances will not necessarily be permissible in another.[321] Article 27(2), however, goes on to further limit the application by providing that certain specific rights are non-derogable[322] and that the 'judicial guarantees essential for the protection of such rights' cannot similarly be derogated from.

In order to determine whether this latter phrase meant that *habeas corpus* was a remedy which could not be suspended in times of emergency, the Court found it necessary to examine certain of the words in detail.[323] The first word to be analyzed was 'guarantee'. The Court defined this as meaning that the concept was 'designed to protect, to ensure or to assert the entitlement to a right or the exercise thereof'.[324] In this context the Court noted that States Parties were under an obligation by virtue of Article 1(1) to ensure the effective exercise of rights and freedoms by means of appropriate guarantees.[325]

In determining the meaning of what judicial remedies might be 'essential' for the protection of the non-derogable rights, the Court observed that these will vary according to the right to be protected. Nonetheless, in the context of Article 27(2) this meant judicial remedies 'that ordinarily will effectively guarantee the full exercise of the rights and freedoms protected by that provision and whose denial or restriction would endanger their full enjoyment'.[326] Further, implicit in the concept of 'judicial guarantees' is 'the active involvement of an independent and impartial judicial body having the power to pass on the lawfulness of measures adopted in a state of emergency'.[327]

The Court then moved to the question of whether the guarantees contained in Articles 25(1) and 7 were to be deemed among the judicial guarantees essential for the protection of non-derogable rights, despite not being mentioned explicitly in Article 27(2). Article 25(1) provides:

> Everyone has the right to simple and prompt recourse, or any other effective recourse, to a competent court or tribunal for the protection against acts that violate his fundamental rights recognized by the constitution or laws of the state concerned to by this Convention, even though such violations may have been committed by persons acting in the course of their official duties.

This the Court took to be a provision which gave expression to the procedural institution of *amparo* which exists in nearly all Latin American states.[328] In this sense it both embraces and subsumes the remedy of *habeas corpus* under which a state's authorities are required by judicial order to bring a detained person before a competent court in order that the lawfulness of the detention might be judicially determined. This remedy is also implicit in Article 7(6) of the Convention, the material part of which proclaims:

> Anyone who is deprived of his liberty shall be entitled to recourse to a competent court, in order that the court may decide without delay on the lawfulness of his arrest or detention and order his release if the arrest or detention is unlawful. In States Parties whose laws provide that anyone who believes himself to be threatened with deprivation of his liberty is entitled to recourse to a competent court in order that it may decide on the lawfulness of such threat, this remedy may not be restricted or abolished...

Taking the two provisions together, the Court found that while *habeas corpus* was simply a species of *amparo*, in some states it stood as an independent remedy, whereas in others it was subsumed by *amparo*.[329] The Court thus ruled that 'since "amparo" can be applied to all rights, it is clear that it can also be applied to those that are expressly mentioned in Article 27(2) as rights that are non-derogable in emergency situations'.[330]

As far as *habeas corpus* was concerned, the Court found that, in order to achieve its purpose, it was necessary that the detained person be brought before a competent judge or tribunal with jurisdiction. Here, especially in Latin America with its history of enforced disappearances, it provided a vital role in ensuring that an individual's life and physical integrity were respected, and also in guarding such individuals against disappearance, torture or other cruel, inhuman, or degrading punishment or treatment.[331] The Court therefore concluded that both *habeas corpus* and *amparo* were among the judicial remedies essential for the protection of various rights, derogation from which was prohibited by Article 27(2), and which also served to preserve legality in a democratic society.[332] The Court also observed that the constitutions and legal systems of States Parties which expressly or impliedly authorized the suspension of *habeas corpus* or *amparo* in emergency situations could not be deemed compatible with their international obligations under the Convention.[333]

A further dimension to the Court's reasoning in the area of derogations was added by its decision in *Judicial Guarantees*. Here Uruguay had asked the Court to examine, *inter alia,* the relationship between Articles 27(2), 25 and 8. While the Court took the opportunity to confirm much of its reasoning in *Habeas Corpus in Emergency Situations,* it also elaborated upon the appropriate mechanisms for giving effect to the non-derogable remedies of *habeas corpus* and *amparo*. Article 8(1) provides:

Every person has the right to a hearing, with due guarantees and within a reasonable time, by a competent, independent and impartial tribunal previously established by law, in the substantiation of any accusation of a criminal nature made against him or for the determination of his rights and obligations of a civil, labor, fiscal or any other nature.

In the Court's view, this provision clearly recognizes the concept of due process of law which is a necessary prerequisite to ensure the adequate protection of those persons whose rights or obligations are pending before a court or tribunal.[334] The Court concluded therefore that the concept of due process of law which is contained in Article 8 is applicable to all the judicial guarantees referred to in the Convention, even where there have been derogations governed by Article 27.[335] Taking Articles 8, 7(6), 25 and 27(2) together, the Court ruled that the principles of due process cannot be suspended in states of emergency[336] 'as they are necessary conditions for the procedural institutions regulated by the Convention to be considered judicial guarantees'.[337] This reasoning was applicable *a fortiori* to the remedies of *habeas corpus* and *amparo* which were themselves 'indispensable for the protection of the human rights that are not subject to derogation'.[338] Thus, while the Court was prepared to hold that the right to due process cannot be suspended in times of emergency, it was not prepared to limit its opinion by indicating which remedies, apart from those of *habeas corpus* and *amparo,* were not susceptible to derogation. As the Court indicated, 'those will depend in each case upon an analysis of the juridical order and practice of each State Party, which rights are involved and the facts which give rise to the question'.[339]

Restrictions and Limitations to the Protocol of San Salvador

Like the American Convention, the Protocol of San Salvador contains provisions dealing with restrictions and limitations to the rights recognized. Unlike the American Convention, however, there is no provision which permits the suspension of these rights. Indeed, Article 4 indicates that, once a right of the kind recognized by the Protocol has been implemented by a State Party, whatever the provenance of that right, it may be neither suspended nor limited, nor may it be the subject of further restriction or curtailment. Article 4 provides:

A right which is recognized or in effect in a state by virtue of its internal legislation or international conventions may not be restricted or curtailed on the pretext that this Protocol does not recognize the right or recognizes it to a lesser degree.

The effect of Article 4 is also further to reinforce the view that the implementation of economic, social and cultural rights is programmatic and progressive.[340] Thus those rights which have been, or are in the process of being, implemented may not be clawed back by a State Party, unless, of course, they fall within the category of rights which are specifically designated as susceptible to restriction or limitation.[341]

Article 5 of the Protocol establishes the conditions under which the rights recognized may be limited or restricted. This provides:

> The States Parties may establish restrictions and limitations on the enjoyment and exercise of the rights established herein by means of laws promulgated for the purpose of preserving the general welfare in a democratic society only to the extent that they are not incompatible with the purpose and reason underlying those rights.

The terminology used in Article 5 is similar to that employed by Article 27 of the American Convention, save that there is a clear reference to the general welfare within the context of a democratic society and an indication that the limitations must be compatible with the 'purpose and reason' underlying the rights established by the Protocol. It is unlikely that the notions of 'general welfare' and 'democratic society' would receive and interpretation different to those in its sibling instrument should the Commission or the Court be called upon to give content to them.

Entry into Force of the American Convention and Reservations

Entry into force of the Convention is governed by Article 74. This provides that 'the Convention shall be open for signature and ratification by or adherence of any Member State of the Organization of American States'.[342] Ratification or adherence is effected by states depositing the appropriate instrument with the General Secretariat of the OAS[343] and the Convention enters into force on the deposit of the eleventh instrument of ratification.[344] Although the American Convention was opened for signature at San José, Costa Rica on 22 November 1969, it did not receive its eleventh ratification, and hence did not enter into force, until 18 July 1978.[345] For those states which ratify or adhere at a later date, the Convention comes into force for them upon the deposit of their instrument of ratification or adherence.[346] Where a state ratifies with reservation, the Convention continues to enter into force in accordance with the provisions of Article 74(2), unless the reservation is incompatible with the object and purpose of the Convention. This latter proposition is derived from the Inter-American Court's advisory opinions in *Effect of Reservations*[347] and *Restrictions to the Death Penalty*.[348]

Article 75 of the American Convention is the basic provision dealing with reservations. It states:

> This Convention shall be subject to reservations only in conformity with the provisions of the Vienna Convention on the Law of Treaties signed on May 23, 1969.

At first glance, this would seem to suggest that Articles 19-23 of the Vienna Convention which deal with multifarious aspects of the law concerning reservations are applicable in their totality to the American Convention, yet careful scrutiny reveals that this cannot be so, since a number of provisions have no direct relevance to the circumstances of the American Convention. Indeed, this became apparent in *Effect of Reservations*. Here, the Commission invoking the advisory jurisdiction of the Court requested the latter to determine the moment at which a state became party to the American Convention when it ratified the Convention with a reservation. Did it become party to the Convention immediately upon making the ratification in accordance with Article 74, regardless of the nature of the reservation, or did its ratification with reservation fail to take immediate effect on the basis of Article 20(5) of the Vienna Convention which makes entry into force of a treaty contingent upon positive acceptance by other States Parties or their acquiescence for a period of twelve months?

In answering these questions, the Court noted that it was required to deal with the complex inter-relationship between the provisions of the American Convention and the relevant provisions of the Vienna Convention. The point of departure was interpretation of Article 74 of the American Convention which stipulates that the Convention enters into force for a ratifying or adhering state 'on the date of the deposit of its instrument of ratification or adherence'. This provision, the Court observed, was silent on the question of reservations. Nonetheless, Article 75 provided that reservations made by ratifying states must conform to the requirements of the Vienna Convention, and therefore an examination of the appropriate provisions contained in this instrument was necessary also. The Court first concluded that the provisions of the Vienna Convention which were relevant to the issue before it were Articles 19 and 20. It noted in particular that since the American Convention neither forbade nor required certain types of reservation, Article 19(c), which requires reservations to be compatible with the object and purpose of the Convention, was alone relevant. Thus states which wished to ratify or adhere to the Convention could do so with reservation as long as such reservation was compatible with its object and purpose. This view that the drafters had intended the Convention to embody a flexible system for the making of reservations was confirmed by the *travaux préparatoires*.[349] Having determined that Article 19(c) was the relevant provision governing the types of reservations which could be made to the American Convention, the Court then turned its attention to which provisions of Article 20 governed the entry into force of the American Convention for reserving states. Only two provisions were *prima facie* relevant here: Article 20(1) or Article 20(4). The Court considered Article 20(2) inapplicable in view of the fact that the object and purpose of the Convention was 'not the exchange of reciprocal rights between a limited number of states, but the protection of the human rights of all individual human beings within the Americas, irrespective of their nationality'.[350] This reasoning also had a direct impact on the question of whether Article 20(1) or 20(4) was applicable to the case. In an application of the principle of effectiveness, the Court declared that it would be 'manifestly unreasonable'[351] to conclude that the reference to the Vienna Convention in Article 75 required the application of Article 20(4) since this would envisage delay of the entry into force of the American Convention until one other state was prepared to accept the reserving state as a party. This, the Court concluded, could hardly be deemed to be the intention of the Convention.[352] Thus, by a process of elimination based upon a combination of techniques of interpretation, the Court arrived at the conclusion that Article 20(1) of the Vienna Convention was the applicable norm which was referred to in Article 75 of the American Convention. The position which therefore emerged was that the Convention entered into force in accordance with Article 74 immediately upon ratification or accession for a state ratifying or acceding with a reservation, as long as that reservation was compatible with the object and purpose of the Convention. This conclusion of course begs the question: who or what is to determine the compatibility of a reservation with the Convention? Would a clearly incompatible reservation, for example, justify other States Parties in refusing to recognize the reserving state as a party? The view of the Court here was unequivocal: if States Parties, which of course had a legitimate interest in barring reservations which were incompatible with the object and purpose of the Convention, wished to contest a reservation, they could do so utilizing the advisory or adjudicatory mechanisms of the Convention. The Court went on to state:[353]

> They [the States Parties] have no interest in delaying the entry into force of the Convention and with it the protection that the treaty is designed to offer individuals in relation to states ratifying or adhering to the Convention with reservations.

In *Restrictions to the Death Penalty,* the Court shed some light on its understanding of the measure of the compatibility of reservations with the Convention. Here, it stated that the object and purpose of the Convention imposed 'real limits' on the effect which reservations could have.[354] In order for reservations to be acceptable they must be compatible with the object and purpose of the Convention, and would be interpreted by the Court in such a manner as to ensure compatibility.[355] A further legal limitation on the interpretation of a reservation was Article 29(a) of the Convention which in the Court's conclusion compelled the view that a reservation 'may not be interpreted so as to limit the enjoyment and exercise of the rights and liberties recognized in the Convention to a greater extent than is provided for in the reservation itself'.[356] In *Restrictions to the Death Penalty,* the practical application of these principles meant that a strict interpretation of the reservation to Article 4 of the Convention reserving the right of Guatemala to extend application of the death penalty for certain common crimes did not permit that State Party to extend, by implication, the death penalty to common crimes associated with political crimes. Furthermore, the Court ruled that any attempt to apply a reservation to one of the Convention's non-derogable rights thereby attempting to limit such a right could never be compatible with the object and purpose of the American Convention.[357]

Entry into Force of the Protocol of San Salvador and Reservations

The Protocol of San Salvador was adopted on 17 November 1988 and is open to signature, ratification or accession by any State Party to the American Convention.[358] Ratification or accession is to be effected by deposit of the appropriate instrument by a Convention State Party with the General Secretariat of the OAS,[359] and the Protocol will enter into force when it receives its eleventh instrument of ratification or accession.[360] To date the Protocol has received fifteen signatures, but only three ratifications.[361] Its early entry into force appears to be unlikely.

Reservations to specific provisions of the Protocol may be made by States Parties at the time of approval, signature, ratification or accession.[362] Such reservations must be compatible with the object and purpose of the Protocol.[363] This provision is clearly less cumbersome than its counterpart in the American Convention and clearly obviates the need for direct reference to the relevant provisions of the Vienna Convention on the Law of Treaties. In interpreting Article 20 and its effects, it is unlikely that the Court would deviate from the observations which it made in *Effect of Reservations* and *Restrictions to the Death Penalty* which were considered in detail above.[364]

Denunciation

Under Article 78(1) States Parties may denounce the American Convention after the expiration of a five year period starting from the date of its entry into force. Notice of denunciation must be given to the Secretary-General of the OAS one year in advance of its taking effect.[365] The denunciation of the Convention by a State Party does not have the effect of releasing it from its responsibility under the Convention for any violation carried out by the State Party prior to the effective date of denunciation.[366] Thus, even if a State Party commits a violation of its obligations within the year prior to the denunciation taking effect, it will still be responsible for that violation.

Other Human Rights Instruments Adopted within the Framework of the Organization of American States

While the instruments considered above comprise the greater part of the inter-American human rights system, treatment of this area would not be complete without mention of three further instruments which have been adopted within the framework of the OAS. These are the Inter-American Convention to Prevent and Punish Torture 1987,[367] the Inter-American Convention on the Forced Disappearance of Persons 1994[368] and Inter-American Convention on the Prevention, Punishment and Eradication of Violence against Women 1994.[369] While the first of these instruments is in force, the latter two are not.

The Inter-American Convention to Prevent and Punish Torture. The Inter-American Convention to Prevent and Punish Torture was adopted on 9 December 1985 and entered into force on 28 February 1987.[370] According to its preamble the Convention records that its adoption is necessary in order to permit the rules prohibiting torture in the OAS Charter, the UN Charter, the American Declaration and the Universal Declaration to take effect.[371] While recognizing the existence of the prohibition on torture in Article 5 of the American Convention on Human Rights,[372] the clear implication of the Inter-American Convention on Torture is that this is insufficient to meet the wider demands of the prevention of torture. Article 2 of the Convention provides a broad definition of torture which will be analyzed below in connection with Article I of the American Declaration and Article 5 of the American Convention.[373] At this point, only the institutional aspects of the Convention will be considered.

Under the Inter-American Torture Convention states are required to take effective legislative, administrative, judicial or other measures to prevent and punish torture and inchoate offences associated with torture within their jurisdiction.[374] They are also required to exercise personal jurisdiction over their own nationals who may commit acts of torture outside their territory[375] and may assume passive personality jurisdiction over persons who may have perpetrated torture against one of their nationals.[376] In addition to these jurisdictional extensions, states area also required to apply the principle of *aut dedere aut iudicare* in relation to fugitive offenders.[377] This creates a comprehensive and interlocking jurisdictional regime for combating torture throughout the territories of the States Parties.

Two further aspects of the Torture Convention relating to extradition require some comment. The first is that Article 15 requires that no provision of the Convention may be interpreted as limiting the right of asylum or as altering the obligation of the Parties in matters of extradition. This raises the unfortunate possibility that a person whose crimes are associated with political offences may well escape prosecution on the grounds of the political offence exception to extradition.[378] To some extent this reflects the political realities of inter-state relations in the Western Hemisphere. Second, as with the United Nations Convention against Torture,[379] States Parties agree not to return or extradite persons to countries where there are grounds to believe they would be in danger of being subjected to torture.[380]

Under the Inter-American Torture Convention States Parties also agree to take measures to ensure that in the training of police officers and other public officials responsible for the custody of persons, special emphasis is placed on the prohibition of the use of torture in interrogation, detention or arrest.[381] It is noteworthy that Article 10 of the Convention stipulates that no statement which has been obtained through torture may be admitted as evidence in legal proceedings, except in proceedings against the alleged torturer him or herself as evidence of the means by which the statement was elicited.[382] Where any person makes an accusation that he or she has been subjected to torture, states are required to guarantee that such a person will have the right to an impartial examination of his or her case.[383] Furthermore, if there is an accusation or well-grounded reason to believe that an act of torture has been committed within the jurisdiction of a State Party, the state must proceed immediately to conduct an investigation into the allegation and initiate the appropriate criminal process to punish any torturer.[384] The Inter-American Convention also lays down the standard of punishment which is to be applied in cases of torture. Article 6(2) provides that States Parties are to make acts of torture 'punishable by severe penalties that take into account their serious nature'. Furthermore, State Parties undertake to incorporate into their national laws a right of adequate compensation for victims.[385] If the domestic legal system should fail the claimant alleging that he or she has been the victim of torture, Article 8(3) makes the rather obvious point that 'the case may be submitted to the international fora whose competence has been recognized by that State'. This also corresponds with Article 16 which makes clear that the Inter-American Convention on Torture does not affect the provisions of the American Convention on Human Rights nor, by implication, the American Declaration on the Rights and Duties of Man nor any other analogous international instrument.

Unlike cognate instruments the Inter-American Torture Convention does not establish a special supervisory institution. It relies instead upon existing OAS institutions to discharge this function. The institution bearing primary responsibility for supervising the Convention is the Inter-American Commission on Human Rights. States Parties are required to inform this body of any legislative, judicial, administrative or other measures adopted in the application of the Convention.[386] The Commission itself is enjoined by Article 17 of the Convention to 'endeavor in its annual report to analyze the existing situation in the Member States of the Organization of American States in regard to the prevention and elimination of torture'. The annual report which is referred to in this provision is that discussed below in the consideration of the Commission's general competences under the OAS Charter.[387] As noted there, this report becomes a matter of public record and is open for discussion by the OAS General Assembly at its annual session. While the specifics of the human rights situation in any particular Member State may or may not be the subject of debate, the report itself becomes a matter of notoriety. Thus state wrongdoing, as well as state progress in combating torture, is exposed to public gaze.

While the institutional aspects of the Inter-American Torture Convention may appear to be weak, it should be noted that this instrument is fundamentally different to other like international instruments, since it is aimed at strengthening the criminal law and law enforcement procedures of its States Parties within the context of an already comprehensive supranational human rights supervision and enforcement system. The aim of the Inter-American Convention on Torture is to alter the penal cultures of the States Parties by reinforcing the ethos of non-violence in dealing with any detained persons whether in time of peace or national emergency. The history of the widespread use of torture in the Western Hemisphere in a variety of circumstances indicates that this has been, and in many instances continues to be, a matter of vital importance.

The Inter-American Convention on the Forced Disappearance of Persons. In many senses the phenomenon of enforced disappearances is synonymous with human rights abuses in many Member States of the OAS. The Commission's annual reports are replete with petitions alleging disappearances, and many of its country reports have been obliged to investigate this practice. While the Commission has ritually condemned enforced disappearances in the strongest terms, the practice persists.[388] In an attempt to reinforce efforts to secure the elimination of disappearances in the Western Hemisphere, the OAS charged the Commission with the task of drafting a convention directed towards such an end. The Convention was adopted at Belém do Pará on 9 June 1994. There are currently twelve signatories to the Convention, but no states have yet ratified the instrument.[389] Under the Convention State Parties undertake not to practise, permit or tolerate the forced disappearance of person.[390] This prohibition is to apply even during states of emergency or during the suspension of individual guarantees protecting human rights.[391] States Parties are further required to punish those within their jurisdictions who commit or attempt to commit enforced disappearances.[392] In order to achieve these ends, States Parties are required create appropriate offences and impose appropriate punishment on those who are convicted of crimes associated with enforced disappearances.[393] Enforced disappearances are not to be considered political offences,[394] and where extradition is not granted, the requested state must investigate and, where appropriate, try those concerned in accordance with its domestic law.[395] Criminal prosecution of enforced disappearances is not to be subject to a limitation period, except in cases where such a limitation period is preserved for grave crimes, in which case the same period of limitation may apply.[396] Superior orders are no defence to prosecutions and the Convention makes clear that 'all persons who receive such orders have the right and duty not to obey them'.[397] Furthermore, Article IX of the Convention provides that the acts constituting enforced disappearance shall be deemed not have been committed in the course of military duties. An obligation is also placed on States Parties to ensure that the training of public law enforcement personnel or officials includes the necessary education on the offence of enforced disappearance of persons.[398]

While the Convention does not of itself possess mechanisms of enforcement, it provides in Article XIII that for its purposes the individual petition procedure of the Commission provided for in Article 44 of the American Convention and the Statute and Regulations of the Commission are to be regarded as applicable. This would seem to suggest that, even if a State Party to the Inter-American Convention on the Forced Disappearance of Persons were not a Party to the American Convention, the Commission's enforcement mechanisms in the latter instrument would nevertheless apply. Whether the Convention on Forced Disappearances is likely to have any significant effect should it eventually enter into force is difficult to predict. It may, however, be pertinent to observe that the strengthening of the law in this area is likely to further underpin existing prohibitions of such practices in the American Declaration and the American Convention.

The Inter-American Convention on the Prevention, Punishment and Eradication of Violence against Women. The question of violence against women not only in the public but also in the private sphere is a matter which has assumed increased importance at the international level.[399] Article 1 of the Inter-American Convention thus provides that:

> For the purposes of this Convention, violence against women shall be understood as any act or conduct, based on gender, which causes death or physical, sexual or psychological harm or suffering to women, whether in the public or the private sphere.

Article 2 then continues to define such violence. Essentially it is that which occurs within the family or domestic unit or within any other inter-personal relationship and includes rape, battery and sexual abuse.[400] Violence is also extended to that which occurs in the community and which is perpetrated by any person.[401] In addition to the specific acts of violence referred to above, violence within the community refers also to torture, trafficking in persons, forced prostitution, kidnapping and sexual harassment in any place.[402] Violence is also perpetrated against women if it is perpetrated or condoned by the state or its agents.[403] Article III of the Convention provides that 'every women has the right to be free from violence in both the public and private spheres' and Article 4 then goes on to list a number of preferred rights which are applicable to women.[404] All these rights may be found in the American Declaration and the American Convention as well as other international instruments which protect first and second generation rights. In addition to placing obligations on states to eliminate violence against women by adopting appropriate legislative and other measures,[405] States Parties are also required to adopted progressive programmes aimed not only at women, but also at men. Article 8(b), for example, requires states to introduce programmes which will 'modify social and cultural patterns of conduct of men ...'.[406]

The mechanisms of protection which will be introduced by the Convention are a system of national reports to the Inter-American Commission of Women outlining the measures taken in pursuit of the Convention's goals.[407] Articles 11 and 12, however, provide practical measures of enforcement. Article 11 permits States Parties and the Inter-American Commission of Women to request advisory opinions from the Inter-American Court of Human Rights[408] while Article 12 allows individuals, groups of individuals or non-governmental organizations to lodge petitions with the Inter-American Commission on Human Rights alleging violation of Article 7 of the Convention. The Commission is to handle such petitions in accordance with its normal practice under Article 44 of the Convention, it Statute and its Regulations.[409]

In accordance with Article 21, the Convention will enter into force on the thirtieth day following the deposit of the second instrument of ratification.

Principles of Treaty Interpretation

In considering the general scope of the various instruments which form the inter-American human rights system, it is appropriate to address the issue of the principles which ought to be, and which have been, applied in the interpretation of their provisions. In a number of decisions both the Commission and the Court have agreed that their primary approach to interpretation of the American Convention and its associated instruments are founded upon the rules contained in Articles 31 and 32 of the Vienna Convention on the Law of Treaties. These provide:

> Article 31(1). A treaty shall be interpreted in good faith in accordance with the ordinary meaning to be given to the terms of the treaty in their context and in the light of its object and purpose.
> Article 32. Recourse may be had to supplementary means of interpretation, including the preparatory work of the treaty and the circumstances of its conclusion, in order to confirm the meaning resulting from the application of Article 31, or to determine the meaning when the interpretation according to Article 31:
> (a) leaves the meaning ambiguous or obscure; or
> (b) leads to a result which is manifestly absurd or unreasonable.

While Article 31 clearly gives primacy to the text in the interpretation of any treaty, that is, the words should be given their plain, ordinary and natural meaning, it is also clear that this may be conditioned by the context in which they appear and construed in the light of an instrument's object and purpose.

As Sinclair points out, however, these latter are secondary factors since the text of the treaty is to be read 'in the light' of the additional criteria.[410] While the context of an agreement may be more or less readily ascertainable by consulting its preamble, questions concerning the object and purpose may not be so easily identifiable. Furthermore, there is also some doctrinal dispute over the extent to which the object and purpose of a treaty should be permitted to dominate the function of interpretation.

There are two ways in which the object and purpose a treaty may be identified: first, recourse may be had to the preamble of the treaty in order to discover the motives which the parties professed for bringing the instrument into being. By using these means, an interpreter ensures the integrity of the instrument by refusing to step outside its four corners in order to identify extraneous factors. Second, interpreters of a treaty may have regard to external issues influencing its origins which may lead to a discovery of the purposes for which it was concluded. These purposes may be further confirmed by an examination of the *travaux préparatoires* which is permitted by Article 32 of the Vienna Convention.

As indicated above, there is some dispute over the degree to which the object and purpose of the treaty should be allowed to influence its interpretation. Those jurists who may be described as 'textualists' consider that the ordinary meaning of the words of a treaty should not be transformed by an undue leaning on the text using criteria derived from its presumed object and purpose.[411] The 'teleologists' maintain, however, that the object and purpose of an instrument ought to be given maximum effect by interpreting its words as broadly as possible. Some teleologists also take the view that the object and purpose of a treaty does not remain static, but is dynamic and must be interpreted to ensure conformity with developing trends or social conditions.[412] The interpretation of the European Convention on Human Rights as a 'living instrument' designed to meet the needs of European society at the time of interpretation rather than the time of the instrument's execution is an example of this latter approach.[413] The major criticism levelled at the teleological approach to interpretation of international agreements is that it leads to judicial legislation thereby distorting or in some cases destroying the purity of the text.[414]

The principle of effectiveness, which is not specifically referred to in the Vienna Convention, should also be mentioned here. During the drafting of the Convention it was thought unnecessary by the International Law Commission to include specifically the variety of principles and so-called canons of interpretation which have been advocated by jurists over the years.[415]

This was not, however, to deny that certain principles enjoyed a lasting influence and legitimacy, but the Commission was of the opinion that the principle of effectiveness, as expressed in the maxim *ut res magis valeat quam pereat*, did not require special mention in the text of the Convention since it believed the principle was subsumed by reference to 'good faith' in Article 31.[416] In practice, the principle requires that the interpretation of a treaty should be such as to make it most effective and useful.[417] Evidence of the principle in action may be found once again in the jurisprudence of the European Court of Human Rights where it has enjoyed a wide and continuing currency.[418]

Although it is possible to identify a number of separate modes of interpretation employed by international tribunals, the reality of the process of interpretation is less clear-cut. Tribunals, rather than employing a single method of interpretation of a treaty, tend to apply a number of interpretative approaches either in sequence or simultaneously to achieve the desired result. It is also noticeable that certain tribunals, such as the European Court of Human Rights, will often declare that they are applying the textual method of interpretation when close analysis reveals that their methods are in fact more teleological or end-orientated.[419] Evidence of this may be found, although to a limited extent given the small number of decided cases, in the work of the Inter-American Court.[420]

As a preliminary matter there is also another factor which needs to be taken into account when considering the approach adopted to interpretation of the American Convention by the Commission and the Court. This is the existence in the Convention itself of Article 29 which places clear restrictions on interpretation. Article 29 provides:

Restrictions Regarding Interpretation

No provision of this Convention shall be interpreted as:
a. permitting any State Party, group or person to suppress the enjoyment or exercise of the rights and freedoms recognized in this Convention or to restrict them to a greater extent than is provided for herein;
b. restricting the enjoyment or exercise of any right or freedom recognized by virtue of the laws of any State Party or by virtue of another convention to which one of the said States is a party;
c. precluding other rights or guarantees that are inherent in the human personality or derived from representative democracy as a form of government; or
d. excluding or limiting the effect that the American Declaration of the Rights and Duties of Man and other international acts of the same nature may have.

The Commission, but more particularly the Court, has referred to this provision on a number of occasions and in so doing has revealed a certain paradox. Indeed, this paradox is contained in Article 29 itself. This is that, rather than functioning to constrain or restrict the breadth of the Court's interpretation of particular provisions or instruments, it has provided the basis for a wider teleological approach. In *Compulsory Membership*, a case involving a Costa Rican law requiring practising journalists to have certain recognized qualifications and to belong to a recognized professional organization,[421] Costa Rica contended that Article 29 demanded that, where a right in another international human rights instrument was more rigorously circumscribed than its American Convention counterpart, the more restrictive interpretation should be given effect within the inter-American system.[422] Failure to do this would mean that what was legal and permissible for states to do on the international plane would constitute a violation under the American Convention.[423] The Court rejected this argument on two grounds: first, that restrictions could not be read into the Convention which were not grounded in the text,[424] and second, Article 29(b) did not permit an interpretation which limited the rights of an individual under the Convention.[425] The Court thus concluded that 'if in the same situation both the American Convention and another international treaty are applicable, the rule most favourable to the individual must prevail'.[426]

A more straightforward application of Article 29 is evident in *Interpretation of the American Declaration*. This advisory opinion, which was requested by Colombia, sought to establish whether or not the 1948 American Declaration on the Rights and Duties of Man was a treaty within the meaning of Article 64 of the Convention.[427] While finding that, as a matter of law, the Declaration was not a treaty, the Court nevertheless held that, by virtue of Article 29(d), which forbade any limitation or exclusion of the Declaration in interpreting the Convention, it was entitled to apply the Declaration when interpreting the Convention.

A less obvious restriction on interpretation, but one to which the Court has referred in conjunction with Article 29, is Article 32(2), a general provision which states that 'the rights of each person are limited by the rights of others, by the security of all, and by the just demands for the general welfare, in a democratic society'. This provision assumes particular importance when analyzing attempted restrictions to the exercise of certain rights which are claimed to be for the general good within the context of a democracy, and will be considered in detail below.[428] It is sufficient to note here, however, that the Court has taken the view that neither Article 29 nor Article 32 may be invoked to deny rights guaranteed by the Convention or to impair or deprive them of their true content.[429] The Court, enunciating the general principle that exceptions must be construed strictly, has stated:[430]

> Those concepts, when they are invoked as a ground for limiting human rights, must be subjected to an interpretation that is *strictly limited* to the 'just demands' of 'a democratic society', which takes account of the need to balance the competing interests involved and the need to preserve the object and purpose of the Convention.

The Literal Approach

Both the Commission and the Court have taken the view that Articles 31 and 32 of the Vienna Convention on the Law of Treaties contain the appropriate rules of international law governing interpretation of treaties.[431] It is within the Court's jurisprudence, however, that the rules principles regarding interpretation of the American Convention have been most fully developed. In *Restrictions to the Death Penalty* the Court stated that Articles 31 and 32 of the Vienna Convention on the Law of Treaties embody 'the relevant international law principles applicable to this subject'[432] and it is this statement which it has cited with approval in subsequent cases.[433] The rationale of the Court for adopting this position is of some interest. In its view, reliance upon the primacy of the text ensures the application of objective criteria to the function of interpretation. This, the Court observed, was particularly appropriate in the case of human rights treaties because, as it had already noted in *Effect of Reservations*, human rights treaties 'are not multilateral treaties of the traditional type concluded to accomplish the reciprocal exchange of rights for the mutual benefit of the Contracting States'.[434] This statement itself, however, suggests an imminent departure from the textuality which the Court itself professed to favour, since it appears implicit that the Court had already identified certain subjective assumptions about the nature and function of multilateral human rights treaties as distinct from other forms of international agreements. Indeed, the seeds of teleology would appear already to have been sown in this case. Nonetheless, the direct application of the textual approach to interpretation is evident in a number of the Court's judgments or at least in parts of those judgments.

The clearest example of the employment by the Court of the literal approach is perhaps to be found in *Right to Reply*.[435] Here, the Court was requested by Costa Rica to render an advisory opinion on, *inter alia*, the extent of the obligation requiring States Parties to grant the right to reply in

Article 14 of the Convention to the persons envisaged by that provision. The Court noted here that Article 14 granted a right to reply or correction to persons who had been the object of defamatory statements which had been disseminated by the mass media. It also noted that this right was absolute, which was why, in the Court's opinion, Articles 14(2) and (3) were so categorical in speaking of the nature of the legal liabilities involved and the requirement that someone within the medium in question should be personally responsible for such statements. The Court therefore ruled that this interpretation was neither ambiguous nor obscure, nor did it lead to a manifestly absurd result. In the Court's view the ordinary meaning of Article 14 was abundantly clear.

In *Other Treaties* the Court was obliged to consider the meaning of 'other treaties concerning the protection of human rights in the American States' in Article 64(1). A number of possible interpretations of this term were put forward by the Court, ranging from a restrictive interpretation which would have limited the phrase to including only treaties concluded within the inter-American system to a broader interpretation which would have embraced treaties of a human rights character to which any American state was party, even though it had been concluded outside the inter-American system. Here the Court noted the broad language employed in Article 64. It concluded from this that the text of the provision did not 'compel the conclusion that it was to be restrictively interpreted'.[436] Thus the ordinary meaning of the text did not permit the Court to rule that certain international treaties were meant to be excluded from the scope of Article 64 because non-American states might be or become party to them. Article 64 spoke simply of treaties concerning the protection of human rights *in* the American states not *between* American states. The Court concluded, 'since such a restrictive purpose was not expressly articulated, it cannot be presumed to exist'.[437]

The Court nonetheless went on to rule that this did not mean there were no limits to its jurisdiction in such matters. There were implied limitations which were not expressly revealed by the words of Article 64 itself. These implied limitations would operate, for example, where a human rights treaty possessed its own autonomous enforcement machinery.[438] This would appear to apply in particular to the International Covenant on Civil and Political Right, the implementation and enforcement of which is supervised by the Human Rights Committee.[439]

In *Effect of Reservations*, the Court again signified its reliance upon the primacy of textual interpretation required by Article 31 of the Vienna Convention. Here, the Court had to consider the meaning of Article 75 which provides that the American Convention is to be 'subject to reservations only in conformity with the provisions of the Vienna Convention on the Law of Treaties'. Relying on the text of Article 75 the Court concluded that the reference to the Vienna Convention must have been intended to be a reference to Article 19(c) of that Convention simply because the American Convention did not prohibit reservations. It held therefore that 'Article 75 must be deemed to permit states to ratify or adhere to the Convention with whatever reservations they wish to make, provided only that such reservations are not "incompatible with the object and purpose" of the Convention'.[440]

It is perhaps appropriate at this point to note that the Court applies precisely the same method of interpretation to reservations to the Convention as it does to the Convention itself. In *Restrictions to the Death Penalty*,[441] the Court indicated that since reservations become part of the Convention they must necessarily be interpreted as an integral part of that instrument. As a result of this it follows that 'a reservation must be interpreted by examining its text in accordance with the ordinary meaning which must be attributed to the terms in which it has been formulated within the general context of the treaty of which the reservation forms an integral part'.[442] The Court also observed, as a general principle, that since a reservation sought to modify a state's obligations within the framework of the Convention, it should be interpreted restrictively and against the state making it.[443]

Context and Object and Purpose

It will be recalled that these are the secondary criteria to which reference may be made when interpreting a treaty. It may also be recalled that the precise extent of the application of the object and purpose of a treaty is not the subject of unanimous agreement between jurists.[444] While the European Court of Human Rights has had considerable recourse to the teleological approach to interpretation, the American Court has had little opportunity to engage in the kind of judicial legislation undertaken by its European analogue. This is not to say that elements of teleology are not evident in the jurisprudence of the American Court, simply that, given the paucity of cases, there has not been the opportunity for that Court to employ it on such a wide scale.

The American Court's earliest recourse to the context of words in, and the object and purpose of, the Convention was in *Other Treaties,* the case in which it was required to fix the limits of its own advisory jurisdiction. Here, the Court looked not only at its institutional competence within the framework of the Convention, but in the context of the inter-American human rights system as a whole.[445] In order to determine this the Court not only examined the text of the Convention, but also its Preamble which refers to the Universal Declaration of Human Rights and other international instruments. The provisions of the Convention itself also refer to other international instruments from which human rights obligations may be derived.[446] The Court also argued that Article 64(2), which empowers it to advise OAS Member States on the compatibility of their domestic laws with human rights obligations assumed under the Convention and other treaties concerning the protection of human rights confirmed this view. From this the Court deduced that the American states had an interest in conforming their domestic laws to international human rights obligations regardless of which other states are parties to the relevant treaties. From these premises the Court deduced that the competence given to it by Article 64 to interpret other treaties for the protection of human rights in the American states did not necessarily mean that its function was restricted simply to interpreting treaties concluded within the inter-American system.

The Court also sought to locate its advisory function within the object and purpose not only of the American Convention, but within the object and purpose of human rights treaties in general.[447] Here it said that the purpose of such treaties was to guarantee the enjoyment of individual human beings of rights and freedoms rather than the establishment of reciprocal relations between states. This emphasis upon the *sui generis* nature of human rights treaties has been a recurring theme in the Court's judgments[448] and has, in Buergenthal's view, weakened traditional concepts in the law of treaties.[449] In order to legitimate its view that human rights treaties are *sui generis,* the Court has had recourse not only to the preamble of the Convention itself,[450] but has also drawn upon the jurisprudence of the ICJ in the *Genocide Convention Case*,[451] Article 60(5) of the Vienna Convention on the Law of Treaties, which provides that treaties of humanitarian character are not to be regarded as having been discharged by breach, and the writings of jurists.[452]

Another case in which the context of a particular word assumed considerable importance was *The Word 'Laws'*. Here Uruguay requested an advisory opinion on the meaning of the word 'laws' in Article 30 of the American Convention. This article provides that restrictions imposed upon the rights and freedoms in accordance with rules established by the Convention may not be applied save in accordance with laws enacted for that specific purpose. The Court held here that the meaning of the word must be sought as a term used in a treaty and could not be defined solely within the context of a state's domestic law. Thus the term had to be interpreted within the context of the system for the protection of human rights and could not be dissociated from that system.[453] Following an analysis of the development of systems for human rights protection the Court concluded that:[454]

> The word 'laws', used in Article 30, can have no other meaning than that of formal law, that is, a legal norm passed by the legislature promulgated by the Executive Branch, pursuant to the procedure set out in the domestic law of each state.

Again in *Habeas Corpus in Emergency Situations,* The Court was requested by the Commission to rule on whether *habeas corpus* was a remedy which could be suspended in emergency situations in accordance with Article 27(2) of the Convention. This required the Court to examine the meaning of the word 'guarantees' in the provision in question. The Court declared:

An analysis of the terms of the Convention in their context leads to the conclusion that we are not here dealing with a 'suspension of guarantees' in an absolute sense, nor with the 'suspension of ... [rights]', for the rights protected by these provisions are inherent to man. It follows therefrom that what may only be suspended or limited is their full and effective exercise.[455]

Supplementary Means of Treaty Interpretation

As indicated above, Article 32 of the Vienna Convention permits the use of supplementary means to interpret treaties in a variety of circumstances in order to confirm the meaning of a provision or to assist in interpretation where an application of the literal or textual approach results in ambiguity or obscurity or leads to a result which is manifestly absurd or unreasonable. Both the Commission and the Court have had resort to the use of Article 32. In the *'Baby Boy' Case,* for example, the majority of the Commission resorted immediately to the *travaux préparatoires* of the American Declaration and the American Convention without even considering the plain meaning of the words in context.[456] In the majority of cases in which the Court has employed the use of supplementary means of interpretation, usually the *travaux préparatoires* of the Convention, this has been to confirm the meaning of the text arrived at by an application of the textual approach to interpretation.[457] In *Other Treaties,* for example, the Court examined the evolution of the text of Article 64 as a means of confirming that the drafters of the Convention had intended to give the Court a broad advisory jurisdiction.[458] In *Effect of Reservations,* however, it is at least arguable that the lack of clarity in the text which simply referred to the Vienna Convention on the Law of Treaties as being the appropriate source of law governing reservations to the American

Convention, was conclusively resolved by recourse to the *travaux préparatoires* of the Convention which revealed that the drafters had intended a liberal system for making reservations to be included in Article 75 of the Convention.[459]

Although not strictly speaking a supplementary means of interpretation, the Court in *The Word 'Laws'* referred to the 'spirit' of the Convention as an aid to interpretation.[460] Rather than being a supplementary means of interpretation, this may rather be viewed as a form of teleology, a recourse to the fundamental rationale for the existence of the Convention. In dismissing the notion that 'laws' meant simply the mechanistic process of creating legal rules, the Court said:

> In the spirit of the Convention, this principle [of legality] must be understood as one in which general legal norms must be created by the relevant organs pursuant to the procedures established in the constitutions of each State Party, and one to which all public authorities must strictly adhere. In a democratic society, the principle of legality is inseparably linked to that of legitimacy by virtue of the international system that is the basis of the Convention as it relates to the 'effective exercise of representative democracy', which results in the popular election of legally created organs, the respect of minority participation and furtherance of the general welfare, *inter alia.*[461]

From this passage it can be seen that the spirit of the Convention is rooted firmly in notions of liberal democratic pluralism in which the notions of legality, as understood by the Court, and legitimacy are intricately intertwined if not, indeed, symbiotic.[462]

The Principle of Effectiveness

While the Court has not yet had significant recourse to the application of this particular principle, it is in evidence in certain decisions. In *Effect of Reservations* the Court was required to decide whether a state ratifying the American Convention with a reservation became party to the Convention from the date of deposit of its instrument of ratification or adherence or whether, in accordance with Article 20(4) of the Vienna Convention on the Law of Treaties, it did not become party until either another contracting party accepted the reservation or until a year had passed without any existing State Party registering an objection. In reaching its decision the Court, without specifically mentioning the principle, declared:[463]

A treaty which attaches such great importance to the protection of the individual that it makes the right of individual petition mandatory as of the moment of ratification, can hardly be deemed to have intended to delay the treaty's entry into force until at least one other state is prepared to accept the reserving state as a party. Given the institutional and normative framework of the Convention, no useful purpose would be served by such a delay.

Further, in *Restrictions to the Death Penalty*, the Court declined to refuse to give an advisory opinion at the request of Guatemala because that state was in actual dispute with the Commission over the meaning of Article 4(2) of the Convention. To decline to give a ruling on that basis said the Court, would deprive the advisory opinion procedure of its utility.[464]

The American Convention as a Treaty sui generis

Another factor which is related to the question of intepretation of the American Convention and its related instruments, and which was referred to briefly above is the way in which the Inter-American Court views the Convention as a treaty *sui generis*. Buergenthal has commented that the emergence of international human rights law as a separate branch of public international law taken together with the emergence of procedural rights for individuals on the international plane has led to a modification in the way in which human rights treaties *qua* treaties are now regarded in the doctrine of international law.[465] There is much to support this argument, especially in the jurisprudence of the European Court of Human Rights and the emerging jurisprudence of the Inter-American Court. The basis for the approach of the Inter-American Court is the identification of the Convention as an instrument which is concerned primarily with the protection of individuals and is which is not particularly concerned with the reciprocal rights and obligations of the States Parties. While the Convention is an agreement between states governed by international law, the traditional concept of reciprocity does not accurately reflect the object of the Convention which is to ensure to the individuals within their jurisdiction the free and full exercise of the rights and freedoms contained therein without discrimination.[466] The obligations of states in this regard do not depend therefore upon the corresponding commitment of the other States Parties to do likewise. The Convention may be the vehicle establishing the legal commitment to ensure rights and freedoms, but the States Parties undertakings have more of a binding unilateral character to them.[467] This theoretical position was enunciated clearly by the Court in *Effect of Reservations* in which the Court emphasized that modern human rights treaties in general, and the American Convention in particular, were not multilateral treaties of the traditional type concluded to accomplish the reciprocal exchange of rights for the mutual benefit of the contracting states, but that their object and purpose is the protection of the basic rights of human beings irrespective of their nationality, both against the state of their nationality and all other contracting states. The Court further held that, in concluding these human rights treaties, the states had submitted themselves to a legal order within which they had assumed various obligations, not in relation to other states, but towards all individuals within their jurisdiction.[468] The Court further observed that the Convention was 'a multilateral legal instrument or framework enabling states to make binding unilateral commitments not to violate the human rights of individuals within their jurisdiction'.[469] In order to support its views, the Inter-American Court referred to the *Genocide Convention Case* in which the World Court had said:[470]

> The Convention was manifestly adopted for a purely humanitarian and civilizing purpose...In such a convention the contracting states do not have any interests of their own; they merely have, one and all, a common interest, namely, the accomplishment of those high purposes which are the *raison d'être* of the Convention. Consequently, in a convention of this type one cannot speak of individual advantages or disadvantages to states, or of the maintenance of a perfect contractual balance between rights and duties...

The Court also cited the judgment of the European Court of Human Rights in *Austria v Italy*[471] in which that court had declared: the purpose of the Parties in concluding the European Convention was not to concede reciprocal rights and obligations to each other in pursuance of their individual national interests but to realize the aims and ideals of the Council of Europe and 'to establish a common public order of the free democracies of Europe with the object of safeguarding their common heritage of political traditions, ideas, freedom and the rule of law'.[472] The Court was further able to refer to Article 60(5) of the Vienna Convention on the Law of Treaties which provides that a fundamental breach of a treaty having a humanitarian character shall not enable the parties to treat the treaty as being discharged by the breach or to suspend its operation between the parties. This provision of the Vienna Convention and the *dicta* of the ICJ and European Court referred to above tend to demonstrate a convergence in the jurisprudence of international tribunals and institutions which indicate that treaties having a humanitarian character are distinct from traditional agreements between states which contain reciprocal rights and duties. As Buergenthal suggests, however, 'no international tribunal has thus far articulated this principle as clearly as the inter-American Court'.[473]

The Inter-American Court's efforts to identify a new framework for human rights treaties, and the Convention in particular, has not been a purely theoretical exercise, but has produced tangible effects in its approach to interpretation. In *Other Treaties*, the Court, in determining whether the Commission could disguise a contentious case by seeking an advisory opinion from it, declared that since the purpose of human rights treaties was to guarantee the enjoyment by individual human beings of rights and freedoms rather than establish reciprocal relations between states, any attempt to weaken the contentious jurisdiction of the Court or undermine its purpose, thereby changing the Convention system to the detriment of the victim, would not be permitted.[474] Again, in *Effect of Reservations* the Court was obliged to consider whether Articles 74 and 75 required the delay of the entry into force of the Convention for a year because of the requirements of the Vienna Convention on the Law of Treaties governing reservations to which Article 75 referred. The Court held that the delay of entry into force because of the ratification or accession by a state with reservation could not be contemplated. This was so because 'the object and purpose of the Convention is not the exchange of reciprocal rights between a limited number of states, but the protection of the human rights of all individual human beings within the Americas, irrespective of their nationality'.[475]

Thus the Court's interpretation of the Convention has much to do not only with the way in which it conceptualizes the nature of the rights protected, but also the way in which it conceptualizes the inter-American system and the application of international law principles to the Convention. Its approach is clearly within the Western liberal democratic tradition which predicates a certain form of political, social and economic organization, which in turn has implications for both the interpretation and application of human rights. Nonetheless, the Court's view of humanitarian treaties, and the Convention in particular, as having a novel quality appears to strengthen the trend in international law of treating such treaties as a *sui generis* group requiring an interpretative approach different to that of traditional multilateral treaties. This might, however, have less to do with new concepts of international law and rather more to do with the development of supra-national systems of human rights protection. Perhaps the key lies in the phrase 'a common public order of the free democracies of Europe' used by the European Court in *Austria v Italy*,[476] which, while not necessarily equating to the European Court of Justice's memorable phrase describing the Treaty of Rome as 'a new legal order',[477] nonetheless signifies that the European Convention may be seen as a distinct system within the general framework of international law. If this is true of the European Convention system, then it ought, in theory, to be true of the American Convention system also.

Notes

[1]   For descriptions of the genesis and structure of the OAS see G. Connell-Smith, *The Inter-American System* (London: OUP, 1966); C.G. Fenwick, *The Organization of American States* (Washington: 1963) (hereafter '*Organization of American States*'); A. van W. and A.J. Thomas, *The Organization of American States* (Dallas: Southern Methodist University Press, 1963); Cecilia Medina-Quiroga, *The Battle of Human Rights* (Dordrecht: Nijhoff, 1988) (hereafter '*Battle of Human Rights*'); D.W. Bowett, *The Law of International Institutions* (London: Sweet and Maxwell, 4th edn, 1982), pp. 215-225; Thomas Buergenthal, Robert Norris and Dinah Shelton, *Protecting Human Rights in the Americas: Selected Problems* (Kehl-am-Rhein: N. p. Engel Verlag, 2nd edn, 1986), pp. 1-12; W.H. Calcott, *The Western Hemisphere: Its Influence on United States Policies to the End of World War II* (Austin, TX and London: University of Texas Press, 1968).

[2]   R.N. Burr and R.D. Hussey, eds, *Documents on Inter-American Cooperation 1881-1948*, Volume II (Philadelphia: University of Pennsylvania Press, 1955), pp. 49-51.

[3]   Ibid., p. 49.

[4]   Ibid., p.51.

[5]   Ibid.

[6]   See Connell-Smith, *Inter-American System*, pp. 1-5.

[7]   Ibid.

[8]   Burr and Hussey, *Documents on Inter-American Cooperation*, pp. 65-8.

[9]   Carnegie Endowment for International Peace, *The International Conferences of American States: First Supplement 1933-40* (Washington: Carnegie Endowment for International Peace, 1940), p.215.

[10]   Ibid., p.129.

[11]   Inter-American Conference on Problems of War and Peace, Chapultepec, Mexico City, February 21-March 8, 1945 in Burr and Hussey, *Documents on Inter-American Cooperation*, pp. 159-61. See also Connell-Smith, *Inter-American System*, pp. 129-38.

[12]   Burr and Hussey, *Documents on Inter-American Cooperation*, pp. 159-61.

[13]   21 UNTS 77.

[14]   Inter-American Conference for the Maintenance of Continental Peace and Security, Quitadihna, Brazil, August 15 - September 2, 1947.

[15]   See J.L. Kunz, 'The Bogota Charter of the Organization of American States' (1948) 42 AJIL 568.

[16]   119 UNTS 4.

[17]   On the Protocol of Buenos Aires see J. Dreier, 'New Wine in Old Bottles: The Changing Inter-American System' (1968) 22 *International Organization* 477; A.H. Robertson, 'Revision of the Charter of the Organization of American States' (1968) 17 ICLQ 345; W. Manger, 'Reform of the OAS: The 1967 Buenos Aires Protocol of Amendment to the Charter of Bogota: An Appraisal' (1968) 10 *Journal of Inter-American Studies* 1; César Sepúlveda, 'Reform of the Charter of the Organization of American States' (1972-III) 137 *Hague Rec* 83.

[18] (1986) 25 ILM 529.

[19] Article 2 of the amended Charter.

[20] Article 116 of the amended Charter.

[21] Protocol of Washington (1994) 33 ILM 1005.

[22] Ibid., p. 1009.

[23] Article I of the Protocol of Managua (1994) 33 ILM 1009. This is not yet in force.

[24] Article 4 OAS Charter. There are currently 35 OAS Member States. They are: Antigua and Barbuda, Argentina, Bahamas, Barbados, Belize, Bolivia, Brazil, Canada, Chile, Colombia, Costa Rica, Cuba, Dominica, Dominican Republic, Ecuador, El Salvador, Grenada, Guatemala, Guyana, Haiti, Honduras, Jamaica, Mexico, Nicaragua, Panama, Paraguay, Peru, Saint Lucia, Saint Vincent and the Grenadines, St Kitts and Nevis, Suriname, Trinidad and Tobago, United States of America, Uruguay, Venezuela.

[25] Article 52 of the UN Charter provides: 'Nothing in the present Charter precludes the existence of regional arrangements or agencies for dealing with such matters relating to the maintenance of international peace and security as are appropriate for regional action, provided that such arrangements or agencies and their activities are consistent with Purposes and Principles of the [UN]' and Article 2 OAS Charter provides 'The [OAS], in order to put into practice the principles on which it is founded and to fulfil its regional obligations under the Charter of the [UN], proclaims the following essential purposes: ...'. An examination of these 'essential purposes' demonstrates that a number of these are entirely consistent with the UN's objectives of maintaining peace and security. Thus Articles 2(a) and (c) of the Charter indicate that two of the Organization's primary purposes are to 'strengthen the peace and security of the continent' by providing mechanisms for cooperation and peaceful settlement of disputes. Article 136 of the OAS Charter further provides, 'None of the provisions of this Charter shall be construed as impairing the rights and obligations of the Member States under the Charter of the UN'.

[26] Article 55 OAS Charter provides: 'All member States have the right to be represented in the General Assembly. Each State has the right to one vote'.

[27] See Article 53 OAS Charter.

[28] Article 56 OAS Charter.

[29] Article 57 OAS Charter.

[30] Article 53(a) OAS Charter provides that General Assembly has as its principle powers: 'To decide the general action and policy of the Organization, determine the structure and functions of its organs, and consider any matter relating to friendly relations among the American States'.

On the potential of the General Assembly to request advisory opinions from the Court under Article 64(1) Convention see infra, p. 234.

[31] Article 60 OAS Charter.

[32] Article 61 OAS Charter. For a description of the Permanent Council see infra, pp. 5-6.

[33] Article 64 OAS Charter.

[34] These are the Permanent Council, the Inter-American Economic and Social Council and the Inter-American Council for Education, Science and Culture. See Articles 69-78 OAS Charter for provisions common to their structure and functioning.

[35] Article 79 OAS Charter. The Permanent Council is composed of one representative of ambassadorial rank from each OAS member State.

[36] Article 90(c) OAS Charter. The General Assembly, however, retains the sole power of decision.

[37] Article 90 OAS Charter.

[38]   Article 92 OAS Charter.

[39]   Article 93 OAS Charter.

[40]   Chapter VII OAS Charter entitled 'Integral Development'.

[41]   Primarily Articles XI-XVI of the American Declaration of the Rights and Duties of Man (hereafter 'Declaration').

[42]   Advisory Opinion OC-10/89 of 14 July 1989, *Interpretation of the American Declaration of the Rights and Duties of Man within the Framework of Article 64 of the American Convention on Human Rights* (hereafter '*Interpretation of the American Declaration*'), Series A, No. 10; (1990) 29 ILM 379; (1990) 11 HRLJ 118.

[43]   Chapter III Convention.

[44]   (1989) 28 ILM 156.

[45]   On states economic, social and cultural rights obligations see infra, pp. 32-3.

[46]   Article 98 OAS Charter.

[47]   It is intended here to give only the briefest of descriptions of the Commission, since its importance as a Charter and Convention institution is considerable, and must be considered in some detail later. See infra, chapter 2.

[48]   See Thomas Buergenthal, 'The Revised OAS Charter and the Protection of Human Rights' (hereafter '*Revised Charter*') (1975) 69 AJIL 828; W. Manger, 'Reform of the OAS: The 1967 Buenos Aires Protocol of Amendment to the 1948 Charter of Bogota: An Appraisal', (1968) 10 *Journal of Inter-American Studies* 1; A.H. Robertson, 'Revision of the Charter of the Organization of American States' (1968) 17 ICLQ 345; César Sepúlveda, 'Reform of the Charter of the Organization of American States' (1972-III) 137 *Hague Rec* 83.

[49]   For more detailed consideration of the role of the Commission see infra, pp. 107-180.

[50]   See infra, chapter 2.

[51]   Article 150 OAS Charter provides: 'Until the inter-American convention on human rights, referred to in Chapter XVI, enters into force, the present Inter-American Commission on Human Rights shall keep vigilance over the observance of human rights'.
The American Convention was not, however, adopted until 1969 and did not enter into force until 1978. For discussion of the Commission's competences under the Charter and the Convention see infra, pp. 107-18.

[52]   Article 127 OAS Charter.

[53]   Article 113 OAS Charter.

[54]   Ibid.

[55]   Article 114 OAS Charter.

[56]   Article 116 OAS Charter.

[57]   Examples include agriculture, cartography, tourism, travel, education and intellectual property.

[58]   'Technical' is to be construed here in the broadest sense.

[59]   The Inter-American Commission of Women has special procedural competences under Article 12 of the Inter-American Convention on the Prevention, Punishment and Eradication of Violence against Women (1993) 33 ILM 1534. This Convention is not yet in force. For further discussion see infra, pp. 66-7.

[60]   The origin and extent of these obligations will be discussed infra.

[61]   See infra, chapter 6.

[62]   Preambular paragraphs 1 and 4.

[63]   Lawrence J. LeBlanc, *The Organization of American States and the Promotion and Protection of Human Rights* (The Hague: Nijhoff, 1977), pp. 8-9 (hereafter '*Promotion and Protection of Human Rights*').

[64]   Previously Article 5(j) of the original Charter and Article 3(j) following the Charter's

1967 amendment by the Protocol of Buenos Aires.
65 Thomas and Thomas, *Organization of American States,* p.223.
66 The original Article 13 of the Charter.
67 Charles Fenwick, 'The Ninth International Conference of American States' (1948) 42 AJIL 553 at 556.
68 Charles Fenwick, 'The Charter of the OAS as the "Law of the Land"' (1953) 47 AJIL 281 at 282.
69 J.L. Kunz, 'The Bogota Charter of the Organization of American States' (1948) 42 AJIL 568.
70 Ibid. at 572.
71 Inter-American Juridical Committee, *Study of the Juridical Relationship Between Respect for Human Rights and the Exercise of Democracy* (Washington DC: Pan American Union, 1960), pp. 13-14.
72 *Organization of American States,* p. 223.
73 Medina Quiroga, *The Battle of Human Rights,* p.43.
74 Resolution XXX, Final Act of the Ninth International Conference of American States, Bogota, Colombia, 30 March - 2 May 1948 at 48.
75 By Resolutions IX and XL of the Conference.
76 Inter-American Juridical Committee, *Draft Declaration of the Rights and Duties of Man and Accompanying Report* (Washington DC: Pan-American Union, 1948) pp. 13-14.
77 Ibid. p. 58.
78 Ibid. p. 59.
79 Ibid.
80 Ibid.
81 As the Committee itself subsequently recognised. See Inter-American Juridical Committee, *Report to Accompany the Definitive Draft Declaration of the International Rights and Duties of Man and Accompanying Report* (Washington DC: Pan-American Union, 1948), p. 12.
82 Inter-American Juridical Committee, *Draft Declaration of the Rights and Duties of Man,* p. 59.
83 Inter-American Juridical Committee, *Report to Accompany the Definitive Draft Declaration of the International Rights and Duties of Man and Accompanying Report* (hereafter *'Definitive Draft Declaration'*), p. 12. The text of the second and final draft of the Committee may also be found in Thomas Buergenthal and Robert Norris (eds), *Human Rights: The Inter-American System* (hereafter *'Buergenthal and Norris'*) (Dobbs Ferry, New York: Oceana, 1984) Vol. 1, Booklet 5, pp. 9-14.
84 Ninth International Conference of American States, *Acta* (Commission VI, 3a. Session, Doc. CB-287-c, c. VI-13), April 21, 1948. For an appraisal of the discussion relating to the draft Declaration in the Sub-Commission A of the Conference's Sixth Commission see Medina Quiroga, *The Battle of Human Rights,* pp. 36-8.
85 Emphasis added.
86 LeBlanc, *Promotion and Protection of Human Rights,* p.16.
87 Ibid.
88 Inter-American Juridical Committee, *Draft Declaration of the Rights and Duties of Man,* pp. 14-15.
89 Article 1(2) of the UN Charter states that the purposes of the United Nations are, *inter alia*: 'To develop friendly relations among nations based on respect for the principle of equal rights and self-determination of peoples'.

90 For a discussion of these issues see LeBlanc, *Promotion and Protection of Human Rights*, pp. 16-17.

91 Advisory Opinion OC-10/89 of 14 July 1989, *Interpretation of the American Declaration of the Rights and Duties of Man within the Framework of Article 64 of the American Convention on Human Rights*, loc. cit., supra, note 42. Discussed in detail infra, pp. 25-30.

92 See infra, pp. 15-25.

93 The use of the term 'generations of rights' to characterise different categories of rights was first proposed by Vasak. See K. Vasak, 'Human Rights: A Thirty Year Struggle', *Unesco Courier*, 1977, pp. 29-32. See further J.S. Davidson, *Human Rights* (Buckingham: Open University Press, 1993), p. 6.

94 See infra.

95 *Definitive Draft Declaration*, p. 14. See also LeBlanc, *Promotion and Protection of Human Rights*, p. 29.

96 Ibid., p. 30.

97 Ibid., pp. 31-8.

98 *Definitive Draft Declaration*, p. 14.

99 LeBlanc, *Promotion and Protection of Human Rights*, pp. 42-6.

100 Thomas and Thomas, *Organization of American States*, p. 230.

101 Fifth Meeting of the Consultation of Ministers of Foreign Affairs, OEA/Ser.F/II.5. Doc. 89 (English) Rev. 2, October 1959.

102 See Medina Quiroga, *The Battle of Human Rights*, pp. 67-8 and LeBlanc, *Promotion and Protection of Human Rights*, pp. 46-50.

103 Resolution II of the OAS Council. See Council of the Organization of American States, *Decisions Taken at the Meetings*, Vol XII, Jan - Dec 1959 (OEA.Ser.G/III/Vol.XII (English)), p. 151.

104 Resolution VII of the OAS Council, ibid. On the adoption of the Statute of the Commission see Anne P. Schreiber, *The Inter-American Commission on Human Rights* (Leyden: Sijthoff, 1970), pp. 31-40.

105 See Article 1 of the Statute of the Inter-American Commission 1960. As Buergenthal notes, 'the Commission was designated as an "autonomous entity" of the OAS, no doubt because this was as good a name as any for a body which was not provided for in the OAS Charter or any other treaty, was established by a simple conference resolution, and qualified neither as an organ of the OAS Council nor as a so-called "specialized organization" of the OAS'. Thomas Buergenthal, 'The Revised OAS Charter and the Protection of Human Rights', (1975) 69 AJIL 828 (hereafter '*Revised Charter*'), p. 833.

106 Article 1 Commission Statute, 1960.

107 These were occasionally supplemented by 'on-site investigations' based on Article 11 of the 1960 Statute which permitted the Commission to meet in the territory of any member state. This, of course, required the consent of the state concerned, see Inter-American Commission on Human Rights, *Report on the Work Accomplished During its First Session, October 3-28, 1960*, OAS Doc OEA/Ser.L/V/II.1, Doc. 32, March 14 1961, p. 10.

108 Ibid., p. 9.

109 Ibid., p. 13.

110 See Medina Quiroga, *The Battle of Human Rights*, pp. 76-77.

111 Resolution XXII, OAS, *Second Special Inter-American Conference, Final Act*, OEA/Ser. E/XIII.1, Doc. 150 (English) Rev., November 1965.

112 LeBlanc, *Promotion and Protection of Human Rights*, p. 95.

113 Inter-American Commission on Human Rights, *Report on the Work Accomplished During*

its Thirteenth Session, April 18 to 28, 1966, OEA/Ser.L/VII.14, Doc. 35 (English), September, 1966, pp. 2-4.

[114] See Regulations 52 and 58 of the Commission's amended Regulations. For discussion see LeBlanc, *Promotion and Protection of Human Rights*, p. 90 and Medina Quiroga, *The Battle of Human Rights*, pp. 80-5.

[115] Ibid., pp. 80-1.

[116] Inter-American Commission on Human Rights, *Report on the Work Accomplished during its Twenty-fourth Session, October 13-22, 1970,* OEA/Ser.L/V/II.24, doc. 32 (English), Rev. corr., 5 April 1971, p. 16.

[117] See below chapter 4 for a full description of the individual petition procedure. The Brazil case is also considered in detail at pp. 19-20.

[118] Inter-American Commission on Human Rights, *Report on the Work Accomplished by the Inter-American Commission on Human Rights during its Twenty-eighth Session (Special), May 1-5, 1972,* OEA/Ser.L/V/II.28, doc. 41 rev. 1 (English), 24 August 1972, p. 16.

[119] Ibid., p. 18.

[120] Dr Dunshee de Abranches dissenting.

[121] Inter-American Commission on Human Rights, *Report on the Work Accomplished by the Inter-American Commission on Human Rights during its Twenty-eighth Session (Special), May 1-5, 1972,* OEA/Ser.L/V/II.28, doc. 41 rev. 1 (English), 24 August 1972, p. 20.

[122] On exhaustion of domestic remedies in the Commission's individual petition procedures under the OAS Charter see below pp. 160-5.

[123] Buergenthal, *The Inter-American System*, p. 474 and *Revised Charter*, p.833.

[124] Buergenthal, *Revised Charter*, p. 833.

[125] Resolution I of the Second Special Inter-American Conference.

[126] See supra, p. 3.

[127] For accounts of the Charter amendments see Margaret Ball, *The Organization of American States in Transition* (Durham, NC: Duke University Press, 1969); John Dreier, 'New Wine and Old Bottles: The Changing Inter-American System' (1968) 22 *International Organization* 47 and César Sepúlveda, 'The Reform of the Charter of the OAS' in (1972) 137-III *Hague Rec* 83.

[128] The Court disposed of this issue in *Interpretation of the American Declaration,* loc. cit., supra, note 42. This will be considered in detail infra, pp. 25-30.

[129] Now Article 52 of the OAS Charter.

[130] Now Article 111 of the OAS Charter.

[131] See Buergenthal, *Revised Charter*, p. 828.

[132] Which was approved by the General Assembly of the OAS in 1979, Ninth Session, La Paz, Bolivia, 1979. See Norris, *New Statute*, pp. 380-81 and Buergenthal, *Revised Charter*, p. 828.

[133] See further infra, Chapter 2.

[134] Buergenthal, *Revised Charter*, p. 835.

[135] See Ball, *OAS in Transition*, pp. 119-20 and Fenwick, *Organization of American States*, pp. 155-57.

[136] Resolution No. 23/81, *Case 2141 (United States)*, March 6 1981, Inter-American Commission on Human Rights, *Annual Report of the Inter-American Commission on Human Rights, 1980-81* (hereafter *1980-81 Annual Report*), 25-54. For comment see Dinah Shelton, 'Abortion and the Right to Life in the Inter-American System: The Case of "Baby Boy"' (1981) 2 HRLJ 309.

[137] Ibid.

[138] *Roe v Wade* 410 U.S. 113 (1973); *Doe v Bolton* 410 U.S. 179 (1973).

[139] Emphasis added. Note that essentially the same reasoning was referred to by the Court in *Interpretation of the American Declaration*, loc. cit., supra, note 42, paras. 39-42.

[140] *Case 9647 (United States)*, (hereafter *'Juvenile Death Penalty Case'*), Inter-American Commission on Human Rights, *Annual Report of the Inter-American Commission on Human Rights 1986-87* (hereafter '*1986-87 Annual Report*'). OEA/Ser.L/V/II.71. Doc. 9 rev. 1, 22 September 1987. Original: Spanish 147. See Christina M. Cerna, 'US Death Penalty tested before the Inter-American Commission on Human Rights' (1992) 10 NQHR 155; Donald T. Fox, 'Inter-American Commission on Human Rights Finds United States in Violation' (1988) 82 AJIL 601.

[141] Ibid., p. 154 at para. 37(b).

[142] Ibid., pp. 158-9 at para. 38(d).

[143] Ibid.

[144] Ibid.

[145] Ibid., p. 166 at para. 48.

[146] Buergenthal, *Revised Charter*, p. 385.

[147] Ibid., p. 835.

[148] *Buergenthal and Norris*, Binder IV, Booklet 21.3, p. 155 at p. 156.

[149] Ibid. at footnote 1.

[150] *Interpretation of the American Declaration*, loc. cit., supra, note 42.

[151] Ibid., para. 2.

[152] Ibid.

[153] See infra, pp. 147-8.

[154] *Interpretation of the American Declaration*, loc. cit., supra, note 42, para. 14(ii).

[155] Ibid., para. 13.

[156] Ibid., para. 11.

[157] Ibid., para. 2.

[158] Ibid., para. 15.

[159] Ibid., para. 12.

[160] Ibid., para. 17

[161] Ibid.

[162] Ibid., para. 25.

[163] Ibid.

[164] Ibid., para. 26.

[165] Ibid., paras. 27 and 28.

[166] Article 2(1)(a) of the Vienna Convention on the Law of Treaties 1969; Article 2(1)(a) of the Vienna Convention on the Law of Treaties among States and International Organizations or among International Organizations 1986. It should be noted that while the former is in force, the latter is not. The definition of a treaty for the purposes of the Vienna Conventions is more restrictive than the definition at customary international law. See I. Brownlie, *Principles of International Law* (Oxford: Oxford University Press, 4th edn, 1990), pp. 604-606. (Hereafter '*Principles*'.)

[167] *Interpretation of the American Declaration*, paras. 32-34. Perhaps a clearer way of expressing this would be to say that the parties did not intend that the Declaration should create legal relation *inter se* or, in the words of the Vienna Conventions, that it was not 'governed by international law'.

[168] Ibid., para. 35.

[169] Ibid., para. 36.

[170] Ibid., para. 37. Here the Court noted that 'the American Declaration has its basis in the

idea that "the international protection of the rights of man should be the principal guide of an evolving American law"'.

[171] Here the Court referred to the statement of the ICJ in *Legal Consequences for States of the Continued Presence of South Africa in Namibia (South West Africa) notwithstanding Security Council Resolution 276 (1970)*, ICJ Rep 1971, p. 16 at para. 31 where it had said: [A]n international instrument must be interpreted and applied within the overall framework of the juridical system in force at the time of the interpretation.

[172] On the approach of the European Court of Human Rights towards interpretation of the European Convention see infra, p. 73.

[173] *Interpretation of the American Declaration*, loc. cit., supra, note 42, para. 38. What these 'certain essential rights' were, the Court did not specify. It is perhaps arguable, however, that they are those first generation rights from which no derogation is permitted in any of the international human rights treaties. The right to be free from torture, inhuman and degrading treatment, for example. See Article 3 ECHR; Article 5 ACHR and Article 5 Banjul Charter.

[174] For this proposition the Court cited *Barcelona Traction, Light and Power Company Limited, Second Phase, Judgment*, ICJ Rep, 1970, p. 3, the *Legal Consequences Case*, loc. cit., supra, note 170, para. 57 and the *Case Concerning United States Diplomatic and Consular Staff in Teheran*, ICJ Rep, 1980, p. 3, para. 42.

[175] See supra, pp. 20-5.

[176] See supra, pp. 23-5.

[177] Buergenthal, *Revised Charter*.

[178] *Interpretation of the American Declaration*, loc. cit., supra, note 42, para. 39. Here the Court referred to the Charter's Preamble (paragraph 3) and Articles 3(j), 16, 43, 47, 51, 112 and 150. (Following consequent amendments to the Charter these are now Preamble (paragraph 4) and Articles 3(k), 16, 44, 48, 52, 111 and 150.)

[179] Ibid., para. 41.

[180] Ibid., para. 42. The resolutions referred to were Resolution 314 (VII-0/77) of June 22, 1977 and Resolutions 370 and 371 (VIII-78) of July 1, 1978.

[181] OASTS No. 67.

[182] *Interpretation of the American Declaration*, loc. cit., supra, note 42, para. 43.

[183] Ibid., para. 43.

[184] Ibid., para. 45.

[185] Ibid., para. 46.

[186] Ibid., para. 47.

[187] Ibid., para. 44.

[188] The possibility of regional customary law was recognized by the ICJ in the *Asylum Case* involving Colombia and Peru.

[189] On this point see also Christina M. Cerna, 'The Structure and Functioning of the Inter-American Court of Human Rights (1979-92) (1993) LXIV BYIL 135 at pp. 199-200.

[190] *Interpretation of the American Declaration*, loc. cit., supra, note 42, para. 12.

[191] Ibid., para. 12.

[192] See Thomas Buergenthal, 'The American Convention on Human Rights: Illusions and Hopes' (1971) 21 *Buffalo Law Review* 121; Buergenthal, *Inter-American System*, pp. 439-451; P.P. Camargo, 'The American Convention on Human Rights', (1970) 3 HRJ 333.

[193] See supra, p. 11.

[194] See supra, p. 12.

[195] *Final Act of the Fifth Meeting of Consultation of Ministers of Foreign Affairs*, Santiago,

Chile, August 12-18, 1959, OEA/Ser.CII.5 (English), 1960, p. 10.
[196] The original draft of the IAJC is reproduced in OAS Secretariat, *Inter-American Yearbook on Human Rights* (Washington DC: OAS, 1973) 236.
[197] See Medina Quiroga, *The Battle of Human Rights*, pp. 95-6.
[198] For a comparison of the two instruments see J. A. Frowein, 'The European and American Conventions on Human Rights' (1980) 1 HRLJ 44 at pp. 64-65; Thomas Buergenthal, 'The American and European Convention on Human Rights: Similarities and Differences', (1980) 30 AmULRev 155.
[199] See Buergenthal, Inter-American System, p. 441; C.D. Dunshee de Abranches, 'Comparative Study of the United Nations Covenants and the Draft Inter-American Convention on Human Rights' [1968] *Inter-American Year Book of Human Rights* 169.
[200] See infra, pp. 260-1.
[201] Buergenthal, *Inter-American System*, p. 442.
[202] Infra, chapter 7.
[203] Supra, pp. 3-4.
[204] AG/RES.836(XVI-0/86), Inter-American Commission on Human Rights, *1986-87 Annual Report,* pp. 18-19. The text of this draft of the Protocol may be found in Inter-American Commission on Human Rights, *Annual Report of the Inter-American Commission on Human Rights 1985-86* (hereafter '*1985-86 Annual Report*'), OEA/Ser.L/V/II.68, Doc.8 rev.1, 26 September 1986, Original: Spanish, pp. 195-211.
[205] AG/RES.887 (XVII-0/87).
[206] The Working Group was composed of delegations from Argentina, Barbados, Bolivia, Colombia, Costa Rica, Ecuador, El Salvador, Guatemala, Honduras, Mexico, Nicaragua, Peru, Uruguay and Venezuela. Present as observers at meetings of the Working Group were representatives of Brazil, Paraguay and the United States.
[207] See Preamble, paragraphs 6 and 8.
[208] Not only are some of the rights novel, but certain categories of rights are more broadly drafted than those of analogous human rights instruments. See, for example, Article 8(3) (no-one may be compelled to join a trade union), Article 11 (right to a healthy environment), Article 16 (rights of children), Article 17 (protection of the elderly) and Article 18 (protection of the handicapped).
[209] While the main mechanism for the supervision of the rights protected in the Protocol is a system of periodic reports, the full institutional system established by Articles 44-51 and Articles 61-69 of the Convention comes into play if Article 8(1)(a) (right to organize and join a trade union) or Article 13 (right to education) are directly violated by a state party: Article 19 Protocol. On the mechanisms of protection see infra, chapters 4 and 5.
[210] See infra, chapters 4 and 5.
[211] See, for example, AG/Res. 742 (XIV-0/84) of 17 November 1984, Inter-American Commission on Human Rights, *Annual Report of the Inter-American Commission on Human Rights 1984-1985,* OEA/Ser.L/V/II.66, doc.10 rev. 1, October 1st 1985, Original: Spanish, pp. 11-14.
[212] See Inter-American Commission on Human Rights, *Annual Report of the Inter-American Commission on Human Rights 1986-87.* (Hereafter '*1986-87 Annual Report*'.) OEA/Ser.L/V/II.71, Doc.9 rev. 1, 22 September 1987, Original: Spanish, p. 273.
[213] This provision was the subject of an advisory opinion by the Inter-American Court in *Advisory Opinion OC-3/83 of September 8, 1983, Restrictions to the Death Penalty.*
[214] Inter-American Commission on Human Rights, *1986-87 Annual Report*, p. 273.
[215] Ibid., pp. 274-5. The Commission referred to the fact that of the States which were then

parties to the Convention, Bolivia, Colombia, Costa Rica, Dominican Republic, Ecuador, Haiti, Honduras, Nicaragua, Panama, Uruguay and Venezuela had abolished the death penalty for crimes. It also noted that the domestic law of Argentina, El Salvador, Mexico and Peru did not impose the death penalty for common crimes and maintained it only for serious military offences committed under exceptional circumstances. Furthermore, the Commission referred to the following international measure: Protocol 6 to the European Convention on Human Rights and the proposed Second Optional Protocol to the International Covenant on Civil and Political Rights.

216 AG/RES.889/XVII-0/87 in [1987] IAYHR 906.

217 AG/RES.943/XVIII-0/88 in [1988] IAYHR 1042.

218 AG/doc.2428/89.

219 See William A. Schabas, *The Abolition of the Death Penalty in International Law* (Cambridge: Grotius Publications, 1993) pp. 281-2. (Hereafter '*Abolition of the Death Penalty*'.)

220 Ibid., p. 282.

221 Article 68 Geneva Convention of August 12, 1949 Relative to the Protection of Civilians (1950) UNTS 135; Geneva Convention of August 12, 1949 Articles 100 and 101 Geneva Convention Relative to the Treatment of Prisoners of War (1950) UNTS 135; Articles 76(3) and 77(5) of Protocol Additional I to the 1949 Geneva Convention and Relating to the Protection of Victims of International Armed Conflicts (1979) 1125 UNTS 3 and Article 6(4) Protocol Additional II to the 1949 Geneva Conventions and Relating to the Protection of Victims of Non-International Armed Conflicts (1979) 1125 UNTS 609.

222 Second Preambular paragraph. Emphasis added.

223 Fourth Preambular paragraph.

224 They are Costa Rica, Ecuador, Nicaragua, Panama, Uruguay and Venezuela.

225 See Organization of American States: Inter-American Commission on Human Rights, *Annual Report of the Inter-American Commission on Human Rights 1992-93* (hereafter '*1992-1993 Annual Report*'), OEA/Ser.L/V/II.83, Doc. 14, corr. 1, March 12, 1993, Original: Spanish, p. 329.

226 Schabas, *Abolition of the Death Penalty*, p. 282.

227 See infra, pp. 77-80.

228 Part I, Chapter III of the Convention.

229 On the concept of progressive implementation see Inter-American Commission on Human Rights, 'Areas in which Steps Need to be Taken towards Full Observance of the Human Rights set forth in the American Declaration of the Rights and Duties of Man and the American Convention on Human Rights' in Organization of American States: Inter-American Commission on Human Rights, *Annual Report of the Inter-American Commission on Human Rights 1993* (hereafter '*1993 Annual Report*'), OEA/Ser.G, CP/CAJP-940/94, 8 March 1994, Original: Spanish, p. 519 at 523-4.

230 *Velasquez Rodriguez*, judgment of 29 July 1988, Series C, No. 4; (1989) 28 ILM 291; (1988) 9 HRLJ 212 at para. 169 and *Godinez Cruz* judgment of 29 July 1988, Series C, No. 5, at para. 178.

231 *Velasquez Rodriguez* at para. 164 and *Godinez Cruz* at para. 173 citing the Court's advisory opinion *The Word 'Laws' in Article 30 of the American Convention on Human Rights*, Advisory Opinion OC-6/86 of May 9, 1986, Series A No. 6 at para. 21.

232 *State and individual responsibility regarding laws which manifestly violate the American Convention/Reintroduction of the death penalty in the Peruvian Constitution, Advisory Opinion OC-14/94* (1995) 16 HRLJ 9 at para. 36.

[233] Buergenthal had already espoused this view in *Inter-American System*, p. 442.

[234] Inter-American Commission on Human Rights, *Report on the Situation of Human Rights in the Republic of Guatemala*, OAS Doc., OEA/Ser. L/V/II. 53, doc. 21 rev. 2, 13 October 1981, Original: Spanish, p. 22, para. 8.

[235] *Velasquez Rodriguez* at para. 166; *Godinez Cruz* at para. 171.

[236] *Velasquez Rodriguez* at para. 167 and *Godinez Cruz* at para. 172.

[237] *Velasquez Rodriguez* at para. 174 and *Godinez Cruz* at para. 179.

[238] *Velasquez Rodriguez* at para. 177 and *Godinez Cruz* at para. 182.

[239] *Velasquez Rodriguez* at para. 172 and *Godinez Cruz* at para. 177.

[240] *Velasquez Rodriguez* at para. 177 and *Godinez Cruz* at para. 182.

[241] Advisory Opinion OC-5/85 of November 13, 1985, *Compulsory Membership in an Association Prescribed by Law for the Practice of Journalism* (hereafter *Compulsory Membership*) Series A, No. 5; (1986) 25 ILM 123; (1986) 7 HRLJ 74.

[242] Ibid., para. 48.

[243] Ibid., para. 56.

[244] Buergenthal, *Inter-American System*, p. 441.

[245] Ibid.

[246] Loc. cit., supra, note 135.

[247] Infra, pp. 263-5.

[248] Communication No. R 13/56 (1981) 2 HRLJ 145.

[249] Article 1 of the Protocol provides that applications may be lodged by 'individuals subject to its [the State Party's] jurisdiction' and Article 2(1) refers to applications by 'all individuals within its [the State Party's] territory and subject to its jurisdiction'.

[250] Communication No. R 13/56, loc. cit., supra n 222 at para. 10.2.

[251] See also *Quinteros v Uruguay*, Communication R No. 24/107, (1983) 4 HRLJ 195 where the same point was made. This case involved the abduction of a Uruguayan citizen from the Venezuelan Embassy in Montevideo.

[252] Buergenthal, *Inter-American System*, p. 446.

[253] Inter-American Commission on Human Rights, *Annual Report of the Inter-American Commission on Human Rights 1990-1991* (hereafter '*1990-1991 Annual Report*') OEA/Ser.L/V/II/79 rev.1, Doc. 12, 22 February 1991, Original: Spanish, p. 237.

[254] Ibid., p. 248.

[255] Ibid.

[256] Ibid.

[257] Supra, p. 32.

[258] Article 2(1) of the Covenant provides: 'Each State Party to the present Covenant undertakes to take steps, individually and through international assistance and cooperation, especially economic and technical, to the maximum of its available resources, with a view to achieving progressively the full realization of the rights recognized in the present Covenant by all appropriate means, including particularly the adoption of legislative measures'.

[259] Emphasis added.

[260] See infra, chapter 4.

[261] A claimant of social security, for example, could not claim that he or she was being discriminated against on grounds of economic status if he or she did not fall within the financial limits set by national legislation for social security applicants.

[262] Organization of American States, *Inter-American Yearbook on Human Rights 1968* (Washington DC: Organization of American States, 1973), p. 191.

[263] Ibid.

[264] See Buergenthal, *Inter-American System*, pp. 443-4.

[265] *Report of the United States Delegation to the Inter-American Conference on Protection of Human Rights*, San José, Costa Rica, November 9 - 22, 1969, p. 17. Copy in Buergenthal and Norris, Binder 3, Booklet 15.

[266] Ibid.

[267] Ibid., pp. 16, 17.

[268] Ibid., p. 17.

[269] Buergenthal, *Inter-American System*, p. 445 and n 25.

[270] Advisory Opinion OC-7/86 of 29 August 1986, *Enforceability of the Right to Reply or Correction (Articles 14(1), 1(1) and 2 of the American Convention on Human Rights)* (hereafter '*Right to Reply*'), Series A, No. 7; (1986) 7 HRLJ 238.

[271] Ibid., para. 13.

[272] Ibid., para. 16.

[273] Ibid., para. 17.

[274] Judges Buergenthal, Nieto-Navia and Nikken.

[275] Article 5.

[276] On the Court's competence to reformulate questions put before it in the context of its advisory jurisdiction see infra, pp. 249-53.

[277] *Dissenting and Concurring Opinion of Judge Thomas Buergenthal*, para. 3.

[278] It should be noted that the word 'ideas' appears only in the English text of the Convention. The Spanish, Portuguese and French texts appear to be concerned primarily with the dissemination of defamatory statements. The texts provide in the material part as follows:
Spanish: '*informaciones inexactas o agraviantes*'.
Portuguese: '*informacoes inexatas ou ofensivas*'.
French: '*données inexactes ou des imputations diffamatoires*'.

[279] See supra, pp. 38-40.

[280] *Right to Reply*, paras. 23 and 25.

[281] Ibid.

[282] Ibid., para. 24.

[283] Ibid., para. 26.

[284] Ibid., para. 27.

[285] Ibid.

[286] Ibid., para. 29.

[287] *The Word 'Laws'*, para. 27.

[288] Ibid.

[289] Ibid., para. 33.

[290] Cf. *The Word 'Laws'* at para. 27 (infra) in which the Court declared that restrictions to any of the protected rights could only be effected by legal norms passed in accordance with the appropriate constitutional procedures of each state.

[291] See generally R. Higgins, 'Derogations under Human Rights Treaties' (1979) 48 BYIL 281.

[292] Advisory Opinion OC-6/86 of May 9,1986, *Restrictions of the Rights and Freedoms of the American Convention - The Word 'Laws' in Article 30* (hereafter '*The Word 'Laws'*') Series A, No 6; (1986) 7 HRLJ 74.

[293] Ibid., para. 14.

[294] Ibid.

[295] Ibid., para. 17.

[296] See below pp. 52-7.

[297] See, for example, Articles 15 and 16. Article 21 introduces a further ground of restriction, namely, the limitation of the right to the use and enjoyment of property which may be subordinated to the interest of society. This opens the way for the application of rules permitting compulsory purchase of private property in circumstances where the public good demands it, for instance, the building of a public highway.

[298] See Article 15 (right of assembly), Article 16 (freedom of association) and Article 22 (freedom of movement and residence).

[299] Article 29(c) provides: 'No provision of this Convention shall be interpreted as: (c) precluding other rights or guarantees that are inherent in the human personality or derived from representative democracy as a form of government'.

[300] In a Commission study on states of siege and protection of human rights, the Commission calculated that there had been over one hundred declarations of or extensions to states of siege in the Americas. See Inter-American Commission on Human Rights, *Preliminary Study of the State of Siege and the Protection of Human Rights in the Americas*, OEA/Ser.L/V/II.8, No 6.

[301] Both the Commission and the Court are clearly competent to determine whether or not a State Party has complied with its obligations under Article 27 of the Convention by virtue of Article 33.

[302] See Article 22 (freedom of movement and residence) which also embodies the possibility of restriction (Article 22(3)).

[303] *The Word 'Laws'*, para. 49.

[304] Ibid., para. 19.

[305] Ibid., para. 21. Here citing the European Court of Human Rights in the *Sunday Times Case*, para. 47.

[306] Ibid., para. 21.

[307] Ibid., para. 22.

[308] Ibid.

[309] See infra, pp. 54-7.

[310] *The Word 'Laws'*, para. 27.

[311] See infra, pp. 313-18.

[312] *Compulsory Membership*, para. 35.

[313] Advisory Opinion OC-8/87 of 30 January 1987, *Habeas Corpus in Emergency Situations (Articles 27(2), 25(1) and 7(6) American Convention on Human Rights)* (hereafter '*Habeas Corpus in Emergency Situations*') Series A, No. 8; (1988) 27 ILM 512; (1988) 9 HRLJ 204.

[314] Ibid., para. 12.

[315] Ibid., para. 1.

[316] Ibid., para. 24.

[317] *Habeas Corpus in Emergency Situations*, para. 26. Cited with approval in Advisory Opinion OC-9/87 of October 6, 1987 *Judicial Guarantees in States of Emergency* (hereafter '*Judicial Guarantees*') Series A, No. 9; (1988) 9 HRLJ 204, para. 35.

[318] *Habeas Corpus in Emergency Situations*, para. 24. Cited with approval in *Judicial Guarantees*, para. 35.

[319] *Habeas Corpus in Emergency Situations*, para. 19.

[320] Ibid.

[321] *Habeas Corpus in Emergency Situations*, para. 22. Cited with approval in *Judicial Guarantees*, para. 36.

[322] These are Article 3 (Right to Juridical Personality), Article 4 (Right to Life), Article 5 (Right to Humane Treatment), Article 6 (Freedom from Slavery), Article 9 (Freedom from Ex Post Facto Laws), Article 12 (Freedom of Conscience and Religion), Article 17 (Rights

of the Family), Article 19 (Rights of the Child), Article 20 (Right to Nationality), and Article 23 (Right to Participate in Government).

[323] *Habeas Corpus in Emergency Situations,* para. 18.

[324] Ibid., para. 25.

[325] Ibid. See also Advisory Opinion OC-11/90 of August 10, 1990, *Exceptions to the Exhaustion of Local Remedies in Articles 46(1), 46(2)(a) and 46(2)(b) of the American Convention on Human Rights* (hereafter '*Exceptions to the Exhaustion of Local Remedies*') Series A, No. 10; (1991) 12 HRLJ 20, para. 23; See also *Velasquez Rodriguez,* para. 166 and *Godinez Cruz,* para. 175.

[326] *Habeas Corpus in Emergency Situations,* para. 29.

[327] Ibid., para. 30.

[328] *Amparo* is a procedural device which provides a remedy for the protection of all rights recognized by a State's constitution.

[329] *Habeas Corpus in Emergency Situations,* para. 34.

[330] Ibid., para. 33. Cited with approval in *Judicial Guarantees.*

[331] Ibid., para. 35.

[332] Ibid., para. 42.

[333] Ibid., para. 43.

[334] *Judicial Guarantees,* para. 28. See also Article 46(2)(a) which uses the same expression to indicate circumstances under which an individual is not required to exhaust local remedies before his case will be considered admissible by the Commission. See supra, pp. 166-9. As the Court noted in the *Velasquez Rodriguez, Fairen Garbi and Solis Corrales* and *Godinez Cruz* cases, Preliminary Objections, Judgments of June 26, 1987, paras. 90, 91 and 92 respectively, states parties are under an obligation to provide effective judicial remedies to victims of human rights obligations which must be in accordance with the rules of due process of law. For these propositions it cited Articles 8 and 25. On matters affecting the right to due process see infra, pp. 285-307.

[335] *Judicial Guarantees,* para. 29.

[336] The term used by the Court in para. 30 is 'states of exception'.

[337] *Judicial Guarantees,* para. 30.

[338] Ibid.

[339] Ibid., para. 40.

[340] On the nature of the obligations under the Protocol of San Salvador see supra, p. 43-4.

[341] The only rights which are specifically designated as being subject to restrictions are those provided for in Article 8 (Trade union rights). This provides, similarly to Articles 15 and 16 of the American Convention that the rights may be subject to restrictions established by law, provided that such restrictions are characteristic of a democratic society and necessary for safeguarding public order or for protecting the public health or morals or the rights and freedoms of others.

[342] Article 74(1) ACHR.

[343] Article 74(2) ACHR.

[344] Ibid.

[345] The eleventh ratification deposited was that of Grenada.

[346] Article 74(2) ACHR.

[347] Advisory Opinion OC-2/82 of September 24, 1982, *Entry into Force of the American Convention for a States Ratifying or Adhering with a Reservation* (hereafter '*Effect of Reservations*') Series A, No. 2; (1983) 22 ILM 37; (1982) 3 HRLJ 153.

[348] Advisory Opinion OC-3/83 of September 8, 1983, *Restrictions to the Death Penalty,* Series

A, No. 3; (1984) 23 ILM 230; (1983) 4 HRLJ 339.

[349]   *Effect of Reservations,* paras. 23 and 25. For further confirmation of this ruling see *Restrictions to the Death Penalty,* para. 60.

[350]   *Effect of Reservations,* para. 27. See also para. 29 where the Court made a statement to the same effect.

[351]   Ibid., para. 34.

[352]   Ibid.

[353]   Ibid., para. 38.

[354]   *Restrictions to the Death Penalty,* para. 65.

[355]   Ibid.

[356]   Ibid., para. 66.

[357]   See further infra, pp. 240-3.

[358]   Article 21(1) Protocol of San Salvador (hereafter 'PSS').

[359]   Article 21(2) PSS.

[360]   Article 21(3) PSS.

[361]   The signatory States are Argentina, Bolivia, Costa Rica, the Dominican Republic, Ecuador, El Salvador, Guatemala, Haiti, Mexico, Nicaragua, Panama, Peru, Suriname, Uruguay and Venezuela. Ecuador, Panama and Suriname are the three States which have ratified the Protocol. See Inter-American Commission on Human Rights, *Annual Report of the Inter-American Commission on Human Rights* 1994 (hereafter '*1994 Annual Report*') OEA/Ser.L/V/II.88, Doc. 9 rev, February 17, 1995, Original: Spanish, p. 245.

[362]   Article 20 PSS.

[363]   Ibid.

[364]   See supra, p. 59.

[365]   Article 78(1) ACHR.

[366]   Article 78(2) ACHR.

[367]   OASTS No 67.

[368]   (1994) 33 ILM 1529.

[369]   (1994) 33 ILM 1534.

[370]   Following deposit of the second instrument of ratification in accordance with Article 22 of the Convention. On the Convention in general see F.H. Kaplan, 'Combating Political Torture in Latin America: An Analysis of the Organization of American States' Inter-American Convention to Prevent and Punish Torture' (1989) XV *Brooklyn Journal of International Law* 399.

[371]   Preamble, para. 4 Inter-American Convention on the Prevention and Punishment of Torture (hereafter 'IACPPT').

[372]   Preamble, para. 3 IACPPT.

[373]   See infra, pp. 276-80.

[374]   Article 6 IACPPT.

[375]   Article 12 IACPPT.

[376]   Article 12(c) IACPPT.

[377]   Article 14 IACPPT.

[378]   For an extensive analysis of the political offence exception in extradition see G. Gilbert, *Aspects of Extradition Law* (1991), pp. 113-82.

[379]   (1984) 23 ILM 1027 and (1985) 24 ILM 535.

[380]   Article 13 IACPPT.

[381]   Article 7 IACPPT.

[382]   Article 10 IACPPT.

383 Article 8 IACPPT.
384 Ibid.
385 Article 6 IACPPT.
386 Article 17 IACPPT.
387 Infra, p. 110.
388 On the issue of enforced disappearances see infra, Chapter 7.
389 Inter-American Commission, *1994 Annual Report,* p. 250. The signatory States are Argentina, Bolivia, Brazil, Chile, Colombia, Costa Rica, Guatemala, Honduras, Nicaragua, Panama, Uruguay and Venezuela.
390 Article I(a) Inter-American Convention on the Forced Disappearance of Persons (hereafter 'IACFDP').
391 Articles I(a) and XIV IACFDP.
392 Article I(b) IACFDP.
393 Articles III and IV IACFDP.
394 Article V IACFDP.
395 Article VI IACFDP.
396 Article VII IACFDP.
397 Ibid.
398 Article VIII IACFDP.
399 See, for example, Part II, para. 38 of the Programme of Action adopted at the United Nations World Conference on Human Rights, Vienna 14-25 June, 1993 (1993) 14 HRLJ 352 at 359.
400 Article 2(a) Inter-American Convention on the Prevention, Punishment and Eradication of Violence against Women (hereafter 'VAW').
401 Article 2(b) VAW.
402 Ibid.
403 Article 2(c) VAW.
404 These are: the right to have her life respected; the right to have her physical, mental and moral integrity respected; the right to personal liberty and security; the right not to be subjected to torture; the right to have the inherent dignity of her person respected and her family protected; the right to equal protection before the law and of the law; the right to simple and prompt recourse to a competent court for protection against acts that violate her rights; the right to associate freely; the right of freedom to profess her religion and beliefs within the law and the right to have equal access to the public service of her country and to take part in the conduct of public affairs, including decision-making.
405 Article 7 VAW.
406 Article 8(b) VAW.
407 Article 10 VAW.
408 On the Court's advisory jurisdiction see chapter xx infra.
409 Article 12 VAW. On the practice of the Commission in individual cases see chapter xx infra.
410 Sir Ian Sinclair, *The Vienna Convention on the Law of Treaties* (Manchester: Manchester University Press, 2nd edn, 1984) p. 130. (Hereafter '*Law of Treaties*'.)
411 On the various approaches to treaty interpretation see Sinclair, *Law of Treaties,* Chapter 5, passim; G. G. Fitzmaurice, 'The Law and Procedure of the International Court of Justice: Treaty Interpretation and Other Treaty Points' (1951) 28 BYIL 1 and 'The Law and Procedure of the International Court of Justice, 1951-4: Treaty Interpretation and Other Treaty Points' (1957) 33 BYIL 220; G. Haraszti, *Some Fundamental Problems of the*

Law of Treaties (Budapest: Akadémia Kiadó, 1973).

[412]   This is what Sinclair refers to as the doctrine of emergent purpose. See Sinclair, *Law of Treaties*, p. 130.

[413]   See J.G. Merrills, *The Development of International Law by the European Court of Human Rights* (Manchester: Manchester University Press, 2nd edn, 1993), pp. 69-119. (Hereafter 'Development'.)

[414]   In the context of the European Convention on Human Rights Judge Sir Gerald Fitzmaurice has been the most outspoken critic of the teleological approach to interpretation. See, for example, his Separate Opinions in *Ireland v United Kingdom,* Eur Ct HR, Series A, No. 25; *Tyrer,* Eur Ct HR, No. 26 and *Marckx,* Eur Ct HR, Series A, No. 31. For commentary on Judge Fitzmaurice's approach see C.C. Morrison, *The Dynamics of Development in the European Human Rights Convention System* (The Hague: Nijhoff, 1981), chapter 1, and Merrills, *Development,* pp. 211-29.

[415]   See YBILC, 1966, vol. ii, p. 1 at p. 25.

[416]   Ibid.

[417]   For examples of the principle in practice see Sir Arnold McNair, *The Law of Treaties* (Cambridge: Cambridge University Press, 1961) Chapter XXI. As Brownlie notes, however, the World Court has generally subordinated the principle to that of textuality. Brownlie, *Principles,* p. 631. See also the judgement of the ICJ in the *Peace Treaties Case,* ICJ Rep 1950, p. 229 where the Court refused to apply the principle.

[418]   See Merrills, *Development,* Chapter 5.

[419]   See, for example, *Golder,* Eur Ct HR, Series A, No. 18, in which the European Court of Human Rights read a right of access to courts into Article 6(1) of the Convention, despite the absence of such a phrase in the article. As Sinclair remarks, it is difficult to escape the conclusion that the Court was engaging in an act of judicial legislation. Sinclair, *Law of Treaties*, p. 128.

[420]   See infra, pp. 138-40.

[421]   On this case see further infra.

[422]   *Compulsory Membership*, para. 51.

[423]   Ibid.

[424]   Ibid.

[425]   Ibid., para. 52.

[426]   Ibid.

[427]   Discussed in detail supra, pp. 25-30.

[428]   See infra, pp. 172-80.

[429]   *Compulsory Membership,* para. 67.

[430]   Ibid.

[431]   The Court's first mention of this was in *Government of Costa Rica (In the Matter of Viviana Gallardo et al)* (hereafter 'Gallardo') No G. 101/81, Judgment of November 13, 1981 (1981) 20 ILM 1424; (1981) 2 HRLJ 328.

[432]   *Restrictions to the Death Penalty,* para. 48.

[433]   See *Proposed Amendments,* para. 22. Here the Court also cited with approval the opinion of the ICJ in the *Admissions Case,* 1950 ICJ Rep, p. 8 in which the ICJ had said that 'the first duty of a tribunal which is called upon to interpret and apply the provisions of a treaty, is to endeavour to give effect to them in their natural and ordinary meaning in the context in which they occur'. See also *Right to Reply,* para. 21 and *Habeas Corpus in Emergency Situations,* para. 14.

[434]   *Effect of Reservations,* para. 29. Note the similar statement of the European Court of Human

Rights in *Austria v Italy*, 6 YB 796, where it said: '[T]he obligations undertaken by the High Contracting Parties in the European Convention are essentially of an objective character being designed rather to protect the fundamental rights of individual human beings from infringements by any of the High Contracting Parties than to create subjective and reciprocal rights for the High Contracting Parties themselves'.

On human rights treaties as novel international instruments see infra, pp. 77-80.

[435] At para. 22.

[436] *Other Treaties*, para. 37.

[437] Ibid.

[438] Ibid., para. 50.

[439] On the Human Rights Committee see D. McGoldrick, *The Human Rights Committee: Its Role in the Development of the International Covenant on Civil and Political Rights* (Oxford: Clarendon Press, 1991) especially chapter 4.

[440] *Effect of Reservations*, para. 22.

[441] *Restrictions to the Death Penalty*, paras. 45 and 62. The Court assumed jurisdiction to interpret reservations to the Convention under Article 64 since in its view the reservation became an integral part of the Convention.

[442] Ibid., para. 63.

[443] Ibid., para. 66.

[444] Supra, pp. 131-2.

[445] *Other Treaties*, para. 19.

[446] Articles 22(7), 27(1), and 29 ACHR, for example.

[447] *Other Treaties*, para. 24.

[448] See also *Effect of Reservations*, paras. 27 and 29.

[449] Thomas Buergenthal, 'The Advisory Practice of the Inter-American Court of Human Rights' (1985) 79 AJIL 1 at p. 20.

[450] *Effect of Reservations*, paras. 29-32.

[451] *Reservations to the Genocide Convention Case*, ICJ Rep, 1974, p. 253. See infra, p. 192-5.

[452] *In casu* E. Schwelb, 'The Law of Treaties and Human Rights' (1973) 16 *Archiv des Volkrechts* 1 , reprinted in W. M. Reisman and B. Weston, eds, *Toward World Order and Human Dignity*, 1976, p. 262.

[453] *The Word 'Laws'*, para. 21.

[454] Ibid., para. 28.

[455] *Habeas Corpus in Emergency Situations*, para. 18.

[456] See infra, pp. 263-5.

[457] For example, in *Restrictions to the Death Penalty*, para. 58. In the words of Fitzmaurice, (1951) BYIL 1, p. 5, the Court's recourse to the use of *travaux préparatoires* has become 'quasi-habitual'.

[458] *Effect of Reservations*, para. 14. It appears that Article 64 had originally been drafted more restrictively.

[459] Ibid., para. 25.

[460] *The Word 'Laws'*, para. 18.

[461] Ibid., para. 32.

[462] See infra, pp. 49-57.

[463] *Effect of Reservations*, para. 34.

[464] *Restrictions to the Death Penalty*, para. 43. See infra, chapter 6.

[465] Buergenthal, *Advisory Practice*, p. 20.

[466] Article 1 ACHR.

[467] See Buergenthal, *Advisory Practice*, p. 22.

[468] *Effect of Reservations*, para. 29.

[469] Para. 33.

[470] *Reservations to the Genocide Convention Case,* ICJ Rep. 1951, p. 15.

[471] 6 YB 796.

[472] Ibid.

[473] Buergenthal, *Advisory Practice*, p. 22.

[474] *Other Treaties,* para. 24. Cited with approval in Advisory Opinion OC-12 of 6 December 1991, *Compatibility of draft legislation with Article 8(2) of the American Convention on Human Rights,* Series A, No. 12; (1992) 13 HRLJ 149.

[475] *Effect of Reservations*, para. 72.

[476] Loc. cit., supra, note 469.

[477] Case 26/62, *Van Gend en Loos v Nederlandse Administratie der Belastingen* [1963] ECR 1 at 12; [1963] CMLR 105 at 129.

2 The Inter-American Commission on Human Rights

Introduction

As we saw in Chapter 1, the Inter-American Commission on Human Rights was created by a simple resolution of the Meeting of the Consultation of Foreign Ministers in 1959 and thus began life as an 'autonomous entity' of the inter-American system. Through a process of amendment to the OAS Charter and incorporation into the inter-American system, however, the Commission acquired a firm constitutional base and became an institution of the Organization of American States. With the entry into force of the American Convention on Human Rights the Commission was called upon to fulfil an additional role under that instrument, necessitating the adoption of a new statute which would allow it perform the functions assigned to it by both the Charter and the American Convention. The Commission thus derives its powers from two sources: the OAS Charter and the American Convention. Under Article 111 of the Charter the Commission is called upon to fulfil promotional, protective and consultative functions. Paragraph one of Article 111 provides:

> There shall be an Inter-American Commission on Human Rights whose principal function shall be to promote the observance and protection of human rights and to serve as a consultative organ of the Organization in these matters.

These functions are elaborated further in the second source of the Commission's powers; the American Convention on Human Rights. Article 41 of this instrument provides:

> The main function of the Commission shall be to promote respect for and defence of human rights. In the exercise of its mandate, it shall have the following functions and powers:
> a) to develop an awareness of human rights among the peoples of America;
> b) to make recommendations to the governments of the Member States, when it considers such action advisable, for the adoption of progressive measures in favour of their domestic law and constitutional provisions as well as appropriate measures to further the observance of those rights;

c) to prepare such studies or reports as it considers advisable in the performance of its duties;

d) to request the governments of the Member States to supply it with information on the measures adopted by them in matters of human rights;

e) to respond, through the General Secretariat of the [OAS], to inquiries made by the Member States on matters related to human rights and, within the limits of its possibilities, to provide those states with the advisory services they request;

f) to take action on petitions and other communications pursuant to its authority under the provisions of Articles 44 through 51 of this Convention; and

g) to submit an annual report to the General Assembly of the [OAS].

The terms of Article 111 of the Charter and Article 41 of the Convention are reflected in the Commission's Statute. Article 18 of the Statute, which is addressed to all OAS Member States, virtually reproduces Article 41(a) to (e) of the Convention but adds the power of the Commission to conduct on-site observations in a state with the consent of that state[1] and to prepare the Commission's budget for presentation to the OAS General Assembly.[2] Articles 19 and 20 of the Statute then elaborate the differentiated functions of the Commission depending upon whether it is acting as a Charter or Convention institution. Article 19 largely reiterates the provisions of the American Convention and applies only to States Parties to the Convention, while Article 20 reproduces Article 9(bis) of the Commission's old Statute.

The fact that Article 41 of the Convention is addressed to all OAS Member States regardless of whether they are party to the Convention or not raises a number of problems. In general the rule that states may not be bound to treaties to which they have not signified their consent would seem to preclude Article 41 from having any effect as far as states not party to the American Convention are concerned. Thus any additional powers conferred on the Commission should, in accordance with the normal rule, not impinge upon the relationship of non-party OAS Member States to the Commission. Buergenthal, however, dissents from this view. He argues that by ratifying the OAS Charter, all OAS Member States agreed that they would be bound by the competences granted to the Inter-American Commission when the American Convention entered into force.[3] In support of this view he cites paragraph two of Article 112 (now Article 111) which provides that 'an inter-American Convention on Human Rights shall determine the structure, competence, and procedure of this Commission, as well as those of other organs responsible for these matters that is, the promotion and protection of human rights'. Whether this view can be maintained is debatable. Cecilia Medina takes a more pragmatic view, arguing that the Article 41 might simply be regarded as another step in the consolidation of the Commission's power.[4] She also takes the view that, while there is no attempt to amend the Commission's Statute or to alter its powers, the problem is likely to remain academic.[5] She points out, however, that it would be desirable to clarify the position since 'it is generally speaking wiser to remove impediments before they actually cause an obstruction'.[6]

This overlapping of institutional powers between the OAS Charter and the American Convention is not, however, unique to the Commission. The Court, which is not mentioned in the OAS Charter, is nonetheless a *de facto* Charter organ since it is empowered by Article 64 to provide advisory opinions on a wide variety of international instruments and a state's own internal law at the request of any Member State of the OAS. This differs somewhat to the position of the Commission, however, in that an OAS Member State which is not a party to the American Convention but which nevertheless requests an advisory opinion from the Court on the compatibility of its domestic laws with the American Declaration might be said to be taking advantage of a rule designed for its benefit within the meaning of Article 36 of the Vienna Convention on the Law of Treaties. Thus the position of the Court can be differentiated from that of the Commission. While states which are OAS members may take advantage of the Court's advisory jurisdiction at their discretion, it seems that the powers of the Commission may be exercised against them without their direct consent.

Composition, Organization and Functioning of the Inter-American Commission on Human Rights

Composition of the Commission

Under Article 34 of the Convention the Inter-American Commission on Human Rights is to be composed of seven members 'who shall be persons of high moral character and recognized competence in the field of human rights'.[7] The members of the Commission are elected in a personal capacity by the OAS General Assembly from a list of candidates proposed by the Governments of the Member States.[8] The procedure for election of Commission Members is that each state may propose up to three candidates who may be nationals of that state or of any other Member State of the OAS.[9] This is qualified by the requirement that, if a state proposes a slate of three nominees, then at least one of them must be a national of another OAS Member State.[10] No two members of the Commission may be nationals of the same state.[11] Commission members are elected for a four year term and may be re-elected for an additional term of office.[12] Their terms of office commence on 1 January of the year following that in which they are elected.[13] In order to provide some continuity in the membership, three members of the original Commission were elected only for a period of two years.[14] The names of these Commission members were chosen by lot.[15] The electoral process for appointing Commission members is governed by Article 5 of the Commission's Statute. This provides that the ballot in the OAS General Assembly must be secret and that the candidate who receives the largest number of votes and an absolute majority of the votes of the Member States is to be declared elected. In the event that it becomes necessary to hold several ballots, the candidates receiving the smallest number of votes are eliminated successively. Where vacancies occur on the Commission for reasons other than the expiration of a Commission member's term of office,[16] the vacancy is filled by the Permanent Council acting in accordance with Article 11 of the Commission's Statute.[17] This requires that in the event of an unforeseen vacancy the Chairman of the Commission is to notify the Secretary-General of the OAS who then notifies the Member States.[18] The governments of the Member States are then to provide the Secretary-General with their proposed candidates within a period of thirty days from the date of receipt of the Secretary-General's communication.[19] Unlike scheduled periodic elections for the Commission, in elections for occasional vacancies Member States are entitled to nominate only one candidate who may, presumably, be one of their own nationals or a national of another OAS Member State.[20] The list of candidates is then sent to the Permanent Council 'which shall fill the vacancy'.[21] Although there is no indication in the Commission's Statute or Regulations about the procedure to be adopted by the Permanent Council, but since the Council is responsible to the General Assembly its *modus operandi* must be the same as the procedure adopted by that body in periodic elections.[22]

Given that Commission members serve in their individual capacity, there are a number of provisions within the Convention and the Commission's Statute and Regulations which are designed to buttress and preserve their independence and impartiality. Article 35 of the Convention, together with certain articles of the Statute[23] and Regulations[24] establish the overarching principle of independence by stipulating that 'the Commission shall represent all the member countries of the Organization of American States'. While this places a general collegial responsibility upon the Commission as a body and establishes the general framework for the protection of the independence and impartiality of Commission members, these instruments also spell out in detail their individual responsibilities in this area. These provide that Commission members may not engage in activities which are incompatible with membership of the Commission, nor may they engage in functions which might affect the independence or impartiality of the member or the dignity or prestige of his or her post on the Commission.[25] Decisions on these matters are within the competence of the Commission itself, which may decide by an affirmative vote of at least five of its members that a case of incompatibility exists.[26] Before taking such a decision, however, the member who is considered to be in a situation of incompatibility must, in accordance with the principle of *audi alteram partem*, be given the opportunity to be heard.[27] If the Commission decides that a member is in a position of incompatibility, that finding is then submitted to the OAS General Assembly for final decision.[28] A decision to remove a Commission member must be taken by two-thirds of the Member States of the OAS in the General Assembly and has immediate effect.[29] Significantly, however, none of the actions in which the Commission member so removed has participated are tainted by invalidity.[30] This presumably applies to actions taken in a period during which it subsequently becomes apparent the Commission members' impartiality may have been in doubt. The adoption of this position by the Statute would appear to be a matter of policy. While it would clearly be inappropriate to reopen decided matters, it is apparent that there may be cases in which a removed Commission member's decision in a particular matter may have been decisive. It may nonetheless be arguable that certainty and finality override other interests in such cases.

In addition to the requirements of impartiality and independence, members of the Commission are required to comply with certain duties.[31] These duties not only include performance of the normal functions of a Commission member such as attendance at meetings[32] and participation in on-site investigations[33] but also 'to maintain absolute secrecy about all matters which the Commission deems confidential'.[34] Furthermore, members of the Commission are enjoined to comport themselves both publicly and privately 'as befits the high moral authority of the office and the importance of the mission entrusted to the Commission'.[35] Should any member of the Commission commit a serious violation of any of these duties then they may be removed from office.[36] The procedure for removing a Commission member for such a breach is the same as that for removal from office on the grounds of incompatibility discussed above.[37]

The impartiality and independence of Commission members is also reinforced by the Convention's requirement that they enjoy throughout the term of their office the immunities extended to diplomatic agents in accordance with international law.[38] This relates not only to their immunity from criminal or civil suit in matters unrelated to their duties as Commission members, but also to the exercise of their functions as such.[39] In addition to this, the Convention provides that members of the Commission may not be held liable for 'any decisions or opinions issued in the exercise of their functions'.[40] In OAS Member States which are not party to the American Convention, the privileges and immunities of Commission members is regulated by Article 12(2) of the Commission's Statute. This provides that members of the Commission shall enjoy in such states 'the privileges and immunities pertaining to their posts that are required for them to perform their duties with independence'. These broad-ranging immunities enable Commission members to carry out their functions free from the constraints of State Party interference. Cecilia Medina argues that in a continent in which force plays a predominant role, and in which state interference with officials is common, the rule on incompatibility and immunity for Commission members is wise.[41]

Internal Organization of the Commission

Article 14 of the Commission's Statute requires that the Commission elect a Chairman and a First and Second Vice Chairman every year by an absolute majority of its members present and voting.[42] Elections are conducted by secret ballot, but there is provision for other methods of election if the members of the Commission who are present agree unanimously.[43] The Commission's officers may be re-elected, but only for one further year in any four year period.[44] Although the mandate of the board of officers extends normally from the date of their election until the holding of new elections on the first day of the Commission's first session of the new calendar year,[45] there may be circumstances in which the Chairman resigns or otherwise ceases to be a member of the Commission. In such cases, the First Vice Chairman serves as Chairman until the Commission elects a new person to that position.[46] The First Vice Chairman also replaces the Chairman if the latter is temporarily unable to perform his or her duties.[47] The Second Vice Chairman fills the corresponding gaps left when the First Vice Chairman is called upon to fulfil the role of Chairman.[48]

The functions of the Chairman are manifold. They comprise, *inter alia*, representing the Commission within the OAS convocation of meetings;

presiding over Commission session; promotion of the work of the Commission; ensuring compliance with decisions of the Commission; organizing the Commission's various committees and sub-Committees and performing any other duties associated with the operation of the Commission which might be required of him or her under the regulations.[49] Some, but not all, of these functions may be delegated to one of the Commission's Vice Chairmen. These are representing the Commission within the OAS, attending meetings of the OAS General Assembly and performing any other functions required by the Commission's Regulations.[50]

The Commission is assisted in its work by a Secretariat. This body is mandated to prepare the Commission's draft reports, resolutions, studies and any other work 'entrusted to it' by the Commission or its Chairman.[51] The Secretariat also prepares the minutes of the Commission's sessions[52] and all other documents,[53] as well as undertaking all the preliminary functions associated with the individual petition procedures under the Charter and the Convention. The Secretariat thus receives petitions from individuals which are addressed to the Commission and seeks the necessary information required from the governments concerned.[54] It also makes the appropriate arrangements to initiate any proceedings to which these petitions may ultimately give rise.[55] The Secretariat is directed by an Executive Secretary and an Assistant Executive Secretary who replaces the former when he or she is unable to act because of absence or disability.[56] The functions of the Executive Secretary are set out in Article 13 of the Commission's Regulations and include, *inter alia*, directing, planning and coordinating the work of the Secretariat, drafting the work schedule for sessions of the Commission in consultation with its Chairman and implementing the decisions entrusted to him or her by the Commission or its Chairman.[57] Given the sensitive nature of much of the Secretariat's work, all its staff, including the Executive and Assistant Executive Secretary, are enjoined to 'observe strict discretion in all matters that the Commission considers confidential'.[58]

Functioning of the Commission

The Commission meets for no more than a total of eight weeks a year divided into however many regular meeting it may decide it needs.[59] This is conditioned by an injunction contained in Article 16 of the Commission's Regulations which provides that the Commission must hold as many meetings during the session as are necessary to allow it to carry out its business.[60] The length of these meetings are determined by the Commission itself,[61] and all such meetings are held *in camera* unless the Commission decides otherwise.[62] The Commission may also convoke special meetings either at the decision of its Chairman or at the request of an absolute majority of all its members.[63] Sessions of the Commission are held at its headquarters in Washington D C, but by an absolute majority vote of its members, it may decide to meet elsewhere.[64] In order to do this, however, the consent of the potential host government must be obtained.[65]

In order to facilitate the execution of its work, the Commission is empowered to establish a number of working groups consisting of three persons designated by its Chairman.[66] This it may do prior to the beginning of every regular session when it considers it 'advisable' to do so.[67] These working groups may be convened in order to prepare draft resolutions and other decisions on petitions and communications before such matters are dealt with by the full Commission.[68] The Commission may also, by a vote of an absolute majority of its members, decide to form other working groups to consider specific subjects again prior to consideration by the full Commission.[69] Such working groups are also to be no larger than three in number, which leaves open the possibility that they may be fewer in number should the Commission Chairman so decide.[70]

In order to constitute a quorum for a meeting of the Commission an absolute majority of its members (i.e. four) must be present.[71] Although most decisions are taken by an absolute majority of the Commission present and voting, in certain circumstances a special quorum is required.[72] As noted above, this is necessitated in the election of the executive officers of the Commission,[73] but it is also demanded when the Regulations of the Commission are to be the subject of either interpretation or amendment.[74] One particularly important matter upon which decision by a special quorum is required is in the adoption of a country report, that is, a report on the situation of human rights in a specific state.[75] Given the importance of such reports and the political sensitivity which attaches to them, the reason for more than a mere majority of Commission members present and voting is self-evident.

Article 19 of the Commission's Regulations establishes the framework for the conduct of discussions and voting. Of particular importance is a category of decisions in which members may not participate if either they have had a certain association with a state or if they have taken part in previous decisions on certain matters. These provisions allow the Commission members concerned to avoid allegations of conflict of interest and may be regarded as an application of the principle of *nemo iudex in sua causa*. Article 19(2) provides that members of the Commission may not participate in 'the discussion, investigation, deliberation or decision of a matter' in the following circumstances:

a) if they were nationals or permanent residents of the state which is [the] subject of the Commission's general or specific consideration, or if they were accredited to, or carrying out, a special mission, as diplomatic agents, on behalf of [the] said state;

b) if previously they have participated in any capacity in a decision concerning the same facts on which the matter is based or have acted as an adviser to, or representative of, any of the parties involved in the decision.

Where a member thinks that he or she may be covered by these rules against participation, he or she must inform the Commission.[76] The Commission then decides whether withdrawal is warranted.[77] Other members of the Commission may also raise the question of whether the withdrawal of a member is warranted on the basis of Article 19(2)(a)-(b).[78] While there is no provision in the Regulations for the procedure following such an allegation, presumably the Commission must also discuss this matter, and, the Commission member against whom this allegation is made should also have the opportunity to present his or her case against withdrawal. This point is probably covered by Article 19(9) which provides:[79]

> Any doubts which may arise as regards the application or interpretation of the present article [19] shall be resolved by the Commission. Members who have withdrawn from the a case are not permitted to participate in any aspect of it, even though the reason for the original withdrawal may have been superseded.

Functions of the Inter-American Commission on Human Rights

As indicated above, the Commission is empowered by the OAS Charter and the American Convention on Human Rights to fulfil a variety of roles. While Article 111 of the Charter states that the principal function of the Commission shall be 'to promote the observance and protection of human rights and to serve as a consultative organ of the Organization in these matters', Article 41 of the Convention provides that its main function is 'to promote respect for and defence of human rights'. Article 41 then goes on to provide a more or less comprehensive list of the detailed functions of the Commission.[80] For the sake of the present analysis, however, the Commission's functions may be divided, somewhat arbitrarily, into those having a promotional aspect and those having a protective quality. In order to assist in drawing a distinction between these two categories of activity, it is, perhaps, useful to quote Karel Vasak who has written:

> The promotion of human rights implies action resolutely directed toward the future: the question of human rights is seen as containing a lacuna, because they are not all, or are only incompletely guaranteed under national legislation or international law, or because they are not sufficiently understood by the persons entitled to them or by the states and their subsidiary bodies which are bound to protect them. In these circumstances, a body for the promotion of human rights will attempt to determine inadequacies and even violations, not so much in order that they may be published by rather that similar situation may be prevented from occurring in the future.
>
> The protection of human rights appears to have, in many respects, a diametrically opposed aim. Intended to ensure the observance of human rights as established under international law, the institution for protection leads, by the sanctions to which protection necessarily gives rise, towards a future that perpetuates the past. It relies mainly on court process whereas the institution for promotion will make use of every available legislative technique, including studies research, reports and the drafting of texts.

While the distinction between the two categories of activities may appear to be somewhat artificial and arbitrary,[81] nonetheless it is possible to identify the various functions gathered under these two heads in the operations of the Inter-American Commission.

Promotion of Human Rights

In this category the Commission carries out a broad range of activities. Since it is enjoined by Article 41(a) of the Convention to 'develop an awareness of human rights among the peoples of America' it may be said to have a broadly educational function as part of its promotional activities. In pursuit of these the Commission has organized conferences and seminars and has published a number of information pamphlets and documents designed to give a broader appreciation of the place of human rights in the Americas.[82] An important initiative in this sphere which the Commission adopted at its very first session, but which has made little impact so far was that of attempting to encourage states to establish national committees on human rights.[83] The function of these committees would be to 'cooperate with the Commission in the task of stimulating an awareness of human rights among the American people, taking advantage of all the cultural and education means available to them ... and [to] suggest to the Commission ways of promoting human rights and guaranteeing their protection through the legislation of the American states'.[84] While there have been fitful attempts to resurrect the idea of forming national committees, a number of impediments have prevented their coming to fruition.[85]

Article 41(c) of the Convention and Article 18(c) of the Commission's Statute also empower it 'to prepare such studies or reports as it considers advisable for the performance of its duties'. This is a power which the Commission has possessed since 1960, and there are numerous examples of its use.[86] In order to prepare such reports, the Commission is entitled to call upon states to provide it with reports on the measures they adopt in matters of human rights.[87] The Commission's role in promoting human rights is also facilitated by Article 18(e) of its Statute which permits it to respond to enquiries made by member states on matters related to human rights and to provide those states with the advisory services they need. Associated with this is the competence of the Commission to consult the Inter-American Court on Human Rights on the interpretation of the Convention or of other treaties concerning the protection of human rights in the American states.[88] This is a power which the Commission has used freely and which has enabled it to clarify the meaning of a number of provisions of the American Convention.[89] While the Court's rulings in requests for advisory opinions are not legally binding, as will be demonstrated below,[90] they are nonetheless of substantial authority and thus capable of influencing the development of human rights in the Americas.

Perhaps the most important of the Commission's promotional activities in terms of concrete results has been its role in drafting a number of inter-American conventions on human rights topics.[91] As noted above,[92] the Commission played a substantial role in drafting the American Convention on Human Rights itself, but it has also taken initiatives in drafting the Inter-American Convention to Prevent and Punish Torture, the Inter-American Convention on the Forced Disappearance of Persons[93] and the Inter-American Convention on the Prevention, Punishment and Eradication of Violence Against Women.[94] Of particular note, however, was the Commission's role in drafting and facilitating the adoption of the Protocol of San Salvador to the American Convention on Human Rights.[95] The Commission had, prior to 1979, implicitly recognized the relationship between respect for first and second generation rights, but in its *1979-80 Annual Report*, it made clear that it would be more active in promoting this field of activity.[96] As a result of the Commission's efforts in promoting economic, social and cultural rights the OAS General Assembly decided not only to affirm that governments of the Member States had a responsibility to undertake the effective protection of such rights, but also mandated that a draft for an additional protocol to the American Convention on Human Rights should be prepared.[97]

The publication by the Commission of its annual report may also be broadly characterized as part of its promotional function. In its annual report, which is submitted to the Permanent Council and General Assembly of the OAS, the Commission provides details of all noteworthy activities which it has carried out in the preceding twelve months. The contents of the report are prescribed by Article 63 of the Commission's Regulations and indicate that in addition to simple matters of report,[98] the Commission is to provide a qualitative assessment of the progress made in attaining the objectives set forth in the American Declaration and the American Convention[99] and a report on the areas in which measures should be taken to improve observance of human rights.[100] Since the Commission's annual report is subject to debate in the General Assembly, and since it is available to the public, it provides the primary mechanism of providing information on the totality of its activities.

Protection of Human Rights

As Vasak observes, the function of protecting human rights is characterized primarily by the action of judicial or quasi-judicial institutions to prevent or redress breaches of rights which exist as a matter of positive law.[101] Vasak also notes that sanctions generally attach to the protective function.[102] Such sanctions may not always be of a pecuniary character and may comprehend interdictive or injunctive action designed to prevent breaches from occurring and, as is common to most human rights systems, widespread publicity and the attendant condemnation which attaches to breaches of positive human rights law. In carrying out its function of protecting human rights, the Inter-American Commission possesses nearly all these characteristics.

As noted above,[103] the Commission's powers to ensure that the American states observe their human rights obligations is derived from two legal sources: the OAS Charter and the American Convention.[104] Under the OAS Charter the Commission is empowered to prepare studies,[105] to request governments to provide information on measures relating to human rights[106] and to conduct on-site investigations with the consent or at the invitation of the government of the state in question.[107] In addition, the Commission under Article 20 of its Statute has the power to receive individual communications and to make recommendations to Member States in order to bring about more effective observance of the rights in question.[108] Under the American Convention the Commission is given the competence to act on individual petitions[109] and inter-state communications[110] and to request the Court to take provisional measures if this is necessary to avoid irreparable damage to persons.[111] Furthermore, if in the course of its procedures under individual petitions and other applications the Commission becomes aware of serious or urgent cases then it may, if such a petition or application fulfils the formal requirements for admissibility,[112] conduct an on-site investigation with the consent of the state concerned.[113]

The Commission's Methods of Inquiry

Central to the Commission's protective function is its competence to engage in wide-ranging inquiries in order to gather facts on the true state of human rights in Member States. It may acquire such information from a variety of sources. As noted above,[114] the Commission is empowered by its Statute to obtain information directly from the governments of Member States in pursuit of its general mandate, but it may also request information in its procedures involving individual cases,[115] and Article 64(2) and (4) of its Regulations gives it power to request annual reports from Member States on the economic, social and cultural rights recognized by the American Declaration of the Rights and Duties of Man. In addition to these sources of information in its role as an inquisitorial body, the Commission also uses individual communications as a source of intelligence in the compilation of its annual and country reports.[116] Cecilia Medina observes that 'the communications thus serve a double purpose: as information to be used by the Commission in defence of human rights, and as an instrument to set in motion the special procedure for individual communications of violation of human rights ...'.[117]

The Commission may also conduct its inquiries by the holding of hearings in certain circumstances defined by its constituent instruments. Under Article 48(1)(e) of the Convention, the Commission in the conduct of its procedures in individual petitions or other applications must, if so requested, 'hear oral statements ... from the parties concerned'. Furthermore, the Commission is granted an extremely broad power to hold hearings *proprio motu*. Article 65 provides:

> On its own initiative, or at the request of the person concerned, the Commission may decide to hold hearings on matters defined by the Statute as within its jurisdiction.

Given that Articles 18, 19 and 20 of the Statute establishes a substantially open-ended mandate in matters of human rights affecting the Americas, the

Commission would appear to be competent to hold hearings on a very wide range of issues. This conclusion is further justified by the terms of Article 66 of the Regulations which establishes the purposes of hearings. Article 66(1) provides that hearings may be held in connection with a petition or communication alleging a violation of a right protected by the Convention or the Declaration or in order to receive information of a general or particular nature related to the situation of human rights in one or more of the American states. Hearings which are called to review individual petitions are held in private, unless the parties or their representative agree otherwise.[118] All other hearings are normally held in private, but the Commission itself may decide otherwise.[119]

Country Studies and On-site Observations

At the very outset of its existence the Commission received complaints from a variety of sources alleging human rights violations in a number of OAS Member States. It will be recalled, however, that the Commission's Statute did not permit it to act on these individual complaints, but Article 9 of its original Statute did allow it to prepare such studies and reports that it considered advisable for the performance of its duties. In addition to this, Article 11 granted the Commission power 'to move to the territory of any American state when it so decides by an absolute majority of votes and with the consent of the government concerned'. As Buergenthal notes, 'these two provisions of the Statute provided the Commission with the legislative authority to develop the system of country studies and "on site" observations'.[120] The country study is a comprehensive investigation of the state of human rights in a particular OAS Member State. It is normally initiated by the Commission when it receives substantial evidence by way of individual complaints, complaints from NGOs or from other credible sources such as churches or aid workers that the government of the state in question is perpetrating large-scale violations of human rights. In such circumstances it may form the view that, while it is able to proceed by way of the individual complaint procedures under either the Charter or the Convention, the magnitude and seriousness of the violations disclosed by such large and well attested numbers of complaints leads it to believe that such a piecemeal approach would not lead to satisfactory results. A country study may also be initiated by the Commission at the request of one of the political organs of the OAS, such as the General Assembly, which may itself be apprised of widespread human rights abuses in one of its Member States. The Commission can also undertake a country study *proprio motu* by way of a follow-up to an earlier study to assess whether recommendations made in that study have been implemented or complied with by the subject state. Furthermore, a government may itself request the Commission to carry out a country study in its own state. The motivation of governments concerned in making such an approach to the Commission may vary. It may wish to pre-empt a country study being initiated by the Commission itself, thereby hoping to convince the Commission that all is well and that it should not expect to find evidence of widespread human rights abuses. A government may, however, genuinely wish to search for solutions to human rights problems within the state and thus engage the Commission as a vehicle through which it might bring pressure to bear on certain sections of the state apparatus, such as the military. Furthermore, the government of a state in which human rights may generally be regarded as reasonably well-protected may wish to use a favourable country report by the Commission to buttress or improve its position domestically. It must be admitted, however, that the majority of country reports have been initiated where the Commission has had good reason to believe that substantial human rights abuses have been taking place in the country in question. As Cecilia Medina has noted, on-site observations have come to be accepted by OAS Member States and that very few of them have rejected a request by the Commission to conduct a visit outright.[121] Indeed, as she correctly observes, most states which have been reluctant to allow observations *in loco* by the Commission have simply found excuses for temporizing.[122]

The Commission's *modus operandi* for the conduct of country studies and the preparation of country reports was established at an early stage in its existence. Its first three country studies on Cuba, Haiti and the Dominican Republic allowed it to develop the procedures and mechanisms for gathering and evaluating information and drafting the report. An important part of the development of this practice was that the Commission decided that it should be permitted, as a matter of course, to carry out on-site investigations when undertaking a country study. While such observations or investigations are extremely valuable for obtaining information or for confirming information already in its possession, they are not absolutely necessary to enable the Commission to fulfil its function here. Indeed, in its first two studies on Cuba and Haiti, the governments of the states in question refused to grant the Commission permission to conduct observations in loco. This, however, did not prevent the Commission from hearing witnesses and gathering information from other sources.[123]

The conduct of on-site observations is governed by the Commission's

Regulations.[124] These provide that such observations are to be carried out by a Special Commission whose numbers and chairman are to be determined by the full Commission.[125] A member of the Commission who is a national or resident of the state which is the subject of an on-site observation is automatically disqualified from participation therein, thus preserving the impartiality and disinterestedness of the Special Commission.[126] The Special Commission, which is supported by personnel from the Secretariat, organizes its own activities and may direct any of its members to perform any activity related to its mission.[127] Before the Special Commission is able to conduct an on-site investigation it must secure an invitation from the subject state.[128] Such an invitation may be secured by a request from the Commission, or it may issue from the state concerned itself.[129] Clearly, as the Cuba and Haiti cases demonstrate, there is no requirement for the state to comply with a request by the Commission to allow the conduct of an on-site observation. Once permission has been granted, however, the state is under an obligation to provide a number of specific guarantees. Article 58 of the Commission's Regulations require that a state giving its consent to on-site observation 'shall furnish to the Special Commission all necessary facilities for carrying out its mission'. Furthermore, the state's primary obligation is to commit itself 'not to take any reprisals of any kind against any persons or entities cooperating with the Special Commission or providing information or testimony'.[130] The imposition of this obligation upon states is crucial to the conduct of an effective on-site observation by the Special Commission, for if individuals or organizations are unable to speak freely and without fear of retaliation by the state or its agents then this would deny the Special Commission much important information. From the Commission's country reports it is evident that states resort to a variety of subterfuges in order to ensure that damaging evidence is not placed before the visiting Special Commission. In Argentina, for example, political prisoners were visited in advance of the Special Commission's visit by state agents who posed as Red Cross representatives. These agents then attempted to identify which of the prisoners were likely to relay damaging evidence against the state to the Special Commission and they were then removed from the prison.[131] Furthermore, when the Special Commission visited Argentina, prisoners were interviewed in places other than those especially set aside for such purposes by the prison authorities since the Commission staff clearly felt that their conversations with the prisoners were likely to be recorded and presumably used against the detainees in future.[132]

The applicable standards for the conduct of on-site observations are established in Article 59 of the Commission's Regulations. These standards, which were initially formulated in 1975[133] to deal with cases of urgency on a largely ad hoc basis, were subsequently refined in 1977 to address the powers of the Commission in dealing with on-site observations.[134] These have been subsequently amended and included in the Commission's Regulations, which now include the following standards:

- The Special Commission or its members must be able to interview freely in private any person, group, institution or other body and the state must provide 'the pertinent guarantees' to all those who provide the Commission with 'information, testimony or evidence of any kind'.[135]
- Members of the Special Commission must be able to travel freely throughout the subject state and to this end the government of the state is to provide the Commission with all necessary facilities, including appropriate documentation.[136]
- The government of the subject state is to provide all local means of transport and accommodation for the Special Commission, as well as ensuring it appropriate measures of security and protection.[137]
- Special Commission members must be allowed access to jails and all other detention and interrogation centres and must be able to interview detainees in private.[138]
- The government of the subject state must provide the Special Commission with any documentation relating to the observance of human rights which that body considers necessary for the preparation of its reports[139] and the Commission must be able to use 'any method appropriate' in the collection, recording or reproduction of information it considers to be useful.[140]

An examination of the conduct of on-site investigations suggests that there is no particular pattern which is followed by the Commission. Generally, however, it may be said that the members of the Special Commission travel throughout the subject state interviewing a wide range of people such as members of the government, opposition members, civil servants, union leaders, church leaders, business groups, non-governmental organizations, eminent persons and private individuals. Special Commissions have also visited prisons, military barracks and other places of detention sometimes precipitating dramatic results.[141] As Buergenthal has also observed, the very presence of the Commission has occasionally stimulated an immediate improvement in the human rights situation.[142]

Regardless of whether or not a country study involves an on-site observation, the Commission in the preparation of a country report follows a certain pattern, part of which is dictated by practice and part by the Commission's own Regulations.[143] An examination of any country report shows that the Commission commences by explaining the reason for the report and its methodology. The Commission then provides background information relating to the political, social, economic and legal situation in the state in question. The legal protection of the rights to be considered by the Commission is then given at the head of the relevant section. The Commission may then refer to individual cases which it has examined or which are in the process of consideration by the Commission. The Commission is at pains in the latter to indicate that such reference does not indicate a predetermination of the issue.[144] The country report then ends with conclusions and recommendations which are a summary of the special conclusions reached at the end of each section considering specific human rights. The country report also usually contains a general appraisal of the human rights situation and the governments responsibility for dealing with it. As indicated above, since 1980 country reports have also included observations on the status of economic, social and cultural rights in a state following the Commission's statement in its *1979-80 Annual Report* that there is an organic relationship between the violation of civil and political rights on the one hand and the lack of promotion of economic, social and cultural rights on the other.[145]

The procedure in drafting a country report is set out in the Commission's Regulations.[146] First, a draft report must be prepared and adopted by the Commission. As noted above,[147] in view of the sensitivity attached to country reports, Article 20(1)(c) of the Commission's Regulations requires a special quorum of a majority of the member of the Commission. Following adoption of the draft report it is then transmitted to the government of the state in question to allow it to make any observations it wishes.[148] Such observations must be made by the state within the time limit established by the Commission.[149] Occasionally, the draft report submitted by the Commission has been subjected to vitriolic attack by the state in question. A notable example of this was the Commission's 1980 report on Argentina which the latter's government characterized as lacking the requisites of fairness and objectivity and suggested that the Commission had violated its duties under its Statute by attempting to discredit the Argentinian government and to put it on trial.[150] Once the Commission has received observations from the government in question, it studies them and may, if it thinks fit, change its report.[151] The Commission in the light of this may then decide whether and how the report is to be published.[152] From this it is clear that the Commission is under no obligation to publish the country report if it thinks that this is an inappropriate way of proceeding. If, for example, the government has indicated that it has already instituted measures and made substantial progress towards rectifying some of the difficulties identified by the Commission, the latter may decide that it would not be productive to publish the report. If, however, the government of the state in question does not respond to the Commission's request for observations on the draft report, the Commission must publish the report 'in the manner it deems suitable'.[153] The implication here would seem to be that the threat of publication of the report operates as a form of sanction against states which are reluctant to participate in the drafting process.

As well as publishing the report, the Commission may also decide to transmit it to the OAS General Assembly for consideration. In a sense this is the ultimate sanction which is attached to the country report process, since the General Assembly discussion of the report may generate considerable publicity and may result in the adoption of a resolution directed against a state. whose human rights record is deemed to be poor. While such resolutions are not legally binding they nonetheless carry substantial political and moral authority. The reality is, however, that states are generally reluctant to engage in full debate over a country report and generally content to allow the subject state and the Commission's representative to debate the merits and demerits of the Commission's methodology and findings. Since the General Assembly is a political body whose composition and attitude change from time to time, its willingness to be critical varies. Occasionally, as in the debate on the country report on Chile in 1975, the states in the General Assembly are willing to conduct a full-blooded debate and to adopt a critical resolution. More often, however, the outcome is simply anodyne and is represented by a simple statement that the General Assembly notes the report and thanks the Commission for its efforts.

Individual Petitions

The development of the Commission's dual competence with respect to individual communications under both the OAS Charter and the American Convention on Human Rights was dealt with in some detail above and the precise mechanics of the procedures are dealt with in chapter 4 below. It is not intended to provide a detailed account of those procedures here, but simply to give a brief indication of the their place in the Commission's overall functions within the inter-American human rights system.

It will be recalled that the Commission initially had no competence under its original Statute to receive individual communications alleging violations of human rights, but that this defect was remedied by an amendment to the Statute and the inclusion of Article 9(bis) which gave the Commission competence to receive individual complaints inasmuch as they related to a specific group of specially designated rights mentioned by the American Declaration. While the Commission's new Statute retains the status of these specially designated rights, its Regulations make no distinction as to the protected rights and the Commission can now receive and act upon any of the rights set forth in the American Declaration.[154] It will also be recalled that the Commission is the body which is competent to receive petitions alleging violations of the rights protected by the American Convention on Human Rights and the Protocol of San Salvador under Article 44 of the former instrument. Whether individual applications arise under the OAS Charter or the American Convention they are processed in the same way. Thus, the Commission screens the applications to determine whether domestic remedies have been exhausted and whether they are timely and well-founded. It is only at the final stages of proceedings that the two types of application are treated differently. Applications lodged under the Charter system are concluded by a report which is normally referred to as a final decision. The Commission has no power to offer compensation or other remedies, although it will generally recommend that specific courses of action be followed. Under the Convention the Commission enjoys the power to dispose of the application itself or to remit it to the Inter-American Court of Human Rights for final determination under its contentious jurisdiction. The Court then has the power to award monetary compensation and to designate other remedial action. A brief comparison of the Charter and Convention-based systems would appear to suggest that the latter has the potential for greater efficacy, since the capacity of the Court to award remedies provides direct relief for victims. Other than inclusion in its annual report or perhaps as part of its country report, a decision by the Commission under the Charter carries little immediate weight.

Notes

[1] Article 18(g) Commission Statute.
[2] Article 18(f) Commission Statute.
[3] Buergenthal, *Inter-American System*, pp. 475-9.
[4] Medina Quiroga, *Battle of Human Rights*, p. 119.
[5] Ibid.
[6] Ibid.

7   Article 2(1) Statute; Article 1(3) Regulations.

8   Article 36(1) ACHR; Article 3(1) Statute.

9   Article 36(2) ACHR; Article 3(2) Statute.

10   Article 36(2) ACHR; Article 3(2) Statute.

11   Article 37(2) ACHR; Article 7 Statute.

12   Article 37(1) ACHR; Article 6 Statute; Article 2(1) Regulations.

13   Article 6 Statute.

14   Ibid.

15   Ibid.

16   Article 5 Regulations refer only to resignation, but clearly vacancies may occur through ill health or death of a Commission member.

17   Article 38 ACHR.

18   Article 11(1) Statute.

19   Article 11(2) Statute.

20   Article 11(1) Statute. This provides in the material part, ' ... each government may propose *a* candidate ...' (emphasis added). The applicable nationality of the candidates is derived from Articles 36(2) ACHR and Article 3(2) Statute.

21   Article 11(3) Statute.

22   See supra.

23   Article 2(2) Statute.

24   Article 1(2) Regulations.

25   Article 71 ACHR; Article 8(1) Statute; Article 4(1) Regulations.

26   Article 8(2) Statute; Article 4(2) Regulations.

27   Article 4(3) Regulations.

28   Article 8(2) Statute; Article 4(4) Regulations.

29   Article 8(3) Statute.

30   Ibid.

31   Article 9 Statute.

32   Article 9(1) Statute.

33   Article 9(2) Statute.

34   Article 9(3) Statute.

35   Article 9(4) Statute.

36   Article 10(1) Statute.

37   See supra.

38   Article 70(1) ACHR; Article 12(1) Statute. These are largely codified in the Vienna Convention on Diplomatic Privileges and Immunities 1961.

39   Article 70(1) ACHR.

40   Article 70(2) ACHR.

41   Medina Quiroga, *Battle of Human Rights*, p. 121.

42   See also Articles 6 and 7(1) Regulations.

43   Article 7(2) Regulations.

44   Article 14(1) Statute; Article 8(1) Regulations.

45   Articles 7(5) and 8(2) Regulations.

46   Article 9(3) Regulations.

47   Article 9(4) Regulations.

48   Ibid.

49   Article 10(a)-(m) Regulations.

50   Article 11 Regulations. These functions are those contained in Article 10(a), (j) and (m).
51   Article 14(1) Regulations.
52   The Commission is required to keep such minutes by Article 22 of its Regulations. The form of these minutes is also dictated by this provision.
53   Ibid.
54   Article 14(2) Regulations.
55   Ibid.
56   Article 13(2) Regulations.
57   Article 13(1)(a)-(e) Regulations.
58   Article 13(3) Regulations.
59   Article 15(1) Regulations.
60   Article 16(1) Regulations.
61   Article 16(2) Regulations.
62   Ibid.
63   Ibid.
64   Article 15(2) Regulations.
65   Ibid.
66   Article 17(1) Regulations.
67   Ibid.
68   Ibid.
69   Article 17(2) Regulations.
70   Ibid.
71   Article 18 Regulations.
72   Article 20(1) Regulations.
73   Supra, p. 104-5.
74   Article 20(1)(d) Regulations.
75   Article 20(1)(c) Regulations.
76   Article 19(3) Regulations.
77   Ibid.
78   Article 19(4) Regulations.
79   Article 19(5) Regulations.
80   Infra, pp. 108-18.
81   Medina Quiroga, *Battle of Human Rights*, p. 122 observes that 'the categorization of human rights activities in promotional and protective functions has no absolute validity, since protective measures always play some sort of protective role and at least a germ of protection can be traced in any promotional activity'.
82   The Commission's own *Annual Report* is a public document which contains much information on the Commission's activities in the promotion and protection of human rights.
83   OAS, *Work Accomplished by Inter-American Commission on Human Rights during its First Session (October 3 to 28, 1960)* OEA/Ser.L/V/II.3, doc. 32, March 14, 1961, p. 15.
84   Ibid, p. 16.
85   See Medina Quiroga, *Battle of Human Rights*, pp. 123-4; Bertha Santoscoy, *La Commission interaméricaine des droits de l'homme et le développement de sa compétence par le système des pétitions individuelles* (Paris: Presses Universitaires de France, 1995), p. 35.
86   See, for example, the Commission's study on desacato laws and strengthening the judicial branch, infra pp. 295-6 and pp. 318-20.
87   Article 18(d) Statute.

[88] Article 19(d) Statute.

[89] See infra, pp. 233-5.

[90] Ibid.

[91] Article 19(e) Statute specifically provides that the Commission has the power 'to submit additional draft protocols to the American Convention ... to the General Assembly, in order progressively to include other rights and freedoms under the system of protection of the Convention'. The Commission is also the body which is empowered to propose amendments to the Convention. See Article 19(f) Statute.

[92] Supra, p. 32.

[93] (1994) 33 ILM 1529.

[94] (1994) 33 ILM 1534.

[95] See supra, pp. 32-3.

[96] Organization of American States, *Annual Report of the Inter-American Commission on Human Rights 1979-80*, OEA/Ser.L/V/II.50, Doc. 13 rev. 1, 2 October 1980, Original: Spanish.

[97] AG/Res 619, XII-0/82.

[98] Such as a list of meetings held by the Commission during the reporting period: Article 63(c) Regulations.

[99] Article 63(e) Regulations.

[100] Article 63(f) Regulations.

[101] Supra, p. 108.

[102] Ibid.

[103] Supra, pp. 99-101.

[104] Article 1(2) Statute.

[105] Article 18(c) Statute.

[106] Article 18(d) Statute.

[107] Article 18(g) Statute.

[108] Article 20(b) Statute.

[109] Article 44 Convention; Article 19(a) Statute.

[110] Article 45 Convention; Article 19(a) Statute.

[111] Article 19(c) Statute; Article 29(2) Regulations.

[112] See infra, chapter 4.

[113] Article 48(2) Convention.

[114] Supra, p. 100.

[115] Article 48(1)(a) Convention; Article 20(b) Statute; Article 34(1)(c) Regulations.

[116] See for example *Case 1684 (Brazil)* Inter-American Commission on Human Rights, *Report on the Work Accomplished during its Twenty-fourth Session, October 13-22, 1970*, OEA/Ser.L/V/II.24, doc. 32 (English), Rev. corr., 5 April 1971, p. 16. For discussion of this case see supra, pp. 19-20.

[117] *Battle of Human Rights*, p. 128.

[118] Article 70(1) Regulations.

[119] Article 70(2) Regulations.

[120] Buergenthal, *Inter-American System*, p 480.

[121] Medina Quiroga, *Battle of Human Rights*, p 134.

[122] Ibid. See, for example, the cases of Paraguay and Guatemala.

[123] In the country study of Cuba the Commission based itself in Miami and took evidence there from refugees and political dissidents.

[124] Articles 55-59 Regulations.

125   Article 55 Regulations.
126   Article 56 Regulations.
127   Article 57 Regulations.
128   Article 58 Regulations.
129   See 'Status of Requests for "On-Site" Visits 1994', Inter-American Commission on Human Rights, *1994 Annual Report,* p. 231.
130   Article 58 Regulations.
131   Inter-American Commission on Human Rights, *Report on the Situation of Human Rights in Argentina,* OEA/Ser. L/V/II.49, doc. 19, corr., 1, 11 April 1980, Original: Spanish, pp. 51-139.
132   Ibid.
133   *Regulations Regarding On-Site Observation*, OEA/Ser.L/V/II.35, doc. 4, rev.1, October 15, 1975.
134   *Resolution on On-Site Observations* in *Handbook of Existing Rules Pertaining to Human Rights,* OEA/Ser.L/V/II.23, doc. 21, rev. 6, 29 March 1979, Original: Spanish.
135   Article 59(a) Regulations.
136   Article 59(b) Regulations.
137   Article 59(c), (g) and (h) Regulations. Article 59(I) provides that the guarantees and facilities which are to be accorded to the Special Commission must also be extended to the accompanying Secretariat staff.
138   Article 59(d) Regulations.
139   Article 59(e) Regulations.
140   Article 59(f) Regulations.
141   Such as the discovery of *desaparecidos* in Argentina. See Inter-American Commission on Human Rights, loc cit, supra, note 131.
142   Buergenthal, *Inter-American System,* pp. 481-2. Here he cites the saving of lives during the Dominican Civil war and the negotiation of hostage releases in Colombia in 1980.
143   Article 62 Regulations.
144   See, for example, Inter-American Commission on Human Rights, *Report on the Situation of Human Rights in Guatemala,* OEA/Ser.L/V/II.53, doc. 21 rev. 2, 13 October 1981, Original: Spanish, p. 7.
145   At p. 151.
146   Article 62 Regulations.
147   Supra, p. 113.
148   Article 62(a) Regulations.
149   Article 62(b) Regulations.
150   Loc cit, supra, note 131.
151   Article 62(c) Regulations.
152   Ibid.
153   Article 62(d) Regulations.
154   Article 51 Regulations.

3 The Inter-American Court of Human Rights

Introduction

The Inter-American Court of Human Rights is the principal judicial organ of the inter-American system which is defined by Article 1 of its Statute as an 'autonomous judicial institution'. Although it is a creature of the Convention, the Court also undertakes certain functions relating to the OAS Charter and other instruments affecting human rights in the Americas. Under Article 33 of the Convention the Court, like the Commission, is charged with ensuring that the States Parties fulfil their obligations under that instrument. By Article 2 of its Statute, however, the Court's purpose is defined as the application and interpretation of the Convention. In order to carry out its various tasks the Court exercises two forms of jurisdiction: adjudicatory and advisory. The Court's adjudicatory jurisdiction, which is more commonly known as its contentious jurisdiction, extends only to the substantive rights protected by the American Convention and the Protocol of San Salvador, while its advisory jurisdiction embraces the Convention, the human rights system established under the Charter. Both categories of jurisdiction will be considered in some detail later in this chapter, but before doing this it is necessary to examine the structure of the Court, as well as its procedure and practice.

The Judges of the Inter-American Court

Titular Judges

The Court is comprised of seven judges who must be nationals of the Member States of the OAS. While they need not possess the nationality of the nominating State, no two judges may be from the same State. Judges are to be elected from among jurists of the highest moral authority and of recognized competence in the field of human rights and they must possess the qualifications which would enable them to exercise the highest judicial functions in conformity with the law of their States. Judges serve in their individual capacity and must, upon appointment, take an oath or swear a solemn declaration that they will exercise their functions 'honourably, independently and impartially' and they will keep secret all the deliberations of the Court. Judges who are elected in the normal way, that is, in accordance with Articles 53 and 54 of the Convention are referred to either as 'elected judges' or 'titular judges'. Such designation distinguishes them from ad hoc and interim judges who may sit from time to time on the bench.

Titular judges are elected for a six year term in secret ballot by an absolute majority of votes of the States Parties to the Convention under the supervision of the OAS General Assembly. They may be re-elected for a further period of six years with no possibility of re-election to the post thereafter. States may propose a slate of up to three nominees, at least one of whom must be a national of a State other than the nominating State where a full slate is proffered. In order to ensure rotation of judges and some continuity on the bench of the Court, half the judges were elected initially for a period of three years only. Should a vacancy occur on the bench outside the normal election period, the new judge must complete the unexpired term of the judge whom he or she is replacing.[1] Judges normally serve until the expiration of their term of office, but Article 54(3) provides that judges whose terms of office have expired should complete hearing cases they have already begun to hear and which are still pending. In such cases, a newly elected judge does not take his or her seat until the case has been concluded. The meaning of this provision was considered by the Court on three occasions. First in the two Honduran cases involving *Interpretation of the Court's Judgment of July 21, 1989, Assessing Compensatory Damages against the State of Honduras*[2] and second in *Neira Alegria et al v Peru*.[3]

The facts of the latter case were that after the Court had heard and ruled upon the preliminary objections lodged by Peru, its session for 1991 came to a close. Before it had the opportunity to rule on the merits of the case, however, the composition of the Court had changed with the election of four new judges. The Ad Hoc Judge appointed by Peru in this case asked the President of the Court to call the old Court to continue hearing the case. In so doing he relied upon Article 54(3) of the Convention and Article 5(3) of the Court's Statute. The relevant articles provide

> The judges shall continue in office until the expiration of their term. However, they shall continue to serve with regard to cases that they have begun to hear and that are still pending, for which purposes they shall not be replaced by the new elected judges.

The Spanish and Portuguese texts of these provisions bear a different meaning when translated. Instead of the term 'still pending' they refer to cases which have reached the judgment stage. The Court was therefore called upon to reconcile the meaning of the different authoritative texts of the Convention. This approach was, however, challenged by the Peruvian judge ad hoc who argued that, since Peru had become a party to the Spanish version of the Convention and since the working language of the case was Spanish, the Court need do no more than examine the meaning of the Spanish text. The Court rejected this view, pointing out that the interpretation to be afforded to the various versions of the relevant article would depend upon the language being used at any time, and that this would 'lead to a result which is manifestly absurd or unreasonable'. The approach adopted by the Court was to apply the rules concerning the interpretation of treaties contained in the Vienna Convention on the Law of Treaties 1969, particularly Article 33 which dealt with multilingual texts. Within Article 33 itself, the Court considered that paragraphs 3 and 4 were of particular significance. These provide:

3. The terms of the treaty are presumed to have the same meaning in each authentic text.
4. Except where a particular text prevails ... when a comparison of the authentic texts discloses a difference of meaning which the application of Articles 31 and 32 does not remove, the meaning which best reconciles the texts, having regard to the object and purpose of the treaty shall be adopted.

Applying these rules of interpretation, the Court noted that since all four texts of the American Convention were authentic, its function was to reconcile the meanings of the texts. In examining the Spanish text the Court found that it had two possible meanings. First, it might mean that a case is at the stage of proceedings when all that remains is for the judgment to be agreed upon and pronounced. Alternatively, it could mean that proceedings are continuing in the sense of moving towards the judgment. In this latter situation the Court might have begun to deal with the legal and factual issues that must be resolved before judgment can be rendered. The English and French versions of the text could also be read in two ways. The term 'proceedings still pending' could mean first, the point at which proceedings in the case were filed and notified or second, the stage of proceedings when the judges have begun to address the merits of the case either totally or in part. In order to reconcile these difference between the texts, the Court considered that it was essential to examine the object and purpose of Article 54(3). Here it noted that the main principle was that 'fairness to the litigants and judicial efficacy require that, whenever possible, only the judges that have participated in all stages of the proceedings should render judgment in the case'. to interpret Article 54(3) to mean that judges could be removed from the Court at any stage in proceedings as long as the case was not ready for judgment would conflict with this principle. This view was also confirmed by a reading of the legislative history of this and analogous provisions.

Returning to the point at issue, the Court found that interpreting the Spanish text to mean 'when the Court is about to vote on a judgment' a 'very extreme rendering' which was difficult to reconcile with the English text. Similarly, a reading of the English text 'still pending' to mean the stage at which the case had been filed and notified was equally extreme. Thus neither of these interpretations satisfied the objective and purpose of the provision which is 'to prevent a succession of judges from disrupting the proceedings'. The Court concluded that the only interpretation which would reconcile the meaning of both texts and be compatible with the object and purpose of the Convention was that judges should continue to hear a case, even though their term had expired, if the court had taken up the merits of a case. The Court cautioned that the phrase 'take up the merits' should not be interpreted restrictively since there was rarely a specific moment at which it could be said that the Court could be said to have 'decided' to do this. The Court also distinguished the practice of the ICJ from its own in this area. After examining Article 13(3) of the ICJ's Statute which is analogous to Article 54(3) of the Convention, the Court noted that the cases heard by the ICJ were different in structure to its own cases. Thus, while the ICJ had to take into account the 'equilibrium of relationships between States', the Inter-American Court of Human Rights was concerned with the 'need to guarantee to the victims the most efficient proceedings possible'. The Court therefore concluded:

> For all these reasons ... the best judge is the Court that began to hear the case. These are the judges who know to what extent they have begun to address the merits, even when oral proceedings have not yet been initiated.

Applying these principles to the instant case, the Court noted that the 'old Court' had rendered judgment on the preliminary objections, but had not yet begun to address the merits of the case. It was therefore appropriate that the 'new Court' should undertake this task. Whether the 'new Court' which was seised of this interlocutory issue was jurisdictionally competent to hear it was a question which was raised by Judge Nieto. Certainly, the 'new Court' appeared to have no doubt that it was competent to rule on this point, but it might be queried that, given the nature of the question, it might have been more appropriate for the 'old Court' to have given a ruling, especially, as the 'new Court' noted in its judgment, the judges of the 'old Court' might have been in a better position to know the exact extent to which they had begun to take up the merits of the case in deciding the preliminary issues.

In *Interpretation of the Court's Judgement of July 21, 1989, Assessing Compensatory Damages against the State of Honduras* the Court was faced with the question of whether Article 54(3) applied to cases involving an interpretation of a judgment previously rendered in accordance with Article 67 of the Convention. Article 67 provides in its material part that 'in case of disagreement as to the meaning or scope of the judgment, the Court shall interpret it at the request of any of the parties, provided the request is made within ninety days from the date of notification of the judgment'. In the Court's view, Article 54(3) also applied to questions concerning the interpretation of judgments under Article 67. Its reasoning here was that 'under general rules of procedural law, a contentious case cannot be deemed to have been concluded until the judgment has been fully complied with'. Although the Court did not take the view that the instant case was necessarily at the judgment stage, it did hold that its reasoning applied by analogy to cases which were still at the enforcement stage. Since the Court had decided in the compensatory damages phase of the *Velasquez Rodriguez* case to supervise compliance with the award by Honduras, it held that the case could not be regarded as having been concluded, and thus Article 54(3) applied in such circumstances. This decision is clearly compatible with that reached by the Court in *Neira Alegria* discussed above. In a sense, it might be argued that the judges in interpreting one of its own judgments which it has undertaken to see through to the conclusion of the enforcement stage, is analogous with a continuing concern by the Court with the merits of the case.

Ad Hoc Judges

The appointment of ad hoc judges is governed by Article 55 of the Convention. This provides that if a titular judge is a national of one of the States Parties to a case, he or she retains a right to hear that case. This would appear to run counter to the doctrine of *nemo iudex in sua causa,* but it should be recalled that judges are obliged to perform their duties impartially and thus, from a technical point of view, nationality should be irrelevant to the matter. In order to preserve balance, however, Article 55(2) provides that if one of the judges called upon to hear a case should be a national of one of the States Parties, the other State Party to a case may appoint a person of its choice to sit as an ad hoc judge. A number of points might be noted here. First, while the process for appointing titular judges should militate against bias, nonetheless the possibility of appointing an ad hoc judge ensures that the Court is seen to maintain an even-handed approach should the States Parties be in conflict. The practical outcome of this may be that the balanced composition of the Court engenders the trust and confidence of not only the States Parties involved in a case, but also in other States Parties to the Convention who have not yet accepted the contentious jurisdiction of the Court. Second, as is the case with the ICJ, ad hoc judges can perform a very useful function by advising the Court on the domestic laws and general conditions in the State Party concerned. Finally, there is no obligation on a State Party to appoint an ad hoc judge since the right to do so is expressed in purely discretionary terms. A refusal to appoint an ad hoc judge when entitled so to do might be seen as a powerful endorsement of the authority and impartiality of the Court by a State Party. It seems, however, that the Convention's concern, at least at the formal level, to protect the interests of States Parties in cases where they may be parties in a case before the Court is a matter of paramount concern since Article 55(3) provides that if none of the titular judges is a national of either of the States Parties, then each may appoint an ad hoc judge. Where, however, a number of States have the same interest in a case they are to be regarded as a single party for the purposes of the proceedings and are thus given the right to appoint only one ad hoc judge to the Court. If there is any doubt or dispute concerning whether the interests of the various States parties is the same, the matter is to be decided by the Court. Where one ad hoc judge only is to be appointed to represent the interests of more than one State, the onus is upon those States to decide who should be their judge. If the States in question are unable to agree on this within thirty days, then the President of the Court chooses a judge by lot from a list of candidates submitted by the States concerned. Where a State Party fails to exercise the right to appoint an ad hoc judge within a prescribed time limit, they are deemed to have relinquished that right. Furthermore, it should be noted that States Parties have a right to appoint ad hoc judges, not simply to nominate them. Such judges must possess the same qualifications as those required for titular judges.

Interim Judges

Reference to interim judges is to be found only in the Court's Statute. They are to be appointed in two circumstances: first, where it becomes necessary to maintain the Court's quorum of five judges and second, where a judge is disqualified from hearing a case. Article 6(3) of the Court's Statute deals with the first situation. Where the appointment of a judge or judges becomes necessary because of the death, permanent disability, resignation or the dismissal of a judge or judges has left the Court below quorum, the President of the Court must request the States Parties to appoint one or more interim judges at a meeting of the OAS Permanent Council. The judges appointed serve until such time as they are replaced by elected judges. The second situation is covered by Article 19(4) of the Statute. In circumstances where a judge or judges are disqualified from taking part in a case, the President may request the Permanent Council to appoint an interim judge. It should be noted that the President's power to request the appointment of an interim judge is discretionary, unless the disqualification takes the Court below its quorum. Although there is no indication of the requisite qualifications for interim judges, it must be assumed that they are the same as those for titular and ad hoc judges.

Rights, Duties and Responsibilities of Judges

Judicial office in the Inter-American Court is held on a part-time basis save for the President of the Court, who is a permanent officer.[4] Although the draft statute of the Court envisaged a permanent body, which the Court thought would enhance its status and credibility in the Americas, the General Assembly of the OAS refused to sanction the creation of a full-time tribunal on the grounds that it would be too expensive to maintain until it had a full case load.[5] At present, the Court only holds two regular sessions each year,[6] although special sessions may be convened at the request of a majority of the judges.[7] There are, however, two provisions of the Court's Statute which would allow the Court to operate on a full-time basis should this prove necessary in the future. The first is Article 16(1) which requires judges to 'remain at disposal of the Court, and shall travel to the seat of the Court or to the place where the Court is holding its sessions as often and for as long a time as may be necessary ..'.. The second provision is Article 18(1)(c) which prohibits judges from taking positions which might prevent them from discharging their duties to the Court. Should it be necessary for the Court to remain in session for the greater part of year because of an increase in its workload, it would appear that the only modification which the Statute would require would be an amendment to Article 17 in order to provide a salary for the judges. Although it would perhaps be wise, for the avoidance of doubt, to amend Article 18 to prevent judges from taking remunerated employment which could interfere with the functioning of the Court.

Although judges may take remunerated employment, there are certain categories of employment which are deemed to be incompatible with judicial status.[8] A general statement to this effect is contained in Article 71 of the Convention which provides that the position of a judge is incompatible with any other activity which might affect their independence or impartiality. This is elaborated in Article 18 of the Court's Statute which contains three categories of activity which are deemed to be incompatible with judicial office.[9] The first two categories include members or high ranking officials of the executive branch of government[10] and officials of international organizations.[11] Persons falling within the former category but who are not under the direct control of the executive branch are excluded from this prohibition as are diplomatic agents who are not Chiefs of Mission to the OAS or to any of its member states.[12] The third category is a catch-all which comprises any other activity which might prevent judges from discharging their duties or that might affect their independence or impartiality or the dignity and prestige of the office.[13] This is a broad formulation which is capable of encompassing a wide range of activities of both a public and private nature. Where there is doubt whether a particular activity is or is not incompatible with judicial office, the Court is given authority to decide the issue.[14] If the Court is unable to resolve the issue, the matter falls to be determined by the OAS General Assembly which has general disciplinary competence over the judges of the Court under Article 73 of the Convention.[15] It should be noted that if a judge has pursued an activity incompatible with his status as a judge during his period of office, the decisions or acts in which he participated are not thereby rendered invalid.[16]

Emoluments

Since judicial office in the Inter-American Court of Human Rights is held on a part-time basis there is no provision for judges to receive a salary. Instead they receive an *honorarium*, which is calculated on the basis of the limitations imposed on their other activities by Articles 16 and 18 of the Statute, and the importance and independence of their office,[17] together with daily and travel allowances where appropriate.[18]

Privileges and Immunities

From the moment of their election, and throughout their term of office, judges enjoy the immunities and privileges accorded to diplomatic agents under international law.[19] In addition to these basic immunities and privileges, judges are also afforded such diplomatic privileges which are necessary for the performance of their duties.[20] Judges are further exempted from all liability for any decisions or opinions issued in the exercise of their functions.[21] Such privileges and immunities are to be accorded by the States Parties to the Convention, but may also be expressly accepted by other member states of the OAS.[22]

The Court, as an institution, and its staff are also to be accorded the privileges and immunities which are contained in the Agreement on Privileges and Immunities of the Organization of American States 1949.[23] Clearly this provision applies primarily to Costa Rica as the state in which the Court has its seat and in which its Secretariat functions, but the provision would also apply automatically should the Court decide to convene in the territory of another state party to the Convention with the consent of that state.[24] While the basic system of privileges and immunities for the judges, the Court and its staff is contained in Article 70 of the Convention and Article 15 of the Statute, there is also provision for the conclusion of additional multilateral or bilateral treaties between the Court, the OAS and its member states in order to supplement those privileges and immunities.[25] To date there has only been one such agreement: the bilateral headquarters agreement between Costa Rica and the Court of 10 September 1981.

Duties, Responsibilities and Disciplinary Regime

It has already been noted that judges may not take employment or engage in activities which are incompatible with their judicial status.[26] The Statute of the Court, however, both prescribes and proscribes certain types of judicial conduct and imposes penalties and liabilities for non-compliance with the standards laid down. Article 20(1), which falls under the rubric 'Disciplinary Regime', provides that in the performance of their duties and at all other times the judges and staff of the Court must conduct themselves in a manner which is in keeping with the office of those who perform an international judicial function. This is a broad prescription which demands the highest standards of conduct from those appointed to the court as titular, ad hoc or interim judges. Not only are judges responsible to the Court for any abrogation of these standards, they are also responsible for 'acts of negligence or omission committed in the exercise of their functions'.[27] The potential ambit of these standards of conduct is difficult to imagine, but it would seem that a judge who does not pay due regard to the conduct of a case might well be found to violate this provision and be held personally responsible for his or her acts.

The exercise of disciplinary authority over the judges of the Court resides in the hands of the OAS General Assembly.[28] This political body may, however, only exercise its disciplinary powers at the request of the Court itself.[29] In making such a request, the Court must be composed only of the judges who are not the subject of the disciplinary action, and it must give reasons for making the request.[30] Such reasons must have a firm foundation in the Statute of the Court, that is they must be based on a breach of either Article 18 or Article 20 of that instrument.[31] There are no specific sanctions contained in either the Convention or the Statute for breach of discipline by a judge. It is left open by Article 73 of the Convention for the Court itself to recommend the sanction to be applied. Presumably this could range from censure to removal from the bench. Whatever sanction is recommended, it must be approved not only by a two-thirds majority vote of the OAS General Assembly, but also by a two-thirds majority vote of the States Parties to the Convention.[32] These requirements are sufficiently substantial to prevent political interference with the operation of the Court by a disgruntled State Party.

Resignation and Incapacity

A judge may resign from the bench at any time after informing the President of the Court of his or her intention to do so.[33] Such resignation does not become effective until the Court has accepted it.[34] Where a judge becomes incapable of performing his or her functions and does not resign, it is open to the Court to make a determination of incapacity.[35] It would seem, given the context, that a determination of incapacity by the Court produces the same effect for the judge in question as a resignation. In both cases, the Secretary-General of the OAS must be informed in order to allow him to take appropriate action either for the appointment of an interim judge if the Court is rendered inquorate, or to invoke the procedures for the election of a titular judge.[36]

Disqualification

Judges in any legal system, whether national or international, must not only be impartial, they must also be seen to be impartial. This is an application of the general principle of law which is expressed in the Anglo-American system as *nemo iudex in sua causa*. The judges of the Inter-American Court are no exception and the Court's Statute makes specific provision for the circumstances in which judges must disqualify themselves or must be disqualified from hearing a case by the Court. Article 19(1) of the Statute provides that judges may not take part in matters in which they or their families have a direct interest. Furthermore, since judges are likely to have been involved in proceedings before the Court as agents, counsel or advocates in a particular case, this also debars them from taking part in that case.[37] Judges who have served as members of a national or international court or an investigatory committee or in any other manner in a case, are similarly prevented from hearing the case should it arise before the Inter-American Court.[38] This would clearly have the effect of preventing a judge who had previously served on the UN Human Rights Committee from hearing a case before the Court which had previously been considered by the Committee. This would appear to be so even if the case had been declared inadmissible before the Committee.

Where the potential for a conflict of interest arises in a specific case, the individual judge may disqualify himself by informing the President of the Court.[39] Should, however, an individual judge not identify a potential ground for disqualification himself, the President of the Court should advise the judge concerned to that effect.[40] Presumably it is open to anyone to draw to the attention of the President of the Court any factors which might lead to disqualification. If a dispute arises between the judge and the President of the Court in either of the two situations envisaged, the Court is given residual power to decide the issue.[41] As indicated above, if the number of disqualified judges leads to the Court becoming inquorate, the President of the Court may request the states parties in a meeting of the Permanent Council of the OAS to appoint an appropriate number of interim judges.[42]

Organization of the Court

In order to ensure the proper functioning of the Court its Statute and Rules of Procedure provide for the appointment of a President, a Vice President, a Permanent Commission and a Secretariat.

The President and Vice President

As we have seen above, the President fulfils a number of functions relating to the appointment and resignation of judges. In such cases, the President provides the link in communications between the Court and the Permanent Council or Secretary-General of the OAS. However, the President and, where the

President is unable to act, the Vice President,[43] also exercises a number of wide-ranging powers and functions which are set down in the Statute and Rules of the Court. These will be examined in detail below.

It will be recalled that the President, by Article 16(2) of the Statute, is the only judge of the Court who is required to serve on a full-time basis.[44] As Buergenthal notes, however, this provision has not been interpreted to require the President to reside in San José or to require him to desist from other compatible remunerated activities.[45] A proposal which would have required the President to reside at the seat of the Court and to refrain from other activities was not approved by the General Assembly in 1979.[46]

The President and Vice President must be elected by the Court from among its members by an absolute majority of votes determined by a secret ballot of the titular judges.[47] If no judge receives an absolute majority in an election for either position a further ballot must be taken between the two judges standing for both the presidency and vice-presidency who have received the largest number of votes.[48] In the unlikely event of a tie, the judge having precedence is deemed elected to office.[49] The President and Vice President serve for a term of two years.[50] There is no limit on the number of times they may be re-elected[51] but, as Buergenthal suggests, the practice of the Court appears to favour rotation of the office of President and Vice President with each being elected only for a single term.[52] He also points out that there appears to be an 'unwritten preference' for a geographical balance with the President and Vice President being elected from different regions of the Americas.[53] The practice of the Court to date indicates that the President and Vice President have tended to alternate between judges from Central America and Latin America.[54]

The duties of the President are contained in Article 12(2) of the Statute which provides that 'the President shall direct the work of the Court, represent it, regulate the disposition of matters brought before the Court, and preside over its sessions'. These duties are further elaborated in Article 4(1) of the Court's Rules. They are:[55]

a)   to represent the Court legally and officially;
b)   to preside over the meetings of the Court and to submit for its consideration the topics of the agenda;
c)   to rule on points of order that may arise during the discussions of the court. If any judge so requests, the point of order shall be submitted to a majority vote;
d)   to direct and promote the work of the Court;
e)   to present, at the beginning of each regular or special session a report on

the manner in which, during the recessions, he has discharged the functions conferred upon him by these Rules;

f) exercise such other functions as conferred upon him by the Statute, these Rules or the Court.

While the main task of the Vice President is to exercise the duties of the President in his absence,[56] he also has the important additional function of acting as President in proceedings in which the President is disqualified from acting as such because the case involves his own state.[57] Where both the President and Vice President are unable to act, their places are taken by the remaining judges in the order of precedence established in accordance with Article 13 of the Statute. Under this provision elected judges take precedence in order of seniority of appointment,[58] while ad hoc and interim judges take precedence after elected judges according to age.[59] If, however, an ad hoc or interim judge has previously served as an elected judge, he takes precedence immediately over other ad hoc and interim judges.[60]

Certain limitations on the President's role were dealt with by the Court in its third advisory opinion, *Restrictions to the Death Penalty.*[61] Here, Guatemala, which contested the jurisdiction of the Court to render an opinion sought by the Commission, requested that either the President or the Permanent Commission[62] rule the case inadmissible.[63] The President, however, admitted the case stating that neither he nor the Permanent Commission was empowered to rule on the question of admissibility, since this was a function of the plenary Court.[64] This view was confirmed by the Court. Relying on Article 56 of the Convention and Article 44(1) of its Rules, it ruled that only the Court convoked in conformity with the quorum requirements was competent to make the necessary binding decisions concerning interlocutory decisions.[65]

The Permanent Commission

This body is composed of the President, the Vice President and a third judge named by the President.[66] Its function is to assist and advise the President in the execution of his duties,[67] and in so doing it is governed by the Rules of the Court.[68] It is also open to the Court to appoint ad hoc commissions to deal with special matters, and the President may appoint commissions *proprio motu* to deal with urgent cases.[69] Buergenthal notes that as a matter of practice the President has always sought to ensure that at least one member of the Permanent Commission resides in Costa Rica, and that he has knowledge of the working languages of the Court.[70]

The Secretariat

In order to carry out administrative functions relating to the operation of the Court, the Court is empowered to establish a Secretariat.[71] The Secretariat is headed by the Secretary who is also appointed by the Court.[72] The Secretary is a full-time officer who not only must possess the legal knowledge and experience necessary to carry out his functions, but must also have knowledge of the working languages of the Court.[73] He serves the Court 'in a position of trust'[74] and is elected by the judges of the Court for a period of five years.[75] Disciplinary authority over the Secretary lies with the Court[76] and his removal may be effected at any time by the vote of no less than four judges by way of secret ballot.[77] This relatively precarious position of the Secretary, together with the obligation of trust placed upon him by the Statute, ensures that his loyalty to the Court as an institution is clearly established.[78]

In order to assist the Secretary, the post of Assistant Secretary is established by the Court's Statute.[79] The Assistant Secretary, whose function is to assist the Secretary and deputize for him in his absence, is appointed by the Secretary in consultation with the Secretary-General of the OAS.[80] If both the Secretary and Assistant Secretary are temporarily absent, the President may appoint an Acting Secretary in their stead.[81] All other members of the Secretariat's staff are appointed by the Secretary-General of the OAS in consultation with the Secretary of the Court,[82] but as Buergenthal points out, in practice the Secretary-General always makes the appointments recommended by the Secretary of the Court.[83]

The functions of the Secretary are set down in Article 10 of the Rules of the Court. A perusal of these functions demonstrates the central importance of the Secretary to the proper functioning of the Court. Of the multifarious administrative tasks which he must carry out, perhaps the most significant is that of communicating the decisions, advisory opinions, resolutions and other rulings of the Court and to announce the times fixed for the hearing of the Court.[84]

The Secretary of the Court and the staff of the Secretariat enjoy the immunities and privileges contained in the Agreement of Privileges and Immunities of the Organization of American States,[85] while disciplinary authority over the staff of the Secretariat is exercised by the Secretary.[86] The Secretary's disciplinary function is governed by disciplinary rules issued by the Court[87] and is overseen by the President of the Court.[88]

The Practice and Procedure of the Court

As indicated above, the Court sits in two regular sessions a year,[89] but the President may convoke a special session of the Court either *proprio motu* or at the request of a majority of the judges.[90] In cases of extreme gravity and urgency and where it is necessary for the Court to adopt provisional measures to prevent irreparable damage to persons,[91] any judge may request that the Court be convened.[92] It will also be recalled that five judges must sit in order to constitute a quorum.[93] All decisions of the Court must therefore be taken by a majority of the judges sitting in plenary session,[94] which means that there is no possibility of the Court sitting in chambers of a lesser number as, for example, does the European Court of Human Rights.[95] At present, the workload of the Court would not seem to suggest that the institution of a system of chambers is required. Should there be a greater use of the Court by the States Parties, member states of the OAS or OAS organs, an amendment of the Statute would be required to enable the Court to sit in chambers.

All hearings of the Court must take place in public unless the Court decides that exceptional circumstances warrant that sessions be held *in camera*.[96] There is no guidance contained in the Court's Rules of Procedure as to what might constitute exceptional circumstances, but an example might be occasions where the lives of witnesses are at risk or where the matter touches on issues of national security claimed by the state concerned. Indeed, this latter ground was invoked by the government of Honduras during proceedings in *Velasquez Rodriguez*[97] where evidence was to be given by the head of the intelligence service of Honduras. Although the Commission objected to the hearing of testimony in secret,[98] the Court nevertheless acceded to the Honduran government's request.[99] Hearings of the Court take place in the working languages of the judges and, if necessary, those of the parties to the case, as long as these latter are official languages of the OAS.[100] However, the Court may authorize anyone in the proceedings to use their own language if they do not have adequate knowledge of an official language of the OAS.[101]

While the hearings of the Court are usually conducted in public, its deliberations generally take place in private and remain secret unless it decides to disclose them.[102] Normally, only the judges and the Secretary of the Court or his or her nominee may take part in such deliberations, but other persons may be admitted following a 'special decision' by the Court and after they have taken an oath.[103] What constitutes a special decision by the Court is not revealed, but it seems to imply that all the judges must concur in deciding to admit any individual who is not entitled to take part in their deliberations as of right. It would be logical to assume that the oath which must be taken by the person so admitted would require him or her not to subsequently divulge the deliberations of the judges. In order further to protect the secrecy of the judges' deliberations all records are kept to a minimum. The minutes of the deliberations are limited to a bare record of the subject of the discussions and the decisions taken, as well as a record of dissenting votes and any declarations made for the record that do not refer to the basis of the vote.[104]

As indicated earlier, decisions of the Court are taken by a majority of the judges as long as the Court is in quorum. An interesting feature of this process is that judges may only vote affirmatively or negatively on any given issue since abstentions are not permitted.[105] If a vote needs to be taken on any issue, votes are cast on the issues set down precisely point by point by the President.[106] Voting takes place in an inverse order of precedence with the President having the deciding vote should a tie occur.[107]

Before examining the conduct of proceedings before the Court, it is important to note that there is a difference in terminology applied by the Convention to contentious cases and to proceedings for advisory opinions. Article 61 provides that only the States Parties and the Commission shall have the right to submit a *case* before the Court,[108] and that in so doing it is necessary that the preliminary procedures established by Articles 48-50 must have been complied with. This would seem to imply that where the word 'case' is used, it refers simply to contentious proceedings. Indeed, the Court itself has confirmed this view in *Restrictions to the Death Penalty*.[109] Thus while Article 61 speaks of the right of the States Parties and the Commission to submit a case, Article 64 merely stipulates that member states and organs of the OAS 'may consult' the Court for advisory opinions or 'request' the Court for an opinion on the compatibility of a member states laws with its international human rights obligations. This permissive language clearly indicates that the Court has a discretion to accept or reject such a request.[110] The procedures to be followed in contentious cases and in requests for advisory opinions are therefore to be differentiated.

Contentious Proceedings

The first point to note about the conduct of contentious proceedings is that individuals have no *locus standi* before the Court.[111] Only the Commission and the States Parties concerned have standing. It would, however, be open to the Inter-American Court to call a petitioner to testify before it under Article 34(1) of its Rules which provides:[112]

> The Court may, at the request of a party or the delegates of the Commission, or *proprio motu*, decide to hear as a witness, expert, or in any other capacity, *any person* whose testimony or statements seem likely to assist it in the carrying out of its functions.

This broad power of the Court to call persons to appear before it is also related to two further provisions. The first of these is Article 22 of the Court's Rules by which the Court is empowered to request the assistance of the government of a State Party in ensuring that communications, notifications or summonses addressed to persons resident within its territory are given effect.[113] The Court is also empowered to request the assistance of the state where it wishes to conduct a fact-finding or investigative visit within the territory of that state, or to secure the attendance of a person it wishes to hear.[114] The second, and vitally important, power possessed by the Court in this field is the power to order interim measures to protect the integrity of persons within the territory of a State Party. The basic provision here is Article 63(2) of the Convention. This provides:

> In cases of extreme gravity and urgency, and where necessary to avoid irreparable damage to persons, the Court shall adopt such provisional measures as it deems pertinent in matters it has under consideration. With respect to a case not yet submitted to the Court, it may act at the request of the Commission.

This basic provision is implemented by Article 23 of the Court's Rules. Where the criteria established by Article 63(2) of the Convention are met, it is clear that the Court may act *proprio motu* or at the request of one of the parties in deciding whether it is necessary for provisional measures to be taken.[115] Where, however, the matter is not before the Court, the Commission may address a request to the President or to any judge of the Court for measures to be taken.[116] As Dunshee de Abranches observes, the use of word 'matters' in Article 63(2) is significant. The term is clearly broader than 'cases' which, in the context of the Convention, signifies a contentious case. He suggests that the use of the term 'matters' justifies the conclusion that Article 63(2) was drafted to enable the Court to take provisional measures in relation to a request for an advisory opinion.[117] Given the circumstances of a request for an advisory opinion, however, it is unlikely that the occasion would arise frequently which would demand the granting of provisional measures by the Court.

Because the Court does not sit in permanent session,[118] provision is made for the immediate convocation of the Court by the President. Pending the meeting of the Court, the President is empowered, in consultation with the

Permanent Commission, or other judges if possible, to request the parties to act in such a manner as to permit any provisional measures granted by the Court to have the necessary effect.[119]

The operation of this procedure was vividly demonstrated by the Court in provisional measures adopted against Honduras in 1988.[120] These measures arose from the assassination of two witnesses, one who had already testified before the Court and one who had been summoned to do so, in three cases involving allegations of 'disappearances' in Honduras. Individuals who had given testimony before the Inter-American Commission in these cases had also had their lives and property threatened. Relying initially on Article 63(2) of the Convention and Article 23(5) of the Rules of the Court, the Court ordered two provisional measures: first, that the government of Honduras adopt, without delay, the necessary measures to prevent infringements of the basic rights of those who had been summoned to appear before the Court in the cases under consideration. This was to be done on the basis of strict compliance with Article 1(1) of the Convention which requires all states parties to ensure to individuals within their jurisdiction the free and full exercise of the rights contained in the Convention. Second, the Court ordered that Honduras conduct a full investigation of the crimes, bring the perpetrators to justice and impose the punishment provided for such crimes by the law of Honduras.

Since the cases in question had been referred to the Court there seems little doubt that the Court was competent under the provisions cited to order the measures in this instance. It is interesting to note, however, that the measures addressed to the government imply two things. First, that it had not taken the necessary measures to investigate the assassinations and threats to witnesses and, second, that it was directly responsible for taking positive measures in accordance with Article 1(1) of the Convention to ensure that the conditions existed in Honduras for the necessary enjoyment of the rights contained in the Convention. This seems to come perilously close to implicating the Honduran government in the assassinations and threats.

While the Court acted *proprio motu* in ordering the first set of provisional measures, it was subsequently requested by the Commission to adopt additional specific measures in order to complement the first order.[121] Here the Court was more precise in the elaboration of its jurisdictional basis for the ordering of provisional measures. In addition to Article 63(2) of the Convention, it also cited Article 33 which, it will be recalled, designates the Court as having the competence with respect to matters relating to the fulfilment of the commitments made by the state parties under the Convention.

Further, it invoked Article 62(3) which indicates that the Court possesses jurisdiction in all cases concerning the interpretation and application of the provisions of the Convention that are submitted to it.[122] Reliance by the Court on these provisions was further supplemented by direct reference to Articles 1 and 2 of the Court's Statute and Article 23 of the Court's Rules.

In the preamble to theOorder the Court noted that Honduras had undertaken to comply with the terms of the First Order, but, in accordance with the Commission's request, ordered the Honduran government to inform the Court on a number of points within a period of two weeks. These points included a description of the measures adopted or to be adopted to prevent harm to witnesses, an indication that judicial investigation had or would be undertaken with respect to cases where individuals had been threatened and a report on the investigations undertaken with respect to the assassinations. An interesting feature of the substantive part of the order was paragraph two which directed the government of Honduras to 'adopt concrete measures' to make clear that the appearance of an individual before either of the Convention institutions 'is a right enjoyed by every individual and is recognized as such by Honduras as a party to the Convention'.

While this development of a right of appearance before the Court is undoubtedly praiseworthy, it is difficult to see how it can be justified by reference to the appropriate legal instruments. It is clear that there is no positive statement of such a right in either the Convention, the Court's Statute or Rules. As indicated above, an individual does not enjoy *locus standi* before the Court, although they may have a duty to appear before the Court when called to do so. This duty as we have seen is supplemented by rules which empower the Court to request states to facilitate the appearance of an individual witness.[123] Clearly this is not a *right* to appear before the Court, since that would seem to imply an automatic right to *locus standi* where the individual concerned could demonstrate an appropriate legal interest. It would perhaps have been more accurate for the Court to have stated that States Parties are under a duty not to interfere with individuals who are called to appear before the Court, although even here, the relevant rules are framed in a permissive rather than a mandatory fashion. If the Court has discovered a new right of individuals to appear before the Convention institutions, it is suggested that the contents and means of invoking this right should be clearly established in the instruments governing the law and procedure of the Commission and the Court.[124]

Institution of proceedings before the Court in accordance with Article 61 of the Convention is effected by either a State Party or the Commission filing an application with the Secretary of the Court indicating, *inter alia*, the object of the application and the human rights involved.[125] If at this stage the applicant does not request the Court to rule in accordance with Article 63(1) of the Convention on the securing of any rights violated or compensation, this can be raised at any point in the written or oral proceedings.[126] On receipt of the application the Secretary notifies the Commission, if necessary, and the States Parties concerned by the case.[127] At that stage, the parties may file preliminary objections stating the facts and law on which the objection is based, together with supporting documentation.[128] The filing of preliminary objections does not cause the suspension of the proceedings on the merits, and the other parties may present their own observations and submissions on the objections.[129] When the Court has received all observations and comments it may either decide on the issue of the preliminary objection or join the preliminary objections to the merits of the case.[130]

Examination of cases is divided into a written stage and an oral stage.[131] The parties, as is consistent with proceedings before international tribunals, must present a memorial and a counter-memorial setting out the relevant facts, a statement of the applicable law and the submissions of the parties.[132] The counter-memorial must, in addition, admit or deny the facts alleged in the memorial.[133] At the discretion of the Court, the parties may be allowed to submit a reply and a rejoinder.[134] It is interesting to note that the Court's Rules specifically enjoin the parties not merely to repeat their contentions but to use the reply and rejoinder to bring out the issues that still divide them.[135] If two cases are presented to the Court which have common elements, the Court enjoys discretion, either at this stage or at any time in the future, to order the cases to be joined.[136]

Oral proceedings are conducted under the authority of the President of the Court. Not only does he fix the date for the opening of the oral proceedings, although he does this in consultation with the agents of the parties and the delegates of the Commission,[137] but he directs the hearings by determining the order in which the parties are to present their cases. During oral proceedings the Court enjoys wide discretionary powers to hear witnesses, independent experts and to receive information from any 'body, office, commission, or authority of its choice'.[138] Judges may also put questions to any person appearing before the Court during the oral stage.[139] Although the Court enjoys wide powers of enquiry and investigation, it is clear that in contentious proceedings the Court is reluctant to extend its powers to intrude upon the Commission's sphere of competence. In *Viviana Gallardo* the Court noted that while it did not lack the power to carry out its own investigations, particularly if these were necessary to allow it to obtain the information it needed to discharge its functions, it was the Commission which enjoyed the primary role of providing all pertinent observations and submissions.[140] Thus it would appear that the Court is content to restrict its power to conduct inquiries and investigations to the judicial process alone.[141] It will be recalled, however, that a provision to facilitate this exists in Article 3(2) of the Court's Statute which permits it to convene on the territory of any state party with the consent of that state.[142]

It will be apparent from the discussion of provisional measures that the calling and hearing of witnesses, experts and other individuals is an important part of the Court's procedure. There are a number of detailed provisions in the Rules of the Court which deal with the calling and treatment of witnesses. As we have seen, the Court may summon any person whose testimony it considers may be useful.[143] The calling of such witnesses may, however, be objected to by the State Party concerned under Article 37 of the Court's Rules.[144] It has also been noted that states are not only under an obligation to facilitate the appearance of such persons, but that they are under a positive obligation not to prevent them from appearing before the Court.[145] Once before the Court, witnesses, experts and other persons must conform to the standards of behaviour required from such persons before domestic courts. They must, if they are witnesses, take an oath or make a solemn declaration to tell the truth or, if they are experts, they must swear or declare that they will discharge their duty as an expert 'honourably and conscientiously'.[146] There are no provisions contained in the Statute itself for the Court to invoke sanctions against witnesses who without good reason fail to appear or who, if they do appear, give false evidence. Article 39(1) of the Court's Rules states that in such circumstances the Court is to inform the state to whose jurisdiction the person is subject of the non-appearance of that person or that, in the opinion of the Court, the testimony which the individual gave was false. By Article 39(2) the Court may then request that the state take measures in accordance with their domestic legislation against those who have violated their oath or solemn declaration. It should be noted that this provision is framed in discretionary and permissive terms: the Court need not ask for action to be taken by the state and the state, even if requested, is not obliged to take action, although this might clearly reflect on the *bona fides* of that state.

While it might be appropriate for a state to take action against persons who have committed acts of perjury before the Court, it would clearly be contrary to the precepts upon which the inter-American human rights system is based if individuals who had testified before it were to be punished simply for having appeared before the Court. Article 39(2) of the Court's Rules therefore provides that States may not try any person on account of their testimony before the Court. The application of this principle to persons who have given truthful testimony would appear to be beyond doubt. Does it apply, however, to persons who had given untruthful evidence? Both the location and broad phrasing of the provision would seem to suggest that it does. Taking Article 39 as a whole, it would appear that the only occasion a state may try a person for giving false evidence to the Court is when the Court requests the state to do so. To allow a state to decide whether or not the evidence of a particular person was or was not false would clearly be open to abuse by states.

Although the non-appearance of an individual may not gravely affect proceedings before the Court, their evidence perhaps being obtainable by other modes of inquiry, the non-appearance of a party, especially the respondent state in contentious proceedings, is highly likely to impair the judicial process. Non-appearance by a state is not an unfamiliar experience in international judicial institutions, and most make provision for this occurrence.[147] The Rules of the Inter-American Court are no exception to this. These provide that if a state fails to appear in or to continue with a case, the Court enjoys a broad discretion to take whatever measures are necessary to complete consideration of the case.[148] Unlike the Statute of the International Court of Justice,[149] there is no provision in the Inter-American Court's Statute which requires the Court to ensure that it provides the presumed legal argument on behalf of the respondent state. Given the broad discretion granted to the Court in the area of non-appearance, it would seem that it might either enter judgment in default, or, if the case raises an important point of law, allow the argument of the appearing party to be heard while providing the argument for the non-appearing respondent itself. This view is further supported by the provisions dealing with discontinuance of a case. While this is not on 'all fours' with the default procedure, there are similarities between them. If a case is discontinued either by agreement between the parties, or by a friendly settlement being reached during proceedings, the Court may decide to strike the case from its list. The Court may decide, however, that the case should not be struck from its list but that it should proceed with the consideration of the case in order to discharge its responsibilities of interpretation and application under the Convention.

Article 44 of the Court's Rules of Procedure provide that 'the judgments, advisory opinions and interlocutory decisions that put an end to a case or proceedings shall be decided by the Court'. While under normal circumstances a case will be disposed of when judgment is given in a contentious case, it appears that Article 44 gives the Court discretion to determine at what stage a case may be deemed to be concluded. Support for this view is to be found in *Interpretation of Compensatory Damages.* Here the Court, in deciding that the judges hearing the interpretation of the judgment in the *Compensatory Damages Case* under Article 67 of the Convention must also, by virtue of Article 54(3), sit in the instant case,[150] ruled that a contentious case could not be deemed to be concluded until the judgment had been fully complied with by the defaulting state party.[151] While some note must be made of Judge Piza Escalante's separate opinion, in which he took the view that a distinction had to be drawn between the rendering of a judgment and the execution of that judgment, it is nonetheless clear that the Court's ruling gives it a useful and potent device for supervising its decisions.

Judgments of the Court must follow a prescribed form[152] and be given in public session.[153] In all cases, reasons must be given for the judgment of the Court,[154] and where the judgment is not unanimous, either in whole or in part, any judge has the right to attach a dissenting or separate opinion.[155] Once judgment is given it is notified to the parties and transmitted to all the Ptates Parties of the Convention for information.[156] Although judgments of the Court are final and admit of no appeal, the Court may be requested to interpret the meaning or scope of any judgment at the request of the parties to the case.[157] Such requests must be made within ninety days of the notification of the judgment.[158] It should be noted, however, that such a request for interpretation does not suspend the effects of the judgment to be interpreted.[159]

In *Interpretation of Compensatory Damages,* the Commission, invoking Article 67 of the Convention and Article 48 of the Court's Rules of Procedure requested the court to clarify its judgment in the *Compensatory Damages Case.* The Commission first enquired of the Court whether its judgment requiring Honduras to pay a lump sum to be managed by a trust fund in favour of the children of Velasquez Rodriguez, the victim of a state-sponsored disappearance, embraced the concept of indexing in order to protect the real purchasing power of the damages.[160] The Commission subsequently made a further request to the Court for 'amplification of the petition for clarification' of the original judgment.[161] Here, the Commission alleged that the potential recipients of compensatory damages had suffered further material damage because of the failure by Honduras to comply with the judgment awarding damages by the date specified.[162] While the Court held that it had jurisdiction to hear and rule upon the application for clarification,[163] it also held that it did not have jurisdiction to consider the request for 'amplification' concerning the further material damage resulting from non-performance of its obligations by Honduras. The rationale for the Court's decision here was that Article 67 empowered it to interpret its judgments whenever there was disagreement as to their 'meaning or scope'. Here, there was no such disagreement. The complaint levelled by the Commission against Honduras was simply one of non-performance, thus the Court could not 'admit the Commission's petition in the guise of an "amplification" of the request for interpretation previously presented'.[164]

What, however, did a request for interpretation of a judgment actually require of the Court? Citing the judgment of the European Court of Human Rights in the *Ringeisen Case*, the Inter-American Court held:

> The interpretation of a judgment involves not only precisely defining the text of the operative parts of the judgment, but also specifying its scope, meaning and purpose based on the considerations of the judgment.[165]

In the instant case, the Court therefore held that since the main purpose of the award of damages was to ensure *restitutio in integrum* to the next-of-kin of the victim based on the projected earnings of the victim throughout his anticipated working life, and since the Court had sought to ensure protection of the real value of the damages by requiring the establishment of a trust fund to be managed 'under the most favourable conditions permitted by Honduran banking practice', indexing was one means under such a system of achieving the results required by the judgment.[166]

It is important to note the effects of the Court's judgment in contentious proceedings since these differ from those of advisory opinions. Article 68 provides that the States Parties to the Convention undertake to comply with the judgments of the Court in any case to which they are parties, and this includes the payment of compensatory damages.[167] As Judge Piza Escalante has indicated,[168] contentious proceedings are condemnatory in nature leading to the classification of the defendant state as a delinquent. This may clearly have an effect on the reputation of that state both regionally and internationally.

Advisory Opinions

The power of the Court to give advisory opinions is extremely wide and will be considered in detail in the chapter devoted to this subject.[169] At this point, however, it is sufficient to note that the Court may be requested to give advisory opinions in respect of three different categories of instrument. *First,* it may be requested to give an interpretation of the Convention by any Member State or organ of the OAS acting within its sphere of competence.[170] *Second*, the same parties may request the Court to give an opinion concerning the interpretation of any other treaties concerning the protection of human rights in the American states.[171] *Third*, any Member State of the OAS may request the Court to give an opinion regarding the compatibility of that state's domestic laws with the Convention or of other treaties concerning the protection of human rights in the Americas.[172]

In the three categories of request for advisory opinions noted above, proceedings are instituted by the relevant parties submitting an application to the Court posing precise questions to which answers or opinions are sought.[173] It is clear, however, that the Court has a residual power to reformulate what it perceives to be defective questions.[174] Where an organ of the OAS seeks an advisory opinion under Article 64(1) of the Convention, however, it must indicate in its application precisely what its spheres of competence are and also the considerations which prompted it to consult with the Court.[175] It is important that in all cases of requests for advisory opinions the Court is given full information since, as will be demonstrated later, the Court has a wide discretion to refuse to comply with a request if it is in reality a disguised contentious case or if it is designed to frustrate the proper functioning of the Convention system.[176]

Although advisory opinions under Article 64(1) of the Convention are essentially declaratory in nature, the Court has nevertheless recognized that its authoritative interpretations may have wider implications for states which are not party to proceedings. This being so, the procedure in requests for advisory opinions contains two important elements. First, the Secretary of the Court transmits copies of the request to any Member State of the OAS 'which might be concerned in this matter'.[177] In practice, all Member States of the OAS are sent copies of the request. The request is sent to the Secretary-General of the OAS for transmission to the appropriate organs of the OAS listed in Chapter VIII of the Charter who might have an interest in the proceedings. Second, all the states and organs so notified are entitled to provide written observations or other documents on the matter which is the subject of the request.

It has also been a feature of proceedings that a number of non-governmental organizations have provided the Court with *amicus curiae* briefs. There is no provision which deals explicitly with the issue of whether the Court is entitled to take notice of such briefs, but Article 34(2) of its Rules would appear to provide an adequate constitutional basis for the Court to receive such briefs. This provides:

The Court may, in consultation with the parties, entrust any body, office, commission or authority of its choice with the task of obtaining information expressing an opinion, or making a report upon any specific point.

To date there has only once been specific mention by the Court of observations made to it in an *amicus curiae* brief. This was in *Compulsory Membership*[178] where, in considering whether compulsory membership and licensing of journalists by an organization prescribed by law violated Articles 13 and 29 of the Convention,[179] the Court referred directly to arguments put to it by the Latin-American Federation of Journalists. There is, however, no evidence, either explicit or implicit, that the Court has adverted to *amicus curiae* briefs submitted by a large number of other organizations in any of its other decisions.[180]

Proceedings in requests for advisory opinions are also divided into a written and oral stage.[181] The Court determines the format which oral proceedings are to take, and fixes the order of hearing and the time limits for the hearing.[182] All other aspects of the procedure are regulated by the rules governing the conduct of contentious proceedings which the Court may apply when the circumstances so require.[183] Hearings on advisory opinions are to be held in public, but there is no indication in the Court's rules as to whether the Court's deliberations are to take place in public or in private.[184] Reference must be made here to Article 14 of the Court's Rules concerning the internal functioning of the Court which seems to suggest that all deliberations must take place in private and that such deliberations must remain secret. The practicalities of the situation clearly supports the secrecy with which judicial deliberation is to be conducted. The opinion of the Court terminates proceedings[185] and the format of the opinion is governed by Article 54 of the Rules of the Court.

Notes

[1]   To date only one female judge has been elected to the Court. This was Sonia Picado-Sotela of Costa Rica who resigned from the Court prior to completing her term of office after accepting a position which was incompatible with that of a member of the Court. See Inter-American Court of Human Rights, *Annual Report of the Inter-American Court of Human Rights 1994*, OAS/Ser.L/V/III.31, Doc. 9, January 17, 1995, Original Spanish, p. 6.

[2]   *Velasquez Rodriguez, Interpretation of the Court's Judgment of July 21, 1989, Assessing Compensatory Damages against the State of Honduras,* Judgment of August 17, 1990, Series C, No. 9; *Godinez Cruz, Interpretation of the Court's Judgment of July 21, 1989, Assessing Compensatory Damages against the State of Honduras,* Judgment of August 17, 1990, Series C, No. 10.

3   Judgment of December 11, 1991, Series C, No. 13.

4   Article 16(2) Statute of the Court (hereafter 'Statute').

5   See Buergenthal, *Inter-American Court*, p. 233.

6   Article 22 Statute; Articles 11 and 12 Rules of the Court (hereafter 'Rules').

7   Article 22(3) Statute; Article 12(1) Rules.

8   On the question of independence and impartiality of members of international human rights supervision and enforcement institutions see H. Cohn, 'International Fact Finding Processes and the Rule of Law' (1977) 18 *The Review of the International Commission of Jurists* 43; F. Ermacora, 'Partiality and Impartiality of Human Rights Enquiry Commissions of International Organizations', in *René Cassin Amicorum Discipulorumque Liber I* (Paris: Pedone, 1969), p. 70; T. H. Franck and H. S. Fairley, 'Procedural Due Process in Human Rights Fact-Finding by International Agencies', (1980) 74 AJIL 313.

9   C.f. Article 16 of the Statute of the ICJ which provides that judges may not exercise any political or administrative function. C.f. also Rule 4 of the European Court of Human Rights' Rules of Procedure which prohibits judges from being members of a government or from practising a profession which could affect their independence. Note that the judges to which these provisions apply are, unlike judges of the Inter-American Court, full-time officials.

10 Article 18(1)(a) Statute.

11 Article 18(1)(b) Statute.

12 Article 18(1)(a) Statute.

13 Article 18(1)(c) Statute. It will be recalled that it is this provision which might be used to facilitate the transfer of the Court from a part-time to a full-time institution.

14 Article 18(2) Statute.

15 Article 18(3) Statute. The disciplinary regime for judges is discussed infra, pp. 131-3.

16 Article 18(3) Statute.

17 Article 72 ACHR; Article 17(1) Statute.

18 Article 17(3) Statute. Ad hoc judges also receive similar categories of emoluments, but their *honorarium* is established by different criteria. C.f. the position of the full-time judges of the ICJ who receive an annual salary. Ad hoc judges of the ICJ receive an *honorarium* for each day of service. See Article 32 of the ICJ Statute.

19 Article 70 ACHR; Article 15 Statute. It should be noted that such immunities and privileges are also accorded to ad hoc and interim judges. Such immunities are codified in the Vienna Convention on Diplomatic Relations 1961, 500 UNTS 195; (1966) 5 ILM 352. On this matter the American Convention does not differ from either the ICJ or the European Court of Human Rights. See Articles 19 and 59 of the respective Courts' Statutes.

20 Ibid.

21 Article 70(2) ACHR; Article 15(2) Statute.

22 Article 15(4) Statute. The relevant privileges and immunities of diplomats codified in the Vienna Convention on Diplomatic Relations which are applicable to Judges of the Court are contained in Articles 29-42 of the Vienna Convention. These establish by inference that judges possess the same immunities enjoyed by diplomatic agents in both the territory of the seat of the Court and that of other states parties to the American Convention. In a judge's own state he has the rights established by Article 38 which ensure the inviolability of his person, staff, archives, correspondence, means of transportation and communication. He also enjoys the legal and fiscal exemptions necessary for the performance of his duties.

23 Pan-American Treaty Series 22; Pan-American Union Law and Treaty Series 31.

24 See supra, pp. 29-30.

25 Article 15(4) Statute.

[26] Supra, pp. 36-7.
[27] Article 20(1) Statute.
[28] Article 20(2) Statute.
[29] Ibid.
[30] Ibid.
[31] Article 73 ACHR.
[32] Ibid.
[33] Article 21 Statute.
[34] Ibid.
[35] Article 21(2) Statute.
[36] Article 21(3) Statute.
[37] Article 19(1) Statute.
[38] Ibid.
[39] Article 19(2) Statute. For an application of this rule, see Judge Hernandez Alcerro's self-disqualification in *Velasquez Rodriguez,* Judgment of 29 July, 1988 (1989) 28 ILM 291; (1988) HRLJ 212, para. 13. The judge's disqualification was accepted, and Honduras informed of the right to appoint an ad hoc judge under Article 10(3) of the Court's Statute.
[40] Article 19(3) Statute.
[41] Articles 19(2) and 19(3) Statute.
[42] Article 19(4) Statute. On interim judges, see supra, pp. 128-9.
[43] Article 12(3) Statute.
[44] Supra, p. 129.
[45] Buergenthal, *Inter-American Court,* p. 233.
[46] Ibid.
[47] Article 12(1) Statute; Article 3(2) Rules.
[48] Article 3(2) Rules.
[49] Ibid., the issue of precedence is dealt with by Article 13 of the Rules of Procedure. This will be considered infra.
[50] Article 3(1) Rules. Their terms of office begins on 1 July of the corresponding year.
[51] Article 3(2) Rules.
[52] Buergenthal, *Inter-American Court,* p. 234.
[53] Ibid.
[54] Ibid.
[55] On the other duties conferred on the President by Statute see supra, pp. 38-41. It should be noted that the President may at any time delegate the official representation of the Court to the Vice President or to any of the Judges or in their absence to the Secretary or Deputy Secretary of the Court: Article 4(2) Rules.
[56] Article 12(3) Statute; Article 5(1) Rules.
[57] Article 5(3) Rules. This happened in *Viviana Gallardo,* where the Costa Rican President of the Court, Judge Rodolfo Piza Escalante yielded the Presidency to the Vice President. However, by the time the Case was heard, Carlos Roberto Reina had been elected President and he therefore assumed the function of presiding over the case. See *Viviana Gallardo,* para. 5.
[58] Article 13(2) Statute. Where judges have the same seniority in office, they take precedence according to age.
[59] Article 13(3) Statute.
[60] Ibid.
[61] Advisory Opinion of September 8 1983, OC-3/83 (1984) 23 ILM 320 (1983) 4 HRLJ

339.

62   On the structure and role of the Permanent Commission see infra, p. 135.

63   *Restrictions to the Death Penalty,* para. 11.

64   Ibid., para. 14.

65   Ibid., para. 17.

66   Article 6(1) Rules.

67   Ibid.

68   Article 6(3) Rules. Note the limitations placed on this role in *Restrictions to the Death Penalty,* supra, p. 43.

69   Article 6(2) Rules.

70   Buergenthal, *Inter-American Court,* p. 234.

71   Article 59 ACHR.

72   Article 58(2) ACHR.

73   Article 7(1) Rules.

74   Article 14(2) Statute.

75   Article 7(2) Rules. He or she may be re-elected for further periods of five years. Elections for the Secretary are conducted in the same manner as those for judges. See supra, p. 124.

76   Article 20(3) Statute.

77   Article 7(2) Rules.

78   Buergenthal, *Inter-American Court,* p. 233, compares the position of the Secretary to the Court with that of the Executive Secretary of the Inter-American Commission on Human Rights who may be removed by the Secretary General of the OAS in consultation with the Commission. See Article 21(3) Statute of the Inter-American Commission on Human Rights.

79   Article 14(3) Statute. The Assistant Secretary is termed Deputy Secretary in the Rules of the Court: Article 8 Rules.

80   Article 8(1) Rules; Article 14(4) Statute.

81   Article 8(2) Rules.

82   Article 14(4) Statute.

83   *Inter-American Court,* p. 234.

84   Article 10(a) Rules.

85   Article 15(3) Statute.

86   Article 20(4) Statute.

87   Such rules must comply with the administrative regulations of the OAS General Secretariat, insofar as they are not incompatible with the independence of the Court: Article 14(4) Statute and Article 59 ACHR.

88   Article 20(3) Statute.

89   Article 22(1) Statute; Article 11 Rules.

90   Article 22(3) Statute; Article 12(1) Rules.

91   Article 63(2) ACHR. See infra, pp. 137-8 on interim or provisional measures of protection.

92   Article 12(2) Rules. Such special sessions are convoke in accordance with the provisions of Article 12(1) Rules.

93   Article 56 ACHR; Article 23(1) Statute; Article 13 Rules. See discussion supra, p. 128.

94   Article 23(2) Statute; Article 15(3) Rules. Dunshee de Abranches, *Inter-American Court,* p. 97, opines that it is a matter of concern that it is possible that 3 judges, a majority of a 5 judges quorum, could make decisions and render opinions of 'significant magnitude' without the support of the other 4 judges who might decide differently in a similar case. He states that 'such a situation could create a continuous instability in the decisions of the Court and weaken the prestige of the Inter-American system'. He takes the view that the Court's

Statute ought to be amended to require that decisions of the Court must be made by an absolute majority of judges.

[95] See Article 43 European Convention on Human Rights.

[96] Article 24(1) Statute; Article 14(1) Rules.

[97] *Velasquez Rodriguez*, para. 32.

[98] Ibid., para. 32.

[99] Ibid., para. 33.

[100] Article 19(2) Rules. The official languages of the OAS are English, Spanish, Portuguese and French.

[101] Article 19(3) Rules. In such circumstances the Court must make arrangements for interpretation.

[102] Article 24(2) Statute; Article 14(2) Rules.

[103] Article 14(2) Rules.

[104] Article 14(4) Rules.

[105] Article 15(1) Rules.

[106] Article 15(3) Rules.

[107] Article 15(4) Rules.

[108] Article 61 ACHR. By Article 57 ACHR the Commission is enjoined to appear before the Court in all cases.

[109] At para. 24.

[110] As, indeed, it has confirmed in subsequent jurisprudence. See infra, Chapter 5.

[111] See M. D. Vargas, 'Individual Access to the Inter-American Court of Human Rights' (1984) *New York University Journal of International Law and Politics*, 601.

[112] Emphasis added.

[113] Article 22(1) Rules.

[114] Article 22(2) Rules.

[115] Articles 23(1) and 23(5) Rules.

[116] Article 23(3) Rules.

[117] *Inter-American Court*, p. 109.

[118] See supra, p. 137.

[119] Article 23(4) Rules.

[120] Order of January 15, 1988 - *Three cases v Honduras: Velasquez Rodriguez / Fairen Garbi and Solis Corrales / Godinez Cruz* - Provisional Measures (hereafter '*First Order*') (1988) 9 HRLJ 104. See also *Velasquez*, paras. 39-49.

[121] Order of January 19, 1988 - *Three cases v Honduras: Velasquez Rodriguez / Fairen Garbi and Solis Corrales / Godinez Cruz* - Provisional Measures (1988) 9 HRLJ 105.

[122] This depends upon the states parties having accepted the jurisdiction of the Court which, in this case, Honduras had done.

[123] Supra, p.139.

[124] The Commission has issued requests for provisional measures in a significant number of cases since the first use of the mechanism in the *Honduran Disappearance Cases*. See Order of the Inter-American Court of Human Rights August 8, 1990, Provisional Measures Requested by the Inter-American Commission on Human Rights Regarding Peru (Bustios - Rojas Case); Decision of the Inter-American Court of Human Rights January 27, 1993, Provisional Measures Requested by the Inter-American Commission on Human Rights Regarding Peru (Peruvian Prisons Case); Decision of the Inter-American Court of Human Rights, January 27, 1993, Provisional Measures Requested by the Inter-American Commission on Human Rights Regarding Peru (Chipoco Case); Decision of the Inter-American Court of

Human Rights January 19, 1994, Medidas Provisionales Solicitadas por la Comision Interamericana de Derechos Humanos Respecto de la Republica Argentina (Caso Reggiardo Tolosa); Decision of the Inter-American Court of Human Rights, June 22, 1994, Medidas Provisionales Solicitadas por la Comision Interamericana de Derechos Humanos Respecto de Guatemala (Caso Colotenango); Decision of the Inter-American Court of Human Rights, August 1, 1991, Medidas Provisionales Solicitadas por la Comision Interamericana de Derechos Humanos Respecto de Guatemala (Caso Chunima); Decision of the Inter-American Court of Human Rights, December 7, 1994, Medidas Provisionales Solicitadas por la Comision Interamericana de Derechos Humanos Respecto del Colombia (Caso Cabellero Delgado y Santana); Caso Carpio Nicolle, Medidas Provisionales Solicitadas por la Comisión Interamericana de Derechos Humanos Respecto de la Republica de Guatemala, Resolución de la Corte Interamericana de Derechos Humanos del 19 de septiembre de 1995.

[125] Articles 25(1) and 25(2) Rules.

[126] Article 43 Rules.

[127] Article 26 Rules.

[128] Articles 27(1) and 27(2) Rules.

[129] Article 27(3).

[130] See infra, chapter 5 on the Court's contentious jurisdiction.

[131] Article 28 Rules.

[132] Articles 30(1) and 30(3) Rules.

[133] Article 30(4) Rules.

[134] Article 30(2) Rules.

[135] Article 30(5) Rules.

[136] Article 31 Rules *in fine*.

[137] Article 32 Rules.

[138] Articles 34 Rules *in fine*.

[139] Article 38(2) Rules.

[140] *Gallardo,* para. 22.

[141] In the *Honduran Disappearance Cases,* however, the Court decided to review *de novo* all evidence presented by the Commission and Honduras. See infra, p. 209.

[142] Supra, p. 137.

[143] Article 34(1) Rules. Cf. Rule 40 of the European Court of Human Rights which provides that the Court may hear 'as witness or expert or in any other capacity any person whose evidence or statements seem likely to assist in the carrying out of its task'.

[144] The government of Honduras made extensive use of this Rule in the *Honduran Disappearance Cases.* See infra, chapter 5.

[145] Supra, p. 139.

[146] Article 36 Rules.

[147] In the case of the International Court of Justice this has happened on five occasions in the *Fisheries Jurisdiction Case* (ICJ Rep. 1974, p. 3.); the *Nuclear Tests Cases* (ICJ Rep. 1974, p. 253; the *Aegean Sea Continental Shelf Case* (ICJ Rep. 1978, p. 3); *Case Concerning United States Diplomatic and Consular Staff in Teheran* (ICJ Rep. 1980, p. 3) and the *Military and Paramilitary Activities Case (Merits)* (ICJ Rep. 1986), p. 98.

[148] Article 24(1) Rules.

[149] Article 53.

[150] See supra, pp. 124-7.

[151] *Compensatory Damages,* para. 12.

[152] Article 45 Rules.

[153]   Article 24(3) Statute.

[154]   Article 66(1) ACHR.

[155]   Article 66(2) ACHR.

[156]   Article 69 ACHR; Article 46 Rules.

[157]   Article 67 ACHR; Article 48 Rules.

[158]   Article 67 ACHR.

[159]   Article 48(4) Rules.

[160]   *Interpretation of Compensatory Damages*, para. 3.

[161]   Ibid., para. 6.

[162]   Ibid.

[163]   Ibid., para. 14.

[164]   Ibid., para. 36. Despite refusing to exercise jurisdiction under Article 67 of the Convention, the Court nonetheless took the view that it remained seised of the case since it was still at the judgment stage and it was therefore competent to rule on the consequences of non-compliance. *Interpretation of Compensatory Damages*, para. 37. As to the Court's position concerning the consequences of non-compliance by Honduras see infra, pp. 97-8.

[165]   Interpretation of Compensatory Damages, para. 26.

[166]   Ibid., paras. 30-32.

[167]   Article 68 ACHR.

[168]   *Gallardo*, Explanation of Vote by Judge Rodolfo E. Piza Escalante.

[169]   See infra, Chapter 6.

[170]   Article 64(1) ACHR.

[171]   Ibid. The meaning of this phrase has been considered in *Other Treaties* and *Interpretation of the American Declaration*. See infra, Chapter 5.

[172]   Article 64(2) ACHR. The meaning of this provision has also been the subject of a ruling by the Court in Advisory Opinion OC-4/84 of January 19, 1984, *Proposed Amendments to the Naturalization Provisions of the Political Constitution of Costa Rica* (hereafter '*Proposed Amendments*') (1984) 5 HRLJ 161.

[173]   See Articles 49, 50 and 51 Rules.

[174]   The Court reformulation of the questions posed by Costa Rica in Advisory Opinion OC-7/85 of August 29, 1986, *Character and Scope of the Right to Reply or Correction Recognized in the American Convention* (hereafter '*Right of Reply*') (1981) 20 ILM 1289; (1986) 7 HRLJ 238, generated some controversy between the judges. A number of judges considered that the majority of the Court had wrongly reformulated the questions put by Costa Rica.

[175]   Articles 49(2)(b) and 50(2) Rules.

[176]   See infra, Chapter 5.

[177]   Article 52 Rules.

[178]   At para. 60.

[179]   Freedom of expression and thought.

[180]   In the preliminary stages of all its judgments, however, the Court refers to all the organizations from which it has received *amicus curiae* briefs.

[181]   Article 52(2) Rules.

[182]   Ibid.

[183]   Article 53 Rules.

[184]   Article 54(1) Rules.

[185]   Article 44(1) Rules.

4 Individual Applications before the Inter-American Commission

Introduction

In chapter 1 the emergence and evolution of the Inter-American Commission on Human Rights as an organ of human rights protection in the Western Hemisphere was examined in some detail. The purpose of this chapter, however, is to analyze the work of the Commission in so far as it relates to individual petitions under both the Charter and the Convention. Before proceeding, it is appropriate to recall that, following the entry into force of the Convention, the competences of the Commission as both a Charter and a Convention organ were largely codified within Article 41 of the latter instrument. It should also be further recalled that the Commission's Statute and Regulations which were adopted under the Convention deal with its practices and procedures under both instruments. This is particularly important when analyzing the Commission's competence to examine individual petitions, for under Article 52 of its Regulations the procedure which is applicable to petitions concerning Member States of the OAS which are not party to the Convention is the same as that which applies to States Parties to the Convention. The rules concerning admissibility are thus identical for petitions made under both instruments. The point of divergence occurs subsequent to the admission of a petition. Under the Convention the Commission moves to the conduct of an optional on-site investigation, engagement of a conciliation procedure and, ultimately, submission of a case to the Court under its contentious jurisdiction if the Commission decides not to dispose of the case itself. Under the Charter, however, it is the Commission which must make a decision in the case without necessarily having recourse to the friendly settlement procedures.[1]

General

Under Article 41(f) of the Convention the Commission is empowered 'to take action on petitions and other communications pursuant to its authority under the provisions of Articles 44 through 51 of this Convention'. A review of these provisions indicates that they apply only to the Convention petition system and are thus concerned with States Parties to the Convention alone. The use of the term 'petition' is reserved for complaints by private individuals, whereas the word 'communications' applies solely to complaints brought before the Commission by States Parties. The use of the former term would seem to suggest that individual applications are a matter of grace, but this is misleading, for the right of individual application under the American Convention is stronger than that under most other species of international human rights enforcement machinery. Under Article 44, 'any person or group of persons, or any non-governmental entity legally recognized in one or more Member States of the Organization may lodge petitions with the Commission containing denunciations or complaints of violation of this Convention by a State Party'.[2] The jurisdiction of the Commission to receive such complaints is not optional but compulsory for all states which become party to the Convention. As the Court itself has acknowledged, this mandatory right of individual petition is 'unique' among international human rights instruments.[3] In contradistinction to the absolute right of individual petition, the competence of States Parties to submit communications alleging a violation of a right protected by the Convention is optional and therefore dependent upon State Party acceptance. Furthermore, the principle of reciprocity applies since the Commission may accept a communication from a State Party only if the state against which a complaint is levelled has similarly accepted the Commission's jurisdiction.[4] Such acceptances of the Commission's jurisdiction must be communicated to the General Secretariat of the OAS which then transmits copies to all Member States.[5] Submission to the jurisdiction of the Commission for the purpose of inter-state complaints therefore becomes a matter of notoriety to all Member States of the OAS and not simply to States Parties to the Convention which are more limited in number.

In making the right of inter-state communication optional rather than mandatory, the American Convention has adopted an approach which is opposite to that of the European Convention.[6] Under Article 24 of the latter instrument, any state which becomes party to the Convention automatically recognizes the right of any other High Contracting Party to make denunciations to the European Commission alleging a violation.[7] It is clear that a number of inter-state complaints brought under Article 24 of the European Convention have been used for partisan political purposes rather than the protection of human rights proper.[8] By making inter-state communications optional rather than compulsory the American Convention has created a situation in which such communications are less likely to be used as vehicles for political intervention.[9]

Individual Petitions

As indicated above, Article 44 provides that the following persons may lodge petitions with the Commission containing denunciations or complaints of violation of the Convention by a State Party:

- Any person;
- Any group of persons;
- Any non-governmental organization (NGO) legally recognized in one or more Member States of the OAS.

It will be immediately apparent that the categories of potential complainants with standing are considerably broader than those in most other international human rights instruments which permit the right of individual complaint. Unlike the European Convention on Human Rights or First Optional Protocol to the International Covenant on Civil and Political Rights there is no primary requirement that petitioners be the actual victims of a Convention violation.[10] It is possible therefore for a person who has no direct interest or standing in a case in a domestic administrative law sense to complain of a breach of the Convention to the Commission. Furthermore, there is no requirement that the complainant be within the jurisdiction of the respondent state. This view is supported by the inclusion of NGOs in the list of potential complainants. The reference to such bodies clearly recognizes the important role which they may discharge in the protection of human rights. Indeed, NGOs such as Americas Watch and Amnesty International have already demonstrated that they are able to play a role in the functioning of the inter-American system by bringing complaints and acting as *amicus curiae* before the Court.[11] It should be noted that it matters not that an NGO be legally present and recognized in the territory of a respondent State Party: it is enough that it is recognized in one or more OAS Member States.[12] Through this device NGOs may still function effectively despite any action which might be taken to outlaw them in the territory of any of the States Parties. A further point which should be made about the classes of private persons who have standing to complain to the Commission is that the Convention clearly contemplates the possibility of persons initiating a class action or *actio popularis*.[13] Again, this differs from the European Convention and the First Optional Protocol to the International Covenant on Civil and Political Rights which do not on their face appear to permit such applications.[14]

Requirements for the Admissibility of Petitions

The conditions for admissibility of a petition or communication are set down in Articles 46 and 47 of the Convention and Articles 31 to 43 of the Commission's Regulations. They have also been further elaborated by the jurisprudence of the Commission and the Court. Article 46 of the Convention and Articles 33 to 39 of the Commission's Regulations stipulate that in order to be admitted a petition must satisfy the following criteria:

> Domestic remedies must have been exhausted in accordance with generally recognized principles of international law;
> The petition or communication must have been lodged within a period of six months from the date on which the party alleging violation of his or here rights was notified of the final judgment;
> The subject of the petition or communication must not be pending in another proceeding for settlement; and
> In the case of individual complainants petitions must contain the name, nationality, profession, domicile and signature of the person or persons or of the legal representative of the entity lodging the petition.

Article 46(2) of the Convention and Article 37(2) of the Commission's Regulations further provide, however, that the first of the two criteria stated above will not be applicable if:

> The domestic legislation of the state concerned does not afford due process of law for the protection of the right or rights allegedly violated; or
> The person alleging violation of his or her rights has been denied access to the remedies under domestic law or has been prevented from exhausting them; or
> There has been unwarranted delay in rendering a final judgment under the aforementioned remedies.

Exhaustion of Domestic Remedies

It is a requirement of all human rights instruments which contain individual application procedures that domestic remedies should be exhausted before a state may be impleaded before an international human rights body with jurisdiction to hear and determine cases.[15] The rationale for this rule is the same as that which is to be found in general international law, namely, that a state should have the opportunity to provide redress for a wronged individual under its own legal system before international proceedings may be invoked against it.[16] As the Court said in the *Gallardo Case*:[17]

The rule which requires the prior exhaustion of local remedies is designed for the benefit of the state, for that rule seeks to excuse the state from having to respond to charges before an international body for acts which been imputed to it before it has had the opportunity to remedy them by internal means.

Furthermore, since the rule is for the benefit or defence of the state, it is open to the state to waive it either expressly or by implication.[18] Such a waiver by a respondent state would have the effect of permitting an applicant to proceed to the next stage of admissibility without impediment. Once a waiver has been effected by a State Party it is irrevocable, but a State Party which seeks to assert the non-exhaustion of domestic remedies as a bar to admissibility must do so in a timely fashion at an early stage in the proceedings before the Commission.[19] This requirement is designed to prevent damage to the victim. As the Court stated in the *Honduran Disappearance Cases,* 'the rule of prior exhaustion must never lead to a halt or delay that would render international action in support of the defenseless victim ineffective'.[20] Indeed, it further observed that this was why Article 46(2) sets out the exceptions to the requirement to exhaust local remedies prior to a person seeking international protection.[21] In proceedings before the Court in *Gangaram Panday,* Suriname claimed that the petitioner had failed to exhaust domestic remedies, and that because of this the Commission ought not to have admitted the petition. The state failed to specify which remedies had not been exhausted, and had not raised this issue in proceedings before the Commission. The Court thus held that by failing to raise the question of exhaustion of local remedies before the Commission, Suriname had effected a tacit waiver of its objection.[22] Furthermore, the Court considered that the respondent state's objection was untimely when it sought to raise it before the Commission. In reaching this conclusion the Court is clearly following a similar path to its European counterpart which has given similar rulings in cases bearing these characteristics.[23]

As noted above, there are three circumstances envisaged by Article 46(2) and Article 37(2) of the Commission's Regulations in which an individual is absolved from demonstrating non-exhaustion of domestic remedies. These circumstances correspond, in fact, to elements of the rules of general international law governing state responsibility, and they therefore go some way to underpinning the requirement of Article 46(1)(a) that domestic remedies be exhausted 'in accordance with generally recognized principles of international law'.[24]

The actual application of the rules concerning exhaustion of domestic remedies has been the subject of considerable discussion by the Commission and has led to the elaboration of a significant jurisprudence by this institution in its conduct of the individual petition procedures under both the OAS Charter and the Convention. The Court has also had the opportunity to clarify the circumstances in which individuals are absolved from the requirement to exhaust domestic remedies under the Convention. The jurisprudence of each of these institutions will be examined in turn.

The Commission's Doctrine on the Exhaustion of Domestic Remedies

It is an axiom of the international law relating to state responsibility that domestic remedies need only be exhausted where there are adequate and effective remedies available to be exhausted.[25] This principle was vividly demonstrated in *Case 9213 (USA)*.[26] This case arose from the US invasion of the Caribbean island of Grenada in October 1983 during which the Richmond Hill Insane Asylum was bombed by US aircraft and a number of inmates killed. A complaint was filed with the Commission on behalf of the victims by the Disabled Peoples' International alleging violation of the American Declaration. Although the US claimed that the complainants should have pursued their claim in the Grenadian courts, the Commission held that domestic remedies could not be exhausted since they were provided for neither by the legislation of Grenada nor the US. Furthermore, the Commission found that the US ad hoc compensation programme had not been implemented in so far as these particular victims were concerned.

While proceedings are in progress it cannot be said that domestic remedies have been exhausted until a final judgment is delivered. In *Case 1740 (Brazil)*[27] an application alleging the arbitrary arrest and mistreatment of two farm leaders was held inadmissible by the Commission on the grounds that the claim was still pending in proceedings before judicial authorities in Brazil. Where a remedy clearly exists which will afford the complainant relief in the cause in question, it is axiomatic that he or she must exhaust that remedy.[28] Furthermore, if the state provides a new remedy which is appropriate to address the infringement complained of, applicants must avail themselves of that remedy.[29] Where, however, the government of a respondent state provides information to the Commission which claims that an applicant has indeed exhausted all available domestic remedies, it will be estopped from subsequently denying that this is indeed the case.[30]

Remedies do not have to be exhausted before agencies which are incapable of granting judicial relief in the cause before them. In *Case 1697 (Brazil)*[31] two Brazilian lawyers alleged that they had been arbitrarily arrested and mistreated by agents of the Brazilian state. Brazil claimed that the applicants had not exhausted domestic remedies because their case was still being considered by the Council for the Protection of Human Rights in Brazil. Further investigation revealed that the Council was not a judicial organ, but a governmental agency charged with advisory functions. While Commissioner Dr Abranches argued that the existence of the Council implied the existence of internal legal remedies in Brazil and that the Commission was therefore not entitled to take cognizance of the case because of the non-exhaustion of domestic remedies, the majority of the Commission took the view that since the Council was incapable of rendering a final judgment in the matter, the applicants were not required to await its determination before the Commission could become seised of the issue. Dr Arechaga, the Chairman of the Commission, argued that the applicants simply had to exhaust all judicial means of redress in order to obtain a final judgment in their cause. It is suggested that the focus of the Commission was misplaced in this case in that it ought to have been concerned with the adequacy and efficacy of the remedies available before the Council rather than upon the nature of the organ itself.

A question associated with whether the tribunal itself is of a judicial character and competent to render a final judgment in any cause, is whether the applicant has standing to lodge an appeal. This is particularly crucial in the Inter-American system where it need not necessarily be the victim him or herself who attempts to obtain redress. Indeed, in cases involving extra-judicial executions and disappearances, a potential applicant may have no direct interest in the case for the purposes of internal legal remedies in a formal sense. Thus the 'remedies' in question may simply be a general interest in ensuring that the investigation of an alleged crime committed by agents of the state is properly carried out in accordance with the formal requirements of the justice system. In a sense these are not real remedies, but are more concerned with the respondent state's respect for the rule of law and the principle of legality. These issues arose in *Case 1683 (Brazil)*.[32] Here an allegation was made that a trade union leader had been arbitrarily arrested, tortured and murdered. A report by the police concluded that the victim had committed suicide by using an industrial poison, and when this report was submitted to the judicial branch (a military magistrate or *Juiz Auditor*), this latter filed the report until new objective evidence modifying the police conclusions came to light. Although it was possible to appeal from the magistrate's decision in the case, it was not clear that the applicants would have enjoyed legal standing to file the appeal. To all intents and purposes therefore, the trial was closed and there was no guarantee it would be reopened. Because of this the Commission held that internal remedies had been exhausted and that it could therefore move to a consideration of the substantive issues raised by the case.

Where an appeal has been denied or where the system of appeals has otherwise been exhausted, the Commission regards this as a proper exhaustion of domestic remedies. In this sense, the denial of appeal represents the final judgment in the issue, and it is from that date which the six month period of limitation begins to run. In *Case 1752 (USA)*[33] the complainants denounced a number of violations of the American Declaration resulting from their alleged arbitrary arrest by trespassing New Mexico law enforcement officials. Their claim for compensation before the US Courts had failed, and an application for *certiorari* to the US Supreme Court had been denied. Initially, the Commission decided that, since the US Courts had properly examined the evidence and had rendered a proper judicial decision, the complainants' claim ought to be rejected. As the applicants pointed out in a request for a revision of the Commission's decision, however, their complaint was not only about the conduct of the law enforcement officials, but also about the failure of the US courts to provide proper redress. Because of this, the Commission, finding that a denial of *certiorari* by the US Supreme Court constituted final judgment in the cause, held that the admissibility of the complaint could be reconsidered. The reasoning of the Commission is worth reproducing at some length here since it states a principle of vital importance to its management of the Inter-American system of human rights protection. It said:

> The mere fact that the internal legal remedies might have been exhausted and that there is a definitive judicial resolution that has examined the evidence presented by the petitioners does not bar the Commission from considering whether that evidence shows a violation of the human right defined in the American Declaration of the Rights and Duties of Man. What the Court of Appeals ... decided was that, in the case of the petitioners, the rights specified in the Constitution of the United States were not violated. Only the revision of this point of its conclusion would be incompatible with the competence of this Commission. It is enough to remember, as an example, that until 1954 the United States Supreme Court maintained the "separate but equal" doctrine in matters of racial discrimination, which would not have barred the IACHR, if it had been in existence at that time, from declaring that such a decision would be contrary to the American Declaration.

Where a system of appeals has been exhausted but there is no evidence of denial of due process or violation of other human rights protected by the American Declaration or Charter, the Commission will, while acknowledging the proper exhaustion of domestic remedies simply communicate the fact of no violation to the respondent state and the claimant.[34] This was the case in a series of complaints by Jamaican citizens who had been properly convicted of crimes in the Jamaican courts and who had been denied the right to appeal to the Privy Council in London; the highest court of appeal for Jamaica. Here the Commission found that their had been no denial of due process nor denial of any other rights protected by the inter-American system.

It seems that domestic remedies must be exhausted before the Commission may exercise its power to consider facts denounced as true unless the respondent state contradicts them within the time limit established by its Regulations. This view is derived by implication from *Case 1688 (Nicaragua)*.[35] In this case it had been alleged that members of the Nicaraguan National Guard had executed all the members of a farming family. The government of Nicaragua claimed that the facts denounced referred most probably to an army unit's encounter with bandits. While the Commission was prepared to defer consideration of the case until a proper investigation was carried out by the Nicaraguan authorities, this did latter did not, in fact, take place. After considerable delay therefore, the Commission decided to act in accordance with Article 51 of its 1967 Regulations[36] and presume the facts denounced to be true. In contradistinction to the above situation where there is some communication with the respondent state, if there is total silence on the part of the state to the Commission's request for information, the Commission will simply presume that internal remedies have been exhausted.[37] In certain circumstances, however, the Commission will exercise this power without requiring the exhaustion of domestic remedies. In *Case 1874 (Chile)*[38] a number of claims were received by the Commission in consequence of its conduct of a study of the human rights situation in Chile denouncing the extra-judicial execution of nine persons. In the absence of the provision of any information on these cases by the government of Chile, the Commission decided to apply Article 51 of its 1967 Regulations. In so doing, however, it made the following observation concerning the necessity of exhausting domestic remedies:

> Given the structure of the corporeal things damaged and the standards that were in force or are in force in Chile on the competence of courts in war time or during a state of siege, it is not fitting to demand of the claimants proof that they have exhausted the recourses provided for under internal law, inasmuch as causing a death constitutes a damage for which the law cannot offer any compensation whatever, except punishment of those individuals responsible for violation of the law.

It would seem therefore that, where the standards in existence in a state at a particular time fall so far short of the normal requirements for the administration of justice, the Commission may take note of this and absolve individuals from the obligation to exhaust domestic remedies, especially when the violation of the human rights in question is the denial of the right to life.[39] It should be acknowledged, however, that the Commission is only likely to take this particular step in extraordinary circumstances and where it has itself garnered direct proof of the standards prevailing in the state in question. It might be further noted that in 'general cases', as opposed to 'individual cases', that is cases in which a large number of denunciations tends to disclose a pattern of widespread human rights violations, the Commission also absolves itself from requiring proof of the exhaustion of domestic remedies.[40]

It is not enough that remedies be extant and technically available to individuals, those individuals must also have the ability to access those remedies. This applies not simply to the question of access to justice in a pure legal sense, but also the physical sense. Thus in *Case 1684 (Brazil)*,[41] Brazil claimed that the applicants, who were complaining, *inter alia,* of arbitrary detention and torture, had failed to exhaust domestic remedies and that the Commission had failed to take cognizance of this in admitting their claim against the state. The Commission's rapporteur Dr Sandifer, arguing against this objection said, 'one can imagine only with difficulty a person isolated in jail and claiming to be the victim of tortures and yet having complete freedom to inform the Commission of his lot'.[42] The rapporteur further observed that *in loco* observation could be used to verify whether or not domestic remedies had been exhausted in cases of this kind. This view is even more pertinent in cases of enforced disappearance. In *Case 7951 (Honduras)*[43] and *Case 8097 (Honduras)*[44] the Commission admitted a petition brought on behalf of two persons who had allegedly been disappeared while travelling through Honduras. Here the Commission, admitting the claim, held:

> 1. That from the information presented in this case, both by the government of Honduras and by the petitioner, it is inferred that those persons whose rights allegedly have been violated, or the person who is submitting the petition in their name and on their behalf, did not have access to the remedies of Honduran domestic law or was prevented form exhausting them.

As Article 46(2)(c) of the American Convention indicates, unreasonable delay in the administration of justice precludes the need to exhaust local remedies. This principle has also been developed independently by the Commission. What is unreasonable will vary from case to case. It was expressly stated in the *Velasquez Rodriguez Case* involving Honduras[45] and in *Case 9425 (Peru)*[46] that in the circumstances of disappeared persons a period of two years during which time the competent courts remained essentially inactive was an unreasonable period of time. In *Case 10.235 (Colombia)*[47] a delay of seven years in the investigation of cases of kidnap and murder allegedly committed by agents of the state was considered to be 'unduly protracted' and therefore absolved the applicants from further pursuing domestic remedies. The application of the principle of unreasonable delay was also evident by implication in the Commission's decision in *Case 9058 (Venezuela)*.[48] In this case a number of Venezuelan citizens had been charged with the sabotage of an Air Cubana aircraft in which 70 persons were killed. In 1977 the charges against the accused persons were dismissed, but they were kept in detention for a period of six years in the absence of a final ruling on the matter by a competent court of review. Given this passage of time and the absence of a final determination by a competent court, the Commission declared the petition admissible, 'because it meets the requirements established in the American Convention on Human Rights'.

The Doctrine of the Inter-American Court on the Exhaustion of Domestic Remedies

The Inter-American Court of Human Rights has ruled on the question of exhaustion of domestic remedies in a number of cases involving both its contentious and advisory jurisdiction. Its earliest pronouncements on this issue can, however, be found in its various rulings in the *Honduran Disappearance Cases,* and it is these which have established the standards which are now currently applied by the Commission in dealing with questions concerning the burden of proof and the adequacy and efficacy of domestic remedies.[49]

Exhaustion of Domestic Remedies: Burden of Proof and Questions of Adequacy and Efficacy

Under Article 37(3) of the Commission's Regulations the burden of proof in demonstrating that domestic remedies have not been exhausted lies upon the respondent state, unless it is apparent from the petition itself that the applicant has failed in this requirement. This view has also been expressed by the Court in the *Honduran Disappearance Cases* in which it stated that 'the state claiming non-exhaustion has an obligation to prove that domestic remedies remain to be exhausted and that they are effective'.[50] The Court has also ruled, however, that if a State Party were able to identify specific remedies which ought to have been pursued by the petitioner, then the burden of proof was shifted to the petitioner who must then demonstrate that those remedies were in fact exhausted or that they fell within the exceptions provided for in Article 46(2). As the Court observed, 'it must not be rashly presumed that a State Party to the Convention has failed with its obligation to provide effective remedies'.[51] It is not enough, however, that a respondent State Party is able to demonstrate the existence of specific remedies; it must also be able to demonstrate that such remedies are both adequate and effective. In this context the Court has interpreted 'adequate' to mean that a remedy must be 'suitable to address an infringement of a legal right'[52] and 'effective' to mean that a remedy must 'be capable of producing the result for which it was designed'.[53] Alleged remedies which are thus simply illusory or incapable of producing practical results will be neither adequate nor effective. Furthermore, the Court has held:[54]

> When it is shown that remedies are denied for trivial reasons or without an examination of the merits, or if there is proof of the existence of a practice or policy ordered or tolerated by the government, the effect of which is to impede certain person from invoking internal remedies that would normally be available to others ... resort to those remedies becomes a senseless formality. The exceptions of Article 46(2) would be fully applicable in those situations and would discharge the obligation to exhaust internal remedies since they cannot fulfil their objective in that case.

This ruling, which is similar to the concept of 'administrative practice' in the law of the European Convention on Human Rights,[55] was made in the *Honduran Disappearance Cases* in which the Court found that, although formal remedies existed in Honduras, they were ineffective in cases of disappeared persons. This was because 'the imprisonment was clandestine; formal requirements made [the remedies] inapplicable in practice; the authorities against whom they were brought simply ignored them, or because attorneys and judges were threatened and intimidated by those authorities'.[56]

Exceptions to the Requirement to Exhaust Domestic Remedies

In *Exceptions to the Exhaustion of Domestic Remedies*[57] the Commission requested the Court to rule on the question of whether domestic remedies needed to be exhausted in circumstances where indigents are unable to avail themselves of legal remedies because of their economic circumstances or where an individuals are unable to secure legal remedies because they are unable to retain legal representation because of 'a generalized fear in the legal community'. In the case of indigence, the Court held that since Article 46(1) is of a general nature, a person claiming indigence must demonstrate that he or she falls within the terms of Article 46(2) in order to be discharged from the obligation to exhaust domestic remedies.[58] This, however, must be seen within the wider context of other provisions of the Convention concerning the prohibition of discrimination and the right to a fair trial. In the view of the Court Article 1(1) and Article 24 are of primary importance in this context.[59] Article 1(1) obliges States Parties to respect the rights and freedoms recognized in the Convention to ensure to all persons subject to their jurisdiction the free and full exercise of those rights and freedoms without any discrimination for reasons of, *inter alia,* economic status. Furthermore, Article 24 provides:

> All persons are equal before the law and entitled to equal protection of the law. Consequently, they are entitled, without discrimination, to equal protection of the law.

The Court therefore ruled that the meaning of discrimination in Article 24 can be determined by reference to the prohibited grounds of discrimination which are contained in Article 1(1) and, as a consequence of this, equal protection of law should be ensured to all persons regardless of their economic status.[60] If, therefore, persons seeking protection of the law in order to vindicate rights protected by the Convention are prevented from doing so because their economic status denies them access to legal counsel or access to justice because the cost of proceedings are beyond their means then, in the Court's view those persons suffer discrimination by reason of their economic status and therefore cannot be regarded as recipients of equal protection before the law.[61] The Court further held that Article 1(1) placed a positive obligation on States Parties 'to organize the governmental apparatus and ... all the structures though which public power is exercised, so that they are capable of juridically ensuring the free and full enjoyment of human rights'.[62] The general obligations established by the preceding provisions are, however, supplemented by Article 8 concerning the right to a fair trial. This provision distinguishes between criminal proceedings and non-criminal proceedings. In the former, individuals are entitled with full equality to 'minimum guarantees'[63] whereas in the latter persons are entitled to 'due guarantees'.[64] The minimum guarantees to which a criminal defendant is entitled are listed in Article 8(2) and include the right of the accused persons to defend themselves or be assisted by legal counsel of their own choosing. In addition to this accused persons are given an 'inalienable right' to be assisted by counsel provided by the state, if they do not defend themselves personally or engage counsel within the time period established by law. Although the Court noted that these provisions did not require a State Party to provide legal counsel free of charge, nonetheless, if an indigent were in need of counsel in order to enjoy a fair hearing and the State Party did not provide such a service free of charge, then it would not be able to assert later that appropriate remedies existed and had not been exhausted.[65] The Court further ruled that, if indigents were forced to defend themselves because they could not afford counsel, a violation of Article 8 might arise if it could be demonstrated that lack of counsel affected the right to a fair hearing.[66] Clearly, this will have to be shown by reference to the facts on a case by case basis.

In non-criminal cases the same principles enumerated above apply to the concept of 'due guarantees' in the context of securing a fair trial in accordance with Article 8(1). In determining whether or not indigence which precludes access to legal counsel obviates the necessity to exhaust local remedies depends in this case upon the circumstances of the particular case or legal proceedings. Here, however, it is not only the right to counsel which might affect the fairness of a trial, but also whether an indigent has the financial wherewithal to institute legal proceedings and thus secure access to justice in the first instance. The Court concluded that in such circumstances, there is no need for an indigent person to exhaust domestic remedies, since the inability to initiate proceedings because of impecuniosity operated to deny access to appropriate remedies.[67]

In cases of unwillingness of lawyers in certain states to accept cases because of a fear that to do so would put their lives or the lives of their families at risk, the Court adopted similar reasoning. Relying upon Article 1(1) in particular, it observed that States Parties were required by that provision 'to take all necessary measures which might exist that would prevent individuals from enjoying the rights the Convention guarantees'.[68] Any State Party which therefore permitted circumstances or conditions which prevented individuals from having recourse to legal remedies not only violated Article 1(1) of the Convention, but also exempted individuals from the necessity to exhaust local remedies.[69] Despite a request by the Commission to the Court to specify the criteria which it should apply in deciding whether or not indigence or fear by legal practitioners to accept cases absolved such persons from exhausting local remedies, the Court nevertheless proceeded only to lay down general guidelines. It stated that:[70]

> It is clear that the test to be applied must be whether legal representation was necessary in order to exhaust the appropriate remedies and whether such representation was, in fact, available.

Although the Court made it clear that it was the duty of the Commission to make this decision on the available facts, nevertheless it stated that it would review the Commission's decision should the case ultimately be referred to the Court.[71]

Exhaustion of Domestic Remedies and Limitation of Time

In *Neira Alegria et al v Peru*,[72] the Court was not only obliged to consider the question of exhaustion of domestic remedies in a more general sense, but it also had to examine its relationship to the six month time limit established by Article 46 of the Convention. In this case, after a number of requests for information to which it did not respond, Peru informed the Commission on 29 September 1989 that the case concerning the disappearance of two terrorist suspects from a prison where a riot had been quelled by the army was being considered by a Special Military Tribunal, and thus domestic remedies had not been exhausted.[73] Following admission of the case by the Commission, however, Peru claimed that domestic remedies in the case had, in fact, been exhausted on 14 January 1987 when the Court of Constitutional Guarantees had denied the applicants' claim, and therefore the application to the Commission was out of time since it had exceeded six months from the date of the final judgment in the case.[74] The Court noted that the claims made by Peru were inconsistent. If the case had been rejected by the Court of Constitutional Guarantees in 1987, then it was not possible for the state to claim that the Special Military Tribunal was still considering the case in 1989.[75] Here the Court observed:[76]

> International practice indicates that when a party in a case adopts a position that is either beneficial to it or detrimental to the other party, the principle of estoppel prevents it from subsequently assuming the contrary position. Here the rule non concedit venire contra factum proprium applies.

Applying this proposition the Court stated that, although it might be argued that the Special Military Tribunal could not provide real remedies, nonetheless the contradictory statements made by Peru regarding the availability of the remedies had affected the procedural position of the other party and had a direct bearing on the admissibility of the application.[77]

Other Admissibility Requirements

Six Month Time Limit

The imposition by Article 46(1)(b) of a six month time limit for the presentation of petitions is elaborated by the Commission's Regulations. While Article 38(1) of the Regulations simply reproduces the Convention provision by instructing the Commission to 'refrain from taking up petitions' which are out of time, Article 38(2) provides that where an individual is absolved from the requirement to exhaust local remedies in accordance with Article 46(20 of the Convention and Article 37(2) of the Commission's Regulations, then the presentation of a petition to the Commission 'shall be within a reasonable period of time ... as from the date of which the alleged violation of rights has occurred'. The question of what amounts to a 'reasonable period of time' is to be determined at the discretion of the Commission having regard to the circumstances of each case which falls for consideration. It is clear that the exercise of this discretion will be subject to review by the Court should the case ultimately be remitted to it either by the Commission or the State Party concerned.

Duplication of Procedures

Article 46(1)(c) provides that the Commission shall not admit a petition or communication which is pending in another international procedure for settlement. This provision is complemented by Article 47 which states that the Commission shall consider inadmissible any petition or communication if it is 'substantially the same as one previously studied by the Commission or by another international organization'. These provisions are not as final as they may seem at first glance, however, for Article 39(2) of the Commission's Regulations further refine the criteria governing admissibility. In essence they provide that, subject to certain conditions, the mere fact that there is apparent duplication of procedures will not necessarily be a bar to admissibility. Thus, where a procedure before another international organization or agency deals with the general human rights situation of the respondent state and there is no decision on the specific facts which form the subject matter of the petition, the Commission may take up and examine the petition. Furthermore, if the procedure is one which will not lead to an 'effective settlement' of the alleged violation, the Commission may also admit the case. While there is no indication of what 'effective settlement' means in this context, it is suggested that it should be interpreted to mean that there must be an effective remedy available to the individual complainant and that the standard of effectiveness should be measured according to the criteria established by the Court in the *Honduran Disappearance Cases*, namely, that it should be 'suitable to address an infringement of a legal right'.[78] From this it is apparent that a petitioner who has made allegations of human rights violations against a State Party to the United Nations, and that State Party then becomes the subject of the UN Economic and Social Council's Resolution 1503 procedure or one of ECOSOC's special procedures, the petitioner will not be precluded from having his or her complaint admitted by the Commission. This conclusion is supported by two cases involving Peru[79] in which the respondent state claimed that, since the UN Working Group on Enforced or Involuntary Disappearances was considering two cases which formed the subject matter of complaints to the Commission, the latter was precluded from admitting the complaints. The Commission rejected this view, stating that 'a decision on the specific facts involved in the present case does not lie with the purview of the Working Group ...'. It appears, however, that a petitioner who has also lodged a complaint with the Human Rights Committee under the First Optional Protocol to the International Covenant on Civil and Political Rights will have his or her case ruled inadmissible, despite the fact that the final views of the Human Rights Committee are not legally binding and are therefore arguably incapable of providing an effective remedy as understood by the Inter-American Court in its jurisprudence.[80] This would seem to indicate, therefore, that the term 'effective settlement' has a wider meaning than 'effective remedy' within the meaning of the Commission's Regulations.

The final circumstance referred to in Article 39(2)(b) of the Commission's Regulations which will not prejudice the admissibility of a complaint is that where the denunciation concerning a petitioner to the Commission is made before another international organization or agency by a third party (including NGOs) without the authority of the petitioner. Presumably when the petitioner has notice of the denunciation made on his or her behalf, he or she is then under an obligation to seek its removal from the other process before the Commission may admit the case. Indeed, in all the cases concerning inadmissibility mentioned above, the Commission is under an obligation to inform the petitioner of such inadmissibility in order to give him or her the opportunity to remedy the situation. This, however, can be done only in cases involving conditional inadmissibility. As Buergenthal points out,[81] Article 39 of the Commission's Regulations posits two different categories of inadmissibility: conditional and unconditional. The fact that a denunciation has been placed before another international system for the protection of human rights does not automatically preclude the Commission from acting on the complaint if the petitioner subsequently withdraws his or her denunciation from the processes of the other system. Furthermore, where a decision on a denunciation by another international organization does not result in effective settlement, this too will not lead to a rejection of the petition by the Commission. In both these circumstances the Commission must, by Article 33 of its Regulations inform the petitioner that the requirements of admissibility have not been met, thus providing them with the opportunity to address the defect and thereby render there petition admissible. Where, however, the decision of another international organization or agency leads to an effective settlement of the violation, the effect will be to render a petition to the Commission absolutely inadmissible and therefore incapable of repair. It is in connection with this latter situation that Buergenthal says, 'the Inter-American Commission, drawing on the universally accepted principles of *res judicata,* very wisely makes absolute inadmissibility dependent, among other considerations, on the existence of a final decision or resolution of the dispute'.[82]

Formalities

Article 46(1)(d) requires that certain formalities must be observed before a petition will be rendered admissible. These are that the petition must include the name, nationality, profession, domicile, and signature of the applicant or applicants or of the legal representative of any entity lodging the petition. This is further elaborated by Article 32 of the Commission's Regulations which provides that in addition to the above-mentioned requirements the following information should be provided:

> An account of the act or situation that is denounced;
> Details of the place and date of the alleged violations;
> If possible, the name of the victims of the alleged violations;
> If possible, the name of any official that might have been appraised of the act or situation denounced;
> The name of the State Party responsible by commission or omission for the alleged violation of human right recognized by the Convention; and
> Information on whether domestic remedies have been exhausted or whether it has been impossible to do so.

Although a model complaint form is available which takes individuals through these requirements step by step, there is no requirement in the

Commission's Regulations that such a form should be used. Indeed, any application which contains the above information will be acceptable. Even if an original document of complaint does not contain all the necessary information, the Commission is obliged to notify the petitioner of the missing information so that this deficiency can be addressed.[83]

Article 47. Even if a petitioner is able to satisfy all the requirements of Article 46, he or she still has to overcome the further conditions laid down in Article 47(b) or (c) of the Convention. These provide that the Commission must reject any complaint which does not on its face disclose any *prima facie* violation of the rights guaranteed by the Convention or if the complaint is 'manifestly groundless or obviously out of order'. Of course, in order to determine whether there has or has not been a *prima facie* violation of any of the rights guaranteed by the Convention, it may be necessary for the Commission to conduct a substantial investigation of the merits of the case.

Declaration of Inadmissibility

If the Commission decides that a petition is inadmissible it must, in accordance with Article 41 of its Regulations, declare it to be so. This requires a formal act on behalf of the Commission.[84] If, however, the petition is declared admissible no formal declaration to this effect is required. The very fact that the Commission continues to the next stage of its procedure in requesting information from the respondent government is a sufficient indication of admissibility to the State Party concerned.[85] Once the Commission has declared a petition or communication inadmissible, it then lacks competence to rule on the merits of the case.[86]

Procedure

Once the Commission has decided that the petition or communication is *prima facie* admissible, the procedure which it must follow is laid down in Articles 48 to 51 of the Convention and Articles 42 to 50 of its Regulations. The way in which the Commission has managed and applied the various procedural rules has been the subject of some controversy among respondent States Parties and has given rise to a number of rulings by the Court. Most of these rulings have arisen in the context of preliminary objections by States Parties to the jurisdiction of the Court which have been based upon alleged procedural impropriety on the part of the Commission. In order to analyze the Commission's post-admissibility procedure, each of its various aspects will be examined in turn. Before doing so, however, some general observations should be made. First, the Court has decided that it is fully competent to review the Commission's procedure in so far as its relates to all matters concerning the submission of a case to it. This view is based upon Article 62(1) by which States Parties to the Convention that recognize the jurisdiction of the Court in contentious cases automatically accept its competence to rule on all matters relating to the interpretation or the application of the Convention.[87] Furthermore, as the Court itself has held:[88]

> Its [the Court's] power to examine and review all actions and decisions of the Commission derives from its character as the sole judicial organ in matters concerning the Convention.

The policy underpinning this view is that it not only affords greater protection to the human rights guaranteed by the Convention, but it also assures States Parties that the provisions of the Convention will be strictly observed. This approach of maintaining a balance between the need to ensure effective protection of human rights and the rights of the States Parties in contentious proceedings is also at the root of the second general point, namely, that the Commission may adopt a flexible approach to the application of its procedures. The guiding principle which has been stated by the Court here is that while failure to observe certain formalities is not necessarily relevant when dealing on the international plane, 'what is essential is that the conditions necessary for the procedural rights of the parties be not diminished or unbalanced'.[89] In addition to this, the Court has also taken the view that procedural rules are essentially a means of attaining justice. In the *Cayara Case*, Peru argued that the Commission had failed to observe Article 25(2) of the Court's Rules of Procedure which provides that the Commission must file, together with twenty copies of its report, a duly signed application indicating the object of the application, the human rights involved and the names of its delegates. In this case the application had arrived four days before the report. The Court held:[90]

> The rule quoted above must not be applied in such a way that distorts the object and purpose of the Convention. It is generally accepted that the procedural system is a means of attaining justice and that the latter cannot be sacrificed for the sake of mere formalities. Keeping within certain and timely limits, some omissions or delays in complying with procedure may be excused, provided that a suitable balance between justice and legal certainty is preserved.

Another procedural defect which had been raised by Peru in the *Cayara Case* was that an application to the Court following the expiration of the three month period provided for in Article 51 of the Convention had arrived by fax three days after the appropriate closing date. Here the Court observed:[91]

> An application containing such serious charges as those which are before us now cannot be deemed to have lapsed simply on those grounds.

Post-admissibility Procedure

Once the Commission has declared a petition admissible it then begins an investigatory phase in its procedure in which the complainant's allegations are evaluated by requesting information from the government of the respondent state and by supplying that state with relevant information from the complaint.[92] Article 48(1)(a) provides that all the information requested from the state must be provided within a 'reasonable period' which is to be determined by the Commission according to the circumstances of each case. Article 34(5) of the Commission's Regulations, however, provide that the respondent government must provide the information requested within ninety days of the request being sent. This period may be extended for a further period of thirty days at the request of the state concerned for 'justifiable cause',[93] but the total period of extensions may not exceed one hundred and eighty days. If the State Party concerned does not provide the pertinent information within the time stipulated then in accordance with Article 42 of the Regulations, 'the facts reported in the petition ... shall be presumed to be true ... as long as other evidence does not lead to a different conclusion'.[94] Following receipt of the relevant information, the Commission then ascertains whether the grounds for the petition or communication still exist.[95] If it considers that they do not, it may close the record.[96] The Commission may also at this stage declare the petition inadmissible or out of order on the basis of information or evidence which it has subsequently received.[97] It would appear that in order to do this the Commission must be satisfied that it would have been justified in ruling the petition inadmissible under Article 47 had it been in possession of the relevant facts at the time of its initial consideration of the petition.[98] As Buergenthal points out, however, this power is not to be used by the Inter-American Commission to adjudicate on the merits of a case.[99] If the Commission decides to proceed with the petition it may hold hearings in which all parties may participate.[100] This, however, is a matter to be determined at the discretion of the Commission, and the Court has decided that the Commission is not obliged to hold such hearings.[101] Article 48(1)(d) of the Convention provides that the Commission shall also carry out an on-site investigation where this is considered 'necessary and advisable'. The language used here appears to imply that such an investigation is a mandatory part of the Commission's procedure, since it does not indicate upon whom the obligation lies to determine whether an on-site investigation is or is not necessary and advisable. When the Commission's Statute[102] and, more particularly, its Regulations[103] are read in context,[104] however, it becomes clear that the question of whether an on-site investigation is deemed necessary is a matter for the Commission to determine solely at its discretion.

It is at this stage in the Commission's proceedings in individual cases that its procedures diverge depending upon whether it is dealing with cases under the Convention or the Charter. Under the Convention the Commission is mandated to attempt to secure a friendly settlement between the parties. This does not mean that the Commission may not seek a friendly settlement within the context of the Charter proceedings, but simply that there is no formal requirement for it to do so. Under the Charter therefore, the Commission proceeds to the compilation of a report which sets out the facts and conclusions relating to the case.[105] It also includes the Commission's recommendations in the case and the period of time within which they have to be implemented.[106] This report, which is usually called a resolution, is then transmitted to the Member State and petitioner.[107] At this stage the report is not published, but if the Member State does not implement the Commission's recommendations within the deadline established by the report, then the Commission may publish the report.[108] Under Article 53(4) of its Regulations, the Commission may also decide to publish its decision in its annual report. Since this report is presented to the General Assembly of the OAS, the decision is assured of notoriety and may even lead to a discussion of the case before the General Assembly. If the Member State concerned implements the Commission's recommendations before the expiration of the deadline established in the report, then it is freed from the sanction of publicity which attends publication of the report. The state may also, however, request a reconsideration of the Commission's report if during the period in which time is running it invokes new facts or legal arguments which had not previously been considered by the Commission.[109] This not only gives the respondent state the opportunity to introduce new material, but it also allows it an opportunity to secure alternative methods of settlement with the petitioner within the time period allowed. Since this is the final stage of proceedings in individual cases under the Charter, the Commission must of necessity secure a conclusion which ensures the proper protection of the rights protected by the American Declaration through the OAS Charter. A report by the Commission will generally require, therefore, that, where possible, the rights of the victim are assured and that compensation be paid either to the victim or to his or her heirs. Where this is not possible, for example in cases of disappearances, the Commission will usually instruct the respondent state to carry out and investigation of the circumstances of the disappearance, to apprehend, try and punish the persons involved and to ensure that it fulfils its obligations to ensure the protection of the rights violated in future.[110]

Friendly Settlement and Subsequent Procedures under the American Convention

Throughout the investigatory stage of its procedure under the Convention the Commission is enjoined by Article 48(1)(f) to 'place itself at the disposal of the parties concerned with a view to reaching a friendly settlement of the matter on the basis of respect for the human rights recognized in this Convention'. This it may do either on its own initiative or at the request of either of the parties.[111] In order for the Commission to be able to execute its task of conciliation the positions and allegations of the parties need to be sufficiently precise, and the subject matter of the dispute must be such as to be susceptible to the use of the friendly settlement procedure.[112] An example of such a case is *Case 11.012 (Argentina)*[113] in which the Argentine government agreed to repeal certain desacato laws criminalizing speech under which a journalist, Horacio Verbitsky, had been convicted. The government also agreed to support Verbitsky's appeal against prosecution and to argue in favour of revocation of the damages he had been ordered to pay. On a number of occasions, however, respondent governments have claimed that the Commission has been in default by not submitting a dispute to conciliation. In the *Honduran Disappearance Cases*, which involved the enforced disappearance of a number of individuals, the Commission decided not to proceed with a friendly settlement and to submit the issue directly to the Court under Article 61(2) of the Convention. Honduras objected to this, claiming that a friendly settlement was a mandatory part of the Commission's procedure. The Court, however, denied this, saying that, while Article 48(1)(f) appeared to establish conciliation as a compulsory procedure, if the provision were interpreted in the context of the American Convention then 'it is clear that the Commission should attempt such friendly settlement only when the circumstances of the controversy make that option suitable or necessary, at the Commission's *sole* discretion'.[114] The Court supported its reasoning here by reference to Article 45(2) of the Commission's Regulations. While it noted that these were not of a higher juridical status than the Convention and could not therefore override it, nonetheless they confirmed the view that the Commission enjoyed discretionary powers which must, however, not be exercised in an arbitrary fashion when deciding whether or not to attempt a friendly settlement.[115] It would appear axiomatic that the exercise of such discretionary powers will ultimately be controlled by the Court where it considers this necessary. In the *Honduran Disappearance Cases,* the Court found that the Commission was quite right not to proceed to a friendly settlement and that its decision could not be challenged.[116] As the Court observed, it is very difficult to secure a friendly settlement when someone has disappeared and the respondent state denies that it has happened.[117] In *Caballero, Delgado and Santana,*[118] however, the Court after confirming its jurisprudence on this point in the *Honduran Disappearance Cases*, held that the Commission's statement in refusing to attempt a friendly settlement that the 'nature' of the case did not render it susceptible to such an approach did not appear to be 'sufficiently well founded'.[119] The Court then went on to say that it believed 'the Commission should have carefully documented its rejection of the friendly settlement option, based on the behaviour of the state accused of the violation'.[120] Despite this, the Court took the view that the Commission's omission did not occasion irreparable harm to the respondent state which had, in any event, been free to solicit a friendly settlement of the dispute at any time during the Commission's proceedings.[121] Nevertheless, the *Caballero et al. Case* serves as a clear indication to the Commission that in exercizing its discretion in this area it should provide adequate reasons when deciding not to attempt a friendly settlement between the parties. It is also suggested that similar considerations apply to the abandonment of conciliation by the Commission under Article 45(7) of its Regulations. This latter provides that if one of the parties does not consent to the application of the friendly settlement procedure or if they do not 'evidence good will in reaching such a settlement', then the Commission may at any stage in the procedure 'declare its role as an organ of conciliation terminated'. The Commission's efforts to secure a friendly settlement may continue even though the case has been submitted to the Court. In *Maqueda v Argentina*[122] the Commission managed to broker a settlement between Argentina and the petitioner consisting of a commutation of the petitioner's sentence and a renunciation of his monetary claims against the state. The Court accepted that Article 49 of its Rules gave it the competence to discontinue its proceedings, but nonetheless reserved the power to reopen proceedings should this become necessary.

If a friendly settlement is reached between the parties, the Commission must draw up a report containing a brief statement of the facts of the case and the solution reached.[123] This report is then transmitted to the concerned parties and to the Secretary General of the OAS for publication. If a friendly settlement is not reached, or if the Commission considers the dispute to be one which is not susceptible to a friendly settlement it must within a period of one hundred and eighty days[124] draw up a report under Article 50 of the Convention. This report should set out the facts which the Commission has gathered during its investigatory phase and the conclusions which it has reached. It should be noted that not every member of the Commission need concur with its report and may append a separate opinion if he or she so wishes.[125] The report is then transmitted to the states concerned, which are not at liberty to publish it.[126] The Commission may, in transmitting the report, make such recommendations as it sees fit.[127] If after a period of three months from the date of transmittal of the Commission's report to the respondent state the matter has neither been settled nor submitted to the Court (if the State Party concerned has accepted its jurisdiction), then the Commission 'may, by an absolute majority of its members, set forth its opinion and conclusions concerning the questions submitted for its consideration'. It may also 'make pertinent recommendations' to the respondent state, prescribe the remedial measures which it must take and the period of time within which this must be done.[128] It should be noted that this is couched in permissive language and does not impose an absolute obligation upon the Commission to take this particular action. It is therefore open to the Commission to determine whether or not this is an appropriate course of action in any given case. After the expiration of the time allotted for the respondent state to take the appropriate measures to remedy the situation investigated by the Commission, the Commission may then decide, again by an absolute majority of its members, whether the state has taken adequate measures and whether to publish its report.[129] If the State Party concerned has not accepted the jurisdiction of the Court then this method of supervision by the Commission remains the most potent weapon at its disposal. Indeed, it may be argued that the 'sanction' of publicity attendant upon the decision to publish the Commission's findings is one of the most powerful devices available to it in the absence of any competence to impose legally binding decisions upon the respondent state. It may also be observed that the sanction of publicity is further intensified by the Commission's Regulations which provides that the report may also be published by its inclusion in the Commission's annual report to the General Assembly.[130] By doing this the Commission ensures that the matter is placed on the General Assembly's agenda for discussion at its annual session at which the behaviour of the recalcitrant respondent government may be discussed.

From the above description of the Commission's procedures, it can be seen that they are lengthy and somewhat convoluted. The reason given by the Court for this is that the proceedings are designed to 'seek a solution acceptable to all parties before having recourse to a judicial body'.[131] They have therefore been designed to escalate 'in stages of increasing intensity'[132] in order to encourage states to fulfil their obligation to cooperate in the resolution of cases. Like the rationale underlying the exhaustion of domestic remedies rule, the Convention's mechanisms, which are designed to facilitate early settlement of a dispute through conciliation, enables the state to rectify its alleged delinquency before the matter gets to court. As the Court has pointed out, however, the susceptibility of cases to this non-judicial form of settlement depends entirely on a number of variables including the rights affected and the willingness of the state to act.[133]

While the procedures contemplated by Articles 50 and 51 appear to be relatively straightforward, they have, in fact, been the subject of some dispute between respondent states and the Commission. In both the *Neira Alegria*[134] and the *Cayara Cases*,[135] the Commission ran into considerable difficulties concerning the timeliness of the presentation of cases to the Court.

In *Neira Alegria*, which involved the alleged disappearance of two terrorist suspects after the military had quelled a riot in a Peruvian prison where the two were being held, the Commission, after several unsuccessful attempts to obtain information from the government of Peru, declared the application admissible under Article 48 of the Convention and on 11 June 1990 informed the respondent state of this. Before the expiration of the three month period provided for in Article 51, however, a new government took office in Peru,[136] and it requested a thirty day extension which would extend the deadline for Commission action to 10 October 1990.[137] The Commission acceded to this request. In its preliminary objections to the Court, however, Peru claimed that the three month period provided for in Article 51 had been exceeded and argued, furthermore, that the Commission had lacked jurisdiction to extend the three month period at the request of a respondent state.[138] It is not surprising perhaps that the Court dismissed these claims, saying, 'in accordance with elementary principles of good faith that govern all international relations, Peru cannot invoke the expiration of a time limit that was extended at its own behest'.[139] And in relation to the Commission's alleged lack of jurisdiction to extend the time limit at the request of a respondent state, the Court ruled that 'principles of good faith dictate that one may not request something of another and then challenge the grantor's power once the request has been complied with'.[140]

A more difficult situation concerning the expiration of the three month time limit arose in the *Cayara Case* in which, after criticism from Peru, the Commission withdrew the case from the Court in order to reconsider its Article 51 report. This action raised not only questions of law about the competence of the Commission to withdraw a case from the Court, but it also raised a question of fact, namely, whether Peru had actually requested the Commission to take such action. Peru's main complaint in this case was that the Commission had not complied with Articles 34(7) and 34(8) of its Regulations by failing to transmit the observations of the applicants to the respondent state. In Peru's view this jeopardized its right of defence and it further argued:[141]

> The investigation of the CAYARA case, which has been rendered invalid, nullifies any other proceeding to which it could give rise and allows Peru to disqualify itself in the future from validating such acts with its participation ...

Peru then asked the Commission to comply with its Regulations and the Convention and decide not to take the case to the Court 'without first weighing the observations made in the present note and making the appropriate procedural corrections'.[142] Following this exchange, the Commission withdrew the case from the Court for reconsideration and informed the President of the Court that it was doing so at the request of the Peruvian government. The Court merely noted the withdrawal of the case and did not comment upon the competence of the Commission to take this action. Although the language used by Peru in its exchange with the Commission might be regarded as either contradictory or, at best, equivocal, it nonetheless maintained in its preliminary objections that it had not requested the latter to withdraw the case from the Court, but had merely pointed out the inadvisability of taking the case to the Court because of the fatal defects in procedure.[143] It also further observed that the withdrawal of the case had allowed time to continue running, so that when the Commission resubmitted its report to the Court after compliance with its Regulations and reconsideration of the substance, it was clearly out of time.[144] The three month time limit for the original report ought to have expired on 31 May 1990, but Peru requested that time should run not from the date of transmission of the report, but from the date of receipt. This was accepted by the Commission and therefore the date was extended to 5

June 1990. After withdrawal of the case, however, the resubmission of the report and application to the Court did not take place until 14 February 1992.[145]

In interpreting the time limits referred to in Article 51 of the Convention, the Court recalled 'the object and purpose of the treaty is the effective protection of human rights and that the interpretation of all its provisions must be subordinated to that object and purpose, as provided in Article 31 of the Vienna Convention on the Law of Treaties'.[146] Thus the Court found no difficulty in confirming the position that it had taken in *Neira Alegria*[147] that the time limit contemplated in Article 51(1) was not final and could be extended. It did, however, seek to place limits upon this saying:[148]

> Nevertheless, legal certainty requires that states know what norms they are to follow. The Commission cannot be permitted to apply the time limits in arbitrary fashion, particularly when these are spelled out in the Convention.

When taken with the Court's flexible approach to procedural issues, the above statement seems to imply that the Commission's actions ought to be governed by the principle of proportionality.[149] Thus, while the rigid application of time limits will not be required by the Court, nevertheless, the Commission must behave in such a way that the twin objectives of maintaining fairness between the parties and ensuring that the object and purpose of the Convention is properly pursued are not jeopardized. Indeed, as the Court observed in the final paragraph of its judgment, failure to ensure the stability and reliability of the mechanism for human rights protection 'would result in a loss of the authority and credibility that are indispensable to organs charged with administering the system for the protection of human rights'.[150]

Reviewing the three month time limit in Article 51(1)of the Convention in the light of these observations, the Court took the view that while the period was running, a number of things might disrupt it or even require the drafting of a new report or the resumption of the period *de novo*. In each case, however, it would be necessary to analyze whether the time limit had expired and what circumstances might reasonably be considered to have interrupted the period.[151] Here, the Court took the view that whatever the reasons for the withdrawal of the case by the Commission, and it did not need to pass on the validity of either of the parties' arguments in this case, the re-presentation of the application on 14 February 1992 substantially exceeded the 'timely and reasonable limits' that govern proceedings.[152] The case could not therefore be heard by the Court. The Court did make it clear, however, that such a finding did not lead to the neutralisation of the other protective mechanisms set forth in the Convention, and that the Commission, in accordance with the object and purpose of the treaty, continued to enjoy all the other powers conferred upon it by Article 51 of the Convention.[153] In practical terms this meant that the Commission could make pertinent recommendations to Peru and prescribe the appropriate remedial action which must be taken by the state.

Articles 50 and 51: One or Two Reports?

The issue of the Commission's practice in making reports under Articles 50 and 51 of the Convention was also the subject of a request for an advisory opinion under Article 64 of the Convention by Argentina and Uruguay in *Certain Attributes*. Here, the requesting states asked whether it was proper that the two reports provided for under the relevant articles should be merged into a single report, and whether the Commission might order the publication of the report to which Article 50 referred before the three month period specified in Article 51 had expired.[154] The Court noted as a preliminary matter that the provisions in question were modelled upon Articles 31 and 32 of the European Convention on Human Rights, but because there was no equivalent to the Committee of Ministers in the American Convention's framework, the Inter-American Commission was empowered to decide whether to submit a case to the Court or to deal with it itself.[155] There were thus two, possibly three, stages to the Commission's procedure under Articles 50 and 51. The first stage is, as noted above, regulated by Article 50. Here, if the Commission has been unable to achieve a friendly settlement, it draws up a report, which the Court characterised as a 'preliminary document', stating the facts and its conclusions.[156] Under Article 50(2) of the Convention the respondent state is not at liberty to publish this report, but the provision says nothing about the Commission's obligations in this matter. The Court held, however, that 'the presumption of equality of the parties' implied that neither was the Commission free to publish the report.[157] The Court did note that this position had been altered by Article 47(6) of the Commission's Regulations which provides that the report shall also be transmitted to the other parties concerned in the case, the applicant and victim, for example, who are also not free to make the report public. Here the Court ruled that the Commission's Regulation did not conform to Article 50 and that its application had altered the confidential nature of the report and the obligation not to publish it.[158] This observation by the Court clearly raises some difficulties. In the interests of the proper operation of the Convention's protective function, it would seem to be both appropriate and necessary that the other parties to a case have access to the Commission's report under Article 50. On the other hand, to maintain the confidence of the States Parties in the operation of the Convention's protective machinery, a degree of confidentiality is clearly necessary. It is submitted therefore that it is the Commission's Regulations which reflect the preferred position, as this clearly meets the needs of both parties for appropriate and timely information and the maintenance of confidentiality. It must be admitted, however, that a change to the Commission's Regulations is likely to be easier to achieve than an amendment to the Convention which would require the consent of two-thirds of the States Parties.[159]

The matter of confidentiality also arose in the *Gangaram Panday Case* where Suriname complained that the Commission had referred to information in the case in its *1990-91 Annual Report* to the OAS, and had thus imposed a 'double sanction' on the state which was not contemplated by the Convention.[160] The Court noted here that what Suriname was complaining about was a simple reference to the existing case in its report; the Commission had certainly not reproduced its Article 50 report. The Court had no difficulty in holding that this did not amount to an infraction either of the Convention or the Commission's Regulations.[161]

The second stage report identified by the Court in *Certain Attributes* is that envisaged by Article 51. It will be recalled that under this provision the Commission has three months in which to decide whether to submit a case to the Court or to continue to examine the matter itself. Here the Court noted that the decision was not discretionary but must 'be based upon the alternative that would be most favorable for the protection of the rights established in the Convention'.[162]

This position is different to that adopted by the Court in its advisory opinion in *Compulsory Membership*.[163] Here the Court took the view that the Commission did have a discretion to refer or to decline to refer a case to the Court, but that this should be informed by whether or not the case raised controversial and weighty issues.[164] It is submitted, however, that the Court's approach in *Certain Attributes* has much to commend it since it rightly places the emphasis upon the protective function of the Convention rather than the potentially controversial nature of the question or issue involved.[165]

If the Commission decides not to submit the case to the Court within the three month period or if, alternatively, the three month period has expired without the Commission having correctly invoked the appropriate procedures, as in the *Cayara Case*, then the Commission is empowered to prepare its second or final report under Article 51 of the Convention. This report must contain the opinions, conclusions and recommendations of the Commission;

it must also stipulate what remedial action should be taken and the period in which this is to be effected.

The Court noted that there is also possibly a third stage in proceedings. If after the production of the second report, the respondent state has failed to comply with its obligations, the Commission is at liberty to publish this report.[166] Here again, the decision whether or not to publish 'must also be based upon the alternative most favorable for the protection of human rights'.[167] The Court thus concluded that there were two reports which were governed separately by Articles 50 and 51 of the Convention. Furthermore, while the report contemplated by Article 50 was to remain confidential throughout the proceedings, this was not the case with the Article 51 report which might be published, depending upon the behaviour of the respondent state. This being so, it was not permissible to merge the two reports into one, even though the contents of those documents might be similar.[168] It would seem therefore that, even where the second report essentially reproduces the conclusions, recommendations and remedial action to be taken by the respondent state which are contained in the first report, the second report must nevertheless be produced in full as a separate document. The Court might have referred here to the different functions of the two reports as a determining factor in denying that they could be joined, but failed to do so.

Referrals to the Court by the Commission

As indicated above, if the Commission is unable to achieve a friendly settlement between a respondent state and an individual who alleges that his or her rights under the Convention have been violated, then either the Commission or the respondent state may, under Article 51, submit the case to the contentious jurisdiction of the Court.[169] Since aggrieved individuals have no standing before the Court they are excluded from this process. It will be evident that a respondent state concerned may be reluctant to submit itself voluntarily to the Court's contentious jurisdiction given the implications which this might hold for it,[170] and this suggests therefore that it will be the Commission which will, as a rule, decide which cases should be remitted to the Court and which should not. There is, however, no indication in the Convention itself as to which cases should be referred to the Court by the Commission. The Court has, however, established the criteria which the Commission should employ in deciding which cases should be submitted to it for determination. In *Compulsory Membership*, the Court was requested by Costa Rica to rule upon whether its laws requiring journalists and reporters to be members of an organization prescribed by law for the practice of journalism were consistent with Articles 13 and 29 of the Convention. Although the question was remitted to the Court under its advisory jurisdiction, the case had its origin in an individual application to the Commission by one Stephen Schmidt, a US citizen who had followed the practice of journalism within Costa Rica without being a member of the *Colegio de Periodistas* as required by Costa Rican law. Costa Rica had, in fact, won the case before the Commission, but the Commission had chosen not to submit the case to the Court's contentious jurisdiction.[171] Costa Rica, however, decided to apply to the Court for an advisory opinion on the issue. In this it attracted the praise of the Court which considered that Costa Rica by referring to the Court a case which it had won had enhanced its moral stature.[172] While the Court noted that Costa Rica could have referred the issue to the contentious jurisdiction of the Court following the Commission's procedures, it did not speculate upon the state's reasons for not doing so. Nonetheless, the Court ruled that although the Convention did not specify the circumstances under which the Commission ought to refer a case to the contentious jurisdiction of the Court, there were certain cases which should be referred to the Court even though there was no explicit legal obligation to do so. In the Court's view the *Schmidt Case* fell clearly into this category. It said:[173]

> The controversial legal issues it raised had not been previously considered by the Court, the domestic proceedings in Costa Rica produced conflicting judicial decisions, the Commission itself was not able to arrive at a unanimous decision on the relevant legal issues, and this subject is a matter of special importance to the hemisphere because several states have adopted laws similar to those of Costa Rica.

Two major criteria governing when the Commission should remit a case to the Court might be extracted from this statement. First, the case should be one of a controversial nature. As the advisory opinion suggests, this might be evidenced by the lack of agreement on the issues raised both in the national courts and in the Commission itself.[174] Second, the matter must be one of importance to the hemisphere. In the instant case evidence of this was provided by the fact that a number of states in the Americas possessed laws similar to those of Costa Rica. Nothing was said in this case about the need to further the protection of the rights contained in the Convention, but this omission was rectified in *Certain Attributes* which arguably gives a sounder indication of the circumstances in which the Commission ought to refer a matter to the Court.

It will be recalled that the advisory opinion in *Certain Attributes* arose from a request by Argentina and Uruguay concerning, *inter alia*, whether Articles 50 and 51 of the Convention required the production of one or two reports. In deciding that two reports were required, the Court also observed that the Commission under Article 51 was obliged to consider whether or not to submit the case concerned to the Court.[175] Here it made no reference to its opinion in *Compulsory Membership,* but held:[176]

> This decision [i.e. whether to submit a case to the Court] is not discretionary, but rather must be based upon the alternative that would be most favorable for the protection of the rights established in the Convention.

This statement clearly marks a retreat from the Court's position in *Compulsory Membership* where it had indicated that there was no legal obligation upon the Commission to submit the case to the Court, thus implying that the decision on this matter was discretionary but governed by the criteria which the Court itself had outlined in its opinion. In *Certain Attributes,* however, the Court took the view that the decision by the Commission to submit or not to submit a case to it was *not* discretionary, but depended upon what would be most favorable for the protection of the rights established in the Convention. This paradox does not, unfortunately, bear scrutiny, for it still remains within the purview of the Commission alone to determine which course of action would best protect the Convention rights. Since the Court has no power to review the Commission's decision in this area, it would still seem that the Commission may still exercise a discretion in deciding whether to submit a case to the Court. Given the competence of the Court to interpret and apply the Convention under Article 62(3), however, it seems that the criteria established by the Court in *Certain Attributes* are authoritative and should be followed by the Commission in the exercise of its functions under Article 51. While it might be considered desirable to have some form of review by the Court of a Commission decision not to submit an individual case to it, this would inevitably require a revision of the Convention which might prove difficult to achieve.[177] It should be remembered, however, that if the Commission decides not to remit a case to the Court, it still retains its competence to make its own rulings.

Waiver of the Commission's Procedures

While it is apparent that a State Party may waive the requirement of exhaustion of domestic remedies in Article 46 of the Convention, the wider question of whether a respondent state may, at its description, waive the Commission's procedures in general. This issue arose directly in *Viviana Gallardo* which was the first case to be presented to the Court. In this case, Gallardo, a Costa Rican citizen, had been shot and killed whilst she was being held as a terrorist suspect in a prison cell. This act had been perpetrated by a member of the Costa Rican Civil Guard who had been assigned to guard her.[178] A number of Gallardo's fellow prisoners were also wounded.[179] The government of Costa Rica indicated that it wished to avoid lengthy proceedings before the Commission and applied directly to the Court requesting it to decide whether the acts of the guard constituted violations of Articles 4 and 5 of the Convention.[180] In so doing the government specifically requested that the Court waive the requirement of exhaustion of local remedies and that the procedures before the Commission should also be waived in order to allow the Court to 'consider the case immediately and without any procedural obstacle'.[181] The main argument adduced by the respondent government was that since the Commission's primary mandate was to seek a friendly settlement under the procedure contained in Article 48(1)(f), it had no juridical interest in this case because the government was only asking the Court to decide whether or not there had been a violation of the American Convention.[182]

The waiver of Article 61(2) which Costa Rica sought to enter involved two separate but related matters: first, the waiver of the exhaustion of domestic remedies, and second, the waiver of the Commission's procedures.[183] As indicated above, the Court had little difficulty in deciding that the respondent state was competent, in accordance with general international law, to waive the procedural requirement of exhaustion of domestic remedies.[184] As regards the waiver of the Commission's procedure in general, however, it held that this could not be effected simply at the request of the state.[185] This latter finding was, however, qualified, for the Court recognized that in certain cases the procedure might be waived if it were demonstrable that the waiver did not impair the function which the Convention assigned to the Commission.[186] This would seem to suggest, for example, that certain inter-state communications might be taken directly to the Court if it could be shown that the institutional integrity of the Convention system was also unlikely to be affected.[187]

Given the importance of the *Gallardo Case* in so far as it relates to the proper conduct of the Commission's procedures and the Commission's place within the Convention structure, it is appropriate to examine the decision in some detail. At the outset the Court noted that 'as an abstract proposition' the case fulfilled the requirements for the exercise of jurisdiction in Article 61(1), and that the alleged violations of the Convention, were within that jurisdiction *ratione materiae*.[188] This, however, raised the question of whether fulfilment of the procedural requirements established by the Convention was an indispensable prerequisite for the Court to be seised of the substantive issues.[189] In considering this, the Court expressly articulated the policy issues underpinning its decision. These were threefold: first, that the interests of the victims in enjoying the rights under the American Convention needed to be assured and protected; second, that the institutional integrity of the Convention system itself required safeguarding; and third, that Costa Rica had a legitimate concern that the case be decided by speedy judicial processes. From the Court's subsequent reasoning, it is clear that it gave considerably more weight to the second and third policy considerations, which it indicated had to be balanced one against the other.[190]

In approaching the question of interpretation of the relevant provisions of the Convention, the Court employed traditional techniques of treaty interpretation.[191] Thus, while there are a number of references in *Gallardo* to the 'very clear language' of Article 61(2) of the American Convention,[192] the Court also expressed its recognition of the object and purpose of the Convention which it stated to be 'to guarantee the individual's basic human dignity by means of the system established in the Convention'[193] and 'the protection of the basic rights of human beings'.[194] Taken together with the need to protect the integrity of the Convention system, the Court concluded that this required that 'the Convention be interpreted in favor of the individual who is the object of international protection, as long as such an interpretation does not result in the modification of the system'.[195] The Court further observed that, as individuals did not have standing before the Court, both the Court and the Commission had an obligation 'to preserve all the remedies that the Convention affords victims of violations of human rights so that they are accorded the protection to which they are entitled under the Convention'.[196]

It is therefore apparent that in *Gallardo* the integrity of the Convention system and the place of the Commission within that system was of supreme importance to the Court. The primary question in this context was whether the role assigned to the Commission was created for the sole benefit of states. If it were, then it would be waivable by them; if it were not, then states would be obliged to follow the procedures established by the Convention.[197] Here the Court took the view that the Commission was required to undertake certain preparatory or preliminary tasks in advance of the Court exercising its task of adjudication. The Commission thus performed a role similar to that of the *Ministerio Publico* (State Attorney) in many American states.[198] Its functions were to investigate allegations of human rights violations and to carry out the very important role of conciliation between the parties involved. This the Court described as 'the fundamental aspect of [the Commission's] role in the system, since it was the channel which the American Convention gave the individual *qua* individual the opportunity to activate the system for human rights protection'.[199] While the Court noted that it possessed the power to conduct investigations and make inquiries itself,[200] a power which it employed extensively in the *Honduran Disappearance Cases*,[201] it nonetheless observed that the Convention entrusted the Commission with the initial phase of the investigation into the allegations made against respondent states.[202] The Court also observed that it was unable to discharge the important function of promoting friendly settlement within a broad conciliatory framework. That function was assigned to the Commission precisely because it was not a judicial body. From this the Court concluded that 'any solution that denies access to these procedures before the Commission deprives individuals, especially victims, of the important right to negotiate and accept freely a friendly settlement arrived at with the help of the Commission and "on the basis of the human rights recognized in [the] Convention." (Article 48(1)(f))'.[203] It further concluded that 'the aforementioned structures have not been concluded for the sole benefit of the states, but also in order to allow for the exercise of important individual rights, especially those of the victims'.[204] Since, therefore, the system had not been created for the sole benefit of states but also for the benefit of individuals, states were not competent to waive those procedures, save, perhaps, in inter-state applications in which individual rights were not threatened.[205]

Some general observations are required about the Court's assumptions in reaching this conclusion. The first is that the Court appears to assume that it possesses a general investigatory power. Such a power is not evident on the face of the Convention or in the Statute or Rules of the Court. The general jurisdiction which is given to the Court by the Convention is to interpret and apply that instrument.[206] The Court's investigatory power would thus seem to derive from the general judicial function assigned to all courts of first instance to determine the facts in cases before them. This, however, is to assume that the Inter-American Court is analogous to a Court of first instance and not an appellate court. Since the Commission does not occupy the position of an adjudicatory agency when it decides to submit a case to the contentious jurisdiction of the Court, it would seem that the Inter-American Court is indeed a court of first instance with extensive fact determining powers. Support for this view might be derived from the very broad powers which the Court possesses to call and examine witnesses and to receive a wide variety of new evidence.

The second point which should perhaps be made is that the jurisprudence in the *Gallardo Case* should not be taken in isolation, and it is appropriate to recall here the observations made by the Court on the function of the Commission in the contentious procedure in the *Honduran Disappearance Cases*. It will be recalled that in those cases the Court took the view that the procedure established by the Convention was designed to designed to 'seek a solution acceptable to all parties before having recourse to a judicial body'[207] and as a consequence they have been designed to escalate 'in stages of increasing intensity'[208] in order to encourage states to fulfil their obligation to cooperate in the resolution of cases. This approach reinforces the position taken in *Gallardo* that the victim has a direct interest in seeing Convention's procedures followed since this allows her or him the opportunity of securing a satisfactory remedy. It also reinforces the notion that the state has a constructive role to play in the resolution of any alleged violation and is not automatically regarded as a criminal in the dock.[209] This observation is particularly important when considering the criticisms levelled at the Convention procedure by Judge Rodolfo E. Piza Escalante of Costa Rica.

While Judge Piza agreed with the decision of the Court[210] to remit the *Gallardo Case* to the Commission because he recognized that the procedures established by the Convention were an indispensable prerequisite to seise the Court of a case, he nevertheless took the opportunity to argue that these procedures were themselves an impediment to the effective protection of human rights. In his view it was possible, 'even imperative', to give individual applicants the status of a party before the Court.[211] Furthermore, he took the view that, while the individual was the active party in a case, the Commission was the passive party and performed a role more in the nature of the *Ministerio Publico* or an *amicus curiae*. Its role was therefore *sui generis* and like that of 'an auxiliary to the judiciary' since it was neither accuser nor accused in the proceedings.[212] He considered the Commission's conciliatory function to be 'tilted' in favour of the state, and that there was 'nothing that the Commission might be able to do, within then the procedures set forth in the Convention, in the interest of an effective protection of human rights, the Court itself cannot do during the proceedings; and do it even better ...'.[213] Judge Piza concluded:

> If I share the reasoning of the decision that, in the instant case, the waiver of the Government of the procedures before the Commission is not admissible, I do not do so because I consider it essential in order to have the best protection of

human rights, but rather I have come to the conclusion that unfortunately the system of the Convention appears to make it impossible since the American states in drafting it did not wish to accept the establishment of a swift and effective jurisdictional system but rather they hobbled it by interposing the impediment of the Commission, by establishing a veritable obstacle course that is almost insurmountable, on the long and arduous road that the basic rights of the individual are forced to travel.[214]

It is clear that Judge Piza's statement evinces a strong frustration with the Commission's procedures. This was induced not, perhaps, by the existence of the procedures *per se,* but rather as a consequence of the failure of the Commission to place one contentious case before the Court in the period since the Convention's entry into force. This, indeed, was frustration which was remarked upon by Judge Maximo Cisneros in *Compulsory Membership* in which he observed in a final note to the opinion:

> Now, whereas in signing this Advisory opinion I am performing my last act as a judge of the Inter-American Court of Human Rights, I wish to say that the "love" that we have put into our work has not been sufficient to avoid the sense of frustration that I feel in leaving the Court before it has had the opportunity to hear a single case of a violation of human rights, in spite of the sad reality of America in this field.

Whether the elimination of the Commission's procedures would enhance the protective and remedial functions of the Convention is debatable. One commentator, for example, considers it 'anomalous'[215] to deny individuals the right to refer a case to the Court 'since the Court's jurisdiction was created to protect individual's human rights'.[216] While this view undoubtedly reflects that of Judge Piza, there exist good legal and policy reasons for limiting direct individual access to the Court in the present state of development of the inter-American human rights system. The first major consideration is that of the need to respect state sovereignty. A number of states in the Western Hemisphere are unaccustomed to international adjudication on matters directly affecting their domestic jurisdiction. Permitting direct individual access to a judicial institution without the opportunity for the state to settle the dispute by way of a friendly settlement brokered by the Commission would be unacceptable to certain states which would see this as an unacceptable erosion of their domestic jurisdiction. Although this might arguably be paying too much deference to the power of the state, it should not be forgotten that the establishment of mechanisms permitting individuals direct access to an international institution with adjudicative powers cannot be achieved without the consent of the states affected. Indeed, it is evident from the preliminary objections cases discussed above that the Court is concerned to maintain a balanced and even handed approach in the management of the petition system in order to engender state respect for the general system for the protection of human rights in the Americas.[217] Second, the Commission acts as a filter to determine whether or not cases are properly founded. While it is always open to the Court to strike out a case that is an abuse of process, it is perhaps more convenient for the Commission to undertake such a task. It might be argued that the inter-American human rights system might traverse the same road as its European counterpart and transfer to the Court the competence to deal with individual applications. Given the current stage of development of the former, however, this is perhaps an unrealistic proposition. The Council of Europe's decision to eliminate the European Commission and its procedures resulted more from the inability of the system to cope with the workload engendered by its own success rather than dissatisfaction with the procedure *per se*. Although the use of the contentious jurisdiction of the Inter-American Court has shown a steady rather than dramatic increase in recent years, it cannot be said that it yet warrants a revision of the system, agreement to which might, in any event, be difficult if not impossible to achieve. It should also be remarked that the Inter-American Commission plays a considerably wider and more interventionist role in the management of the system than does its European analogue. The Inter-American Commission with its competence to conduct observations *in loco* and on-site investigations, together with its own individual petition system under the Charter, does not make comparison with the European Commission particularly appropriate. Furthermore, it is arguable that the Inter-American Commission has over a period of some thirty years developed a *modus operandi* with which the states of the region are familiar and willing to accept. It would necessarily take a considerable amount of time for a restructured Court permitting direct individual access to build up a similar stock of acceptance and respect. This is not to say that the current Convention structure and institutional procedures are not in need of reform. The most obvious considerations are perhaps the need for the Commission to remit more of its cases to the Court and to bring them before it with considerably more expedition than is currently the case. This is most likely to be achieved, however, by improving the Commission's procedures rather than facilitating direct individual access to a reformed Court.

It may be argued, however, that the Court missed an opportunity in *Gallardo* to take a small step in potentially expediting the procedure in contentious cases. In this case, as we saw above,[218] Costa Rica wished to waive the admissibility requirements set down in the Convention in order to allow it to take a case directly to the Court. Its motive for so doing was to secure a speedy judicial decision in the case in question. The Court, it will be recalled, refused to permit direct access because, *inter alia,* failure to comply with the conditions governing procedures before the Commission might damage the institutional integrity of the Convention system, and it would interfere with the interest of the victims in utilizing all the available Convention procedures to ensure the effective protection of their rights. The disagreement of Judge Piza with these arguments has already been referred to above, but it is once again worth pointing to his view that the Commission's procedures are an impediment to effective protection of human rights. While it might not be desirable to extend direct access to the Court by individuals, there would seem to be no pressing objection to allowing a state to waive the Commission's procedures and take an individual case directly to the Court with the *consent* of a potential petitioner. It is the issue of consent to which the Court did not allude in the *Gallardo* case which might prove decisive in such circumstances. It would probably be the case, however, that a state which wished to waive the Convention's procedural requirements is also likely to be a state which would be most inclined to redress the violation of individual rights under its own domestic law. The more likely scenario in contentious cases is that states may wish to use the potentially lengthy and cumbersome procedures of the Commission to delay or even frustrate an individual's access to the Court. Indeed, an examination of the preliminary objections cases placed before the Court discloses a number of arguments deployed by States Parties which might be viewed as both frivolous and vexatious.[219] The fact that the Court has listened to such arguments and considered them carefully in its judgments indicates that it is particularly concerned to convey the message to States Parties that it will be scrupulously fair in its assessment of the issues presented to it. Indeed, as the *Cayara Case* amply demonstrates, the Court is particularly solicitous to ensure that the authority and credibility of the Convention's organs and their role in the protection of human rights in the Americas is both maintained and enhanced.[220] Unfortunately, the desire to enhance the reputation of the Convention's organs is perhaps being achieved at the cost of retarding the delivery of justice to individual complainants.

In the *Honduran Disappearance Cases* for example, petitions were lodged with the Commission on behalf of the victims in 1981, but it was not until 1988 that the Court's judgment on the merits of these cases were delivered. A further delay of two years was occasioned by the failure of the Commission to plead precise grounds for the calculation of compensatory damages.[221] The judgment in that case was delivered in 1990. Much of the blame for the excessive delay in the case is attributable to Honduras, whose procrastination in all aspects of the Commission's procedure was excessive. Initially, Honduras requested the Commission to consider its first resolution on the case because domestic remedies were allegedly still pending, and subsequently requested two extensions for the delivery of information to the Commission. Neither the Convention nor the Commission's rules of procedure provide for this possibility. The Court, however, found that the states interests were not affected by the extensions because it had already enjoyed considerable latitude by the Commission in responding to its demands and because it had seriously affected the petitioner's right to expeditious process.[222]

As indicated above, it may be arguable that the tardiness of proceedings under the Convention may, in itself, be a denial of justice to individual petitioners. The legitimate expectations of persons who petition the Commission might be that they can expect prompt and effective consideration of their case. Indeed, Article 25 of the Convention provides that individuals should be guaranteed 'the right to a simple and prompt recourse, or any other effective recourse, before a competent court or tribunal for protection against acts that violate one's fundamental rights'. It can hardly be said that the management of the Convention's procedures by the Commission and the Court achieve this. States may, however, take a contrary view. It will undoubtedly be their opinion that denunciations by individuals should be thoroughly investigated by the Commission before the issue is submitted to the Court for a binding decision under its contentious jurisdiction. Again, the main concern here is balancing the dignity and sovereignty of the state against the need for speedy and efficacious redress for individuals whose rights may have been violated. Since, however, states are in the position to delay or retard the process as they are likely to be in possession of most of the relevant information affecting the case, it is perhaps important that the Commission exercises more direct control over its use of extensions. One commentator suggests[223] that the Court could exercise control over the Commission's discretion in this area, but this would only increase the general length of the proceedings if the Court had to hear arguments on this matter also.

Notes

1   There may, however, be some opportunity for this under the Commission's Regulations. See infra, pp.177-83.
2   For discussion of this provision see infra, p. 157.
3   *Gallardo*, para. 22.
4   Article 45(1) ACHR. Cf Article 24 European Convention on Human Rights (hereafter 'ECHR') and the optional procedure under Article 40 of the United Nations International Covenant on Civil and Political Rights (hereafter 'ICCPR').
5   Article 45(4) ACHR.
6   For a comparison of the American and European Conventions see A.G. Mower, *Regional Human Rights: A Comparative Study of the West European and Inter-American Systems* (New York: Greenwood Press, 1991); T. Buergenthal, 'The American and European Conventions on Human Rights: Similarities and Differences' (1980) 30 *American University Law Review* 155; J. Frowein, 'The European and American Conventions on Human Rights: A Comparison' (1980) 1 HRLJ 44.
7   On inter-state applications under the ECHR see D.J. Harris, M. O'Boyle and C. Warbrick, *Law of the European Convention on Human Rights* (London: Butterworth, 1995), pp. 626-30. (Hereafter '*Law of the European Convention*'.) See also P. van Dijk and G.J.H. van Hoof, *Theory and Practice of the European Convention on Human Rights* (Deventer: Kluwer, 2nd edn, 1991), pp. 33-36. (Hereafter '*Theory and Practice*'.)
8   See, for example, *Greece v United Kingdom* 2 YB 182 and 186; *Ireland v United Kingdom* 21 *YB* 602, Eur. Ct. H. R., Sr. A, No. 21; *Austria v Italy* 6 YB 742; *Cyprus v Turkey* 18 *YB* 82 and 20 *YB* 98. For comment see Davidson, *Human Rights*, pp. 103-5.
9   See Buergenthal, *Inter-American System*, pp. 454-5.
10   See Article 25 of the European Convention on Human Rights and Articles 1 and 2 of the Optional Protocol to the International Covenant on Civil and Political Rights. The jurisprudence of the European Court of Human Rights and the United Nations Human Rights Committee have enlarged upon the concept of 'victim' within their respective instruments. On the meaning of 'victim' within the European Convention see Harris, O'Boyle and Warbrick, *Law of the European Convention*, pp. 630-8; van Dijk and van Hoof, *Theory and Practice*, pp. 39-49 and Beddard, *Human Rights in Europe*, pp. 43-9. On the meaning of 'victim' within the Optional Protocol see McGoldrick, *Human Rights Committee*, pp. 168-77. See also Davidson, *Human Rights*, pp. 80-2 and pp. 105-6 for an overview of both systems.
11   See supra, p. 157.
12   See *Case 9213 (USA)* infra in which the US based Disabled Peoples' International lodged a claim against the US for alleged violations of human rights in Grenada.
13   Buergenthal, 'The Inter-American Court of Human Rights' (1982) 76 AJIL 231 at 237.
14   The apparent rigour of the ECHR and ICCPR have, however, been mitigated to some degree by the jurisprudence of their various interpretative agencies which permit applications of an abstract nature under certain conditions. See McGoldrick, *Human Rights Committee*, pp. 172-7 and van Dijk and van Hoof, *Theory and Practice*, pp. 39-48.
15   The relevant provisions of the universal and regional instruments which allow a right of individual application are Article 5(2)(b) ICCPR; Article 26 ECHR and Article 56(5) OAU Charter. For a review of these instruments see M. Tardu, *International Petition Procedures*; Trindade, *The Application of the Local Remedies Rule* (1984); C. Trindade, 'Coexistence and Coordination of Mechanisms of International protection of Human Rights' (1987 - II)

202 *Hague Recueil.*
16 See the *Interhandel Case (Preliminary Objections)*, ICJ Rep (1959) 27.
17 At para. 26. See also *Velasquez Rodriguez Case*, Judgment of July 29, 1988, Series C, No. 4, para. 61; *Godinez Cruz, Fairen Garbi and Solis Corrales Case*, Judgment of March 15, 1989, Series C, No. 5, para. 85, *Gangaram Panday (Preliminary Objections)*, Judgment of 3 January 1993, Series C, No. 12, para 38. and *Case 10.205 v Dominican Republic*, Resolution 15/89 of April 14, 1989, Inter-American Commission on Human Rights, *Annual Report 1988-89*, 67.
18 *Gallardo*, para. 26. See also *Velasquez Rodriguez Case (Preliminary Objections)*, Judgment of June 26, 1987, para. 88; *Fairen Garbi and Solis Corrales Case (Preliminary Objections)*, Judgment of June 26, 1987, para. 87; *Godinez Cruz Case (Preliminary Objections)*, Judgment of June 26, 1987, para. 90; *Gangaram Panday (Preliminary Objections)*, para. 39.
19 *Velasquez Rodriguez Case (Preliminary Objections)*, para. 88; *Fairen Garbi and Solis Corrales Case (Preliminary Objections)*, para. 87; *Godinez Cruz Case (Preliminary Objections)*, para. 90.
20 *Velasquez Rodriguez Case (Preliminary Objections)*, para. 93; *Fairen Garbi and Solis Corrales Case (Preliminary Objections)*, para. 92; *Godinez Cruz Case (Preliminary Objections)*, para. 95.
21 *Velasquez Rodriguez Case (Preliminary Objections)*, para. 93; *Fairen Garbi and Solis Corrales Case (Preliminary Objections)*, para. 92; *Godinez Cruz Case (Preliminary Objections)*, para. 95.
22 *Gangaram Panday (Preliminary Objections)*, para. 39.
23 See J.G. Merrills, *The Development of International Law by the European Court of Human Rights* (Manchester: Manchester University Press, 2nd edn, 1993), pp. 192-8.
24 *Velasquez Rodriguez Case (Preliminary Objections)*, para. 87; *Fairen Garbi and Solis Corrales Case (Preliminary Objections)*, para. 86; *Godinez Cruz Case (Preliminary Objections)*, para. 89. Here, the Court observed that it did not need to decide whether the grounds listed in Article 46(2) absolving individuals from exhausting domestic remedies was 'exhaustive or merely illustrative' since the reference to 'generally recognized principles of international law' was sufficient to overcome most of the difficulties associated with the identification of the content of the domestic remedies rule.
25 *Robert E Brown Claim* (1923) *RIAA vi, 120.*
26 Inter-American Commission on Human Rights, *Annual Report 1986-87*, 184.
27 22 March 1972, Inter-American Commission on Human Rights, *Annual Report 1973*, 115.
28 *Case 9706 v Mexico*, Res. No. 24/88 of March 23, 1988, Inter-American Commission on Human Rights, *Annual Report 1987-88*, 163 in which the petitioner had failed to exhaust the remedy of *amparo*. See also *Case 10.208 v Dominican Republic*, Res. No. 15/89 of April 14, 1989, Inter-American Commission on Human Rights, *Annual Report 1988-89*, 67 in which the complainant was still entitled to appeal against a conviction entered during a trial *in absentia*.
29 *Case 2966 v Honduras*, Resolution 27/81 of March 9, 1982. Reproduced in *Buergenthal and Norris*, vol. 3, booklet 21, 131.
30 *Case 1967 v Uruguay*, August 5 and 16, 1975, Inter-American Commission on Human Rights, *Annual Report 1977*, 55; *Case 9726 v Panama*, Res. No. 25/87 of September 23, 1987, Inter-American Commission on Human Rights, *Annual Report 1987-88*, 174.
31 22 December 1970, Inter-American Commission on Human Rights, *Work Accomplished*

by the Inter-American Commission on Human Rights in its Twenty Sixth Session, 9.

[32]   9 June 1970, *Work Accomplished by the Inter-American Commission on Human Rights in its Twenty Sixth Session, 9.*

[33]   7 September 1972, *Work Accomplished by the Inter-American Commission on Human Rights in its Thirty First Session, 44.*

[34]   See *Case 2175 v Jamaica*, Res. No. 25/82 of March 9, 1982, OEA/Ser.L/V/II.55, doc. 40, 9 de marzo, 1982, reproduced in *Buergenthal and Norris, Binder 3, Booklet 21*, p. 125; *Cases 3101 and 3103 v Jamaica*, Res. Nos. 9 and 11/81 of March 6, 1981, OEA/Ser.L/V/II.52. doc. 19, 6 March 1981, reproduced in *Buergenthal and Norris, Binder 3, Booklet 21*, p. 43; *Cases 3115 and 3102 v Jamaica*, Res. Nos. 24 and 25/81 of June 25, 1981, Inter-American Commission on Human Rights, *Annual Report 1981-82*, 89; *Case 7512 v Jamaica*, Res. No. 26/82 of March 9, 1982, OEA/Ser.L/V/II.55, doc. 41, 9 marzo 1982, reproduced in *Buergenthal and Norris, Binder 3, Booklet 21*, p. 164.

[35]   15 August 1970, *Work Accomplished by the Inter-American Commission on Human Rights in its 25th Session*, 32, reproduced in *Buergenthal and Norris, Binder 3, Booklet 19*, p. 37.

[36]   Article 42 of the current Regulations.

[37]   *Case 2563 v Haiti*, Res. no. 43/82 of March 9, 1982, OEA/Ser.L/V/II.55, doc., 67, 9 marzo 1982, reproduced in *Buergenthal and Norris, Binder 3, Booklet 21*, p. 122; *Case 3519 v Haiti*, Res. No. 46/82 of March 9, 1982, ibid., p. 137; *Case 7824 v Bolivia*, Res. No.33/82 of March 8, 1982, ibid., p. 187.

[38]   22 July - 2 August, 1974, Inter-American Commission on Human Rights, *Annual Report 1975*, 125.

[39]   See, for example, *Case 10.235 v Colombia*, Report No. 1/92 of February 6, 1992, Inter-American Commission on Human Rights, *Annual Report 1991-92*, 41 in which the Commission held that 'in the instant case it is obvious that the petitioners have been unable to secure effective protection from the internal jurisdictional organs which, in spite of the irrefutable evidence available to them, cleared the responsible police officers of all charges by ordering that the case be dismissed; therefore, whether or not the remedies under domestic law have been exhausted, the Government of Colombia cannot invoke those remedies to argue in favor of suspending the Commission's processing of this case ...'.

[40]   *Case 1684 v Brazil, Buergenthal and Norris, Binder 3, Booklet 19*, 22.

[41]   Inter-American Commission on Human Rights, *Annual Report 1973*, p. 115.

[42]   Ibid.

[43]   Res. No. 16/84 of October 4, 1984, Inter-American Commission on Human Rights, *Annual Report 1984-85*, 84.

[44]   Res. No. 32/83 of October 4, 1984, reproduced in *Buergenthal and Norris, Binder 3, Booklet 21.1*, p. 99.

[45]   *Case 7920 v Honduras*, Res. No. 22/86 of April 18, 1986, Inter-American Commission on Human Rights, *Annual Report 1985-86*, 40.

[46]   Res. No. 17/87 of June 30, 1987, Inter-American Commission on Human Rights, *Annual Report 1986-87*, 114.

[47]   Report No. 1/92 of February 6, 1992, Inter-American Commission on Human Rights, *Annual Report 1991-92*, 27.

[48]   Resolution 2/84 of May 17, 1984, Inter-American Commission on Human Rights, *Annual Report 1983-84*, 127.

[49]   See infra, pp.165-6.

[50]   *Velasquez Rodriguez (Preliminary Objections)*, para. 88; *Fairen Garbi and Solis Corrales (Preliminary Objections)*, para. 87; *Godinez Cruz (Preliminary Objections)*, para. 90. Cited

with approval in *Exceptions to the Exhaustion of Domestic Remedies*, para. 41.

51 *Velasquez Rodriguez*, para. 60; *Fairen Garbi and Solis Corrales*, para. 84; *Godinez Cruz*, para. 63. Cited with approval by the Court in *Exceptions to the Exhaustion of Domestic Remedies*, para. 44.

52 *Velasquez Rodriguez*, para. 64; *Fairen Garbi and Solis Corrales*, para. 88; *Godinez Cruz*, para. 67. Cited with approval by the Court in *Exceptions to the Exhaustion of Domestic Remedies*, para. 36.

53 *Velasquez Rodriguez*, para. 66; *Fairen Garbi and Solis Corrales*, para. 91; *Godinez Cruz*, para. 69. Cited with approval by the Court in *Exceptions to the Exhaustion of Domestic Remedies*, para. 36.

54 *Velasquez Rodriguez*, para. 68; *Fairen Garbi and Solis Corrales*, para. 71; *Godinez Cruz*, para. 63.

55 On the doctrine of 'administrative practice' in the European Human Rights system see van Dijk and van Hoof, pp. 39-40 and 82-5.

56 *Velasquez Rodriguez*, para. 80; *Fairen Garbi and Solis Corrales*, para. 102.

57 Advisory Opinion OC-11/90 of August 10, 1990.

58 Ibid., para. 20.

59 Ibid., para. 21.

60 Ibid., para. 22.

61 Ibid.

62 Ibid., para. 23. See also *Velasquez Rodriguez*, para. 166 and *Godinez Cruz*, para. 175.

63 Article 8(2).

64 Article 8(1).

65 *Exceptions to the Exhaustion of Domestic Remedies*, para. 25.

66 Ibid., para. 26.

67 Ibid., para. 30.

68 Ibid., para. 34.

69 Ibid., para. 36.

70 Ibid., para. 38.

71 Ibid., para. 39.

72 Order of 29 June 1992 - Article 54(3) American Convention on Human Rights (1992) 13 *HRLJ 407*.

73 Ibid., para. 18.

74 Ibid., para. 22.

75 Ibid., para. 28.

76 Ibid., para. 29.

77 Ibid., para. 30.

78 See Buergenthal in *Meron*, p. 456.

79 Case *9748 v Peru*, Res No. 30/88 of September 14, 1988 and *Case 9786 v Peru*, Res. No. 33/88 of September 14, 1988, Inter-American Commission on Human Rights, *Annual Report 1988-89*, pp. 30-33.

80 *Case 10.235 v Colombia*, Inter-American Commission on Human Rights, *Annual Report 1991-92* 27. On the legal status of the HRC's 'final views' see McGoldrick, pp. 150-6.

81 Buergenthal in *Meron*, p. 457.

82 Ibid.

83 Article 33 Regulations.

84 *Velasquez Rodriguez (Preliminary Objections)*, para. 40; *Fairen Garbi and Solis Corrales (Preliminary Objections)*, para. 45; *Godinez Cruz (Preliminary Objections)*, para. 43.

85   Ibid.

86   *Certain Attributes*, para. 42.

87   *Velasquez Rodriguez (Preliminary Objections)*, para. 29; *Fairen Garbi and Solis Corrales (Preliminary Objections)*, para. 34; *Godinez Cruz (Preliminary Objections)*, para. 32.

88   Ibid.

89   *Velasquez Rodriguez (Preliminary Objections)*, para. 33; *Fairen Garbi and Solis Corrales (Preliminary Objections)*, para. 38 and *Godinez Cruz (Preliminary Objections)*, para. 36; *Gangaram Panday (Preliminary Objections)*, para. 18.

90   *Velasquez Rodriguez (Preliminary Objections)*, para. 42; *Fairen Garbi and Solis Corrales (Preliminary Objections)*, para. 47 and *Godinez Cruz (Preliminary Objections)*, para. 45. This formula was approved by the Court in, *Certain Attributes*, para. 43.

91   Ibid., para. 40.

92   Art 48. In the *Cayara Case* one of the complaints by Peru was that the Commission had failed to furnish the State with the appropriate portion of the applicant's petition. This omission was subsequently rectified by the Commission. By Article 34(4) of the Commission's Regulations the identity of the petitioner must be withheld as must any other information that could identify him or her.

93   Article 34(6) Regulations.

94   For examples of this approach see the cases against Peru in Inter-American Commission on Human Rights, *Annual Report 1987-88*.

95   Article 48(1)(b) Convention.

96   Ibid.

97   Article 48(1)(c) Convention.

98   See Buergenthal in *Meron*, p. 457.

99   Ibid., p. 458.

100   Article 48(1)(e) Convention; Article 43 Regulations.

101   *Velasquez Rodriguez (Preliminary Objections)*, para. 53; *Fairen Garbi and Solis Corrales (Preliminary Objections)*, para. 57.

102   Article 18(g) Statute.

103   Articles 44 and 55-9.

104   See *Velasquez Rodriguez (Preliminary Objections)*, para. 49; *Fairen Garbi and Solis Corrales (Preliminary Objections)*, para. 54; *Godinez Cruz (Preliminary Objections)*, para. 52.

105   Article 53(1) Regulations.

106   Ibid.

107   Article 53(2) Regulations.

108   Article 53(3) Regulations.

109   Article 54(1) Regulations.

110   See for example *Case 10.581 v Colombia*, Report No. 33/92 of September 25, 1992, Inter-American Commission on Human Rights, *Annual Report 1992-93* 61.

111   Article 45(1) Regulations.

112   Article 45(2) Regulations.

113   Inter-American Commission on Human Rights, *1994 Annual Report* 40.

114   *Velasquez Rodriguez (Preliminary Objections)*, para. 44; *Fairen Garbi and Solis Corrales (Preliminary Objections)*, para. 49; *Godinez Cruz (Preliminary Objections)*, para. 47. Emphasis added.

115   *Velasquez Rodriguez (Preliminary Objections)*, para. 45; *Fairen Garbi and Solis Corrales (Preliminary Objections)*, para. 50; *Godinez Cruz (Preliminary Objections)*, para. 48.

116   *Velasquez Rodriguez (Preliminary Objections)*, para. 46; *Fairen Garbi and Solis Corrales*

(Preliminary Objections), para. 51; *Godinez Cruz (Preliminary Objections)*, para. 49.

[117] Ibid.

[118] *Judgment of January 21, 1994 - Preliminary Objections.*

[119] Ibid., para. 27.

[120] Ibid., para. 28.

[121] Ibid., para. 29. See also *Genie Lacayo v Nicaragua* [1995] 16 HRLJ 414 in which the Commission expressly approved its reasoning in *Caballero et al.*

[122] [1995] 16 HRLJ 151.

[123] Article 49 Convention; Article 45(6) Regulations.

[124] Article 23(2) Statute.

[125] Article 50(1) Convention; Article 47(4) Regulations.

[126] Article 50(2) Convention; Article 47(6) Regulations.

[127] Article 50(3) Convention; Article 47(1) Regulations.

[128] Article 51(1) and (2) Convention; Article 47(2) Regulations.

[129] Article 51(3) Convention; Article 47(3) Regulations.

[130] Article 48(2) Regulations.

[131] *Velasquez Rodriguez (Preliminary Objections)*, para. 58; *Fairen Garbi and Solis Corrales (Preliminary Objections)*, para. 58; *Godinez Cruz (Preliminary Objections)*, para. 61.

[132] *Velasquez Rodriguez (Preliminary Objections)*, para. 60; *Fairen Garbi and Solis Corrales (Preliminary Objections)*, para. 53; *Godinez Cruz (Preliminary Objections)*, para. 51.

[133] Ibid.

[134] *Order of 29 June, 1992 - Article 54(3) American Convention on Human Rights.*

[135] *Judgment of 3 February 1993 - Preliminary Objections.*

[136] This was the government of President Alberto Fujimoro.

[137] *Neira Alegria*, para. 21.

[138] Ibid., para. 32.

[139] Ibid., para. 34.

[140] Ibid., para. 35. See also *Velasquez Rodriguez (Preliminary Objections)*, para. 72; *Fairen Garbi and Solis Corrales (Preliminary Objections)*, para. 72 and *Godinez Cruz (Preliminary Objections)*, para. 75.

[141] *Cayara Case*, para. 25. Emphasis as in the original.

[142] Ibid.

[143] Ibid., para. 29.

[144] Ibid., para. 36.

[145] Ibid.

[146] Ibid., para. 37. See also *Velasquez Rodriguez Case, Preliminary Objections*, Judgment of June 26, 1987, Series C, No. 1, para. 30.

[147] At paras. 32. 33 and 34.

[148] *Cayara Case*, loc. cit., supra, note 11, para. 38.

[149] See supra, pp. 173-5.

[150] Ibid., para. 63.

[151] Ibid., para. 39.

[152] Ibid., para. 60.

[153] Ibid., para. 61.

[154] *Certain Attributes*, para. 3.

[155] Ibid., para. 46. On the competences of the Committee of Ministers of the Council of Europe under the European Convention on Human Rights see R. Beddard, *Human Rights and Europe* (1993), pp. 55-60 and J.S. Davidson, *Human Rights* (1993), pp. 113-15.

[156]   Ibid., para. 48.
[157]   Ibid.
[158]   Ibid., para. 49.
[159]   See Article 76(2) of the Convention.
[160]   *Gangaram Panday (Preliminary Objections)*, para. 32.
[161]   Ibid., para. 33.
[162]   At para. 50.
[163]   Advisory Opinion OC-5/85 of November 13, 1985, *Compulsory Membership in an Association Prescribed by Law for the Practice of Journalism (Arts. 13 and 29 American Convention on Human Rights)*, Series A, No. 5 (1986) 25 ILM 123 (1986) 7 HRLJ 74.
[164]   Ibid., para. 25. For discussion see Davidson, *Inter-American Court*, pp. 26-7.
[165]   See further, *infra*, pp. 185-7.
[166]   Ibid., para. 54.
[167]   Ibid.
[168]   Ibid., paras. 55 and 56.
[169]   See supra, pp. 22-7.
[170]   That is a finding of violation, a binding ruling and the award of compensatory damages.
[171]   *Case 9178 v Costa Rica*, Resolution No. 17/64 of October 3, 1984, Inter-American Commission on Human Rights, *Annual Report 1984 - 85* 51 (1985) 6 *HRLJ* 211.
[172]   At para. 23. The Commission, however, attracted general criticism for its failure to submit cases to the Court both in past and present instances in a Declaration appended by Judge Maximo Cisneros. See infra, p. 192.
[173]   At para. 26.
[174]   The *Schmidt Case* attracted a strong dissenting opinion from Commissioner Bruce McColm.
[175]   *Certain Attributes*, para. 50.
[176]   Ibid.
[177]   See the suggestions made by A. S. Dwyer, 'The Inter-American Court of Human Rights: Towards Establishing an Effective Regional Contentious Jurisdiction' (1990) 13 *Boston College International and Comparative Law Review* 127 at 154-6.
[178]   *Gallardo*, para. 1.
[179]   Ibid.
[180]   Article 4 (right to life); Article 5 (right to humane treatment).
[181]   *Gallardo*, para. 2.
[182]   Ibid., para. 8.
[183]   Supra, pp. 63-4. See discussion supra, pp. 22-7.
[184]   *Gallardo*, para. 18.
[185]   Ibid., para. 25.
[186]   Ibid.
[187]   Buergenthal posits the situation where two states are in dispute over the meaning of a provision of the Convention which does not involve human rights, for example a dispute over the diplomatic immunities to be ascribed to a judge. He suggests that this might not fall within the terms of the *Gallardo* ruling and that the procedure before the Commission could be dispensed with, since it does not affect the integrity of the system. *Inter-American Court*, pp. 238-9.
[188]   Ibid., para. 28.
[189]   Ibid.
[190]   *Gallardo*, para. 13.
[191]   The Court referred in particular to Articles 31 and 32 of the Vienna Convention on the

Law of Treaties as providing the basis for its approach. See *Gallardo*, para. 20.

192 See particularly *Gallardo*, para. 20.
193 Ibid., para. 15.
194 Ibid., para. 16.
195 Ibid.
196 Ibid., para. 15.
197 Ibid., para. 21.
198 Ibid., para. 22.
199 Ibid., para. 23.
200 Ibid., para. 22.
201 See infra, pp. 206-9.
202 Ibid., para. 22.
203 Ibid., para. 24.
204 Ibid., para. 25.
205 Ibid.
206 Article 63(2) Convention.
207 *Velasquez Rodriguez (Preliminary Objections)*, para. 58; *Fairen Garbi and Solis Corrales (Preliminary Objections)*, para. 58; *Godinez Cruz (Preliminary Objections)*, para. 61.
208 *Velasquez Rodriguez (Preliminary Objections)*, para. 60; *Fairen Garbi and Solis Corrales (Preliminary Objections)*, para. 53; *Godinez Cruz (Preliminary Objections)*, para. 51.
209 On the non-criminal nature of contentious proceedings see infra, p. 209.
210 Which, in consequence, was taken unanimously.
211 Under Article 61(1) only States Parties and the Commission have a right to submit cases to the Court. C.f. Article 48 ECHR which states that only the European Commission or a High Contracting Party may bring a case before the Court. Protocol 11 of the ECHR (which is not yet in force) eliminates proceedings before the Commission and allows the individual victim or a High Contracting Party to bring a case before the Court.
212 *Explanation of Vote*, para. 4.
213 *Explanation of Vote*, para. 10.
214 Ibid., para. 11.
215 A. S. Dwyer, 'The Inter-American Court of Human Rights: Towards Establishing an Effective Regional Contentious Jurisdiction' (1990) 13 *Boston College International and Comparative Law Review* 127 at 145.
216 Ibid.
217 See supra, pp. 175-85.
218 Supra, pp. 180.
219 See, for example, *Neira Alegria et al (Preliminary Objections)*, supra, p. 180 and the *Cayara Case*, supra. p. 181.
220 See the *Cayara Case*, para. 63.
221 On the compensatory damages phase see supra, pp. 88-98.
222 *Velasquez Preliminary Objections*, para. 70.
223 At p. 152.

5 Individual Applications before the Inter-American Court of Human Rights

Introduction

In the previous chapter the role of the Inter-American Commission on Human Rights in the consideration and disposal of individual applications under both the Charter and Convention systems was considered in some detail. It will be recalled that under the Convention system the Commission has a discretion to submit a case to the Court if it finds that there has been a *prima facie* breach of the rights protected by the Convention and, in the case of certain designated rights, the Protocol of San Salvador. The discretion of the Commission to remit an individual case to the Court is, however, circumscribed by two factors. First, if the State Party concerned has not accepted the contentious jurisdiction of the Court, then the Commission must dispose of the application itself. Second, in cases in which the respondent State Party has accepted the jurisdiction of the Court, the Commission must follow the guidelines laid down in *Compulsory Membership* and *Certain Attributes* concerning the desirability of submitting cases bearing certain characteristics to the Court. It is the consideration and disposal of such cases by the Court with which the present chapter is concerned.

Judge Piza Escalante has described contentious proceedings as the Court's 'ordinary jurisdiction'[1] in the sense that it is likely to be relied upon most frequently in guaranteeing the rights protected by the Convention.[2] Indeed, both the Convention and the format of the Court's Statute and Rules of Procedure would seem to confirm this view.[3] The early experience of the Court, however, demonstrated both a reluctance on the part of States Parties to accept its contentious jurisdiction and a failure by the Commission to remit cases to the Court which ought to have been placed before it. This is beginning to change as the democratic impulse becomes more firmly embedded in a number of States Parties who have committed themselves to effective human rights protection through a variety of measures, including greater participation in the region's human rights instruments and a willingness to allow the Court to adjudicate on human rights violations. The steady increase in the number of cases in the Court's docket in recent years bears witness to the progress which has been accomplished.

Acceptance of the Court's Contentious Jurisdiction

The main objective of the Court's contentious jurisdiction is to rule on whether a state has violated any of the rights contained in the Convention and to secure redress for the victims of such violations. While Judge Piza Escalante has taken the view that contentious jurisdiction has 'an obvious condemnatory nature, as in penal jurisdiction, whose specific object is not that of defining the right in question but rather that of re-establishing the violated right, specifically deciding whether there has been a violation of the rights guaranteed by the Convention that can be imputed to a State Party ...',[4] the Court itself has refused to characterize its contentious procedure as penal in nature.[5]

Before the Court may exercise its jurisdiction to hear and determine a case, the State Party or States Parties concerned must have accepted its jurisdiction under Article 62(3) of the Convention. Such acceptance of the Court's jurisdiction is optional and may be made by declaration at the time of ratification or adherence to the Convention or at any time thereafter.[6] Declarations may be unconditional, in which case the Court's jurisdiction is *ipso facto* binding and does not require any special agreement, or conditional.[7] Where conditions are attached to a State Party's acceptance of the Court's jurisdiction, they may restrict matters *ratione temporis, ratione materiae,* or simply on the basis of reciprocity.[8] It is nevertheless always open to States Parties to accept the jurisdiction of the Court in an individual case by effecting a special agreement.[9] The Commission is also empowered by Article 50 of its Regulations to call upon a state which has not accepted the jurisdiction of the Court to accept it in a specific case. The state concerned is clearly not obliged to accede to the Commission's request, since submission to the jurisdiction of any international tribunal is an exercise of sovereignty requiring the consent of the state.[10]

Acceptance of the Court's jurisdiction either absolutely or conditionally by a State Party is not the sole criterion for the exercise of that jurisdiction in any case. As discussed above,[11] Article 61(2) of the Convention provides that, before the Court can hear a case, the procedures contained in Articles 48 to 50 of the Convention must have been completed.[12] The procedures contained in the appropriate articles have already been considered in some detail, but it is worth reiterating their salient aspects. *First,* a petitioner must have pursued and exhausted all remedies under domestic law in accordance with generally recognized principles of international law.[13] *Second,* the petition must be timely, that is within six months of notification of the final judgment to the victim.[14] *Third,* the subject of the petition must not be pending in another international proceeding for settlement.[15] In addition to these substantive requirements, there are a number of technical details relating to the form of the petition which must be satisfied.[16] Failure to comply with any of these requirements will lead to the dismissal of the petition as inadmissible by the Commission.[17] Further grounds for inadmissibility contained in Article 47 are the non-disclosure of a violation of any rights protected by the Convention,[18] that the petition is manifestly groundless or out of order,[19] or that the petition is substantially the same as one previously considered by the Commission or another international organization.[20] Once a case is declared admissible, it then proceeds to the second stage, the major feature of which is the Commission's conciliatory function of attempting to secure a friendly settlement between the parties.[21] Should a friendly settlement not be achieved, the Commission draws up its report in accordance with Article 50 of the Convention and submits it to the Court, if it has previously decided not to act or if the state party concerned has not already submitted the case to the Court.[22] As the *Gallardo* case made clear, these procedures are not optional but must be followed in all individual cases.

Proceedings in Contentious Cases[23]

The first contentious cases heard by the Inter-American Court were three cases against Honduras concerning the alleged disappearance of four persons. The Commission argued that, since the government of Honduras tolerated the practice of disappearances, it was responsible for the violations of the American Convention which that entailed. These cases raised a number of difficulties for the Court, many of which might have been avoided with a little foresight. As Cerna rightly argues,[24] the Commission had not given 'serious thought' to the presentation of these cases to the Court. First, it had neither revised its Regulations since the entry into force of the Convention to accommodate the creation of the Court, nor had it considered what the relationship between itself and the Court should be in contentious proceedings. Second, the subject matter of the cases was of a particularly intractable nature involving as they did the definition and proof of a crime which was 'not typified in the criminal code of any country in the hemisphere'.[25] As Cerna cogently observes:

> The very nature of the crime - a 'disappearance' - eludes the tools of investigation and fact finding. With no proof, how was the Commission to demonstrate the responsibility of the Honduran Government to the Court?'

Since this was so, the Court was faced with acute problems in establishing evidence and determining where the burden of proof was to lie in contentious cases of this kind. As indicated above, the major reason for this was that the cases concerned the government tolerated practice of 'disappearing' political dissidents or opponents. Enforced disappearance was a practice used by a number of Central and South American governments during the 1970s and 1980s and is still allegedly employed in a number of Latin American states today.[26] The *modus operandi* in the practice of disappearances displays a remarkable consistency.[27] Suspected political opponents and, in certain cases, those who associated with such opponents, were usually picked up by armed military personnel wearing civilian clothes and using unmarked civilian vehicles. The 'disappeared' were then taken to military barracks or secret prisons where they were tortured in order to extract information from them. Attempts by relatives and friends to seek the release of detainees were usually ineffective since judicial remedies such as *habeas corpus* or the writ of *amparo* often proved to be merely illusory. Although some of the 'disappeared' did reappear, more often than not they were eventually executed (if they had not died at the hands of their torturers) and buried in unmarked graves. These were precisely the methods proven to the Court's satisfaction to have been used by the Honduran security forces in *Velasquez Rodriguez and Godinez Cruz*. The Court found that the disappearances alleged in the *Fairen Garbi and Solis Corrales* case had not been proved.

Before examining the approach adopted by the Court to the finding of evidence in the *Honduran Disappearance Cases*, it is perhaps appropriate to examine the factual situations in each case. In *Velasquez Rodriguez*, the victim was a university student who was arrested in Tegucigalpa by members of the Honduran national security service and members of the armed forces. He was taken to a national security service establishment where he was allegedly tortured. Some days later Velasquez Rodriguez was reported to have been transferred to a military barracks. Nothing further was heard of his whereabouts thereafter. Honduras denied that the victim had ever been detained. Similarly, in *Godinez Cruz*, it was alleged that the victim, a school teacher, had been disappeared while on his way to work. A witness claimed to have seen someone of the victim's description being detained by three men; one in plain clothes and two in military uniforms. Despite attempts to obtain Godinez Cruz's release by two applications for *habeas corpus,* no information on his whereabouts was forthcoming from the Honduran authorities. Finally, in *Fairen Garbi and Solis Corrales,* the victims were Costa Rican nationals who disappeared while travelling through Honduras to Mexico. Honduras informed the Commission that the alleged victims had left its territory and had entered Guatemala. The Guatemalan representative in San José, Costa Rica, informed the Costa Rican government that Guatemala had no record of Fairen Garbi and Solis Corrales having entered Guatemala. There was some evidence that the two had been seen in Tegucigalpa, but this was not without contradiction. In all these cases the Commission asked Honduras to furnish it with further information, and in all the cases Honduras failed to do so. The Commission therefore found that Honduras had violated Articles 4 and 7 of the Convention, but asked the Court to rule that there had been violations of Article 4, 5 and 7.

It will be readily apparent that, when faced with the practice of enforced disappearance, the Court is likely to encounter substantial difficulty in finding evidence. The fundamental reason for this is that the practice is, if not instigated by the government of a state, at least tolerated by it. In both cases, however, the state has an interest in ensuring that the practice remains secret.[28] There is usually no useful evidence forthcoming from the state either because no documentary evidence is available or because it is suppressed. Furthermore, witnesses and their families may also be subjected to threats, harassment or even death if they agree to testify in proceedings relative to disappearances.[29] In circumstances such as these, conventional concepts of evidence and the burden of proof developed in the context of domestic judicial proceedings require modification. Considerable recourse must be had to circumstantial evidence and to inference as means of proving fact.[30] Indeed, these are methods which have already been employed in international adjudication, particularly in the practice of the ICJ where they were used in both the *Corfu Channel (Merits) Case*[31] and in the *Military and Paramilitary Activities (Merits) Case.*[32] It is also significant that both these cases involved non-appearance by the respondent states, and therefore in accordance with Article 53 of its Statute the ICJ was required to satisfy itself that the applicants' cases were well-founded in fact and law. In both cases it did so by finding evidence *proprio motu.*[33] While the government of Honduras did appear in the *Honduran Disappearance Cases,* it only offered documentary evidence in support of its preliminary objections to the Court's jurisdiction, and no evidence on the merits. In a sense, this was the equivalent of non-appearance since, as the Court itself observed, it was compelled to reach its decision 'without the valuable assistance of a more active participation by Honduras, which might have resulted in a more adequate presentation of its case'.[34] In the *Honduran Disappearance Cases* therefore, the Court reviewed all questions of fact and law *de novo*. Although the Commission argued against this course of action,[35] the Court held that the Convention gave it full jurisdiction over all issues, and that it was not bound by previous decisions on matters by the Commission.[36] The Court was the sole judicial institution with the power of decision and not a court of appeal from decisions of the Commission.[37]

Before assessing the Court's approach to determining the burden of proof and the nature of the probative evidence admitted, it is appropriate to examine the precise nature of contentious proceedings before the Court. A preliminary question is whether such proceedings have more in common with criminal processes where the respondent state is placed in the dock, or whether they are more in the nature of a tortious or delictual action in domestic proceedings or whether they are *sui generis*. The temptation is perhaps to see contentious procedure as analogous to the domestic criminal process in which the Commission prosecutes the state for violation of the law.[38] In the *Honduran Disappearance Cases*, however, the Court was chary of such a view, preferring to find that international adjudication in human rights cases was of a *sui generis* nature. It ruled:[39]

> The international protection of human rights should not be confused with criminal justice. states do not appear before the Court as defendants in a criminal action. The objective of international human rights law is not to punish those individuals who are guilty of violations, but rather the to protect the victims and to provide for the reparation of the damage resulting from the acts or omissions of the responsible state.

Such a view seems to recognize the sovereignty of the state and continues to safeguard, to a certain degree, the rights and privileges associated therewith. In general, therefore, it would appear that a finding of violation or delinquency on behalf of the respondent state will not be reached lightly by the Court.[40] It thus seems that the Court recognizes the narrow path it must tread between respect for state sovereignty and protection of individual rights. It is apparent that both these concerns manifest themselves in the approach taken by the Court with respect to both the burden of proof and to the weight to be accorded to probative evidence.

Burden of Proof

It will be apparent from the discussion of the burden of proof in connection with the exhaustion of local remedies[41] that the allocation of the burden has a significant effect on the position of the parties to proceedings. Since contentious proceedings cannot be considered the international analogue of either criminal or tortious proceedings in domestic law, the parties in such cases are presumed to stand, at the outset, on an equal footing. This presumption of equality of the parties, or equality of arms as it sometimes known, led the Court to adopt the proposition generally taken in international proceedings that it is for the party seeking to adduce a point to prove that point.[42]

As far as the burden of proof is concerned, the Court observed in the *Disappearance Cases* that, since it was the Commission which was accusing Honduras of 'disappearing' the victim, it should 'bear the burden of the facts underlying its petition'.[43] This, however, raised the problems referred to above, namely, that if the policy of disappearances enjoyed government sanction or tolerance, it would be impossible to prove as an absolute fact that the individuals concerned had disappeared in accordance with such a policy since conclusive evidence would not be available.[44] The only way to proceed in such circumstances would be to rely on circumstantial and presumptive evidence. In order to do this, however, it would have to be proved that a policy of 'disappearances' existed in Honduras, and that the disappearance of the individuals concerned bore the indicia of that policy.[45] This approach, which was advocated by the Commission, found explicit approval from the Court[46] and implicit approval from the government of Honduras,[47] although the latter argued that no policy of government-sanctioned or tolerated disappearances could be proved as a matter of fact.[48] In order to deal with this problem, the Court transferred the burden of proof to the government, requiring it to produce evidence to refute the petitioners' claims.[49] In approving such an approach to the allocation of the burden of proof, however, the Court added the caveat that all the evidence presented must meet the standard of proof required.[50] What then was the appropriate standard of proof? Here the Court adopted a pragmatic response, indicating that international jurisprudence recognized the right of the Court to weigh evidence freely and to avoid rigid rules concerning the proof necessary to support a judgment.[51] It also noted that the standards of proof were 'less formal' in international proceedings than in domestic proceedings.[52]

As indicated above, the evidence available to the Court in the *Disappearance Cases* was comprised of documentary evidence, the testimony of witnesses and press reports. The documentary evidence supplied by the Commission was not refuted by Honduras, and the testimony given by witnesses, both friendly and hostile to the Commission's case, tended to prove the existence of a policy of disappearances in Honduras. In the case of every friendly witness called by the Commission, the government of Honduras sought either to challenge the witness under Article 37 of the Rules of the Court or to discredit their testimony on the grounds of partiality, lack of objectivity or hearsay.[53] None of the challenges was allowed by the Court and, in the cases of witnesses whose impartiality or objectivity was challenged, the Court declared that it was capable of making the necessary adjustments in determining the evidentiary value of statements made by such witnesses.[54] With respect to the use in evidence by the Court of newspaper reports, the Court, citing the ICJ in the *Military and Paramilitary Activities Case*,[55] declared that, although such reports could not be considered as documentary evidence *per se,* they were of evidential value where they merely reproduced public and well-known facts.[56] Indeed, they were of particular importance when they corroborated prior testimony.[57]

A matter of particular concern which arose during the course of the trial, and which was also manifested in the orders of interim protection,[58] was the fact that witnesses appearing for the Commission were characterized as disloyal to the state and subjected to verbal and physical harassment. Citing the American Declaration of the Rights and Duties of Man and the Preamble to the Convention, the Court stated:[59]

> The insinuation that persons who, for any reason, resort to the inter-American system for the protection of human rights are disloyal to their country is unacceptable and cannot constitute a basis for any penalty or negative consequence.

Taking into account all the evidence available to it the Court found as proved that there was a practice of disappearances in Honduras during 1981-4 which was either carried out or tolerated by the Honduran government; that disappearances at the hands of officials within the framework of that policy and the Honduran government failed to guarantee the human rights affected by the practice of disappearances.[60] These findings were clearly derived from the two stage process advocated by the Commission and accepted by the Court in determining by inference the disappearance of an individual within the existence of a state-sponsored or tolerated practice of disappearances. Thus, in the cases of *Velasquez Rodriguez* and *Godinez Cruz*, the Court found that the victims had been disappeared and that the government of Honduras was responsible therefor. In the case of *Fairen Garbi and Solis Corrales*, however, the Court found that the Commission had not produced sufficient evidence to lead to the conclusion that the Honduran government was responsible for the disappearances. While there was evidence from eyewitnesses in the first two cases that the victims had been arrested or detained, there was no such evidence in the third case. Given that lack of evidence, there was nothing to link Honduras directly with the disappearances of the individuals and, as the Court pointed out, it was unwilling to create a legal presumption in the absence of such evidence that the state was responsible for the disappearances.[61]

It is arguable that the Court could not have been confronted with a more difficult issue in its first contentious cases. The practice of disappearances and the recalcitrance of the respondent state in providing evidence and in assisting the Court during the hearing of the merits of the case created obstacles which required the Court to develop through its jurisprudence what the standard of proof was to be and where the burden of such proof was to lie. Nonetheless, the complexity of the cases meant that the Court was obliged to state its rules of evidence rather more fully than would perhaps have been required had the case been more tractable.

Judgments in Contentious Cases and Their Effects

As indicated above,[62] a contentious case normally terminates with a judgment by the Court that there has or has not been a violation of one or more of the rights protected by the Convention.[63] It is, however, within the Court's discretion to determine when a judgment closes a case in order to ensure effective supervision and enforcement of a judgment.[64] While the judgment of the Court is final and admits of no appeal,[65] it may be interpreted by the Court at the request of any of the parties within ninety days from the communication of the judgment to the parties if there is disagreement about its meaning or scope.[66] If a breach of any of the rights contained in the Convention is found, the Court must rule that the party be ensured of the enjoyment of the rights denied and, where appropriate, the circumstances which gave rise to the breach be remedied and fair compensation be paid.[67] States Parties to the Convention undertake to comply with the judgment of the court in cases to which they are parties;[68] thus judgments are binding upon them. Not only are parties to the case notified of judgments, but so also are all other states parties to the Convention.[69] This has the effect of making the Court's decision notorious, and non-compliance less likely for fear of adverse publicity on the part of the delinquent state.

Judgments of the Court are clearly declaratory in nature in that they are technically binding only on the parties to the case and do not produce effects *erga omnes*. Nonetheless, it is clear that the Court's interpretation of the rights contained in the Convention are authoritative and therefore have a greater practical significance than their formal status would seem to suggest. While states not party to proceedings are obviously not under an obligation to comply with rulings in cases to which they are not parties, such rulings will certainly function as statements of the Court's understanding of the law and thus constitute useful guide-lines for state practice. The formal position of decisions of the European Court under the European Convention is identical to that of the American Court. Of the former Merrills has said:[70]

> [E]ach ruling is not an isolated episode; it is also a contribution to the jurisprudence of the European Convention. In each decision the Court is not just spelling out the obligations of the state which happens to be involved in the particular case. It is interpreting the Convention for all states which are parties to it. Naturally, the main impact of a decision will usually be in the state immediately concerned but every party to the Convention must stay abreast of developments.

This effect of declaratory judgments by the European Court is made even more apparent by the development of a *jurisprudence constante*. Although there is no system of precedent in the European Court, its jurisprudence is developed and refined in cases by reference, where applicable, to previous decisions. The same process is evident in the practice of the Inter-American Court in both contentious and advisory proceedings. In both categories of jurisdiction, the Court has demonstrated a willingness to refer to principles enunciated in previous decisions which represent the Court's settled approach to particular issues. In the field of remedies, however, the Court has also demonstrated a willingness to depart from or modify principles stated in its earlier decisions where this has proved necessary.

Remedies

Article 63(1) of the American Convention provides:

> If the Court finds that there has been a violation of a right or freedom protected by this Convention, the Court shall rule that the injured party be ensured of his right or freedom that was violated. It shall also rule, if appropriate, that the consequences of the measure or situation that constituted the breach of such a right or freedom be remedied and that fair compensation be paid to the injured party.

This provision subsumes two categories of judicial remedy. The first is a ruling which requires a State Party to bring an end to the violation of a substantive right protected by the Convention by ensuring the enjoyment of that right by the victim. This may require the state to enact legislation to bring its domestic legal system into line with the Convention or it may simply require the state to afford victims the full range of existing domestic remedies in order to allow them to vindicate their rights. The second remedy is that which is most commonly employed in international tribunals, namely, the award of pecuniary damages to compensate the victim for the breach suffered. Despite the apparent exclusivity of Article 63(1), however, there is a third category of remedy which may be termed satisfaction. While there is no explicit legal basis for the award of such a remedy, the Court has nonetheless given indications that it is prepared to award such redress where it considers it appropriate. In general terms, however, the Court has, to date, been presented with few opportunities to rule on the question of remedies, but the cases in which it has delivered judgment on this issue have raised a number of interesting theoretical and practical problems. Before examining these, however, it should be noted that the Court does not have to make a formal finding of violation of the Convention before it can proceed to the damages phase. In the *Aloeboetoe*[71] and *El Amparo Cases*,[72] both Suriname and Venezuela accepted responsibility for the alleged violations. In both cases, the Court instructed the Commission and the state to agree the level of damages while retaining the cases in its docket pending a satisfacory conclusion to the negotiations between the parties. In *Aloeboetoe*, agreement could not be reached between Suriname and the Commission and therefore, the Court was required to rule on the issue. At the time of writing, the position in the *El Amparo Case* is unknown.

Basis of Compensation

In the *Velasquez Rodriguez* and *Godinez Cruz* cases the Court was first obliged to deal with an argument by the Honduran government that compensation ought to be calculated on the basis of its domestic legal provisions concerning social security. The Court quickly rejected this argument, holding that, since Honduras was in breach of its international legal obligations under the Convention, the question of damages was to be determined solely be reference to international law. In support of this view, the Court referred not only to the fact that the payment of monetary compensation was supported by a number of international human rights instruments, but that there was a general tenet of international law which required that every violation of an international obligation which results in harm creates a corresponding duty to make adequate reparation. Thus it held that international reparation operates independently of a delinquent state's local law. Furthermore, in the *Aloeboetoe Case*,[73] the Court held that, since Article 63(1) was a codification of customary international law, the scope and characteristics of the provision must be interpreted in accordance with the norms of that system. Because this was so, a delinquent state could not modify or suspend the operation of Article 63(1) by attempting to invoke provisions of its own domestic law.

In characterizing the remedy available to the victims and their successors in the *Honduran Disappearance* cases, the Court stated:[74]

> Reparation of harm brought about by the violation of an international obligation consists in full restitution (*restitutio in integrum*) which includes the restoration of the prior situation, the reparation of the consequences of the violation and indemnification for patrimonial and non-patrimonial damages, including emotional harm.

The characterization of the remedy by the Court as *restitutio* raises a number of difficulties both of a practical and theoretical nature, not least what form of restitution is possible where the issue is the unlawful deprivation of life. As the Court itself observed, given the corporeal nature of the things damaged, the only possible remedy was the payment of damages. In *Aloeboetoe,* the Court appeared to be unhappy with its original characterization of the remedy contained in Article 63(1) and decided to modify its approach. While affirming that in cases involving violation of the right to life the appropriate reparation must of necessity be in the form of pecuniary compensation, the Court appeared to be more content to describe the effects of the remedy available under Article 63(1) rather than terming it *restitutio in integrum* together with all the theoretical assumptions that such a characterization might imply. The Court said, 'regardless of the term employed ... the compensation to be paid by Suriname [the delinquent state] shall be in an amount sufficient to remedy all the consequences of the violations that took place'.[75] The focus then seems to have shifted from attempting to return the victims and their beneficiaries to the position which they would have been in had the violation not occurred, to providing redress for all the effects of a breach of the Convention. This is not to say that there will not be occasions when *restitutio* may be an appropriate form of remedy. As the Court itself observed that, while *restitutio* might be one way in which the effects of an unlawful international act may be redressed, it is not the only way in which it must be redressed, since in certain circumstances, such as those present in this case, reparation might not be 'possible, sufficient or appropriate'.[76]

Heads of Damage

In both the *Honduran Disappearance* cases and the *Aloeboetoe* case the Court has been consistent in its identification of the heads of damage. The primary ground for assessing damages in the Court's view is that of direct and indirect damage actually suffered. Such damage must also be sufficiently proximate to the damage suffered. Damage which is too remote cannot be the subject of reparation. In *Velasquez Rodriguez* and *Godinez Cruz*, the identification of damage actually suffered was a relatively simple matter. The victims themselves had suffered, *inter alia*, loss of life, inhumane treatment and deprivation of personal liberty, while the victims' dependants had been deprived of the primary wage-earner and the loss or damage suffered thereby was readily calculable. The same was true of the victims in the *Aloeboetoe* case who had been abducted and summarily executed by the armed forces of Suriname. Here the Court held that the victims had suffered actual damage by virtue of their loss of life.

The Inter-American Court has also been consistent in awarding damages for moral and emotional damage. This is in sharp distinction to the European Court of Human Rights which has refused to allow moral damage as a basis for its awards. In the *Honduran Disappearance Cases*, moral damage was held to be payable to the victims' next-of-kin because of the suffering occasioned by them as a direct result of the trauma arising from the disappearance of the victim. Similarly, in *Aloeboetoe*, the Court held that moral damages were payable to the heirs of the victims because of the particularly cruel way in which the victims had been killed.[77]

The Court has, however, refused to grant punitive damages to victims, despite an invitation by the Commission to do so. Although it's approach here is consistent with the practice of other international tribunals, the Court derives its view from the wording of Article 63(1) which refers to the award of 'fair compensation'. In the Court's view this implies that damages should be compensatory and not punitive. It is also consistent with the Court's conception of its view of contentious proceedings which is that they are not penal in nature. To introduce a penal element into that procedure by awarding punitive damages against a delinquent State Party would clearly run counter to that view.

Identification of Beneficiaries

While the identification of the beneficiaries of reparation was not a problem for the Court in the *Honduran Disappearance* cases, this issue raised matters of considerable complexity in *Aloeboetoe*. Here certain members of the Saramaca tribe living in a remote part of Suriname were abducted and executed by members of the armed forces who suspected them of belonging to a rebel organization known as the Jungle Commando. The Saramaca, who were descended from runaway slaves, were largely illiterate and therefore kept no formal records of births, deaths or marriages. The tribe also had a complex social structure which the Court described thus:[78]

> ... the tribe displays a strong matriarchal familial configuration where polygamy occurs frequently. The principal group of relatives appears to be the bêê composed of the descendants of one single woman. This group assumes responsibility for the actions of any of its members, who, in theory, are each in turn responsible to the group as a whole.

As a consequence of this social structure the Commission claimed that it was not only the immediate relatives and dependents of the victims who should be the beneficiaries of any compensation, but the Saramaca as a whole.[79] In determining the identity of the beneficiaries the Court considered that the issue was governed primarily by international law, but that reference to Suriname's family law might be appropriate to resolve any difficulties.[80] Following an investigation of Suriname's domestic law, the Court took the view that the Saramaca enjoyed autonomy within Suriname on the basis of a treaty concluded between the tribe and the Dutch in 1762 and that as a result of this the beneficiaries of reparations should be identified according to the custom of the tribe in so far as this conformed to general principles of law identified by reference to Article 38(1)(c) of the Statute of the ICJ and in so far as it did not contradict the American Convention.[81] The Court therefore concluded that the beneficiaries of any award should be the successors of the victims, that is their children, spouses and ascendants.[82] Furthermore, the Court held that the obligation to make reparation also extended to dependent persons who might not necessarily be in a familial relationship with the victim.[83] The burden of proof in such circumstances lay upon the state to disprove the entitlement of a claimant successor, but it was for non-relative dependants to show that they were entitled to damages. In order to do this they had to demonstrate, first, that they were the recipients of regular periodic payments either in cash or in kind which were actually made to them by the victim; second, that such payments would have continued had the victim not been killed; and third, that the claimant experienced a financial need that was met by the victim. In the present case, the Commission had been unable to satisfy the Court as to the dependency status of any of the persons whom it had listed in its application.[84]

Although the Court was content to allow Saramacan customary law to inform its decision on the entitlement of heirs and dependants to receive compensation, it was unwilling to accept that the tribe as an entity was entitled to damages. The Commission's argument to this effect was rejected by the Court on the basis of both fact and law. On the facts the Court held that the Commission had not proved that there had been a racial factor involved in the killings; rather it preferred to view the human rights violations as response to suspected subversive activity alleged by Suriname. As the Court said:[85]

> It is true that the victims of the killings all belonged to the Saramaca Tribe, but this circumstance of itself does not lead to the conclusion that there was a racial element to the crime.

This finding by the Court does not mean that, where proof of a racial motive for human rights violations can be proved in the future, the Court will necessarily ignore it. Furthermore, the Court intimated that, where direct damage could be shown to a tribe as such, then this might be the subject of compensation.[86] The rejection of the claim for moral damage to the Saramaca tribe does, however, raise a number of difficulties. In particular, the Court took the view that all persons, in addition to being members of their own families and citizens of a state, also belong to intermediate communities, and that, in practice, the obligation to pay compensation for moral damage does not extend to such communities.[87] In the Court's view moral damage to intermediate communities can be rectified by the enforcement of the state's system of laws.[88] This approach appears to leave little room for distinguishing between different kinds of intermediate community. A small, unique, community, such as the Saramaca, will clearly be affected in a much more direct way by human rights violations affecting a significant number of its members, than will a community which is simply a subset of a much more homogeneous social structure. This problem of moral damage to intermediate communities can be brought into sharper focus by postulating two distinct situation. First, if a community is the victim of genocidal action on the part of the state, it is clear that there will be direct, actual moral damage both to the community and to the individuals of which it is comprised. Second, moral damage to a community may simply be incidental to a broader range of state actions, as the Court assumed to be the case in *Aloeboetoe*.

Quantum

In the *Honduran Disappearance* cases the moral and material damage suffered by the victims' next-of-kin was undertaken by the Court with considerable care and precision. On the question of material damage, the Court rejected the contention of Honduras that the calculation ought to be based on the most favourable conditions to the victims' next-of-kin under domestic law concerning the payment of social security for accidental death. It will be recalled that the Court had already dismissed the argument that the *quantum* of damages for breach of the Convention should be calculated on the basis of domestic law. Here, however, it observed, perhaps ironically, that the disappearance of the victims 'could not be considered an accidental death' and could not therefore be calculated on an insurance basis.[89] The method adopted by the Court for calculating material damage was based on the victims' lost income from the date of their disappearance to the time they would have met their possible natural death.[90] In so doing, however, the Court took account of the beneficiaries which, it noted, might have the actual or future possibility of working or receiving income of their own.[91] In both cases, the Court held that victims' children should be guaranteed an opportunity of education until the age of 25 which would delay the date at which they might begin remunerated work. In the *Velasquez Rodriguez* case the Court determined that damages of five hundred thousand *lempiras* should be paid to Velasquez's wife and three children.[92] In the *Godinez Cruz* case, the Court awarded the victim's widow and child four hundred thousand *lempiras*.[93]

As far as moral damage was concerned, the Court received expert documentary evidence and testimony from a psychiatrist who testified that the victims' next-of-kin had suffered symptoms of fright, anguish, depression and withdrawal resulting from the enforced disappearance of their respective spouses and fathers.[94] This trauma, the Court concluded, resulted directly from the violation of the rights and freedoms guaranteed by the American Convention, and especially by the 'dramatic characteristics' of the involuntary disappearance of the victim.[95] The amount awarded by the Court for moral damage to the families of *Velasquez Rodriguez* and *Godinez Cruz* was two hundred and fifty thousand *lempiras* to each family.[96]

An additional problem facing the Court was that, while in these cases Honduras had accepted the victims' wives and families as the sole beneficiaries for the purposes of proceedings before the Court, it nevertheless insisted that payment of damages could only proceed once the next-of-kin had fulfilled the requirements of Honduran law concerning recognition of heirs.[97] The Court rejected this contention unequivocally, stating:[98]

> The obligation to indemnify is not derived from internal law, but from violation of the American Convention. It is the result of an international obligation. To demand indemnification the family members of Manfredo Velasquez need only show their family relationship. They are not required to follow the procedure of Honduran inheritance law.

In its judgment the Court also determined how the damages were to be paid to the victims' next-of-kin. Execution of the judgment was to take place within ninety days from the date of its notification, and the payment of the damages was to be without deduction of tax.[99] A quarter of the sum was to be paid directly to the victims' wives directly, while the remaining three-quarters was to be placed in a trust fund for the children. In the case of the Velasquez Rodriguez family, the children would receive monthly payments from the trust fund until the age of 25 when they would receive equal proportions of the capital.[100] In the case of Godinez Cruz's daughter, she would receive monthly payments until the age of 25 at which time she would be entitled to the totality of the capital.[101] Supervision of these judgment was to be undertaken by the Court itself, and the case was to remain open until Honduras had complied with its requirements.[102]

Subsequent to the Court's decisions in the *Compensatory Damages,* phases of the *Velasquez Rodriguez* and *Godinez Cruz* cases, the Commission acting under Article 67 of the Convention,[103] requested the Court to clarify its judgment. In particular it asked the Court to direct that the portion of damages transferred to the Trust fund for the benefit of victims' children should be indexed to protect the purchasing power of such monies. The Commission's rationale for making such a request was the high rates of inflation which had been experienced in recent years which, if it continued, 'might cause irreparable damage to the injured parties'.[104]

In its ruling the Court noted once again that the purpose of compensatory damages under Article 63(1) was to provide *restitutio in integrum*, in so far as this was possible given the nature of the breaches in question, for the damage caused by the state's violation of human rights. Thus the fact that the award had been calculated on a 'prudent estimate' of Velasquez's income for the remainder of his probable life indicated that the concept was linked to the possibility of maintaining the real value of the damages stable over a long period of time. Although indexing was one way of achieving this stability, the Court considered that such a device would normally only apply in cases where damages were payable in instalments over a lengthy period.[105] Nevertheless, the Court took the view that it could see no reason why in these cases the notion of preserving the real value of the damages by such a method should be ignored. Indeed, the Court indicated that this purpose was facilitated by requiring a trust fund to be established 'under the most favorable conditions permitted by Honduran banking practice'. Here the Court interpreted the term 'under the most favorable conditions' as 'referring to the fact that any act or measure by the trustee must ensure that the amount assigned maintains its purchasing power and guarantees sufficient earning or dividends to increase it'.[106] It further interpreted 'permitted by Honduran banking practice' to mean that 'the trustee must faithfully perform his task as would a good head of family and that he has the power and the obligation to select diverse types of investment' to achieve this purpose.[107]

It would thus appear that the Court took the implicit view that the measures it had ordered in *Compensatory Damages* incorporated a sufficient element of 'indexing' to allow the real value of the damages to be maintained over a long period of time. It was perhaps for this reason that the Court rejected the Commission's request that Honduras should be ordered to pay 'top up' disbursements to the trust fund in favour of the victims' children at periodic intervals in order to maintain the real value of the fund. In the Court's view, to make such an order would have been to impose upon Honduras an obligation not provided for in the respective judgments.[108]

The experience of the European Court of Human Rights in this field has not been particularly encouraging. Under Article 50 of the European Convention the Court has power to award 'just satisfaction' to a victim for breaches of the Convention. This does not mean, however, that the European Court necessarily awards damages to victims of a violation in all circumstances. Indeed, as Gray points out,[109] no consistent pattern can be found in the European Court's approach to this issue. In a number of cases, the Court has granted damages for non-material moral injury,[110] whereas in others it has been content to find that a declaration of breach of the Convention was a sufficient remedy for the victim.[111] It does not appear that the divergent approach of the Court can be explained by the assumed intensity of the moral damage suffered by the victim nor by the particular article of the Convention which has been violated. The European Court's approach in this area seems to be simply arbitrary.

Awards for material loss resulting from a violation of the Convention have not been particularly common, largely because of the difficulty which a victim encounters in demonstrating that the loss is a direct result of the violation. Where direct loss can be shown, compensation will be awarded, but as Gray has pointed out, the Court has always taken a strict view of the causation requirement.[112] It might be argued that in *Velasquez* the issues were so well-defined that few courts, whether domestic or international, would have had difficulty in determining the existence of a causal connection between the acts of the government and the damage to the victims. Within the European Convention system the Court has also awarded compensation for loss of opportunity,[113] but again it must be demonstrated that the loss is real and attributable directly to the state.[114]

When the problem of *quantum* is addressed, the practice of the European Court is also unpredictable. The European Court has taken the view that it is almost impossible to quantify moral damage in any meaningful sense.[115] Although the Inter-American Court can be congratulated for at least attempting to come to terms with this issue, it is noticeable that reasons underlying the amount given for the moral damage suffered by the next-of-kin in the two *Honduran Disappearance* and *Aloeboetoe* cases are conspicuous by their absence. Again, however, the stand of the Inter-American Court on this issue might be explicable on the grounds of the kind of human rights violation with which it was required to deal. The case in question involved unambiguous breaches of human rights leading to readily discernible moral damage. Most domestic private law systems have formulae for calculating damages for such matters as nervous shock, therefore it is realistic to expect that international human rights tribunals should, in theory, be able to establish criteria for dealing with similar symptoms arising from human rights abuses where a causal connection can be shown between the abuse and the symptoms of the claimants. It is unfortunate that the Court in the *Compensatory Damages* and *Aloeboetoe* cases did not disclose either the rationale or the formula employed for calculating the amount of the award.

While it might be expected that the European Court's approach to calculation of material damage has been more logical and predictable than its treatment of moral damage, this has not, in fact, proved to be so. The Court has on no occasion given an indication of the indicia which it uses to calculate *quantum*, but seems to have been satisfied simply to state an arbitrary amount by way of compensation. The issue has been further complicated in that, where a monetary award is made for both moral and material loss, there has been no indication of the amount awarded for each head of damage.[116] The Inter-American Court has made a good start in this area by signifying quite precisely its basis for calculating material loss in the cases which it has considered. One blemish on its record, however, is its award in *Gangaram Panday*.[117] In this case the Court decided that Suriname had violated Article 7(2) of the Convention and simply decided to award nominal damages of US$10,000 for the breach.[118] The Court gave no indication of how it reached its decision on quantum in this case.

A question not answered by the various compensation decisions is how an award of compensation is to be enforced against a delinquent State Party. Article 68(2) of the Convention provides:

> That part of a judgment that stipulates compensatory damages may be executed in the country concerned in accordance with domestic procedure governing the execution of judgments against the state.

This presupposes that the execution of the Court's judgment should be a function of public law within the state adjudged in breach of its obligations under the Convention. Clearly, the manner of enforcement will vary from state to state depending on national procedures. It is also clear that since enforcement depends on state action, in the absence of any measures for automatic payment of damages which a state might implement by domestic legislation, there may be problems with enforcing damages against a recalcitrant state. Non-payment of damages would therefore raise the same issues concerning enforcement which were referred to above in the context of declaratory judgments.[119]

The solution adopted by Costa Rica in Article 27 of its headquarters agreement with the Court of 10 September 1981 is instructive here. This provides:

> The decisions of the Court, and in its place those of its President, as soon as they have been communicated to the appropriate administrative or judicial authorities of the Republic [of Costa Rica], shall have the same effect and executory force as those adopted by Costa Rican Courts.

Article 27 thus removes the possibility of executive interference with the payment of damages by the state should these be adjudged against it by the Court. Buergenthal notes that the Court plans to incorporate similar provisions in agreements with other states.[120]

This does not, however, dispose of all problems relating to the payment of compensation to victims or their assignees. What, for example, would be the position if the victim of a violation of the Convention was the national of another state? The relevant provisions of the Convention give no indication of whether the award of compensatory damages against a state may be enforced in a third state by a non-national or whether compensation may be demanded in foreign currency. Article 68(2) and, indeed, the Costa Rican headquarters agreement, seem to imply that judgments must be executed within the jurisdiction of the respondent state, but give no indication as to whether payment may be ordered in foreign currency. The European Court has given awards of damages payable in currency other than that of the respondent state,[121] and has indicated that the nature of the award is personal to the victim. Such awards cannot therefore be the subject of attachment proceedings by the respondent state.[122]

A problem which emerged in the compensatory damages phase of the *Honduran Disappearance* cases was the consequences of non-payment of damages by a State Party against whom an award had been made under Article 63(1). Subsequent to the Commission's request for an interpretation by the Court of its judgments in the *Compensatory Damages* cases, it became clear that, although the government of Honduras had ordered that the damages be paid to victims' next-of-kin and had published this order in the state's official gazette, no payment had, in fact, been made. The Commission therefore petitioned the Court to allow it to amplify its request for interpretation in order to deal with the consequences of non-payment. As indicated above,[123] the Court took the view that the 'petition for amplification' exceeded the function of interpretation, going instead to the question of enforcement of the judgment. Since, however, the Court had undertaken to supervise enforcement of the judgments in *Velasquez Rodriguez* and *Godinez Cruz*,[124] it considered itself competent to deal with the question of Honduran non-compliance *proprio motu*. Thus the Court held that, since payment of damages had not been effected, it was appropriate to demand that Honduras pay interest on the entire amount of the capital due at the regular banking rate in effect in Honduras at the time of actual payment.[125] It also held that other damage resulting from non-payment was to be compensated, namely, the loss in real value of the damages originally awarded which had to be made good in order to give effect to the principle of *restitutio in integrum*.[126]

Other Remedies

As noted above, Article 63(1) appears to subsume another category of remedy under which the Court might require a delinquent State Party to take appropriate measures to ensure that an injured party be assured of the right or freedom which was violated. This raises the question of whether Article 63(1) may be interpreted by the Court to allow it to order injunctions or specific performance. There is no doubt that the provision is ambiguous. Not only is the Court empowered to declare that the injured party shall be ensured the enjoyment of the right or freedom violated, but it may also rule 'that the consequences of the measure or situation that constituted the breach ... be remedied'. This seems to imply that the Court may rule not only upon specific redress, but also upon rectification of the law or circumstances which gave rise to the breach. The *Aloeboetoe* case is particularly instructive on these points. The claimants had requested as part of the reparation that the Court should require the President of Suriname to make a public apology to the Saramaca, that a park or square or street in a prominent section of Paramaribo be named after the Saramaca and that the persons guilty of the murders be punished. Although the Court did not address these claims specifically, it nonetheless required Suriname to make certain non-pecuniary forms of reparation. It required the government to reopen a school for the Saramaca and to staff it with teaching and administrative personnel to enable it to function on a continuous basis. The Court also ordered the respondent state to open a medical dispensary and to make it operational by a specific date. In addition to these orders, the Court also ruled that Suriname was obliged to use all the means at its disposal to inform the complainants of the fate of the victims and the location of their remains. These are clearly far-reaching orders made by the Court and seem to confirm the opinion that it is competent to require not only rectification of the circumstances which gave rise to any breach, but also to order specific performance of non-pecuniary forms of satisfaction.

Non-compliance with the Court's Judgment

There is only one provision which refers directly to the question of non-compliance by a State Party with a judgment of the Court: Article 65. This provides that, when making its annual report to the regular session of the OAS General Assembly, the Court shall specify the cases in which a state has not complied with a ruling. As Buergenthal points out,[127] although Article 65 refers to regular sessions of the OAS, this does not mean that an issue of non-compliance may not be raised at a special session of the General Assembly at the request of either a member state or the Permanent Council. The significance of this becomes apparent when non-compliance or threat of non-compliance, especially with provisional measures, is likely to lead to serious prejudice to individuals.

Since the issue of non-compliance is essentially one to be resolved by the General Assembly, it will be apparent that the question becomes a political matter to be determined through the political processes of the OAS. While there is no provision in the OAS dealing with the ultimate sanction of expulsion of a state from the Organization as is the case in the Statute of the Council of Europe,[128] it seems that the Organization's practice with regard to Cuba suggests that there is a *de facto* power to exclude a government which fails to comply with its obligations under the Charter, although this is by no means firmly established at law.[129]

Notes

[1]   *Gallardo, Explanation of Vote.*

[2]   Ibid.

[3]   Note in particular Article 53 of the Court's Rules which indicates that the rules governing proceedings in contentious cases are to be used in proceedings for advisory opinions where this is deemed necessary.

[4]   Ibid.

[5]   See infra, p. 209.

[6]   Article 62(1) ACHR.

[7]   Article 62(2) ACHR.

[8]   Ibid. In this respect the American Convention is wider than both Article 36 of the Statute of the International Court of Justice and Article 46 of the European Convention on Human Rights, both of which restrict declarations to those concerning restrictions to jurisdiction *ratione temporis* or on the basis of reciprocity. On declarations accompanying acceptance of the ICJ's jurisdiction see Shabtai Rosenne, *The World Court: What it is and How it Works* (Dordrecht: Kluwer, 4th edn., 1989), pp. 89-92.

[9]   Article 62(3) ACHR.

[10]   Should the case raise a question involving the interpretation of the Convention, it may nevertheless be possible for the Commission to request an advisory opinion from the Court under Article 64(1) without the consent of a state which might be affected by such a ruling. See infra, chapter 6.

[11]   Supra, chapter 4.

[12]   For a comparison of the procedures contained in both the American and European Conventions see C. Gray, *Judicial Remedies in International Law* (Oxford: Clarendon Press, 1987), pp. 149-63 (hereafter '*Judicial Remedies*'); A.G. Mower, *Regional Human Rights: A Comparative Study of the West European and Inter-American Systems* (New York: Greenwood Press, 1991); J.A. Frowein, 'The European and American Conventions on Human Rights' (1980) 1 HRLJ 44 at pp. 64-5; T. Buergenthal, 'The American and European Convention on Human Rights: Similarities and Differences' (1980) 30 *The American University Law Review* 155.

13 Article 46(1)(a) ACHR. Article 46(2) establishes a list of circumstances where this provision will be deemed to have been complied with. See supra, p. 158.

14 Article 46(1)(b) ACHR.

15 Article 46(1)(c) ACHR.

16 Article 46(1)(d) ACHR. The petition must contain the name, nationality, profession, domicile, and signature of the person or persons or of the legal representative of the entity lodging the petition. See supra, pp. 172-3.

17 Articles 46(1) and 47(1) ACHR.

18 Article 47(b) ACHR.

19 Article 47(c) ACHR.

20 Article 47(d) ACHR.

21 Article 48(1)(f) ACHR.

22 Article 51 ACHR. On the Commission's discretion to refer a case to the Court see infra, pp. 204-6.

23 See D.L. Shelton, 'Judicial Review of State Action by International Courts'(hereafter 'Judicial Review') (1989), 12 Fordham *International Law Journal* 361.

24 Cerna, *Structure and Functioning*, p. 206.

25 Ibid.

26 See Inter-American Commission on Human Rights, *1994 Annual Report, passim.*

27 The analysis of the practice of disappearances by the Commission in its Country Report for Argentina provides a useful insight. See *Report on the Situation of Human Rights in Argentina*, OEA/Ser.L/V/II.49, doc. 19. corr. 1, 11 April 1980, Chapter III. On the substantive rights protected by the ACHR which are violated by the practice of enforced disappearances see infra, pp. 155-8.

28 See *Velasquez Rodriguez*, para. 131; *Fairen Garbi and Solis Corrales*, para. 137; *Godinez Cruz*, para. 137.

29 As indicated above, interim measures of protection may be taken in such cases. See supra, chapter 3.

30 See *Velasquez Rodriguez*, para. 124. See also the observation of the Court at *Velasquez Rodriguez*, para. 131; *Fairen Garbi and Solis Corrales*, para. 130; *Godinez Cruz*, para 137; Circumstantial or presumptive evidence is especially important in allegation of disappearances, because this type of repression is characterized by an attempt to suppress all information about the kidnapping or the whereabouts and fate of the victim.

31 ICJ Rep, 1949, p. 4. Here the Court said (at p. 18) 'indirect evidence is admitted in all systems of law and its use is recognized by international decisions'. See S. Rosenne, *The Law and Practice of the International Court* (hereafter *'Law and Practice'*) (Dordrecht: Nijhoff, 1985) pp. 582-3.

32 ICJ Rep 1986, p. 98.

33 Rosenne, *Law and Practice*, pp. 590-91.

34 *Velasquez Rodriguez*, para. 137; *Godinez Cruz*, para. 143.

35 *Velasquez Rodriguez (Preliminary Objections)*, para. 28; *Fairen Garbi and Solis Corrales (Preliminary Objections)*, para. 33; *Godinez Cruz (Preliminary Objections)*, para 31.

36 *Velasquez Rodriguez (Preliminary Objections)*, para. 29; *Fairen Garbi and Solis Corrales (Preliminary Objections)*, para. 34; *Godinez Cruz (Preliminary Objections)*, para 32.

37 Ibid. As Shelton points out, 'Judicial Review', p. 372, it was necessary for the Court to undertake review of the evidence *de novo* since the government of Honduras had not responded to the Commission's requests for information. The Commission, relying on Article 42 of its Statute had simply presumed the facts denounced by the petitioners to be true. Although, the

Court could, in Shelton's view, have relied upon the doctrine of estoppel as regards Honduras's subsequent claims, it preferred to base its judgment on proof and not presumption.

[38] See the view of Judge Piza Escalante, supra.

[39] *Velasquez Rodriguez*, para. 134; *Fairen Garbi and Solis Corrales*, para. 136; *Godinez Cruz*, para. 140.

[40] *Velasquez Rodriguez*, para. 129.

[41] Supra, pp. 165-6.

[42] This proposition is usually expressed in the maxim *ei incumbit, qui dicit, non qui negat.* See *Diversion of the Water from the Meuse Case* (The Netherlands v Belgium) (1937) PCIJ Ser A/B, No. 70 at 30; *Minquiers and Ecrehos Case* (France v United Kingdom), ICJ Rep 1953, p. 47 at p. 52, *The Temple of Preah Vihear* (Cambodia v Thailand), ICJ Rep 1962, p. 6 at pp. 15-16. C.f., however, the position of the European Court of Human Rights which takes the view that there is no question of burden of proof in cases before it: *Ireland v United Kingdom*, 21 YB 602; Eur Ct HR Series A, No. 25, paras. 160-61; *Artico*, Eur Ct HR, Series A, No. 37, paras. 29-30. In the former case the Court declared that it was empowered to examine all evidence whether or not originating from the Commission, parties or other sources. It also held that it could obtain information *proprio motu*. This would seem to suggest that the victim (the object of the proceedings) could be called upon to supply evidence. Indeed, in *Lawless*, Eur Ct HR Series A, No. 1, the Court permitted the applicant to append his written observations to the European Commission's submissions. In *Artico* the Court took the view that neither the victim nor the Commission had the status of party to the proceedings. Thus, the state was the only party, and since it had no adversary, there was no question of allocating the burden of proof. In practice the Court has required the Commission to prove the applicant's allegations.

[43] *Velasquez Rodriguez*, para. 123; *Fairen Garbi and Solis Corrales*, para. 126; *Godinez Cruz*, para. 131. Shelton, 'Judicial Review', p. 383, correctly states that the Court's decision here not only reflects the practice of international tribunals, but also the presumption that states not only should, but do, carry out their international obligations in good faith. She further argues that this view implies a presumption of innocence on the part of the state impleaded.

[44] *Velasquez Rodriguez*, para. 124; *Fairen Garbi and Solis Corrales*, para. 127; *Godinez Cruz*, para. 130.

[45] *Velasquez Rodriguez*, para. 126; *Fairen Garbi and Solis Corrales*, para. 133; *Godinez Cruz*, para. 129.

[46] *Velasquez Rodriguez*, para. 124; *Fairen Garbi and Solis Corrales*, para. 127; *Godinez Cruz*, para. 130.

[47] *Velasquez Rodriguez*, para. 125; *Fairen Garbi and Solis Corrales*, para. 128; *Godinez Cruz*, para. 131.

[48] *Velasquez Rodriguez*, para. 124; *Fairen Garbi and Solis Corrales*, para. 127; *Godinez Cruz*, para. 130.

[49] *Velasquez Rodriguez*, para. 138; *Fairen Garbi and Solis Corrales*, para. 130; *Godinez Cruz*, para. 132.

[50] *Velasquez Rodriguez*, para. 124; *Fairen Garbi and Solis Corrales*, para. 127; *Godinez Cruz*, para. 130.

[51] *Velasquez Rodriguez*, para. 127; *Fairen Garbi and Solis Corrales*, para. 130; *Godinez Cruz*, para. 133. C.f., the holding of the ICJ in the *Military and Paramilitary Activities Case*, para. 29, that the claim adduced must show that 'the facts on which it is based are supported by convincing evidence'. In *Ireland v United Kingdom*, para. 161, the European

Court of Human Rights applied the standard of proof 'beyond reasonable doubt'. See Shelton, 'Judicial Review', pp. 384-5.

[52] *Velasquez Rodriguez*, para. 128; *Fairen Garbi and Solis Corrales*, para. 131; *Godinez Cruz*, para. 134.As to the standards of proof required in other international tribunals see D.V. Sandifer, *Evidence Before International Tribunals* (1975). The ICJ in particular has exercised considerable liberality in admitting evidence. It has, however, applied *post hoc* controls in weighing the value of evidence after its presentation. See in particular the *Military and Paramilitary Activities (Merits) Case*. The European Court of Human Rights has also adopted a liberal approach in admitting evidence. Rule 40(1) of the European Court's rules of procedure states that 'the Court may obtain any evidence which it considers capable of providing clarification of the facts of the case'.

[53] Hearsay evidence is usually treated with caution by international tribunals. See *Corfu Channel Case* (United Kingdom v Albania), ICJ Rep 1949, p. 1 at p. 16.

[54] Ibid., paras. 141 and 143. The Court also observed (at para. 141) that where testimony was challenged the challenging party bore the burden of refuting that testimony.

[55] Loc. cit., supra, n. 52.

[56] *Velasquez Rodriguez*, para. 146; *Fairen Garbi and Solis Corrales*, para. 145; *Godinez Cruz*, para. 152.

[57] *Velasquez Rodriguez*, para. 146; *Fairen Garbi and Solis Corrales*, para. 145; *Godinez Cruz*, para. 152.

[58] Discussed supra, pp. 139-41.

[59] *Velasquez Rodriguez*, para. 144; *Fairen Garbi and Solis Corrales*, para. 142; *Godinez Cruz*, para. 150.

[60] *Velasquez Rodriguez*, para. 148; *Godinez Cruz*, para. 156. On the substantive rights affected by the policy see infra, chapter 7.

[61] At para. 159.

[62] Supra, pp. 144-5.

[63] Article 63 ACHR.

[64] *Interpretation of Compensatory Damages*, supra, pp. 144-6.

[65] Article 67 ACHR.

[66] Ibid. See also *Interpretation of Compensatory Damages*, supra, pp. 144-6.

[67] Article 63(1) ACHR.

[68] Article 68(1) ACHR. The same obligation is placed upon Contracting States under the European Convention which provides that they must 'undertake to abide by the decision of the Court in any case to which they are parties'.

[69] Article 69 ACHR.

[70] J.G. Merrills, *The Development of International Law by the European Court of Human Rights* (Manchester: Manchester University Press, 2nd edn, 1993), p. 12.

[71] *Aloeboetoe et al. Case, Reparations (Article 63(1) of the American Convention on Human Rights)*, judgment of 10 September 1993, Series C, No. 15. See Scott Davidson, 'Remedies for Violations of the American Convention on Human Rights' (1995) 44 ICLQ 405.

[72] Judgment of January 18, 1995, Series C, No. 19 (1995) 16 HRLJ 149.

[73] Loc. cit., supra, note 91.

[74] *Velasquez Rodriguez, Compensatory Damages (Article 63(1) American Convention on Human Rights)*, Judgment of July 21, 1989, Series C, No. 7, para. 24; *Godinez Cruz, Compensatory Damages (Article 63(1) American Convention on Human Rights)*, Judgment of July 21, 1989, Series C, No. 8, para. 26.

[75] *Aloeboetoe*, para. 47.

[76]   Ibid., para. 49.

[77]   Ibid., para. 51.

[78]   Ibid., para. 59.

[79]   Suriname objected to the claim on behalf of the tribe since it alleged that this was the introduction of new facts which had not hitherto been before the Court and which Suriname had not had the opportunity to contest. It claimed that it had been denied its right of defence. The Court citing the ICJ in the *Chorzow Factory Case*, PCIJ, Series E, No. 9, p. 163 ruled, however, that 'in proceedings before an international court a party may modify its application provided that the other party has its opportunity to state its views on the subject'. It also held that any disagreement on the facts between the parties related only to reparations and their scope, and thus declared that it had jurisdiction to resolve the issue in the current proceedings.

[80]   *Aloeboetoe*, para. 55.

[81]   Ibid., paras. 61 and 62.

[82]   Ibid., para. 62.

[83]   Ibid., para 138.

[84]   Ibid., para. 68. This was apparently due in part to the failure of the Commission to place adequate evidence before the Court. As the Court remarked, 'the Court is aware of the difficulties presented by the intrant case: the facts involve a community that lives in the jungle, whose members are practically illiterate and do not utilize written documents. Nevertheless, other evidence could have been produced'.

[85]   *Aloeboetoe*, para. 82.

[86]   Ibid., para. 84.

[87]   Ibid., para. 83.

[88]   Ibid.

[89]   *Velasquez Rodriguez (Compensatory Damages)*, para 46; *Godinez Cruz (Compensatory Damages)*, para. 44.

[90]   *Velasquez Rodriguez (Compensatory Damages)*, para 46; *Godinez Cruz (Compensatory Damages)*, para. 44.

[91]   *Velasquez Rodriguez (Compensatory Damages)*, para. 48.

[92]   Ibid.

[93]   *Godinez Cruz (Compensatory Damages)*, para. 47.

[94]   *Velasquez Rodriguez (Compensatory Damages)*, para. 51; *Godinez Cruz (Compensatory Damages)*, para. 49.

[95]   *Velasquez Rodriguez (Compensatory Damages)*, para. 50; *Godinez Cruz (Compensatory Damages)*, para. 49.

[96]   *Velasquez Rodriguez (Compensatory Damages)*, para. 52; *Godinez Cruz (Compensatory Damages)*, para. 50.

[97]   *Velasquez Rodriguez*, para. 53.

[98]   Ibid, para. 54.

[99]   *Velasquez Rodriguez (Compensatory Damages)*, para. 57; *Godinez Cruz (Compensatory Damages)*, para. 52. The Court offered Honduras the facility to pay the damages in six equal monthly instalments in successive months, with interest being added to the outstanding balance in accordance with the prevailing interest rate in Honduras.

[100] *Velasquez Rodriguez*, para. 58.

[101] *Godinez Cruz (Compensatory Damages)*, para. 53.

[102] *Velasquez Rodriguez (Compensatory Damages)*, para. 59; *Godinez Cruz (Compensatory Damages)*, para. 54.

[103] See supra, pp. 145-6.

[104] *Velasquez Rodriguez (Interpretation of Compensatory Damages)*, para. 18; *Godinez Cruz (Interpretation of Compensatory Damages)*, para 18. The Commission stated that Honduras had suffered 263% inflation in the last decade.

[105] *Velasquez Rodriguez (Interpretation of Compensatory Damages)*, para. 29; *Godinez Cruz (Interpretation of Compensatory Damages)*, para 29.

[106] *Velasquez Rodriguez (Interpretation of Compensatory Damages)*, para. 31; *Godinez Cruz (Interpretation of Compensatory Damages)*, para 31.

[107] *Velasquez Rodriguez (Interpretation of Compensatory Damages)*, para. 31; *Godinez Cruz (Interpretation of Compensatory Damages)*, para 31.

[108] *Velasquez Rodriguez (Interpretation of Compensatory Damages)*, para. 32; *Godinez Cruz (Interpretation of Compensatory Damages)*, para 32. The Court held that this part of the Commission's request exceeded the scope of a 'mere interpretation'.

[109] *Judicial Remedies*, p. 155.

[110] See, for example, *Artico*, Eur Ct HR Series A, No. 37; *Van Droogenbroeck*, Eur Ct HR Series A, No. 53; *De Jong, Baljet and Van den Brink*, Eur Ct. HR Series A, No. 77.

[111] See, for example, *Silver*, Eur Ct HR Series A, No. 67; *Campbell and Fell*, Eur Ct HR Series A, No. 80 and *Marckx*, Eur Ct HR Series A, No. 31; *Johnston*, Eur Ct HR Series A, No. 126.

[112] *Judicial Remedies*, p. 157.

[113] See, for example, *Artico*, loc. cit., supra, note 94 and *Goddi*, Eur Ct HR Series A, No. 76.

[114] *Goddi*, loc. cit., supra, note 97 at para. 35.

[115] See *X and Y v The Netherlands*, Eur Ct HR Series A, No. 91 at para. 40 where the Court said: The damage in question does not lend itself even to an approximate basis of calculation.

[116] See Gray, *Judicial Remedies*, pp. 155-60 and CD Gray, 'Remedies for Individuals under the European Convention on Human Rights' (1980) *Human Rights Review* 153.

[117] Judgment of 21 January 1994, Series C, No. 16.

[118] Ibid., para. 4 of the operative part of the judgment.

[119] Supra, p. 213.

[120] *Inter-American Court*, p. 240.

[121] See, for example, *Ringeisen*, Eur Ct HR Series A, No. 16 in which an award of 20,000 Deutschmarks was made against Austria.

[122] Ibid.

[123] Supra, pp. 145-6.

[124] Ibid.

[125] *Velasquez Rodriguez (Interpretation of Compensatory Damages)*, para. 40; *Godinez Cruz (Interpretation of Compensatory Damages)*, para 40.

[126] Ibid., para. 41. A major part of the loss of purchasing power of the award resulted from the devaluation of the *lempira* against other currencies during the period of non-payment. The Court observed that one of the 'easiest and most accessible ways' of preserving the purchasing power of the award had been lost by non-payment on the due date, namely, conversion of the *lempira* into 'hard' currencies such as the US Dollar. Ibid., para. 42.

[127] *Inter-American Court*, pp. 240-41.

[128] Articles 3 and 8. On the Council of Europe's power of expulsion see Francis G. Jacobs, *The European Convention on Human Rights* (Clarendon Press, Oxford, 1975), pp. 269-71.

[129] See *Exclusion of the present Government of Cuba from participation in the inter-American system*, Res. VI of the 8th Meeting of Consultation of Ministers of Foreign Affairs, Punta del Este, January 1962, OEA/Ser.F/II.8, Doc. 68, O.14. The argument that it was the *government* of Cuba and not the *state* of Cuba which was excluded would appear to be casuistic.

6 The Advisory Jurisdiction of the Inter-American Court of Human Rights

Introduction

The advisory jurisdiction of the Inter-American Court is complementary to its contentious jurisdiction. Its role is to enable the States Parties and certain designated organs of the OAS to seek rulings on the interpretation of a broad range of human rights instruments concerning the protection of human rights within the western hemisphere and to allow states to test the compatibility of their domestic laws with these instruments. It will be noticed immediately that the right to consult the Court on these matters is not limited to States Parties to the Convention, but is open to any Member State of the OAS. For these reasons, the Inter-American Court might be regarded as an OAS institution in fact if not in law. It should also be noted at the outset that whereas the Court's decisions in contentious cases are legally binding, advisory opinions are merely declaratory in nature. As will be suggested below, this does not mean that advisory opinions are negligible in their effect since they have considerable persuasive effect not only for the states which are party to such proceedings, but for the entire inter-American system. A number of the Court's advisory opinions, as we have already seen, have provided the Commission with guidance on various important procedural aspects, such as the exhaustion of local remedies, and, as we shall see below, have begun to contribute to the Court's development of a jurisprudence in the field of the system's substantive rights.

Basis of the Court's Advisory Jurisdiction

Article 64 of the American Convention provides the Inter-American Court with an advisory jurisdiction which the Court itself has observed 'is more extensive than that enjoyed by any international tribunal in existence today'.[1] A brief glance at Article 64 certainly suggests a jurisdiction which is broader than that of either the ICJ[2] or the European Court of Human Rights.[3] Article 64 provides:

232

1. The member states of the Organization may consult the Court regarding the interpretation of this Convention or of other Treaties concerning the protection of human rights in the American states. Within their spheres of competence, the organs listed in Chapter X of the Charter of the Organization of American States, as amended by the Protocol of Buenos Aires, may in like manner consult the Court.
2. The Court, at the request of a member state of the Organization, may provide that state with opinions regarding the compatibility of any of its domestic laws with the aforesaid international instruments.

It will be apparent that the advisory jurisdiction exercised by the Court under Articles 64(1) and 64(2) are different in nature. Whereas the former deals with the question of interpretation in general, the latter concerns the rather more concrete issue of compatibility of a state's domestic law with the appropriate instruments. In both cases, however, a number of questions arise as to the application of the provisions *ratione personae* and *ratione materiae*.

Who May Request an Advisory Opinion?

First, it will be noted that *any* member state of the OAS may request an advisory opinion from the Court under Article 64(1) or 64(2) whether or not it has become party to the Convention.[4] Although a state which is not party to the Convention is unlikely to be concerned with the meaning of that instrument, it may well be interested in the meaning of 'other treaties concerning the protection of human rights in the American states', especially since the Court has ruled that the standards contained in the American Declaration of the Rights and Duties of Man are an authoritative interpretation of the references to human rights contained in the OAS Charter.[5]

The second group of entities which are competent to seek an advisory opinion from the Court are the organs listed in Chapter VIII of the OAS Charter as amended by its subsequent protocols. These, however, are restricted to seeking rulings within their spheres of competence. As indicated above,[6] Chapter VIII contains only a single provision, Article 52, which refers either directly or indirectly to the majority of OAS organs, including the Specialized Organs which are defined by Article 130 of the Charter. While the right of these organs to consult the Court is conditional, it is also clear that certain of the organs, such as the Commission and the General Assembly, will generally have a broader competence than, say, one of the Specialized Organs. Indeed, the Court dealt with this very question in its second advisory opinion: *Effect of Reservations*.[7] Here the Commission sought a ruling from the Court as to the date on which a state ratifying or adhering to the Convention with a reservation could be regarded as a party to it.[8] As a preliminary matter the Court considered it was obliged to determine whether the Commission had *locus standi* to seek a ruling.[9]

The Court observed that, while member states in general enjoyed an absolute right to seek an advisory opinion, OAS organs were restricted to matters within their competence. Thus, in order for the latter to obtain *locus standi*, they had to demonstrate a 'legitimate institutional interest'.[10] While OAS organs could decide initially whether or not they were competent to seek a ruling, the question was to be determined ultimately by the Court which would refer to the appropriate constituent instruments and the 'legal practice' of the organ in question.[11] As far as the Commission was concerned, however, the Court, referring to the very broad competence enjoyed by that organ in the field of human rights[12] declared that:[13]

> Unlike some other OAS organs, the Commission enjoys, as a practical matter, *an absolute right* to request advisory opinions within the framework of Article 64(1) of the Convention.

It is clear then that the Commission will always be able to demonstrate the necessary legitimate institutional interest to seek an advisory opinion from the Court, but since this is only a 'practical matter', it would appear that the Court might still refuse the Commission standing should this be deemed necessary.[14]

If the Commission enjoys a pre-eminent position before the Court, it is also arguable that the General Assembly of the OAS should enjoy a similar status. As the supreme organ of the Organization with the competence to oversee all matters concerning human rights, including the issue of non-enforcement of the Court's own judgments, it will also generally be able to demonstrate the necessary 'legitimate institutional interest'.[15] Indeed, this conclusion may be implied from the Court's opinion in *Restrictions to the Death Penalty* where it indicated that the General Assembly would be 'in a similar position' to the Commission were it to seek an advisory opinion on a question concerning human rights.[16] As far as the other organs of the OAS are concerned it is clear that applications for advisory opinions from the Court will be treated individually on their merits. It is likely, for example, that a request for a ruling by the Inter-American Commission of Women on an issue of sexual equality would be admissible, while it is unlikely that the Pan-American Institute of Geography and History on an issue of freedom of movement for academics would be able demonstrate the necessary legitimate institutional interest.

What May Be the Subject of an Advisory Opinion?

While it is clear that Article 64 *in fine* permits the designated entities to seek an advisory opinion from the Court on the conditions established, it also raises a number of problems concerning precisely which instruments the Court is entitled to rule upon. The problems may be expressed thus:

1. Is the Court required to render an advisory opinion in all cases where the applicant appears to have *locus standi*?
2. Is the Court competent to render an advisory opinion on the meaning of one or more of the rights protected by the Convention when the request for such an opinion is in reality a disguised contentious case?
3. What is the meaning of 'other treaties concerning the protection of human rights in the American states' in Article 64(1)?
4. Does 'domestic laws' in Article 64(2) include not only laws in force in a Member State but draft laws also?
5. Which agency of the state is entitled to seek a ruling on the compatibility of domestic laws with the human rights instruments designated in Article 64?

1. Is the Court required to render an advisory opinion in all cases where the applicant appears to have locus standi?

It is a general principle of law that judicial institutions have a residual discretion to refuse to admit a case for consideration where to do so would amount to an abuse of process by one or more of the parties. Numerous examples of this can be found in domestic legal systems and also in the legal system established by the Treaty of Rome.[17] It is also clear that the European Commission and the Inter-American Commission, functioning as quasi-judicial organs, are empowered to reject cases which are manifestly ill-founded or abusive of the right of petition. The Human Rights Committee, while not empowered by any of its constituent instruments to reject communications on such a basis, has nevertheless developed this concept through its jurisprudence.

Similarly, while there is nothing in the constituent legal instruments of the Court empowering it either expressly or implicitly to reject cases which it considers to be an abuse of process, the Court has nevertheless made it clear that, although an application appears to comply with the formal requirements of Article 64, it retains discretion to refuse to admit a case. In its first advisory opinion, which concerned a case brought by Peru on the meaning of the phrase 'other treaties for the protection of human rights in the American states' in Article 64(1), the Court was required to define the limits of its own jurisdiction.[18] Here the Court noted that, although the language of Article 64 conferred very broad powers upon the Court, these were not limitless and were required to be viewed in the context of the Convention and taking into account its object and purpose.[19] There were, in the Court's view, essentially two broad categories of limitation on its discretion to exercise its advisory jurisdiction. The first category of limitations was derived from the place of the Court in the inter-American system taken as a whole.[20] As an inter-American institution, therefore, there were certain limitations on its jurisdiction *ratione materiae*. It could exercise neither its contentious nor its advisory jurisdiction in order to determine the scope of treaties, whether of a human rights character or not, which had been concluded by states which were not members of the OAS, nor could it interpret provisions governing the structure or operation of international organizations or institutions not belonging to the inter-American system.[21] The Court noted, however, that it possessed the power 'to interpret any treaty as long as it is directly related to the protection of human rights in the American states of the inter-American system'.[22]

Other limitations on the Court within this first category derived from the Court's status as a Convention institution.[23] Here the Court referred directly to an issue with which it was required to deal in its Second Advisory Opinion, *Effect of Reservations,* namely, the problem of contentious cases being disguised as requests for advisory opinions. Although the Court was not required to rule upon this matter specifically in the instant case, it nevertheless made some general observations which indicated the line which it was likely to follow in subsequent cases where this issue was raised. Here the Court noted that states in general had opposed the application of advisory jurisdiction in a number of cases before the ICJ since they saw such an extension as eroding the principle that the consent of states party to a dispute was required before they could become subject to international adjudication.[24] The Court, however, was able to refer to the jurisprudence of the ICJ in which such arguments had been effectively overruled.[25]

The Court also noted the obverse of this particular problem in the case of human rights proceedings, namely, the use by states of the Court's advisory jurisdiction to weaken or undermine the purpose of its contentious jurisdiction, thus modifying the system to the detriment of the victim.[26] Since the advisory jurisdiction of the Court was closely related to the purposes of the American Convention, and since that jurisdiction was also intended to assist the American states and the organs of the OAS to fulfil their functions, it was 'obvious' that 'any request for an advisory opinion that has another purpose would weaken the American Convention system and distort the advisory jurisdiction of the Court'.[27]

The second group of limitations upon the Court's jurisdiction stem from the context in which it was granted advisory jurisdiction and from the object and purpose of the American Convention.[28] Unlike Protocol II of the European Convention,[29] Article 64 of the American Convention does not specifically exclude any matter relating to the protection of human rights in the American states; it is therefore for the Court to determine the limits of its jurisdiction on a case by case basis.[30] Like the ICJ, however, whose advisory jurisdiction is similarly permissive, the Court has the power to determine whether the circumstances in which a request for a ruling is made justifies the acceptance or rejection of that request.[31] While the Court has a broad appreciation over whether to admit a case, it has held that this should not be equated with an 'unfettered discretion' to grant or deny a ruling:[32]

> The Court must have compelling reasons founded in the conviction that the request exceeds the limits of its advisory jurisdiction under the Convention before it may refrain from complying with a request for an advisory opinion.

The Court's ruling in *Other Treaties*, which has been consistently reaffirmed in subsequent opinions,[33] clearly establishes the way in which it will exercise its discretion to admit or refuse a request for an advisory opinion. As far as the Court's jurisdiction *ratione materiae* is concerned, only treaties which impact directly on the protection of human rights in the American states will be admitted for interpretation. This of course raises problems of interpretation itself which will be dealt with in section 3 below. On the question of the Court's policy, it is apparent that the maintenance of its contentious jurisdiction and the protection of the integrity of the Convention system and the protection of a victim from human rights violations within that system are paramount. It is equally apparent that the Court will determine the admissibility of each request for an advisory opinion on a case by case basis, guided by the considerations outlined above. To date the Court has only ruled one request for an advisory opinion inadmissible. That ruling is based quite clearly on the principles described above.

In *Compatibility of Draft Legislation*,[34] Costa Rica requested the Court to rule upon whether or not certain proposed amendments which affected the appeal structure in criminal cases in Costa Rica were compatible with Article 8 of the American Convention.[35] In particular, Costa Rica wished to know whether its legislative proposal complied with Article 8(2)(h) which guarantees the right of a convicted person to appeal to a higher court.[36] This legislation had, in fact, been introduced to deal with certain problems in Costa Rica's criminal appeal structure which had resulted in the submission of a number of applications by Costa Rican citizens to the Commission alleging breaches of the Convention. The Commission had declared certain of these applications admissible and had instructed Costa Rica to rectify the position by adopting the appropriate legislative measures to ensure compliance with Article 8(2)(h). Despite many serious delays in implementation of the Commission's report, Costa Rica had still not fulfilled its obligations at the time the request for the advisory opinion was submitted to the Court.[37] The Commission was therefore still in a position to submit the case to the Court, although it had not yet done so, and might not do so if the problem were rectified to its satisfaction by the proposed legislation. The Court nonetheless held that:[38]

> ... a reply to the question presented by Costa Rica could produce, under the guise of an advisory opinion, a determination of contentious matters not yet referred to the Court, without providing the victims with the opportunity to participate in the proceedings. Such a result would distort the Convention system.

The Court went on to state that contentious proceedings provided a venue where matters could be dealt with in a much more direct way than advisory proceedings, and this was not an opportunity which could be denied to individuals who did not have the chance to participate in the latter proceedings.[39] Furthermore, the Court noted that the Commission played different roles in contentious and advisory proceedings. In the former, it represented the interests of the individual victim or applicant, whereas in the latter its interests were those of an inter-American institution. The Court therefore took the view that this was one of the occasions on which it should invoke its power to refuse an advisory opinion in order to avoid undermining the contentious jurisdiction in a way which might impair the human rights of the applicants with cases pending before the Commission.[40]

2. Is the Court competent to render an advisory opinion on the meaning of one or more of the rights protected by the Convention when the request for such an opinion is in reality a disguised contentious case?

As we have seen above, this issue is not unique to the Inter-American Court of Human Rights. The propriety of rendering an advisory opinion in cases which appear to have a contentious element has been raised in a number of cases before the World Court. In the *Eastern Carelia Case*,[41] the PCIJ refused to give a ruling at the request of the League of Nations Council concerning a dispute between Russia and Finland. The primary reason for the refusal to give an advisory opinion was that Russia was not a member of the League of Nations, nor had it consented to the issue being submitted to the Court. The *Eastern Carelia Case* has, however, been consistently distinguished in subsequent cases before the ICJ. In the *Interpretation of Peace Treaties Case*,[42] the Court found that the PCIJ had declined to give an opinion in the *Eastern Carelia Case* because it had involved an actual dispute between the two parties. In the instant case, the Court took a broader view of the function of advisory opinions as addressing underlying issues of law in order to assist the UN in performing its functions.[43] The *Eastern Carelia Case* was further distinguished by the ICJ in the *Western Sahara Case*,[44] in which it stated that the absence of Russian consent to judicial proceedings and the fact that Russia was not a member of the League of Nations appeared to be central to the PCIJ's determination. The ICJ based its own competence to give an opinion in the *Western Sahara Case* on the General Assembly's need for such an opinion to assist it in the proper performance of its functions. It appears therefore that the persuasive influence of the *Eastern Carelia Case* has been considerably marginalized and that the dominant feature of the ICJ's jurisprudence has been its willingness to offer opinions if these will guide the UN its work.[45]

In the context of the inter-American human rights system, it is apparent that a state might seek to contest the Court's jurisdiction to render an advisory opinion where the subject matter of that opinion forms the basis of a dispute either between that state and another state or that state and the Commission. The problem becomes especially acute when the contesting state has not accepted the contentious jurisdiction of the Court under Article 62 of the Convention. A request for an advisory opinion in these circumstances might very well appear to be a means of circumventing the jurisdictional requirements of the Convention in an attempt to implead a recalcitrant state before the Court.

The question of whether the Court would refuse to give an advisory opinion following a request by the Commission because it was alleged to be a contentious case in disguise was faced squarely in *Restrictions to the Death Penalty*. Here, the Commission, acting on the basis of Article 64(1), had requested an interpretation of the final sentence of Article 4(2) of the Convention concerning the extension of the death penalty to crimes to which it did not currently apply. The motivation for the request was the existence of a difference of opinion between the Commission and Guatemala during the compilation by the former of a country report on the latter.[46] The essential difference was over whether this provision was capable of modification by way of a reservation by Guatemala, thus allowing extension of the death penalty to crimes to which it did not previously apply. Guatemala, which had not accepted the jurisdiction of the Court, argued that the dispute which existed between it and the Commission should not be heard by the Court because of lack of jurisdiction.[47]

Before the Court could proceed to consider the question of jurisdiction in the present case, it was required to deal with a prior procedural objection by Guatemala that the question of jurisdiction should have been considered separately from the merits. This claim was dealt with in some detail by the Court since it considered it to be of some importance and likely to arise in future contentious or advisory opinions. The primary focus of the Court in dealing with this procedural issue was the nature of its advisory jurisdiction as distinct from its contentious jurisdiction. Whereas the states in contentious cases became parties to proceedings and were obliged to comply with the judgments of the Court, this was not so in advisory proceedings.[48] Here 'all the proceeding is designed to do is to enable OAS Member States and OAS organs to obtain a judicial interpretation of a provision embodied in the Convention or other human rights treaties in the American states'.[49] Nonetheless, the Court recognized that a state's interests might be affected by an advisory opinion in that it might weaken or strengthen a state's position in some present or future legal controversy.[50] The Court might also have mentioned that an interpretation of the Convention or some other relevant human rights treaty during the course of advisory proceedings is authoritative, and although it may not be binding on states *stricto sensu*, it certainly provides a clear guide as to the standard of conduct required by States Parties to the Convention or Member States of the OAS. A prudent state might well wish to modify its domestic laws to bring them in line with an advisory opinion which it had not itself requested.[51]

The Court also observed that the purpose of advisory proceedings was to obtain a ruling on a question of law and as a consequence such proceedings raised no question of fact.[52] As a consequence Guatemala was in a position no different to that of other states who were entitled to make their observations on the question known to the Court.[53]

As a practical matter, the Court expressed concern over the likely delay a separation of the consideration of the preliminary jurisdictional issues and the merits of a case might occasion. This, it felt, would interfere with the fundamental purpose of advisory opinions which was to enable OAS organs to 'fulfil [their] mission within the inter-American system'.[54] The need for expedition here was essential since delay might defeat the object of the request, especially where the issue concerned the right to life.[55] The Court therefore held that for all the reasons enumerated, there was no basis for refusing to join the jurisdictional objections of Guatemala to the case.

Turning to the question of whether the Court possessed jurisdiction to render an advisory opinion on a question which related directly to an actual dispute between the Commission and a state, the Court indicated that a fundamental distinction had to be drawn between the Court's two types of jurisdiction.[56] The primary differences were, in the Court's view, that contentious proceedings were primarily fact-driven and resulted in a binding decision upon the delinquent state, whereas in advisory proceedings the Court was simply called upon to 'render opinions in interpreting legal norms'.[57] These distinctions were further distinguished by the procedures applicable to contentious and advisory proceedings. The only entities capable of bringing a contentious case concerning the Convention were the states parties and the Commission. However, as far as advisory proceedings were concerned, a much broader range of applicants was potentially competent to seek a ruling upon a much broader range of instruments.[58] From this the Court deduced:

> It is obvious, therefore, that what is involved here are very different matters, and that there is no reason in principle to apply the requirements contained in Articles 61, 62 and 63 to the consultative function of the Court, which is spelled out in Article 64.

This did not mean, however, that the Court was obliged to give an advisory opinion every time it was requested to do so. Recalling its judgment in *Other Treaties* the Court indicated that it had a discretion whether or not to render an opinion and could refuse to do so if it appeared that would either interfere with the proper functioning of the system or if it were likely to affect the interests of a victim adversely.[59] In *Other Treaties* the Court had said:[60]

The advisory jurisdiction of the Court is closely related to the purpose of the Convention. This jurisdiction is intended to assist the American states in fulfilling their international human rights obligations and to assist the different organs of the inter-American system to carry out the functions assigned to them in this field. It is obvious that any request for an advisory opinion which has another purpose would weaken the system established by the Convention and would distort the advisory jurisdiction of the Court.

The Court therefore held that the instant case did not demand that it exercise its discretion to refuse to render an advisory opinion, since it involved a legitimate request from the Commission to interpret a provision of the Convention in order to allow that organ to fulfil its functions as an OAS organ.[61] Thus the 'mere fact' that there existed a dispute between the Commission and Guatemala concerning the meaning of Article 4 of the Convention did not justify the Court in refusing to exercise its advisory jurisdiction.[62]

While it might be thought that this reasoning was adequate to sustain the conclusion reached, the Court nonetheless referred to the jurisprudence of the ICJ in order to support its finding. Here it noted that the critical question had always been whether the organ requesting the opinion had 'a legitimate interest in obtaining the opinion for the purpose of guiding its future action'.[63] Applying this reasoning to the Inter-American Commission, the Court reaffirmed its decision in the *Effect of Reservations* that the Commission enjoyed as a practical matter an absolute right to request advisory opinions within the framework of Article 64(1).[64]

The Court also took the opportunity in this case to deal with some wider issues concerning the exercise of its advisory jurisdiction. First, it noted that its advisory jurisdiction operated in parallel to its contentious jurisdiction. It thereby offered 'an alternate judicial method of a consultative nature which was designed to assist states and OAS organs to comply with and to apply human rights treaties without subjecting them to the formalism and sanctions associated with the contentious judicial process'.[65] Here the Court appeared to utilize the principle of effectiveness in interpreting the treaty,[66] ruling that it would be incompatible with the object and purpose of the Convention to interpret Article 64 as being subject to the jurisdictional requirements of Article 62 merely because there was a dispute over the meaning of the provision subject to the request.[67] This, said the Court, would 'rob' the process of its utility.[68]

Second, the Court, referring to the ICJ's judgment in *Interpretation of the Agreement of 25 March 1951 between WHO and Egypt*,[69] observed that rules of law do not operate in a vacuum and therefore it was necessary to understand the legal and factual context in which the interpretation was required.[70] Thus the Commission had not exceeded its mandate simply because it indicated in the considerations giving rise to the request that there existed a dispute between itself and Guatemala concerning the interpretation of Article 4 of the Convention.[71]

It is important to determine whether the reasoning of the Court in *Restrictions to the Death Penalty* is restricted solely to the competence of the Commission to seek an advisory opinion in circumstances where there is a dispute between it and a member state of the OAS. If it can be so limited, then, as Buergenthal argues,[72] it is possible that the advisory route may not be used to avoid the procedures inherent in contentious cases involving individuals and state parties to the Convention. However, the Court's language does not seem to imply such a restriction, especially when one has regard to its statement that advisory proceedings constitute a system parallel to contentious proceedings. Here, it might be appropriate to refer back to the definition by the Court of the limits of its advisory jurisdiction in *Other Treaties*. It may be recalled that there the Court said that it would not permit the use of its advisory jurisdiction if this was likely to undermine its contentious jurisdiction or if it would weaken or alter the Convention system in a manner that would impair a victim's rights.[73] Thus, if a petitioner had commenced proceedings before the Commission, it is unlikely that the Court would accede to a request by the affected state that the issue in dispute should be the subject of advisory proceedings since this would offend against its stated policy.[74]

3. What is the meaning of 'other treaties concerning the protection of human rights in the American states' in Article 64(1)?

Not only is the Court competent to give opinions on the meaning of the Convention, it is also empowered by Article 64(1) to interpret 'other treaties concerning the protection of human rights in the American states'. It is important to determine what this phrase itself means for two major reasons. First, all member states of the OAS may request an opinion on the interpretation of such instruments, whether or not they are parties to the Convention.[75] It is crucial therefore for these states to know exactly which instruments the Court is competent to interpret, since it may affect their obligations under the relevant treaties. Second, and this matter is directly related to the first issue, such states may also request a ruling from the Court under Article 64(2) to determine whether their domestic laws are compatible with the instruments in question.

Again, this may have important consequences for all states within the inter-American system.

In its first advisory opinion, *Other Treaties,* the Court was requested by Peru to rule directly upon the meaning of the phrase at present under consideration. In so doing, Peru also offered three possible solutions to the question. These were that the phrase comprehended:

a) Only treaties adopted within the framework or under the auspices of the inter-American system; or
b) The treaties concluded solely among the American states; or
c) All treaties in which one or more American states are parties.[76]

While not wishing to exclude any of these possibilities at the outset, the Court determined that in interpreting the phrase it must 'resort to traditional international law methods relying both on general and supplementary rules of interpretation which find expression in Articles 31 and 32 of the Vienna Convention on the Law of Treaties'.[77] In so doing, the Court observed at the outset that it mattered not whether any potential treaty subject to interpretation was bilateral or multilateral in character. Equally irrelevant was the source of the treaty obligation or its main purpose, which seems to suggest that the treaty in question need not be concerned solely or, indeed, *prima facie,* with 'human rights'.[78] From this the Court deduced that the ordinary meaning of the text did not permit the Court to exclude treaties, *a priori,* simply because they were concluded outside the inter-American system or because non-American states were or might become party to them.[79] The only restriction contained in Article 64(1) was that the treaties in question must be for the protection of human rights *in* the American states; this did not mean that the treaties themselves were required to be *between* the American states, nor that they be regional in character, nor that they were adopted within the inter-American system. As the Court said:[80]

> Since such a restrictive purpose was not expressly articulated, it cannot be presumed to exist.

Thus the limitations upon the Court's jurisdiction to interpret treaties under Article 64(1) are imposed by geopolitical considerations, namely, whether the state requesting the interpretation is affected by the treaty as an American state. Furthermore, the principal purpose of the request must relate to the implementation or the scope of the obligations assumed by a Member State of the OAS.[81] If the principal purpose of the request is to enquire about the scope of the obligations assumed under such a treaty by a non-American state, the Court will decline jurisdiction.[82] Buergenthal has also suggested that the Court might be reluctant to comply with requests for advisory opinions on interpretations of other treaties if they have their own enforcement mechanisms.[83] Given the Court's subsequent statements however, while this might be a matter of which it would take cognizance, it does not appear that it would constrain the Court unduly.[84]

The main rationale for Article 64(1) was, in the Court's view, to assist the American states in fulfilling their various human rights obligations. From this point of departure the Court observed that an American state was 'no less obliged to abide by an international agreement merely because non-American states are or may become parties'.[85] While it was true that regional methods of protection were better suited to hemispheric conditions and likely to be more acceptable to states, the Court nevertheless observed that the nature of human rights militated against a strict distinction between regionalism and universalism and that it would therefore be improper to make a distinction between treaties on this basis.[86] The Court also noted a tendency to integrate the regional and universal human rights systems in the American Convention, which refers throughout to a variety of human rights instruments having a provenance other than the inter-American system.[87] To support this view, the Court also referred to Article 29(b) of the Convention which makes clear that the Convention itself must not be interpreted to restrict the enjoyment of rights or freedoms originating from other treaties to which states may be party. Thus the Court declared:

> The function that Article 64 of the convention confers on the Court is an inherent part of the protective system established by the Convention. The Court is of the view, therefore, that to exclude from its advisory jurisdiction international human rights treaties that are binding on American states would weaken the full guarantee of the rights proclaimed in those treaties and, in turn, conflict with the rules enunciated in Article 29(b) of the Convention.

It followed from this that the regional system needed to be complemented by the universal system and that, indeed, this could be discerned in the practice of the Commission. This view was 'entirely consistent with the object and purpose of the Convention; the American Declaration and the Statute of the Commission'.[88]

The practice of the Commission in interpreting and applying international human rights conventions itself also raised, in the Court's view, the possibility that the Commission might render an erroneous interpretation of such an instrument. As a practical matter therefore, it was necessary for the Court to exercise jurisdiction over interpretation of these treaties in order that a state might be able 'to challenge' the Commission's interpretation.[89]

While it might be thought that it was sufficient for the Court to refer simply to Article 31 of the Vienna Convention in support of its findings, it nevertheless had recourse to Article 32 of the same Convention in order to confirm its interpretation. It may be recalled that Article 32 permits an interpreter to have recourse to a treaty's *travaux préparatoires* for the purposes of, *inter alia*, confirming the meaning the provision subject to the interpretative process. Here, the Court declared that the preparatory work of the American Convention demonstrated a clear tendency 'to conform the regional system to the universal one, which is evident in the text of the Convention itself'.[90]

Two objections were raised concerning the extension of the Court's jurisdiction by interpreting 'other treaties' in such a broad way. The first was that a broad interpretation would lead the Court into giving opinions on matters which had nothing to do with the Convention or the member states of the OAS, and which could not, in the ordinary course of events, be brought before the Court. This was rejected by the Court on two grounds. First, such a scenario was hypothetical and did not raise sufficient grounds for the Court concluding *a priori* that it lacked power to render an opinion on a treaty merely because its provenance was outside the inter-American system.[91] The second objection was that an extension of the Court's jurisdiction might lead it to render interpretations of international instruments which conflicted with those given by institutions established by those treaties. The most obvious source of potential conflict here would be with the UN Human Rights Committee established by the International Covenant on Civil and Political Rights which, under the First Optional Protocol to that instrument, is empowered to receive individual petitions and give its views on whether a state has violated its obligations under the Covenant. It is also conceivable that the ICJ might be asked to give an advisory opinion on a 'human rights' treaty which might conflict with an opinion delivered by the Inter-American Court. This argument did not find favour with the Court which offered two reasons for rejecting it. First, it observed that the possibility of conflicting interpretations was a phenomenon common to all legal systems which do not have courts which are hierarchically integrated. It was not unusual in such systems to find differing interpretations of the same rule. Second, even if conflicts did occur, they would not be serious, since decisions in advisory opinions did not have the same binding force as decisions in contentious cases.[92] It may be noted here, however, that the Court perhaps underplayed the importance of a possible conflict between itself and another international institution having competence to rule on human rights issues. While it is true that advisory opinions lack the same mandatory force as decisions in contentious cases, it is also true, as we have seen above, that such opinions are strongly persuasive since they are authoritative interpretations of the legal instruments in question. Indeed, the Court itself has also noted in *Restrictions to the Death Penalty* that advisory opinions may strengthen or weaken a state's position in relation to some actual or potential legal controversy.[93] The possibility of conflicting interpretations might therefore hold a very real fear for some states which may be unsure which particular interpretation they should follow. It is likely, however, that the Court would strive to avoid conflicting interpretations for a number of reasons. First, Article 29(b) enjoins it not to interpret the Convention in a manner which restricts rights acquired under other international instruments. It is therefore unlikely to offer a more restrictive interpretation of a particular right than that given by the institution competent to interpret the rights under its own constituent Convention. Second, and this is a matter of policy, it would reflect badly upon the status and authority of the Court if it consistently undercut, or deliberately deviated from, interpretations offered by other international tribunals. Third, as we have seen above,[94] the Court may decline to exercise its discretion to render an advisory opinion if the purpose for which it is sought is to seek a ruling on the legal position of extra-hemispheric states. The Court may also exercise this discretion if, perhaps, the purpose for which a state sought the opinion was an attempt to seek 'review' of an opinion rendered by the ICJ or some other international human rights institution.

Two questions which were neither asked of the Court in *Other Treaties,* nor which it sought to answer were:

(a) What is a treaty *'concerning the protection of human rights in the American states'*? and;
(b) Is the American Declaration of the Rights and Duties of Man a *treaty concerning the protection of human rights in the American states?*

While the answer to question (a) still leaves considerable room for speculation, question (b) has already been answered by the Court in *Interpretation of the American Declaration,* and has already been considered in some detail above.[95]

The point of departure in attempting to answer question (a) might be an examination of the terminology employed in Article 64(1). Buergenthal has noted,[96] that the phrase does not refer to treaties concerned exclusively with human rights but to treaties, which may be bilateral or multilateral which possess a human rights content. It may be further observed, however, that the phrase also refers to treaties concerning the *protection* of human rights. This might imply that a treaty which simply mentions human rights in passing or which is not focused primarily on the protection of human rights may not fall within the meaning of the phrase. Thus, to take Buergenthal's possible examples of an extradition treaty or a bilateral commercial agreement, it may be queried whether these are treaties concerning the *protection* of human rights or whether they are treaties concerning criminal or commercial matters which incidentally *affect* human rights. While this might be a matter for dispute, it does not answer the question of what exactly a human rights treaty is or what is a human rights provision within a treaty concerned also with other matters.

It is possible, without becoming embroiled in a jurisprudential discourse, to identify a range of human rights upon which states are generally agreed. Such rights are contained in a number of international instruments both binding and non-binding which can be located with ease. It should be noted, however, that such instruments, which might be said to articulate the widely recognized 'core rights', embrace not only what are known as civil and political rights, but also economic, social and cultural rights. While the former are usually characterized by their immediate and mandatory qualities, the latter are generally drafted in a programmatic and hortatory style. This does not, however, make the latter any less 'human rights': it is simply concerned with their mode of implementation.[97] One can therefore point to the Universal Declaration of Human Rights, the two International Covenants, the European Convention on Human Rights, the European Social Charter, the African Charter on Human and People's Rights, the UN Convention on the Elimination of All Forms of Racial Discrimination, the UN and European Conventions on the Prohibition of Torture and so on, which collectively comprise identifiable and widely agreed 'human rights'. The difficulty arises when treaties which are not specifically aimed at protecting 'human rights', but which nevertheless have such a component, are identified. Take extradition treaties, for example. Such treaties are designed not only to facilitate cooperation between states in criminal matters, they are also, as a rule, intended to ensure that the rights of an alleged fugitive offender are protected. Thus extradition treaties generally incorporate the speciality principle whereby a fugitive may not be tried for a crime other than the one for which he was extradited. Of greater importance, however, may be provisions concerning the non-extradition of fugitive offenders for political offences. Such treaties between OAS states might be said to fall within Article 64(1) of the Convention and therefore susceptible to interpretation by the Court.

Of more immediate concern to OAS member states is whether the OAS Charter itself is a treaty concerning the protection of human rights in the American states. As we have seen, there are a number of references to human rights in the Charter which have been authoritatively interpreted by the American Declaration of the Rights and Duties of Man. There are also, however, several references to economic and social standards within the Charter.[98] Given the Court's ruling in *Interpretation of the American Declaration,* there would seem to be no reason in principle why the Charter itself should not be regarded as falling within the term under discussion.

4. What is the meaning of 'domestic laws' in Article 64(2)?

Article 64(2) of the Convention permits OAS member states to request the Court for an advisory opinion on the compatibility of its domestic laws with the human rights treaties referred to in paragraph one of the same article. As a preliminary, it may be remarked that this article only permits states to seek advisory opinions on the compatibility of its own laws with those of the pertinent international human rights instruments. Since the request is for an interpretation of the state's domestic laws themselves, it would be inappropriate for a state to seek an opinion on the compatibility of another state's laws with the appropriate conventions. Nevertheless, an interpretation given at the request of one state may produce effects for another state. This may occur in one of two ways. First, a ruling on a state's laws will usually involve an interpretation of the rules established by the international instrument in question. Although such an interpretation does not produce effects *erga omnes* it does, as noted above, provide an authoritative interpretation of the relevant instruments for other states of which they must, if they are prudent, take appropriate notice.[99] Second, as Buergenthal notes,[100] human rights treaties may constitute the appropriate 'domestic law' for a number of states which possess monist constitutions.[101] An interpretation of a treaty for one such of these states will, in effect, constitute an interpretation for all of them.

The major questions arising from the term 'domestic laws' are whether it comprehends all laws within a state ranging from basic constitutional provisions to subordinate or delegated legislation, and also whether it includes not only laws in force but also draft or potential laws. Both these questions were considered by the Court in its Fourth Advisory Opinion.[102] Here the question arose whether certain draft amendments to the constitution of Costa Rica concerning the acquisition of Costa Rican nationality by naturalization would violate Articles 17, 20 and 24 of the Convention if they entered into force. The Court was able to dispose of the first question concerning the laws affected with some ease. It simply noted:

> Whenever an agreement speaks of 'domestic laws' without in any way qualifying that phrase, either expressly or by virtue of its context, the reference must be deemed to be to all national legislation and legal norms of whatsoever nature, including provisions of the national constitution.

This broad view would seem to embrace all legal provisions adopted within the context of a state's national legal order no matter from which source they arise. It is questionable, however, whether the Court's formulation is sufficiently wide to include quasi-legal devices, such as the administrative practices of government departments, which operate in an insidious way but which nevertheless often affect human rights directly and decisively. Given these effects, it is arguable that the Court should be competent to rule on such devices if requested to do so by a member state.

The second question referred to above required the Court not only to interpret the Convention, but also to identify the salient issues of policy informing its decision that it was competent to render advisory opinions on the compatibility of proposed laws with the human rights treaties referred to in Article 64(1).

The policy underpinning the Court's decision to admit, in principle, cases concerning draft or proposed laws for interpretation, is to be found in the general rationale concerning the function of advisory opinions as a whole. As indicated above,[103] the Court has defined the broad purpose of its advisory jurisdiction to be that of assisting states to fulfil their international human rights obligations,[104] and to assist the organs of the OAS to fulfil their functions.[105] To refuse to admit a request for an advisory opinion on the grounds of compatibility of a draft or proposed law with the Convention would hardly be assisting states to comply with their international obligations and would frustrate the purposes of the process. As the Court also noted, Costa Rica could, simply by rephrasing the questions asked in the instant case, have brought the request under Article 64(1) of the Convention. The only difference with respect to a case brought under Article 64(1) and 64(2) is that the latter does not require notification of other member states for solicitation of their comments on the issues raised.[106]

These policy issues were, in the Court's view, supported by a proper construction of the Convention. In the process of interpretation, the Court applied Article 31 of the Vienna Convention on the Law of Treaties. Here, however, it was not content simply to apply the rule of textuality, but sought also to identify the object and purpose of the agreement.[107] Citing its own decision in *Restrictions to the Death Penalty* the Court found that it could not interpret the Convention in a way which would weaken its system of protection.[108] Furthermore, it reiterated that the Convention must be interpreted in favour of the individual.[109] Since, therefore, the advisory jurisdiction of the Court had been established to safeguard individual rights, its jurisdiction was 'as extensive as may be required to safeguard such rights, limited only by the restrictions that the Convention itself imposes'.[110] In order to determine these limits in the instant case, the Court examined Article 2 of the Convention which requires states 'to give effect' to the rights and freedoms established. Applying the principle of effectiveness,[111] it held that, if it were to decline to hear a case concerning the proposed laws of a state, this would not assist the state to give effect to the rights and freedoms concerned, since if a state were required to pass laws before the Court could rule on them, this would mean that the state would be required to violate the Convention before the Court would be able to render an opinion to that effect.[112] The Court further noted that, once a law was promulgated, it might take 'a very substantial amount of time before it could be repealed or annulled'.[113] It therefore held:[114]

> A restrictive reading of Article 64(2), which would permit states to request advisory opinions under that provision only in relation to laws already in force would unduly limit the advisory functions of the Court.

Nonetheless, the Court once again drew attention to its discretionary powers to admit or decline to admit a case if it considers that this would be an abuse of process.[115] In exercising this discretion in the context of laws proposed but not yet adopted, the Court made it clear that it would decline jurisdiction if the parties resorted to this procedure 'in order to affect the outcome of the domestic legislative process for narrow partisan political ends' that is, if it were likely to lead to the Court becoming 'embroiled in domestic political squabbles'.[116] To determine whether such is the case would require the Court to make an investigation into the internal affairs of a state which might not always be welcomed by the government making the request. In *Proposed Amendments* the Court was able to assess the divergent views prevailing in

Costa Rica by inviting, *proprio motu*, interested groups to submit their views and to be heard by the Court. In this case, however, the Court was able to rely on the support of the Costa Rican government which selected the appropriate groups in consultation with it.[117] The Court may not always be able to rely on the full cooperation of a state which may decide to dispute the Court's power to solicit the views of other parties or groups interested in the outcome of proceedings.[118] Although Buergenthal comments that the procedure adopted in *Proposed Amendments* was well suited to Article 64(2) proceedings he also acknowledges that Costa Rica did not contest the Court's jurisdiction in this case.[119] He therefore concludes:

> The Costa Rica case is not the strongest precedent ... for according private groups or individuals an opportunity to be heard in advisory proceedings, particularly when their views differ from those of the government.

An analogous question to that considered in *Proposed Amendments* is whether or not the Court may render an advisory opinion on draft reservations formulated by member states in advance of their becoming party to the Convention. While such reservations are neither draft legislation nor a treaty concerning human rights, it would seem that there are good policy reasons for allowing the Court to interpret proposed reservations by a potential contracting state. A reservation which seeks to modify or exclude certain obligations of a State Party to the Convention is subject to interpretation by the Court. Indeed, the Court has already had occasion to rule on the compatibility of reservations to the Convention in *Effect of Reservations*. Here the question arose whether a state making a reservation could be considered a party to the Convention from the date of deposit of its instrument of accession to which the reservation was attached or whether the state could only be a party from a later date in accordance with the relevant provisions of the Vienna Convention on the Law of Treaties. Although this case has been considered in detail above,[120] it is appropriate to reiterate here that the Court ruled that a state was permitted to adopt any reservation to the Convention as long as it was not incompatible with its object or purpose, and that, as long as these requirements were fulfilled, the Convention entered into force from the date of deposit of its instrument of accession. While this opinion was requested by the Commission, it is clear that it had concrete effects for the states factually concerned. Thus, at the time of the opinion their precise status *vis-à-vis* the Convention was in doubt. Rather than perpetuating such doubt in future cases and passing *post hoc* judgment on the effects of a reservation, it would seem to be both prudent and appropriate to allow a state which is contemplating becoming party to the Convention to be able to seek the Court's opinion on the legality of any proposed legislation *propter hoc*. Buergenthal, who takes this view, further argues that: [121]

> This conclusion follows because a reservation that has not yet been adopted and attached to an instrument of ratification is the conceptual analogue of draft legislation.

This position has much to commend it, although whether the Court will be prepared to extend the meaning of 'domestic laws' in Article 64(2) to increase the effectiveness of its role under the Convention remains to be seen.

5. Which agency of the state is entitled to seek a ruling on the compatibility of domestic laws with the human rights instruments designated in Article 64?

Article 64(2) provides that a Member State of the OAS may request an opinion from the Court on the compatibility of its domestic laws with the human rights treaties referred to in Article 64(1). The article does not, however, indicate which organ of government is competent to seek a ruling from the Court. In *Proposed Amendments*, the initial request to the Court for an advisory opinion was lodged by a Committee of the Legislative Assembly of Costa Rica and not the government of Costa Rica itself. The Court noted that the Committee was 'not one of the governmental entities empowered to speak for Costa Rica on the international plane'[122] and that it only became seised of the issue when the Costa Rican Minister of Foreign Affairs formally filed the request for an opinion.[123] From this it would appear that the only persons competent to request an opinion on behalf of the state are those who are empowered to represent it at the international level. Such persons may be identified by reference to Article 7 of the Vienna Convention on the Law of Treaties which deals with persons competent to represent states in all matters concerning the conclusion of a treaty.

In an earlier comment Buergenthal suggested that Article 64(2) might be used by national tribunals which might be required to decide questions involving interpretation of either the Convention or human rights treaties to which their state was party.[124] The model envisaged here was that of Article 177 of the EEC Treaty which permits the courts and tribunals of EC member states to seek a preliminary ruling from the European Court of Justice where an interpretation of EC law is necessary in order to allow such a court to decide a case.[125] While the uniform interpretation of human rights treaties is undoubtedly a commendable objective, it would seem that, in the light of the

Court's decision in *Proposed Amendments*, this is not legally possible without the state in question signifying that it is willing to allow all or some of its courts to resort directly to the Court without having to secure transmittal of the request through the executive branch of government. As Buergenthal points out,[126] such a procedure might be facilitated by an agreement between states and the Court under Article 27(2) of its Statute.

Notes

[1]   *Other Treaties*, para. 14. The Court's advisory jurisdiction was also described as 'unique' in contemporary international law by the Court itself in *Restrictions to the Death Penalty*, para. 43.

[2]   Article 65 of the ICJ's Statute provides that the Court 'may give an advisory opinion on any legal question at the request of whatever body may be authorized by or in accordance with the Charter of the United Nations to make such a request'. Article 96 of the UN Charter grants only the General Assembly and the Security Council power to request advisory opinions on legal questions as of right. Other organs and specialized agencies may only request advisory opinions with the authorization of the General Assembly 'on legal questions arising within the scope of their activities'.

[3]   Protocol II to the European Convention on Human Rights. Article 1 of the Protocol provides:
1. The Court may, at the request of the Committee of Ministers, give advisory opinions on legal questions concerning the interpretation of the Convention and the Protocols thereto.
2. Such opinions shall not deal with any question relating to the content or scope of the rights or freedoms defined in Section I of the Convention and in the Protocols thereto, or with any other question which the Commission, the Court or the Committee of Ministers might have to consider in consequence of any such proceedings as could be instituted in accordance with the Convention.
3. Decisions of the Committee of Ministers to request an advisory opinion of the Court shall require a two-thirds majority vote of the representatives entitled to sit on the Committee.

[4]   Presumably this might be construed as a provision in a treaty for the benefit of third states which is governed by Article 36 of the Vienna Convention on the Law of Treaties.

[5]   See *Interpretation of the American Declaration*, supra, pp. 25-30.

[6]   Supra, p.5.

[7]   Advisory Opinion OC-2/82 of September 24, 1982, *Entry into Force of the American Convention for a State Ratifying or Adhering with a Reservation* (hereafter '*Effect of Reservations*'), Series A, No. 2 (1983) 22 ILM 37 (1982) 3 HRLJ 153.

[8]   Ibid., para. 8.

[9]   Ibid., para. 14.

[10]   Ibid.

[11]   Ibid.

[12]   See Article 112 OAS Charter.

[13]   Ibid., para. 16. Emphasis added. This dictum was cited with approval by the Court in *Restrictions to the Death Penalty*, para. 42 and in Advisory Opinion OC-8/87 of January 30, 1987, *Habeas Corpus in Emergency Situations* (hereafter '*Habeas Corpus in Emergency Situations*'), Series A, No. 8 (1988) 27 ILM 512 (1988) 9 HRLJ 94, para. 8.

14   For example, where the issue clearly does not raise a question of the interpretation of a right protected by the Convention.

15   See Thomas Buergenthal, 'The Advisory Practice of the Inter-American Human Rights Court' (hereafter 'Advisory Practice') (1985) 79 AJIL 1 at p. 4.

16   At para. 38.

17   See Case 104/79, *Foglia v Novello* [1980] *European Court Reports* 745. See Hartley, *Foundation,* pp. 258-60 and Freestone and Davidson, *Institutional Framework*, pp. 158-9.

18   M. C. Parker, 'Other Treaties: The Inter-American Court of Human Rights Defines its Advisory Jurisdiction' (1983) 33 *AmULRev* 211.

19   *Other Treaties*, para. 18.

20   Ibid., para. 19.

21   Ibid., para. 21.

22   Ibid.

23   Ibid., para. 22.

24   Ibid., para. 23.

25   Here the Court referred to the *Interpretation of Peace Treaties Case*, ICJ Rep. 1950 , 65; *International Status of South West Africa Cases*, ICJ Rep. 1950, 128; *Certain Expense of the UN*, ICJ Rep. 1962, 151; *Legal Consequences Case*, ICJ Rep. 1971, 16.

26   *Other Treaties*, para. 24.

27   Ibid., para. 25.

28   Ibid., para. 26.

29   See supra, p. 100, note 4.

30   Ibid., para. 27.

31   Ibid., para. 28. See on this point the decision of the ICJ in the *Interpretation of Peace Treaties Case*, 1950 ICJ Rep., 65.

32   Ibid., para. 30. The Court further observed that under Article 66 of the Convention, it was obliged to give reasons for its decision declining to give an advisory opinion.

33   *Habeas Corpus in Emergency Situations;* Advisory Opinion OC-9/87 of October 6, 1987, para. 11; *Judicial Guarantees in States of Emergency* (hereafter '*Judicial Guarantees*') (1988) 9 HRLJ 204, para. 16; *Interpretation of the American Declaration*, para. 27.

34   Advisory Opinion OC-12/91 of 6 December 1991, *Compatibility of draft legislation with Article 8(2)(h) of the American Convention on Human Rights* (1992) 13 HRLJ 149.

35   The right to a fair trial.

36   Ibid., paras. 1-3.

37   Ibid., paras. 11, 24-7.

38   Ibid., para. 28.

39   Ibid.

40   Ibid.

41   PCIJ, Series B, No. 5, 1923.

42   ICJ Rep., 1950, p. 6.

43   This view was reiterated in *Reservations to the Genocide Convention Case*, ICJ Rep., 1951, p. 15.

44   ICJ, Rep., 1975, p. 12.

45   See Rosenne, *Law and Practice,* pp. 708-18.

46   The Report was eventually produced in 1981. See Inter-American Commission on Human Rights, *Report on the Situation of Human Rights in the Republic of Guatemala*, OEA/Ser.L/V/II.53, doc.21, rev.2, October 13, 1981.

47   *Restrictions to the Death Penalty*, paras. 11 and 30.

48   Ibid., paras. 21 and 22.

49   Ibid., para. 22.

50   Ibid., para. 24.

51   On the status of advisory opinions see supra, p. 59.

52   *Restrictions to the Death Penalty*, para. 27.

53   Ibid. In fact, Guatemala restricted its observations on the issue to the preliminary questions of jurisdiction and did not address the merits of the case.

54   Ibid., para. 25. The Court here specifically referred to the modification of the practice of the ICJ by Article 103 of the Rules of the Court which was designed to accelerate its procedure in advisory opinions. The Court also noted that Article 79 of the ICJ's Rules requiring the Court to hear objections to jurisdiction prior to the hearing of the merits in advisory proceedings had not been applied by the ICJ in the *Western Sahara Case*, ICJ Rep. 1975, p. 12. See also E. J. de Arechaga, 'The Amendments to the Rules of Procedure of the International Court of Justice' (1973) 67 AJIL 1.

55   *Restrictions to the Death Penalty*, para. 26.

56   Ibid., para. 31.

57   Ibid., para. 32.

58   Ibid., para. 34.

59   Ibid., para. 36.

60   At para. 25.

61   *Restrictions to the Death Penalty*, para. 37.

62   Ibid., para. 39.

63   Ibid., para. 40.

64   Ibid., para. 42. See supra, p. 102.

65   Ibid., para. 43.

66   On the principle of effectiveness in treaty interpretation see supra, pp. 76-7.

67   *Restrictions to the Death Penalty*, para. 43.

68   Ibid.

69   1980, ICJ Rep., 73.

70   Ibid., para. 44. The Court here referred to Article 49(2)(b) of its Rules which provide that the request for an advisory opinion by an OAS organ must indicate, *inter alia*, how the consultation relates to its sphere of competence and the considerations giving rise to the consultation.

71   Ibid., para. 44.

72   'Advisory Practice', p. 10.

73   See supra, p. 104.

74   See the hypothetical problem stated by Buergenthal in 'Advisory Practice', p. 11.

75   This much is clear from *Other Treaties*, para. 35.

76   Ibid., para. 8.

77   Ibid., para. 33. On the Court's approach to treaty interpretation see supra, pp. 77-80.

78   Ibid., para. 34.

79   Ibid., paras. 36 and 37.

80   Ibid., para. 37.

81   Ibid., para. 38.

82   Ibid.

83   'Advisory Practice', p. 6.

84   See supra, pp. 235-8.

85   *Other Treaties*, para. 39.

86 Ibid., para. 40.
87 See the Preamble to the Convention which refers to the Universal Declaration of Human Rights, and Articles 22, 26, 27 and 29 which refer to international treaties and general international law.
88 *Other Treaties*, para. 43.
89 Ibid., para. 44.
90 Ibid., para. 48.
91 Ibid., para. 49.
92 Ibid., paras. 50 and 51.
93 Supra, p. 108.
94 Supra, p. 115.
95 See supra, pp. 25-30.
96 'Advisory Practice', p. 7.
97 On this see D. M. Trubeck, 'Economic, Social and Cultural Rights in the Third World: Human Rights Law and Human Needs Programs', in Meron, *Human Rights,* p. 205.
98 See in particular Chapters VII and VIII.
99 See supra, p. 146.
100 'Advisory Practice', p. 12.
101 That is, constitutions which permit treaties to be self-executing under certain conditions and thus enforceable in those states courts.
102 Advisory Opinion of January 19, 1984, No. OC-4/84, *Proposed amendments to the Naturalization Provisions of the Political Constitution of Costa Rica* (hereafter '*Proposed Amendments*'), Series A, No. 4 (1984) 5 HRLJ 161.
103 Supra, p. 237.
104 See *Other Treaties*, para. 39.
105 *Restrictions to the Death Penalty*, para. 43.
106 Buergenthal notes in *Advisory Practice* p. 16, note 65, that the outcome of Article 64(1) and Article 64(2) procedures will be essentially similar and that states will have an interest in opinions offered under both articles. He therefore suggests that states 'should routinely receive the requisite notice in both instances'.
107 *Proposed Amendments*, paras. 21, 22 and 23.
108 Ibid., para. 24.
109 Ibid.
110 Ibid., para. 25.
111 On the principle of effectiveness see supra, pp. 76-7.
112 *Proposed Amendments*, para. 26.
113 Ibid., para. 27.
114 Ibid., para. 28.
115 Ibid., para. 29. Citing its earlier decisions in *Other Treaties* and *Restrictions to the Death Penalty*. Discussed supra, pp. 103-6.
116 *Proposed Amendments*, para. 30.
117 See Buergenthal, 'Advisory Practice', p. 16.
118 Although the Court's wide power to call 'witnesses, experts and any other persons' under Article 35 of its Rules would be a suitable counter-argument to such a claim.
119 'Advisory Practice', p. 17.
120 See supra, pp. 58-61.
121 *Inter-American Court,* p. 13.
122 *Proposed Amendments*, para. 11.

[123]   Ibid.
[124]   *Inter-American Court*, p. 243.
[125]   Ibid.
[126]   Ibid., p. 244.

7 The Rights Protected

Introduction

This chapter is concerned primarily with the way in which the Inter-American Commission and Court have interpreted and applied the human rights protected by the various instruments which form the inter-American human rights system. At the outset it should be noted that there is comparatively little in the way of detailed jurisprudence which has arisen from the Commission and Court in this area. This is in stark contrast to the European human rights system where both the quantity and quality of the jurisprudence of the European Commission and Court are substantial and significant. The reason for the existence of such a disparity between Europe and the Americas resides largely in the different political and social environments in which their human rights institutions have been, and continue to be, obliged to labour. The European human rights system functions in a predominantly homogeneous political and social milieu in which there are relatively few widespread or gross violations of human rights, and in which the principles of legality and the rule of law are largely respected, even by the recently democratized former Eastern bloc states which have become party to the European Convention on Human Rights. Human rights cases in Europe therefore tend to focus on individual violations which may be characterized as marginal in nature: the decisions by the Commission and the Court have more in common with the finely reasoned decisions of municipal constitutional courts than with those of truly international courts.[1] The inter-American institutions are, however, faced with a far less tractable situation. At various times in the recent history of the Americas, a significant number of states has experienced governments which have committed gross and widespread violations of human rights as pretexts for maintaining the political status quo. The context in which such violations have occurred is also significant. In many instances they have been perpetrated in states with poor records of economic and social justice, prompting the Commission to observe on more than one occasion that violations of first generation human rights are usually intimately linked with a denial of second generation rights.

259

An examination of the work of the Commission and the Court reveals that there has been little juridical analysis of the content of the rights protected by the various inter-American human rights instruments. The reason for this is that in the face of massive and widespread violations, these institutions have been preoccupied with questions of fact and the proof of fact relating to breaches of human rights norms, rather than with the content of those norms. The vast preponderance of individual cases, for example, have involved instances of arbitrary detention, physical and mental mistreatment, denial of due process and loss of life; or what is otherwise known as the phenomenon of enforced disappearance. The Commission and the Court have, occasionally, been confronted by the need to elaborate upon the content and meaning of a particular right or rights, but such decisions have been limited in number.

The Rights Protected

The substantive rights which are recognized and protected within the inter-American system are contained in three major documents: the American Declaration on the Rights and Duties of Man, the American Convention on Human Rights and the Protocol of San Salvador. As noted above in chapter 1, the American Declaration is comprised of both first and second generation rights which are set down in a relatively exiguous manner. The American Convention on the other hand, elaborates first generation rights in a much more comprehensive way, spelling out the rights and their limitations in some detail. Although Article 26 of the Convention refers to the progressive implementation of economic, social and cultural rights, the description of such rights is to be located either in the American Declaration, to which Article 26 refers obliquely, or in the additional optional protocol of San Salvador. It should also be noted that despite the differences in the drafting of the Declaration and the Convention, the relationship between them is preserved and developed by Article 29(d) of the latter instrument. This provides that 'no provision of this Convention shall be interpreted as ... excluding or limiting the effect that the American Declaration of the Rights and Duties of Man ... may have'. Thus, where the right protected by the American Declaration is broader than that protected by the American Convention, it appears that the broader interpretation must be preferred.[2] Furthermore, the Commission has taken the view that in interpreting the rights protected by the American Declaration it will employ the 'most accepted doctrine' which is that set forth in the more detailed provisions of the American Convention on Human Rights.[3]

While it is possible to analyze each of these rights individually, this does not fully convey the flavour of the jurisprudence of the inter-American institutions. As noted above, the rights, with some exceptions, have generally been considered by the Commission and the Court within the context of widespread and gross violations and have, for the most part, not yielded to precise individual juridical analysis. Instead, it is noticeable that the treatment of the rights by the inter-American institutions has led to descriptions of the kinds of activities by states and their agents which violate certain clusters of separate rights. The general methodology adopted by the Commission is to state the facts as found and then to declare whether the given facts violate certain protected rights. More often than not, the Commission is less than explicit in relating the facts to the violation of a specific article, but is rather content to treat the rights violated as a seamless complex. Such an approach inevitably hinders effective analysis, since certain assumptions and inferences must be derived from undifferentiated assemblages of fact and legal obligation. It should be noted, lest the foregoing appears to be too critical of the Commission, that very often it has been confronted by states which have either been unwilling to respond to the Commission's request for information or have supplied an insufficiency of information. The Commission has therefore frequently been obliged to fall back upon the use of Article 42 of its Regulations (and the predecessors of that regulation) which requires it to presume as correct the facts denounced if a state does not comply with its obligation to furnish appropriate and timely information. There have nevertheless been circumstances where the Commission has engaged in extended juridical analysis of certain rights which has shed considerable light on that institutions understanding of the rights protected under the Charter and the Convention. Due attention will be given to these decisions below.

The Right to Life

There is little doubt that the Inter-American Commission regards the right to life as fundamental and pre-eminent among other rights. In its report on Nicaragua in 1993, the Commission cited with approval the observation by the independent expert appointed to report on the right to property by the United Nations Commission on Human Rights that 'a trend has been observed to consider the right to life as a broader and more general concept, characterized not only by the fact of being the legal basis of all the rights, but also by forming an integral part of all the human rights that are essential for guaranteeing access for all human beings to all goods, including legal possession of same, necessary for the development of their physical, moral and spiritual existence'.[4] Furthermore, the Commission regards the right to life as being intimately related to a range of economic and social rights. In its report on the 'Status of the Rights of Minors in the Hemisphere',[5] the Commission observed:[6]

> In light of declarations collected recently the stark fact is apparent that, primarily for reasons of extreme poverty, deprivation, abandonment and lack of resources, the inhabitants of the hemisphere cannot be assured of enjoyment, even at an early age, of their most elementary human rights, namely the right to life and the right to physical integrity.

The right to life is protected by Article I of the American Declaration of the Rights and Duties of Man and Article 4 of the American Convention on Human Rights. Article I of the Declaration simply declares that 'every human being has the right to life' while Article 4(1) of the Convention provides that 'every person has the right to have his life respected'. Article 4 continues to provide that the right shall be protected by law and 'in general, from the moment of conception'. It further provides that no one shall be arbitrarily deprived of his or her life. The remainder of Article 4 is devoted to matters concerning the abolition and regulation of the death penalty in those states which maintain it. The difference in the drafting of the Article I of the Declaration and Article 4(1) of the Convention is noteworthy. While the former guarantees the right to life absolutely, the latter provides only that persons have the right to have their right to life 'respected'. This would seem to suggest that there may be a degree of conditionality about the right as expressed in the Convention. Furthermore, when coupled with the final sentence of Article 4(1) which provides that no one shall be 'arbitrarily' deprived of his or her life, it is clear that the American Convention envisages circumstances in which the non-arbitrary deprivation of life will be permissible. This may seem strange when read alongside Article 27(2) of the Convention which makes the right to life non-derogable, but given the preoccupation of the remainder of Article 4 with the death penalty, it would seem that this provides the context within which Article 4(1) must be read. Since therefore the right to life is non-derogable, and since the only exception to the right to life is the exercise of the death penalty in the circumstances described by the remainder of Article 4, a proper reading of the provision would seem to suggest that there can be no other justification for deprivation of right to life. Support for this view is to be found in the case of *Neira Alegria* v *Peru*.[7] In this case three detainees had been killed during an uprising in a Peruvian prison. Here the Court held that the inclusion of the word 'arbitrarily' in Article 4(1) of the Convention clearly excluded legal proceedings leading to the death penalty. The Court also held that although the state had both a right and duty to guarantee its security, it must do so in a manner which conforms to 'law and morality'.[8] Given that it had found the use of force by the Peruvian authorities in quelling the prison riot had been disproportionate, the Court held that 'it may reasonably be concluded that [the victims] were arbitrarily deprived of their lives by the Peruvian forces in violation of Article 4(1) of the Convention'.

Note should also be taken of the fact that Article I of the Declaration states that the right to life belongs to the 'human being', whereas Article 4(1) states that the right pertains to the 'person'. For most purposes this difference in the drafting of the two instruments will make little difference in the application of the right to life, since Article 1(2) of the Convention provides that for its purposes '"person" means human being'. Neither the Declaration nor the Convention, however, define the point at which life begins or ends. In other words they do not reveal when the foetus becomes a 'human being' nor do they indicate the point at which a human being ceases to be so. In short, neither the Declaration nor the Convention deal explicitly with the questions of abortion or euthanasia. While the Commission has had occasion to consider the former question, it has not yet had to analyze the latter.

In *Case 2141 (United States of America)*, otherwise known as the *'Baby Boy' Case*, the Commission was faced with the question of whether the termination of a male foetus in accordance with the liberalized abortion law of the United States was compatible with the right to life protected by Article I of the Declaration. Following a review of the *travaux préparatoires* of the American Declaration and the American Convention, the majority of the Commission came to the conclusion that the United States' abortion laws were not incompatible with Article I. The Commission's analysis of the *travaux* revealed that during the drafting of Article I explicit language which would have protected the unborn foetus was dropped from the final formulation of this provision. The original draft of Article I had read:[9]

> Every person has the right to life. This right extends to the right to life from the moment of conception, to the right to life of incurables, imbeciles and the insane. Capital punishment may only be applied in cases in which it has been prescribed by pre-existing law for crimes of exceptional gravity.

The reason for the removal of the sentences relating to protection of the foetus and the application of the death penalty was that the draft was incompatible with the domestic laws governing these matters in a majority of American states and would require such states to derogate from laws already in force. From this excision of the offending language the Commission concluded that the United States was correct in challenging the applicants' assumption that the protection of Article I of the Declaration exists from the moment of conception. As the Commission observed, 'the conference faced this question but chose not to adopt language which would clearly have stated that principle'.[10] As the two dissenting Commissioners pointed out, if this reasoning were adopted, it would lead to the possibility that incurables, imbeciles and the insane had also lost their right to life as a consequence of their deletion from the original text of Article I. In fact, a reading of the *travaux* does not lead to the unequivocal conclusion adopted by the Commission. The better view is perhaps that of Dr Aguilar who in his concurring decision expressed the opinion that Article I 'sidesteps the very controversial question of determining at what moment human life begins'.[11] From this Dr Aguilar concluded:[12]

> The legislative history of this article permits one to conclude that the draft which was finally approved is a compromise formula, which even if it obviously protects life from the moment of birth, leaves to each state the power to determine, in its domestic law, whether life begins and warrants protection from the moment of conception or at any other point in time prior to birth.

In this case the petitioners had also relied on Article 4(1) of the Convention to support their interpretation of Article I of the Declaration. While the Commission declined to employ the Convention as a means of interpreting the Declaration on the grounds that 'it would be impossible to impose upon the United States Government or any other member state of the OAS, by means of an "interpretation", an international obligation based upon a treaty that such state has not duly accepted or ratified' it was nonetheless, prepared to analyze the provision from a theoretical standpoint. Again the Commission resorted immediately to a consideration of the *travaux préparatoires* of the Convention without considering the ordinary meaning of the words within their context as required by the provisions concerning interpretation contained in the Vienna Convention on the Law of Treaties 1969. From the *travaux* the Commission was able to deduce that the text represented a compromise between states which supported abortion and those which did not. The insertion of the crucial phrase 'in general from the moment of conception' represented an important element in the compromise between pro- and anti-abortion states which enabled the former to continue to apply their own domestic law on this issue. As the Commission said:

In the light of this history, it is clear that the petitioners' interpretation of the definition given by the American Convention on the right to life is incorrect. The addition of the phrase 'in general, from the moment of conception' does not mean that the drafters of the Convention intended to modify the concept of the right to life that prevailed in Bogota, when they approved the American Convention.

Shelton is critical of the way in which the Commission arrived at its conclusion in this case on the grounds that it was too quick to resort to the *travaux préparatoires* of the Declaration and Convention in analyzing the compatibility of abortion with these instruments. In her view, the Commission could have reached the same conclusion, namely that abortion was inconsistent with neither Article I of the Declaration or Article 4(1) of the Convention, by using the traditional textual canons of interpretation contained in Article 32 of the Vienna Convention on the Law of Treaties. She also criticizes the minority on the same grounds, although she does acknowledge that Drs Tinoco and Monroy came closer to relying on traditional methods of interpretation.[13] In particular, they sought to answer the meaning of 'human being' by reference to medical science and theology. Whether such an approach is consistent with the 'ordinary meaning of the words in their context' approach inherent in the Vienna Convention on the Law of Treaties may be open to some doubt. It is also significant that by adopting this method of interpretation, together with different inferences drawn from the *travaux préparatoires*, the two dissenting Commissioners were able to come to a diametrically opposite conclusion to that of the majority by holding that abortion is forbidden by Article I of the Declaration. This position is also criticized by Shelton who observes that the dissenting opinions did not take into account the competing rights of the mother in such circumstances.[14]

Whether Article I of the Declaration or Article 4(1) of the Convention would permit euthanasia is a moot point for which little assistance may be derived from other human rights instruments or institutions. Presumably in circumstances of brain death it might be argued that an individual has ceased to be a 'human being ' or a 'person' and that there is consequently no need to continue to maintain the physical existence of these people by the use of medical technology. In general terms life is already at an end and cannot therefore be terminated by such an act. The question of whether intentional termination of life in order to relieve or foreshorten suffering or euthanasia proper might be a violation of the right to life is a question of a different order, especially where the conditions for such termination are established by the state. Given the fundamental character of the right to life and the overriding public interest in the unabridged maintenance of this right, it might well be that the Commission and the Court would not wish to see a weakening of this provision by accepting so-called mercy killing as an exception. This might even be so despite evidence of the individual's consent to termination of life in such a case either through 'living wills' or some other medium.[15] Certainly in terms of Article 4(1) of the Convention, termination of life would avoid characterization as 'arbitrary' if it were carried out in accordance with well-defined criteria established by the state, but whether either the Commission or Court would countenance a weakening of the right is, as suggested above, open to question.

The vast majority of cases which the Commission and Court have been obliged to consider have raised few issues concerning the interpretation of either Article I of the Declaration or Article 4(1) of the Convention. This is because the violations in question have largely been clear and unambiguous. Extrajudicial executions, assassinations and enforced disappearances, copious examples of which appear throughout the Commission's Annual Reports, have been classified without further analysis as distinct breaches of the right to life protected in both the Declaration and the Convention. Of these, the most common form of violation with which the inter-American institutions have had to deal is the enforced disappearance. While there is no prohibition on disappearances within either the Convention or the Declaration, the OAS political organs and the Commission have on a significant number of occasions denounced this practice as 'an affront to the conscience of the hemisphere' which 'constitutes a crime against humanity' and as a cruel and inhuman practice which 'mocks the rule of law, and undermines those norms which guarantee against arbitrary detention and the right to personal security and safety'. Furthermore, the Court has observed that 'the forced disappearance of human beings is a multiple and continuous violation of many rights under the Convention that the States Parties are obligated to respect and guarantee',[16] while the Commission has remarked that disappearances 'constitute a serious violation of the right to life'.[17] While the characteristics of disappearances vary in detail they usually consist of the kidnapping of a person by agents of the state, detention incommunicado without trial or other judicial safeguards, the infliction of torture and, ultimately, execution. In the *Honduran Disappearance Cases,* the Court found that disappearances violated Articles 4, 5 and 7 of the Convention. It is of course Article 4 which is of primary concern in the present context. The Court noted here:[18]

> The practice of disappearances often involves secret execution without trial, followed by concealment of the body to eliminate any material evidence of the

crime and to ensure the impunity of those responsible. This is a flagrant violation of the right to life, recognized in Article 4 of the Convention.

Indeed, the Court also continued to observe that the practice of disappearances, as well as violating the provisions of the Convention referred to above, constituted a 'radical breach of the treaty' as it demonstrated 'a crass abandonment of the values which emanate from the concept of human dignity and of the most basic principles of the inter-American system and the Convention'.[19] This of course adds little to an understanding of the juridical nature of the right to life, save to reinforce the view that it represents a fundamental aspect of the inter-American human rights system. As with most of the Commission and Court proceedings in questions involving disappearances, much of the Court's concern centred upon questions of proof of violation. Although it could not be proved definitively that the victims had been killed in the *Honduran Disappearance Cases,* the Court held that the context in which the victims had been disappeared and the lack of knowledge of their fates over a lengthy period of time created a 'reasonable presumption' that they had been killed. As the Court further observed 'even if there is a minimal margin of doubt in this respect, it must be presumed that [their] fate was decided by authorities who systematically executed detainees without trial and concealed their bodies in order to avoid punishment'.[20]

The Death Penalty

While Article 4 of the Convention contains extensive provisions concerning the death penalty, Article 1 of the American Declaration makes no mention of this issue at all. The history of this instrument shows, however, that Article I of the original draft contained a specific reference to the death penalty by providing that 'the right to life may be denied by the state only on the ground of a conviction of the gravest of crimes, to which the death penalty has been attached'.[21] Following a series of drafting amendments which were designed to ensure that Article I fully reflected the practice of American states without taking a partisan stance on the question of the abolition of the death penalty, it was decided to remove any reference to this matter. As Schabas suggests, deletion of the reference to the death penalty 'was in the interests of succinctness, and the qualifications found in earlier drafts, that the death penalty can only be permitted as an exception to the right to life where provided by pre-existing law for crimes of exceptional gravity, must nevertheless be considered implicit in the text'.[22] Article 4 of the Convention is, however, much more specific in its treatment of the death penalty. Article 4(2) places limitations on both the type of crimes for which, and the procedure by which, the death penalty may be imposed. It may only be imposed by states which have not abolished capital punishment for the 'most serious crimes' and 'pursuant to a judgment rendered by a competent court'. Article 4(4) further provides that capital punishment may not be imposed for political offences or related common crimes. Article 4(2) places additional restrictions on the imposition of capital punishment by prohibiting the retroactive application of any law relating to the death penalty by providing that it must be 'in accordance with a law establishing such punishment, enacted prior to the commission of the crime'.[23] Limitations are also imposed on the categories of persons to whom the death penalty may be applied. Article 4(5) of the Convention requires that capital punishment may not be imposed upon persons who were under eighteen or over seventy years of age at the time the relevant crime was committed, not may it be imposed upon pregnant women. A progressive abolitionist intent is also evinced by Articles 4(2) and 4(3) of the Convention. The former provides that in states in which the death penalty still exists, it may not be extended to crimes to which it does not at present apply while the latter stipulates that 'the death penalty shall not be re-established in states that have abolished it'. As the Court observed in *Restrictions to the Death Penalty*:[24]

> On this entire subject, the Convention adopts an approach that is clearly incremental in character. That is, without going so far as to abolish the death penalty, the Convention imposes restrictions designed to delimit strictly its application and scope, in order to reduce the application of the penalty to bring about its gradual disappearance.

Furthermore, as was indicated in chapter 1 above, the abolitionist imperative in the inter-American system is further evidenced by the Protocol to the American Convention Abolishing the Death Penalty. The Commission has also been quite forthright in its condemnation of capital punishment. In its report on Peru in the 1993 Annual Report the Commission stated:[25]

> For the Inter-American Commission on Human Rights, there is no premium that can be placed upon human life. The death penalty is a grievous affront to human dignity and its application constitutes cruel, inhuman and degrading treatment of the individual sentenced to death.

The Commission has also observed in connection with the death penalty that the right to life can never be suspended and 'under no circumstances can persons be executed to restore public order'.[26]

Both the Commission and the Court have been confronted with issues concerning the death penalty under both the Declaration and the Convention. *Case 9647 (United States of America)* before the Commission concerned the execution of two seventeen year old minors in South Carolina and Texas. In accordance with the laws of those states, both minors were transferred to adult courts at the discretion of the juvenile courts before which they had been arraigned. Before the adult courts, one petitioner had been convicted of rape and murder, while the other had been convicted of attempted rape and murder. The United States of America was not party to the American Convention on Human Rights and was therefore not bound by the provisions of Article 4(5) which, as indicated above, specifically prohibits the imposition of the death penalty on minors below the age of eighteen. The petitioners contended, however, that the application of the death penalty to minors below the age of eighteen was contrary to customary international law and that such customary international law was comprehended by the right to life in Article I of the American Declaration. As we have seen above,[27] the Commission had already established that the American Declaration was binding upon the United States of America. Whether or not Article I of the Declaration did comprehend a norm of customary international law prohibiting the application of capital punishment to minors necessitated an investigation by the Commission into the creation of such law. After reviewing the doctrinal aspects of customary law creation, the nature of *ius cogens* and state practice in the field of capital punishment in the Americas the Commission held:[28]

> The Commission finds that in the member states of the OAS there is recognized a norm of *ius cogens* which prohibits the state execution of children. This norm is accepted by all the states of the inter-American system, including the United States. The response of the U.S. Government to the petition in this case affirms that all states, moreover, have juvenile justice systems; none permits its juvenile courts to impose the death penalty.

The Commission took the view that the instant case arose not because of doubt concerning the existence of an international norm which prohibited the execution of children but because there was a lack of consensus about the age of majority in the Member States. Having decided that the prohibition on the execution of minors qualified as a norm of *ius cogens* but denying that such a peremptory norm specified the age of majority certainly seems strange, but the Commission went on to say that consequent upon its analysis:[29]

> The Commission is convinced by the US Government's argument that there does not now exist a norm of customary international law establishing eighteen to be the minimum age for imposition of the death penalty. Nonetheless, in light of the increasing numbers of states which are ratifying the American Convention on Human Rights and the United Nations Covenant on Civil and Political Rights, and modifying their domestic legislation in conformity with these instruments, the norm is emerging.

The Commission further held that, even if there were such an emergent norm stipulating eighteen as the age of majority, the United States would not be bound by it because by proposing to enter a reservation to Article 4(5) upon ratification of the Convention, it had signified its intention not to be bound by this provision.[30] Again, this sits uneasily with the Commission's characterisation of the prohibition of applying capital punishment to minors as a norm of *ius cogens*, since it is the hallmark of such a peremptory norm that it may not be derogated from. The result of the Commission's deliberations therefore was the conclusion that there exists a norm of *ius cogens* which prohibits the imposition of the death penalty upon minors, but without fixing the age of majority for these purposes. The Commission held, however, that the question of age was not dispositive of the issue before it. The issue was rather whether the absence of a federal prohibition within United States domestic law on the execution of juveniles who were under the age of eighteen when they committed serious crimes was in violation of Article I of the American Declaration.[31] As it observed, 'what needs to be examined is the United States law and practice, as adopted by different states, to transfer adolescents charged with heinous crimes to adult criminal courts where they are tried and may be sentenced as adults'.[32]

The Commission therefore investigated the discrepancy between states in the treatment of juvenile offenders in the United States in the absence of any federal legislation on the matter. It noted that thirteen states had abolished the death penalty and that the remaining states divided into two groups. The first group of states comprised those that prohibited the application of the death penalty to persons under the age of eighteen, and the second group of states were those which allowed juveniles to be transferred to the jurisdiction of adult criminal courts where they may be sentenced to death. It was the discretion and practice of this second group of states which occupied the Commission. It described the situation in the United States as 'a hodge podge of legislation'[33] and noted that the result of this was that, while some states forbade the application of the death penalty altogether, the Indiana state statute potentially allowed a ten year old to be judged before an adult criminal court and sentenced to death. This, it said, 'shocks this Commission'.[34]

As a result of the Commission's inquiry into the imposition of the death penalty in the United States, it concluded that the diversity of practice in each of the states resulted in very different sentences for the commission of the same crime. It therefore observed: [35]

> The deprivation by the state of an offender's life should not be made subject to the fortuitous element of where the crime took place. Under the present system of laws in the United States, a hypothetical sixteen year old who commits a capital offense in Virginia may potentially be subject to the death penalty, whereas if the same individual commits the same offense on the other side of the Memorial Bridge, in Washington, DC, where the death penalty has been abolished for adults as well as for juveniles, the sentence will not be death.

The Commission concluded that for the federal government of United States to leave the issue of the application of the death penalty to juveniles to the discretion of state officials resulted in a 'patchwork scheme of legislation' which rendered the severity of punishment dependent not primarily on the nature of the crime committed but on the location where it was committed. The Commission further observed that permitting states to determine whether juveniles may be executed was not in the same category as granting states the discretion to determine the appropriate age of majority for the purposes of buying alcohol or marrying. As a consequence of the disparity in the various states' laws relating to the application of the death penalty to juveniles and because of 'the failure of the federal government to pre-empt the states as regards this most fundamental right - the right to life - results in a pattern of legislative arbitrariness throughout the United States which results in the arbitrary deprivation of life and inequality before the law, contrary to Articles I and II of the American Declaration ... respectively'.[36]

It cannot be said that the Commission's decision in *Case 9647 (United States)* is satisfactory either in terms of its analysis or its conclusion. The incorporation of customary international law into an instrument which is designated the 'principal guide of an evolving American law' seems to go further than is warranted, and the designation of the prohibition of the imposition of capital punishment on minors as a species of *ius cogens* begs more questions than its answers. Furthermore, in the Commission's view it is the arbitrariness of the imposition of the death penalty rather than capital punishment *per se* which appears to be the object of concern. The rationale which the Commission applied to the question of the death penalty for minors applies *mutatis mutandis* to the imposition of the death penalty on any person of any age in the United States. If one takes the Commission's hypothetical person committing crimes at either end of the Memorial Bridge, it would not matter whether the individual in question was sixteen or sixty; the imposition of the death penalty would still be arbitrary. Thus, if the Commission's reasoning were taken to its logical conclusion, the federal government of the United States would have to choose whether to abolish capital punishment in all states of the Union or to require it in all states of the Union. Since the Declaration is silent on the matter of capital punishment, it would seem, as Commissioner Cabra pointed out in his dissenting opinion, that its application remains permitted by that instrument. Furthermore, as the Commission itself observed, even if there were general agreement on the age of eighteen as the age of majority, the United States, having adopted the position of persistent objector, would not be bound by it. In addition to this, the United States is not bound by the constraints of Article 4(5) of the Convention since it has not yet become a party to this instrument. If, however, one were to adopt the Commission's doctrine in employing the Convention to elaborate upon the more sparsely worded rights in the Declaration, it might well be possible to arrive at the opposite conclusion. Whatever the difficulties associated with the Commission's analysis, it would seem that the final conclusion which must be drawn from the decision in the instant case is that capital punishment is a legitimate exception to the right to life which is protected by Article I of the Declaration, but that it must not be applied arbitrarily in the case of juveniles.

While the Commission has not had other opportunities to analyze capital punishment in such detail in the context of Article I of the Declaration, it appears by implication that any imposition of the death penalty as an exception to the right to life protected by this Article is circumscribed by the requirements that it may only be imposed in accordance with pre-existing laws and due process. In the Commission's *1988-89 Annual Report* it condemned Cuba for the execution of a number of military officers following conviction for drug trafficking and the commission of hostile acts against third countries. The Commission noted that these crimes were not capital crimes under Cuban law and that the speed with which they were carried out raised 'well-founded doubts as to compliance with fundamental guarantees of due process'.[37] Furthermore, it appears that Article I of the Declaration also incorporates the notion that having been abolished, capital punishment may not be reintroduced,[38] nor may it be imposed for politically related offences under that provision.[39]

Both the Commission and the Court have been confronted with issues concerning the death penalty under Article 4 of the Convention. The Court has been requested to give two separate advisory opinions dealing with the relationship between reservations and the death penalty. In the first of these cases the Court was asked by the Commission to respond to the question concerning the point at which a state became party to the American Convention when it ratified the Convention with a reservation. This request for an advisory opinion, which has been discussed in some detail above,[40] did not raise substantive questions about the precise form or compatibility of the reservations to Article 4 of the Convention which had been lodged by a number of states upon ratification. It was, however, the reservation made by Guatemala to Article 4 that gave rise to the Court's third advisory opinion which raised particular issues relating to the compatibility of that reservation with the object and purpose of the Convention. The Guatemalan reservation in this case provided that its ratification of the Convention was subject to Article 54 of the Guatemalan constitution which excluded from the application of the death penalty political crimes, but not common crimes related to political crimes.[41] It will be readily apparent that this was in clear contradiction to Article 4(4) of the Convention which provides that capital punishment may not be inflicted either for political offences or related common crimes. Furthermore, as the Court itself observed, the practical effect of the reservation to Article 4(4) would be to allow Guatemala to extend the death penalty to crimes to which it had not previously applied. Such an effect was, of course, in violation of the provisions of Article 4(2) of the Convention to which Guatemala had not sought to enter a reservation. The Court therefore noted that a state which had not made a reservation to Article 4(2) could not extend the death penalty to offences to which it had not previously applied. It further observed that it did not believe that it could be 'reasonably argued that a reservation to Article 4(4) can be extended to encompass Article 4(2) on the grounds that the reservation relating to the prohibition of the death penalty for political offenses and related common crimes would make no sense if it were inapplicable to new offenses not previously punished with that penalty'.[42] As a consequence of this analysis the Court concluded that that the Guatemalan reservation 'failed to manifest its unequivocal rejection of the provision'.[43]

Despite the Court's ruling in *Restrictions to the Death Penalty*, the Commission has been faced with circumstances in which States Parties have reintroduced the death penalty for crimes to which it did not previously apply. A notable example of this occurred in 1993 when the government of Peru amended its 1979 constitution to add crimes of terrorism to those carrying the death penalty.[44] Art 140 of the amended Peruvian Constitution provided that 'the death penalty may only be applied for the crime of treason in case of foreign war and for the crime of terrorism, in accordance with the laws and treaties to which Peru is party and by which it is bound'.[45] The Commission took the view that this new constitutional provision was directly contrary to Article 4 of American Convention on Human Rights and could not be reconciled with that provision. Citing Articles 1, 27 and 29(a) of the Convention and *Proposed Amendments* the Commission held that the interpretation of the Convention must be done in such a way that it does not in any way weaken the system, and must always take into account that its object and purpose is to protect the fundamental rights of the individual.[46] The Commission also cited *Restrictions to the Death Penalty* in which, as noted above, the Inter-American Court of Human Rights had confirmed that Article 4(2) of the Convention forbade the extension of the death penalty to crimes for which it was not provided previously under domestic law. The Commission concluded:[47]

> Obviously, now that terrorism is being criminalized, the purpose of this amendment is to extend the death penalty to a crime for which it was not provided in the 1979 Constitution. This is a violation of Article 4 paragraphs 2 and 4 of the American Convention.

The Commission also cited Advisory Opinion OC-13/93 and held that Peru had violated Convention 'by enacting provisions that are contrary to what its obligations under the Convention require of it'.[48]

Right to Humane Treatment

The right to humane treatment is comprehended by Article I of the American Declaration and Article 5 of the American Convention. As with the right to life, the Declaration's provision is short and simply provides that every person has the right to 'liberty and the security of his person'. Article 5 is much more elaborate and deals with a range of issues which give substance to the right. These include the protection of the physical, mental and moral integrity of persons; the prohibition of torture, inhuman and degrading punishment or treatment and matters affecting trial and punishment. In a large number of cases, the Commission has not differentiated between the various aspects of Article I of the Declaration and Article 5 of the Convention because, as explained above, in many instances the Commission has been concerned with questions of evidence and proof of violation in the absence of cooperation or in the face of hostility on the part of a number of states. As is the case with the right to life, the right to humane treatment protected by Article 5 may not be subject to derogation.[49]

In *Neira Alegria*,[50] the Court indicated that the sphere of operation of Article 5 is different from that of Article 4(1) which deals with the arbitrary deprivation of life. In this case three inmates had been killed during the suppression of a prison riot in which excessive force had been used by the Peruvian authorities. The Commission claimed that as well as constituting a violation of Article 4(1), the deaths of the individuals also amounted to a violation of Article 5. The Court rejected this view saying:[51]

> While the deprivation of a person's life could also be understood as an injury to his or her personal integrity, this is not the meaning of [Article 5] ... In essence Article 5 refers to the rule that nobody should be subjected to torture or to cruel, inhuman and degrading treatment or punishment and that all persons deprived of their liberty should be treated with respect for the inherent dignity of the human person. It has not been proved that the three persons to which this matter refers had been subjected to cruel treatment or that the Peruvian authorities had damaged their dignity during the time they were being detained ...

Disappearances

In addition to being a violation of the right to life, the Commission and the Court have held that enforced disappearances also violate Article I of the Declaration and Article 5 of the Convention. The vast bulk of individual cases considered by the Commission have involved this issue and the Commission faced with the absence of information or assistance from states, has simply relied on the powers of presumption in Article 42 of its Statute to consider the facts denounced as true.[52] In the *Honduran Disappearance Cases* the Court found that the evidence of those victims who had been disappeared and who had regained their liberty tended to show that they had often been 'subjected to merciless treatment including torture and other cruel, inhuman and degrading treatment, in violation of the right to physical integrity recognized in Article 5 of the Convention'.[53] In particular, the Court found that prolonged isolation and deprivation of communication, which were in themselves cruel and inhuman treatment, were harmful to the psychological and moral integrity of the persons detained.[54] While the Court could find no direct evidence that the victims in these cases had been tortured, it nonetheless held that Honduras had violated its obligation under Article 1(1) of the Convention to ensure in general the rights guaranteed by Articles 5(1) and 5(2).[55] As regards the other aspects of these articles that is, respect for the physical, mental and moral integrity of the person and freedom from torture inhuman and degrading treatment, the Court found that these had been violated by Honduras in the very act of disappearing the victim.[56] The Commission has cited the criteria established in the *Honduran Disappearance Cases* in a number of its recent pronouncements on enforced disappearance[57] and has even held that temporary disappearance is itself a violation of Article 5.[58] In one case,[59] the Commission has stated that disappearances are not only cruel and inhuman but that they constitute 'a true form of torture for the victims' family and friends, because of the uncertainty they experience as to the fate of the victim and because they feel powerless to provide legal, moral and material assistance'.

Personal Integrity, Torture and Related Practices

As can be seen from the discussion of disappearances above, the Commission and the Court have tended not to differentiate the violation of the physical, mental and moral integrity of the person and the subjection of individuals to torture, inhuman and degrading treatment or punishment, but rather to treat them as compound violations of Article I of the Declaration and Article 4 of the Convention. Indeed, it will be noted that Article I nowhere refers to the prohibition of torture and related practices, but the Commission has nonetheless always subsumed treatment amounting to torture under that provision. It is also significant that the Commission and the Court have never attempted to provide a definition of the concept of torture and its related practices, but have simply assumed that certain factual situations fall within the general prohibition. Indeed, on occasion the Commission has simply stated quite baldly that a state has committed torture without revealing the conduct which it is categorizing in this way. It is, however, possible under both Article I of the Declaration and Article 4 of the Convention to establish a catalogue of prohibited activity, without actually having any definition of the concepts which such activities violated. It should be mentioned, however, that the Inter-American Convention to Prevent and Punish Torture may provide an appropriate definition since in its preamble it recognizes the existence of the prohibition in Article 5(2) of the Convention.[60] Article 2 of the Torture Convention provides:

> For the purposes of this Convention, torture shall be understood to be any act intentionally performed whereby physical or mental pain or suffering is inflicted on a person for purposes of criminal investigation, as a means of intimidation, as personal punishment, as a preventive measure, as a penalty or for any other purpose. Torture shall also be understood to be the use of methods upon a person intended to obliterate the personality of the victim or to diminish his physical or mental capacities, even if they do not cause pain or mental anguish.

Article 2 then goes on to exempt physical or mental pain or suffering which is inherent or solely the consequence of lawful measures, providing that they do not include the acts or use of methods referred to above. The purpose of this provision is to preclude the definition of torture from applying to measures which are incidental and inherent to lawful detention and punishment. Article 5 of the Inter-American Torture Convention also makes clear that torture may not be justified on grounds of national emergency. It further provides that 'neither the dangerous character of the detainee or prisoner, nor the lack of security of the prison establishment or penitentiary shall justify torture'. This is consistent with the non-derogable quality of the right as expressed in Article 27(2) of the American Convention. Furthermore, Article 4 of the Torture Convention precludes superior orders being advanced as a defence to any criminal liability for the commission of torture.

One further aspect of the definition of torture in the Inter-American Convention which requires some comment is the final sentence which indicates that torture may be committed in circumstances where there is no pain or mental anguish if the intention of the torturer is to obliterate the personality of victims or to diminish their physical or mental capacities. This would clearly comprehend drug-based techniques under which the victims are not aware of pain or mental anguish because of the soporific nature of the drugs, but which nonetheless lead to mental or physical incapacity. This takes torture beyond the narrower definition which includes the deliberate inflicting of physical or mental *pain* and suffering to the realms of the intentional causing of *harm* to a victim. Given that torture may be used as a punishment rather than simply as an interrogation device, the extension of the definition of torture into this area is to be commended. It makes clear that any attack upon the physical or mental integrity of a victim is unacceptable, whether it actually causes perceptible pain to that victim or not.

An analysis of the cases characterized by the Commission as torture would find ready classification according to the definition of torture contained in Article 2 of the Inter-American Torture Convention. Examples of practices held to be violations of Article I of the Declaration or Article 5 of the Convention by the Commission include sitting a victim half-naked and wet in a metal tub and applying electric shocks, standing on his body, beating him on the chest and abdomen, putting a hood over his head so he could not breathe and burning him with lighted cigarettes,[61] rape,[62] mock burials, mock executions, deprivation of food and water,[63] threats of removal of body parts, exposure to the torture of other victims,[64] keeping prisoners naked for lengthy periods of time, denial of appropriate medical treatment,[65] submarine,[66] keeping detainees naked in cells, hooding, interrogation under the drug pentothal (truth drug), restricted diet leading to malnutrition and simulation of early release.[67]

In one case, the Commission has differentiated cruel and inhuman treatment from that of torture. Here the Commission found that Panama had breached Article 5 'by the Government's violent and disproportionate responses to the peaceful demonstration organized by opposition groups'. [68] This included the use of birdshot to put down such protests which resulted in a considerable number of injuries. The Commission also found that Article 5 had been violated 'by the degrading and at times cruel and inhuman treatment that members of the opposition have received in jails when detained'.[69] Such treatment included 'beatings with rubber hoses, and blows with fists and rifle butts'.[70] The Commission stated explicitly that this was not torture, but that 'the rule has been indiscriminate brutality combined with the withholding of food and drink'.[71] It is difficult to see how this case can be reconciled with the many situations referred to above in which the Commission has found similar acts to amount to torture. It is perhaps because of the absence of a clear and workable definition of torture and its related practices that the Commission's approach lacks an element of consistency.

As indicated above, the Commission has on very few occasions seen fit to analyze in detail the different constituent provisions of Article 5. In certain recent cases, however, it has been more specific concerning the application of these elements to concrete cases. In *Case 10.772 (El Salvador)*[72] a girl of seven years of age was raped by a soldier. Despite clear evidence to the contrary, the local military Commandant told the mother that the rapist was in fact a guerrilla. El Salvador did not respond to the Commission's requests for further information, leading the Commission to presume the facts denounced to be true. It therefore held that the rape of the girl was a violation of Article 5(1) of the Convention.[73]

Article 5(2) has received similar treatment by the Commission. The majority of the cases which have concerned the Commission here have involved the treatment of prisoners in a number of states. In its follow-up report on El Salvador in the 1994 Annual Report, the Commission observed that 'the crowding and lack of minimum services [in Salvadoran penitentiaries] affects the rights of prisoners to be treated with respect for the inherent dignity of the human person (Article 5(2))'.[74] Similar concerns have been expressed regarding the treatment of prisoners in Cuba. In this case, the conditions of prisoners were reported to be particularly severe in terms of the disciplinary regime and general conditions, including insanitary conditions in prison, poor food and lack of appropriate medical treatment. None of the relevant provisions of the

American Declaration or American Convention dealing with humane treatment of prisoners were actually mentioned, but the Commission held that the complaints which it had received about prisons in Cuba 'constitute evidence of the serious prison conditions and the deliberately severe and degrading treatment meted out to prisoners by the Cuban Government and that these conditions and the treatment inflicted amount to serious violations of human rights'.[75]

Article 5(3) provides that 'punishment shall not be extended to any person other than the criminal'. Again, the Commission has had little opportunity to consider this issues in substantial detail. In *Case 10.006 (Peru),*[76] however, the Commission discovered a violation of this provision. This case arose following the attempted arrest of former Peruvian President Alan Garcia by his successor Alberto Fujimori. Although Garcia managed to escape an attack upon his home by the military who had been despatched to arrest him, his family were held under detention by armed military personnel. The Commission held that this was a violation of Article 5(3). It stated:[77]

> The Commission wishes to point out that there is a special prohibition in the Convention that proscribes extending punishment to the family of the person alleged to be guilty of a crime. And so while the Peruvian Government believes that Dr Garcia Perez should have been arrested for the commission of a criminal offense, the inability to apprehend him did not justify applying punishments intended for him to his wife and children instead.

Although the Peruvian Government attempted to pass the detention off as a form of protective custody in its replies to the Commission, the latter was unwilling to accept this characterization. Whether the detention can be properly classified as 'punishment' within the terms of Article 5(3) is, however, a moot point. While detention without due process will clearly violate Articles 8 and 25, it is doubtful whether it falls within the notion of punishment within the context of the right to humane treatment in Article 5. Clearly this would have benefited from further analysis. If, for example, members of Garcia's family had been placed in fear of their lives, this would presumably have aggravated the conditions attached to the detention and thus arguably would have rendered it inhumane.

Article 5(4), (5) and (6) all deal with aspects of imprisonment and conditions associated therewith. These correspond not only to Article I of the Declaration but also to Articles XXV and XXVI of that instrument. As a general proposition the Commission has stated that 'the necessary mechanisms must be implemented to keep a national record of detainees in order to make certain that the civil rights and judicial guarantees of every individual detained are respected'.[78]

Article 5(4) provides that, save in exceptional circumstances, accused persons are to be segregated from convicted persons and should be accorded separated treatment appropriate to their status as unconvicted persons. This provision is clearly related to Article 8(2) which requires that every person accused of a criminal offence should be presumed innocent so long as his or her guilt has not been proven according to law. There has been little comment on this provision by the Commission. In its 1994 Annual Report on El Salvador the Commission observed that problems within the penitentiary system in that country had led to absence of segregation of convicted and unconvicted prisoners contrary to Article 5(4). The Commission also commented upon this issue in the wider context of serious overcrowding of prisons in Panama. The Commission held that not only was such overcrowding a systematic violation of the prison population's right to minimum living conditions, but that it also lent itself to uprisings and rebellions.[79] The Commission also noted that there was a clear violation of Art 5(4) in that there was no segregation of convicted and unconvicted prisoners and stated:

> The Commission should point out that, on the whole, for both convicted and unconvicted persons alike, the prison conditions are an affront to the dignity that every human being deserves.

Freedom from Slavery

Article 6(1) of the American Convention prohibits slavery and involuntary servitude 'in all their forms' as well as the slave trade and traffic in women. There are no comparable provision in the American Declaration, although Article XXXIV of the Declaration deals with one of the exceptions to the prohibition, namely the duty of able bodied persons to render civil or military service to their state in cases of public emergency or disaster. As is the case with torture, the concepts of slavery, servitude and related practices are not defined in the Convention, nor is the practice of the Commission or Court of much assistance in this area. The appropriate point of departure for defining these terms for the purposes of the American Convention would seem to be the 1926 Slavery Convention as amended by its Protocol of 1953. Article 1 of the Convention defines slavery as 'the status or condition of a person over whom any or all of the powers attaching to the right of ownership are exercised'.[80] It further defines the slave trade as including 'all acts involved in the capture, acquisition or disposal of a person with intent to reduce him to slavery; all acts involved in the acquisition of a slave with a view to selling or exchanging him; all acts of disposal by sale or exchange of a slave acquired with a view to being sold or exchanged, and, in general, every act of trade or transport in slaves'.[81] In essence slavery and the slave trade deal with the ownership of, and trade in, human beings.

Similar problems also emerge in defining the terms 'traffic in women', and 'involuntary servitude' which are also prohibited by Article 6(1) of the American Convention. Again, assistance may be derived from the 1956 Supplementary Convention on the Abolition of Slavery, the Slave Trade and Institutions and Practices Similar to Slavery. While the term 'traffic in women' is not explicitly defined in this instrument, it is clear from Article 1(c) that the characteristics of such a concept are clearly defined. Article 1 provides that institutions and practices similar to slavery are:

(a) debt bondage, that is to say, the status or condition arising from a pledge by a debtor of his personal services or of those of a person under his control as security for a debt, if the value of those services as reasonably assessed is not applied towards the liquidation of the debt or the length and nature of those services are not respectively limited and defined;

(b) serfdom, that is to say, the condition or status of a tenant who is by law, custom or agreement bound to live and labour on land belonging to another person and to render some determinate service to such other person, whether for reward or not, and is not free to change his status;

(c) any institution or practice whereby:
   (i) a woman, without the right to refuse, is promised or given in marriage on payment of a consideration in money or in kind to her parents, guardian, family or any other person or group; or
   (ii) the husband of a woman, his family, or his clan, has the right to transfer her to another person for value received or otherwise; or
   (iii) a woman on the death of her husband is liable to be inherited by another person;

(d) any institution or practice whereby a child or young person under the age of eighteen years is delivered by either or both of his natural parents or by his guardian to another person, whether for reward or not, with a view to the exploitation of the child or young person or of his labour.

Further assistance in interpreting 'traffic in women' in Article 6(2) of the American Convention may be derived from the Convention for the Suppression of Traffic in Persons and the Exploitation of the Prostitution of Others. Here the States Parties agree to punish those 'who, to gratify the passions of another procures, entices or leads away, for the purposes of prostitution another person, even with the consent of that person' or those who exploit the prostitution of others even with their consent.

While neither the Commission nor the Court has been confronted with the issue of slavery and its related practices, the question of forced or compulsory labour which is prohibited by Article 6(2) of the Convention has arisen for consideration. Article 6(2) requires that 'no one shall be required to perform forced or compulsory labour'. Again, there is no definition of what amounts to forced or compulsory labour in the Convention, although certain categories of activity are expressly excluded from its ambit. These include forced labour where this is part of the penalty established in connection with a custodial sentence upon conviction by a competent court for certain crimes. There are, however, limits to this in that forced labour must not adversely affect the dignity or intellectual capacity of the prisoner. This provision clearly relates to Article 5(2) which requires prisoners to be 'treated with respect for the inherent dignity of the human person'. It is also relevant to mention Articles XXV and XXVI of the American Declaration at this point since these also require that individuals should enjoy humane treatment during the time they are in custody, and that no-one should receive 'cruel, infamous or unusual punishment' following conviction. Article 6(3) of the Convention provides a list of activities which 'do not constitute compulsory or forced labour'. These are:

(a) Prison labour following part of court sentence properly handed down, so long as such work is carried out under the 'supervision and control' of public authorities. Prisoners performing such work or service may not be placed at the disposal of any private party, company, or juridical person.

(b) Military service or national service in lieu of military service.

(c) Service exacted in time of danger or calamity that threatens the existence or the well-being of the community. This provision has its analogue in Article XXXIV of the American Declaration.[82]

(d) Work or service that forms part of normal civic obligations. Included in this might be the requirement that lawyers take on a certain amount of *pro bono* work in the early years of their careers.

While these exceptions to the prohibition on forced and compulsory labour in Article 6(2) are tolerably clear, they still do not shed much light on the nature of such labour. Some assistance may be had in this area from the work of the International Labour Organisation. ILO 29 and 105 both deal with this issue. Article 2(1) of ILO 29 defines 'forced labour' to mean 'all work or service which is extracted from any person under the menace of any penalty and for which the said person has not offered himself voluntarily'. Article 2(2) then goes on to provide a series of exceptions similar to those contained in Article 6 itself. The 1957 ILO 105 supplements ILO 29 by providing a list of reasons for which the imposition of forced or compulsory labour is unacceptable. In some respects these have the effect of modifying the prison exceptions contained in ILO 29. They may also be interpreted as elaborating the qualification contained in Article 6(2) of the American Convention in so far as it relates to the protection of the dignity and physical and intellectual capacities of prisoners. Thus forced labour in prison as part of a political re-education regime would be unlikely to be permissible under ILO 29. This instrument requires States Parties to suppress and not to make use of any form of forced or compulsory labour for the following reasons:

(a) as a means of political coercion or education or as a punishment for holding or expressing political views or views ideologically opposed to the established political, social or economic order;

(b) as a method of mobilizing and using labour for purposes of economic development;

(c) as a means of labour discipline;

(d) as a punishment for having participated in strikes;

(e) as a means of racial, social, national or religious discrimination.

Assistance in interpreting Article 6 of the American Convention may also be derived from decisions of the European Commission and Court on Article 4 which is, in essence, similar to the former provision. One notable point of difference in the drafting of the two provisions is that while the European Convention prohibits servitude *per se*, the American Convention prohibits only involuntary servitude. This would suggest that voluntary servitude would be permissible, but such a view is not in accord with the tenor of the international instruments reviewed above.

In its Report on the Situation of Human Rights in Panama [83] the Inter-American Commission was required to consider certain alleged practices in Panama concerning the use of prison labour for the personal benefit of commanding officers of the Panamanian National Guard. While the Commission was unable to find sufficient evidence to support such an allegation, it nonetheless concluded that forced and unremunerated labour was required of unsentenced detainees and that the economic goals of the government acted as an incentive to maintain an adequate work force by the use of these methods. The use of unsentenced detainees for forced labour would clearly be contrary to Article 6(3)(a) of the Convention as this states that such labour may only be required of persons imprisoned in execution of sentence passed by a competent judicial authority.

Right to Personal Liberty

The right to personal liberty is protected by Article 7 of the American Convention and Articles I, XVIII and XXV of the American Declaration. These provisions seek to protect the integrity of the individual from a wide range of abuses and deal in some detail with aspects of due process in criminal cases. The remaining aspects of due process are dealt with by Article 8 of the Convention and Article XXVI of the Declaration respectively. Given the complexity of these provisions, each of their constituent elements will be considered in seriatim. Before doing this, however, it should be noted that Article 7 is also one of the rights which the Court has declared forms part of the complex series of violations of human rights protected by the Convention in cases of enforced disappearance. In the *Honduran Disappearance Cases*, the Court held that the kidnapping of an individual in such circumstances, together with the denial of access to the judicial authorities by which the legality of the arrest could be reviewed constituted a clear violation of Article 7. The Court declared in the *Velasquez Rodriguez* case that 'as a result of the disappearance, Manfredo Velasquez was the victim of an arbitrary detention which deprived him of his physical liberty without legal cause and without a determination of the lawfulness of his detention by a judge or competent tribunal'.[84] The Disappearance Cases add little to an understanding of the meaning of Article 7, since the Court's judgments in these cases are not fully analytical. Again, the Court was clearly more occupied with questions of evidence and proof of fact than with precise juridical analysis of the relevant provision. A strict analysis of enforced disappearances discloses, however, that the various elements of Article 7 are violated in their entirety. It should also be noted that the Commission, as well as following the jurisprudence of the Court in the *Honduran Disappearance Cases* in its recent decisions, has also consistently taken the view that disappearances constitute violations of Article I and XXV of the Declaration. The Commission has also held that temporary disappearances constitute a violation of Article 7. In *Case 10.508 (Guatemala)*[85] the petitioners were kidnapped and detained by members of the military. and threatened that they would be killed if they did not reveal certain information. The Commission formed the view that this treatment amounted to a temporary disappearance and held that such an illegal arrest constituted an act in violation of Articles 5 and 7 of the Convention. It said, 'the forced causing - even temporary - of the disappearance of person by agents of the state constitutes a complex of human rights violations'.[86] The Commission has also decided that forcible recruitment of an individual into the army without his consent is a violation of Article 7 *in toto*,[87] as is detention of an individual by the military without a court order.[88]

Deprivation of Physical Liberty

Article 7(2) provides that persons may not be deprived of their physical liberty except for the reasons and under the conditions established in advance by a State Party's constitution or by a law established in accordance with the constitution. Article XXV of the Declaration similarly provides that no person may be deprived of his or her liberty except in the cases and according to the procedures established by pre-existing law. Article 7(2) of the Convention were examined in some detail in *Case 10.006 (Peru)*[89] which involved the attempted arrest of the former President of Peru, Alan Garcia, at his home by members of the Peruvian armed forces. The arrest was carried out by armed military personnel equipped with tanks who surrounded, and fired upon, Garcia's home. While Garcia was able to escape, his children and wife were kept imprisoned in their home for a number of days. The Peruvian Government attempted to justify the action not as an arrest, but as measures for the protection of the ex-President and his family. The Commission, however, readily recognized the transparency of this justification. Citing European Commission on Human Rights decision in the *Winer Case*,[90] the Commission held that while liberty and security must be taken to mean physical liberty,[91] nevertheless, threatening persons with arbitrary and unjustified detention can infringe the right to security of the person.[92]

Furthermore, in the *Garcia Case*[93] the attempted arrest was carried out by soldiers who had no constitutional authority to perform such actions. The Commission took the view that any arrests must be made by the competent authority under the domestic laws of the state and that the procedures must comply with the minimum requirements under international law for making an arrest. In the absence of these the Commission said that '... arrests cease to be arrests per se and become kidnappings'.[94] The Commission therefore held that 'the acts of violence ... for the purposes of arresting [Garcia], lead the Commission to conclude that in the instant case, his right to personal security which is protected under Article 7 of the American Convention , was violated by the measures taken by the Peruvian Armed Forces ...'.[95]

Arbitrary Arrest or Imprisonment

Article 7(3) of the American Convention prohibits the arbitrary arrest and imprisonment of any person. Similarly, while the text of Article XXV of the Declaration does not explicitly prohibit arbitrary arrest, its side heading reads 'right to protection from arbitrary arrest'. A reading of this provision therefore indicates that deprivation of liberty in circumstances other than where it is provided for in pre-existing law will be arbitrary. There are many examples of these practices contained in the Commission's reports. Clearly enforced disappearances, since they are conducted in a manner which is contrary to the due process provisions of the constitutions of states in which this practice occurs, are by definition arbitrary and have been so characterised by the Commission. neither the Commission nor the Court have been compelled to give a definition of what constitutes 'arbitrary' in the context of arrest or imprisonment. This is in contrast to the UN Human Rights Committee and the European Convention institutions which have been compelled to elaborate this concept in their case law. It would seem, however, that any arrest or imprisonment which is carried out in violation of fundamental domestic norms governing these matters will be *ipso facto* arbitrary. In the *Garcia Case*[96] discussed above, the ex-President's wife was detained in a manner which was clearly contrary to Peru's constitutional provisions. There was no written arrest warrant from a competent judge stating the reasons for the arrest, nor was she brought before a competent court authority, nor was she informed of the reasons for her arrest.[97] The Commission therefore held that her arrest was unlawful and consequently arbitrary.

Notification of Charge

Article 7(4) provides that detained persons must be informed of the reasons for their detention and promptly notified of the charges against them. This provision relates also to Article 8(2)(b) which states that individuals accused of criminal offences are entitled to the guarantee of prior notification in detail of charges against them. This aspect of due process will be dealt with in the context of Article 8 below.

Presentation before a Judge and Pre-trial Release

Article 7(5) provides that detained persons must be brought before a judge or other appropriate person promptly and shall be entitled to trial within a reasonable time or to be released without prejudice pending the continuation of proceedings. Such release may be made subject to guarantees to assure the detainees appearance for trial at a future date. The third paragraph of Article XXV provides in similar terms that a detained person has the right to be tried without undue delay or otherwise to be released.

Article 7(5) of the Convention has been subjected to extensive and detailed analysis by the Commission in a follow-up report on Panama and in an individual case involving Argentina. In the report on Panama the Commission was confronted with circumstances in which pre-trial detention in Panama was an average length of two to four years, after which the detained individual was sometimes found innocent. This was held by Commission to be a violation of Article 7(5).[98] The implication to be drawn from this is that the criterion of reasonableness in Article 7(5) had been exceeded given the delay in bringing the persons to trial. Whether there might be other criteria which might render such a lengthy period of pre-trial detention unreasonable was not considered by the Commission, nor was there consideration of other criteria apart from the temporal element which might render pre-trial detention unreasonable. These, however, were analyzed to some degree in the case involving Argentina.

This case involved the question of the circumstances in which an individual should be released pending trial. Here, the petitioner had allegedly committed the crimes of homicide, kidnapping and extortion and had been remanded in prison for three and a half years. Article 380 of Argentine Code of Criminal Procedure provided that in determining whether to release such a person pending trial, the judge could take into account the characteristics of the case and the personal characteristics of the accused in order to ascertain whether there were reasonable grounds for believing that accused would not attempt to evade justice. The Commission said of this provision that it was 'not per se a violation of Article 7(5) of the Convention, in that the said power could lend itself to the application "of particular criteria of the judge called upon to apply the law"'.[99] Had the petitioner therefore been brought to trial within a reasonable time? Here Commission used criteria established by the European Court of Human Rights in the *Stögmuller Case*.[100] Of the concept of reasonable time the Commission said that it was not possible to define this period *in abstracto*, but that it must instead be defined according to the circumstances extant in each case after considering the criteria mentioned in Argentine criminal code. The Commission thus agreed with Argentina which had argued that the state was not bound by the Convention to fix a valid period for all cases independently from the circumstances. The Commission held that the release of prisoners in pre-trial detention 'cannot be done based on a simple chronological consideration of years, months and days'. As it noted, this same point had been made explicit in *Stögmuller*. Applying that point to the present case, the Commission stated that 'the concept of "reasonable period" is left to the consideration of "the seriousness of the violation," when determining whether the detention has ceased to be reasonable'.[101] The Commission thus concluded that the reasonableness of the period in question must be established by Article 380 of the Argentine Code of Criminal Procedure taken together with assessment of the criteria identified as relevant by trial judge. The Commission also agreed with the position taken by the European Court of Human Rights in *Neumeister*.[102] It said:[103]

> The Court also believes that to decide whether, in a given case, the detention of the accused does not exceed the limits of what is reasonable, it behooves the national judicial authorities to investigate all circumstances which, because of their nature, lead them to acknowledge or reject the existence of true public interest which justifies the repeal of the rule of respect for individual liberty.

The Commission considered it necessary to consider three criteria to determine what constituted a 'reasonable period' for the purposes of Article 7(5) of the Convention. These were:

(a)   the duration of imprisonment;
(b)   the nature of acts which led to criminal proceedings; and
(c)   the difficulties or judicial problems encountered when conducting trials.

Applying these criteria to the present case it was clear there had been delays because of the conduct of extradition proceedings in Brazil which the applicant had contested. Second, the nature of the crimes were such that the Commission took the view that 'the characteristics of the (punishable) actions ... and the penalties which could be imposed on the accused make it possible to assume, on a solid basis, that measures must be taken to forestall an avoidance of justice and that, hence, a request for release must be turned down'.[104] Third the length of proceedings had been complicated by a variety of factors, including negligence on the part of the defence. The Commission thus concluded:[105]

> The foregoing makes its possible to draw the conclusion that although four years is not a reasonable period, in this case because of its unique features and the complexity of the reasons affecting its progress such a period is not an unjustified delay in the administration of justice.

It will be noted that Article 7(5) also states that a person's release from pre-trial detention may also be made subject to guarantees to assure appearance for trial Such guarantees will presumably be those which are evident in most states' criminal processes such as forms of bail or monetary assurance and restrictions on freedom of movement, such as being required to live in a particular area, reporting to the police on a periodic basis or the surrender of one's passport.

Recourse to a Competent Court

Article 7(6) is a lengthy provision which gives persons deprived of their liberty the right of recourse to a competent court for the purposes of determining the lawfulness of their arrest or detention. If the arrest or detention is unlawful, then the court must order the detainee's release. Article 7(6) also provides that in states which provide a remedy for the purposes of challenging the lawfulness of arrest or detention, such remedy may not be 'restricted or abolished' and may be sought either by the interested party or a person acting on behalf of that party. While the question of what constitutes a competent court will be considered under Article 8 below, it is appropriate at this point to mention that the Court has clearly ruled against the possibility of the remedies of *habeas corpus* and *amparo* being suspended in emergency situations. Such action, it has held, would be incompatible with the obligations imposed on States Parties by the Convention. This issue has been discussed in detail in chapter 1 above in so far as it relates to the suspension and restriction of guarantees in general and need not be rehearsed here. Nonetheless, it is worth noting that the Commission has had occasion to apply the principles enunciated by the Court in this area. In a follow-up report on Panama, the Commission observed that Art 51 of that state's Political Constitution empowered the executive to suspend procedural guarantees protecting right to personal liberty and remedy of *habeas corpus* which were guaranteed by art 21 of the Panamanian constitution. The Commission held:[106]

> This violates the American Convention on Human Rights and is at odds with what the Inter-American Court has expressly stated in its Advisory Opinion 8 concerning the sense and scope of Articles 7(6) and 25(1) in relation to Article 27 of the American Convention.

Detention for Debt

While Article XXV of the American Declaration provides that no person may be deprived of liberty for non-fulfilment of obligations of a purely civil character, Article 7(7) of the American Convention prohibits detention for debt alone. The latter prohibition is narrower in scope than the former, which would appear to prohibit loss of liberty on the grounds that an individual might be unable to perform a contractual obligation other than that of payment of money owing. Article 7(7) would, however, seem to countenance such a possibility. This provision also explicitly excepts from the prohibition of imprisonment for debt circumstances in which a person fails to fulfil duties concerning the payment of support following the orders of a competent judicial authority. The support which is referred to here is presumably that which must be paid to a former spouse for their own maintenance or the maintenance of the children of a marriage.

Right to a Fair Trial

The right to a fair trial is covered in detail in Article 8 of the American Convention and in Article XXVI of the American Declaration where the right is referred to as that of due process. Both the Court and the Commission have indicated, however, that Article 8 of the Convention itself recognizes the concept of due process of law which they have also held to be a necessary prerequisite to ensure the adequate protection of those persons whose rights or obligations are pending determination before a court or tribunal.[107] The Court has also observed that the concept of due process of law which is recognized in Article 8 is applicable to all the judicial guarantees referred to in the American Convention, even where there have been derogations from certain of the rights protected by the Convention under Article 27. The fundamental nature of Article 8 and the right to judicial protection in Article 25 has also been recognised by the Commission. In *Case 9850 (Argentina)* the petitioner had been charged with politically motivated offences and his confession had been extracted by torture. This was followed by a trial in which certain irregularities occurred.[108] Finding that there had been a violation of Article 8 the Commission observed: [109]

> The principles established in these articles [Articles 8 and 25] - the right to judicial protection and judicial guarantees - rank as fundamental rights within our Convention, because they protect individuals in their complex relationship with the state. Consequently, enforcement of these principles cannot be confined to a mere formal verification of procedural requirements.

The meaning of the last sentence is not explained by the Commission, but presumably it means that there must be due process in a substantive sense as well as in the formal laws enacted by States Parties in order to give effect to these rights.

Article 8(1) of the Convention establishes the basic conditions for the right to a fair trial, while Article 8(2) establishes the minimum criteria for the proper conduct of criminal cases. Article 8(1) provides that 'every person has the right to a hearing with due guarantees and within a reasonable time, by a competent, independent, and impartial tribunal, previously established by law, in the substantiation of any accusation of a criminal nature made against him or for the determination of his rights and obligations of a civil, labour, fiscal or any other nature'. Article 8(2) further provides that persons accused of criminal offenses have the right to be presumed innocent so long as their guilt has not been proven according to law. Such persons are also entitled to certain minimum guarantees such as the right to a free translator, prior notification of charges, adequate time and means for the preparation of a defence, the right to counsel, the right to examine witnesses, the right against self-incrimination and the right to appeal to a higher court. As the Commission has stated, Article 8(2) provides a list of certain minimum guarantees in criminal proceedings, the enumeration of which should not be regarded as exhaustive. Because of this, it is the Commission's view that there are other guarantees recognised in the domestic law of States Parties which, although not explicitly included in the text of the Convention. are equally protected under the broad wording of Article 8(1) of the Convention.

Articles 8(1) and 8(2) involve a multiplicity of issues which will be considered in turn below. Before doing this, however, it should be noted that the Commission has on many occasions found breaches of Article 8 *in toto* in several kidnapping and disappearance cases. The approach which seems to be adopted by the Commission is that in such cases, the complex of violations which include deprivation of the right to life, humane treatment and the right to personal liberty also raise the presumption that due process has been denied. In *Case 10.508 (Guatemala)*[110] the petitioners had been kidnapped by the military and threatened with death if they did not divulge certain information. The Commission held that 'had the victims been accused of any crime, they should have been brought to trial legally, in accordance with the provisions of the national legislation and Article 8 of the Convention'.[111]

In an interesting variation on the interpretation of Article 8(1) of the Convention the Commission has also held that the provision is violated in cases where amnesty is granted to those who were being tried for the human rights violations of a previous regime. This interpretation arose in a number of cases involving the passage of a law in Argentina terminating *criminal* proceedings against members of the armed forces who had been involved in the 'dirty war'. This law closed off the possibility of continuing further criminal proceedings against such persons. The petitioners in these cases, who were either victims or the relatives of victims, claimed that their rights which were protected by Articles 8(1) and 25 had been violated. It will be noted here that it was not the persons who were to be subject to the criminal trials who were claiming that the right to due process had been violated, but rather the alleged victims of those persons who had been granted amnesty. The Commission placed this argument in context of the role and participation of victims or their relatives in criminal process. It pointed out that in a good number of the criminal law systems in Latin America, the victim or his or her attorney has the right to be the party making the charge in a criminal proceeding. Furthermore, the Commission noted that in legal systems which permit it - such as Argentina's - the victim of a crime has a fundamental civil right to go to the courts. As the Commission observed, 'that right plays an important role in propelling the criminal process and moving it forward'.[112] The Commission thus held that Articles 8(1) and 25 were indeed violated by the Argentinian amnesty law. It said:[113]

> The laws and the Decree sought to, and effectively did, obstruct the exercise of the petitioners' right under Article 8.1 ... With enactment and enforcement of the laws and the Decree, Argentina has failed to comply with its duty to guarantee the rights to which Article 8.1 refers, has abused those rights and has violated the Convention.

In assessing whether due process has been complied with, the Commission has stated strongly that it is not concerned with whether or not the decision of the national court is correct, but whether the principles of due process have been followed. Clearly the Commission is wary of trespassing upon those areas which still remain within a States Party's reserved domain. In *Case 9850 (Argentina)* the Argentine Supreme Court had dismissed that the petitioners' claim without hearing their evidence. The Commission stated here that it was not within its competence to decide whether Argentine law had been properly applied by the country's courts, but on the evidence before it (in this instance the file of the applicant's case) the Commission found that the Argentine judiciary's failure to review the trial evidence was 'inconsistent with the letter and the spirit of the Convention as regards judicial guarantees and the principle of due process'.[114] The Commission also made it clear that it was not competent to pass judgment upon the final evidentiary weight of the new evidence in a new criminal trial. Here it referred to cases decided by the European Commission on Human Rights[115] where it (the European Commission) had stated that it may examine how evidence has been obtained, but not how it has been assessed by the Court, unless there has been gross unfairness.[116] The Commission further agreeing with the European Commission said it was not called upon to decide whether or not domestic courts had correctly assessed evidence before them, 'but whether evidence for and against the accused has been presented in such a manner and the proceedings in general have been conducted in such a way that he has had a fair trial'.[117]

Competent, Independent and Impartial Tribunal

As indicated above, this element of due process also coincides with the requirements of Article 7(6) that persons deprived of their liberty should be entitled to recourse to a competent court. In analysing the independence and impartiality of the judiciary, the Commission has emphasised the doctrine of the separation of powers as its primary rationale. In a follow-up report on Cuba, the Commission stated: [118]

> The effective observance of [judicial] guarantees is based on the independence of the judiciary, which derives from the classic separation of the three branches of government. This is the logical consequence of the very concept of human rights. In effect, to protect the rights of individuals against possible arbitrary actions of the state, it is essential that one of the branches have the independence that permits it to judge both the actions of the executive branch and the constitutionality of the laws enacted and even the judgments handed down by its own members. Therefore, the Commission considers that the independence of the judiciary is an essential requisite for the practical observance of human rights in general.

A clear example of the subordination of the judicial branch to the executive appears in *Case 11.084 (Peru)*.[119] In this case the Commission considered that the Peruvian Special Military Court was not a competent, independent and impartial tribunal according to Article 8(1) because under Peru's Laws of Military Justice it was supervised by the Ministry of Defence. This meant that it was a special court subordinated to the executive branch of government.[120]

While it is possible at a theoretical level to state that the judiciary should enjoy independence and be free from interference by the executive, this has proved to be notoriously difficult to maintain in practice in certain American states. In its follow-up report on Nicaragua in 1994[121] the Commission observed that it continued to receive complaints about 'the compartmentalization, politicization and slowness of the Judicial Branch' and observed that these were factors which 'unquestionably affect the exercise of the right to justice and due process'.[122] The Commission noted in particular that this led to the lack of investigation and punishment of serious crimes and that in certain cases justice officials tended to adopt the *a priori* position that investigatory proceedings could not be commenced. Furthermore, in the case of Panama, the Commission investigated the judicial institution of the *Corregidor* and found that it was 'incompatible with the principles and standards embodied in the American Convention on Human Rights ...'.[123] The Commission described the institution in the following way:[124]

> The *Corregidor* is a special police official, designated by the Mayor of the respective township who may remove him from his post at any time. Under the Constitution, the *Corregidor* must be 18 years of age in order to be appointed; hence, *Corregidores* are generally illiterate young men who have neither the preparation nor the independence necessary and are easily influenced.

The *Corregidores* were granted jurisdiction over petty crime, but they had, in fact, extended their jurisdiction to include those citizens who were involved in political demonstrations and those who had allegedly disobeyed or wronged members of the armed forces. Sentences imposed by the *Corregidor* could in theory be appealed to the Mayor, but in practice this did not happen. As the Commission noted, even if an appeal were filed the matter remained within the purview of the executive, thus violating the separation of powers and usurping responsibilities that rightly belonged to the judiciary. Given these characteristics of the institution of *Corregidor* the Commission held that it violated Articles 8 and 25 of the American Convention on Human Rights.

Similarly, in Peru military courts were granted jurisdiction in criminal matters in emergency zones which had been established in approximately half the country. The Commission held that the existence of such courts was incompatible with the guarantee of trial by an independent and impartial court in Art 8(1).[125] This case seems to indicate, therefore, that the existence of military courts which purport to exercise criminal jurisdiction over the civil population are *per se* a violation of Article 8.

It should also be observed that it is not enough that the separation of powers and the independence of the judiciary should be formally guaranteed by the constitution or fundamental law of the state in question. It is crucial that the physical conditions should be maintained in which judges and judicial officers are able to pursue their tasks free from external influences. As the Commission stated in its report on Guatemala:[126]

> Apart from the fact that the rule of law must be in full effect with the principle of separation of powers duly observed, and the fact that administrative measures are needed to provide judges with suitable material means for protecting their security, the autonomy, independence and integrity of the members of the judiciary calls for measures that will ensure unrestricted access to the courts and legal remedies, trials conducted in accordance with the principles of due process of law, and the conclusion of such trials within a reasonable time and with judgments that address all points involved.

In its *1992-93 Annual Report*, the Commission published a report entitled 'Measures Necessary for rendering the autonomy, independence and integrity of the member of the Judicial Branch more effective'. In this, it provided a checklist of criteria which relate to the guarantees that should characterize the administration of justice, 'the implementation of which, and their adaptation to the particular circumstances of each state, being the responsibility of its authorities'.[127] The checklist included the following requirements:[128]

- guaranteeing that the executive and legislative branches will not interfere in matters that are the purview of the judiciary;
- providing the judiciary with the political support and the means needed for it to be fully able to perform its function in guaranteeing human rights;
- ensuring the exclusive exercise of jurisdiction by the members of the judiciary, and eliminating special courts;
- guaranteeing that judges cannot be removed from office as long as their conduct remains above reproach, and ensuring that panels are set up to consider the cases of judges who are accused of unethical conduct or corruption;
- preserving the rule of law and declaring states of emergency only when absolutely necessary, in keeping with Articles 27 of the American Convention on Human Rights and Article 4 of the International Covenant on Civil and Political Rights structuring this system in such a way that it does not affect the independence of the different branches of government;
- ensuring unrestricted access to the courts and legal remedies and enabling the victim, when called for , to take action to bring those responsible to justice;
- ensuring the effectiveness of the judicial guarantees essential for the protection of human rights, and removing the obstacles that prevent their swift and appropriate application;
- guaranteeing due process of law - indictment, defense, evidence and conviction - in public trials;
- returning to judges the responsibility for disposition and supervision of persons detained;
- guaranteeing that judges will be immediately notified of all facts and situation in which human rights are restricted or suspended regardless of the legal status of the accused;
- removing the procedural obstacles that cause trials to run on for extended periods of time, so that cases may be tried within a reasonable period and settled by means of judgments covering all points involved.

The Commission clearly regards this list as an authoritative statement of the criteria necessary for the maintenance of the independence and impartiality of the judicial branch of government since it reiterated the measures in its 1993 follow-up report on Nicaragua.[129] Many of the elements in this list have already been referred to by the Commission and the Court, particularly the need to maintain the separation of power and the maintenance of the rule of law, and it might be argued that other criteria might be subsumed under these headings. The practical application of certain aspects relating to the independence and impartiality of tribunals were considered by the Commission in *Case 10.006 (Peru)* [130] concerning the trial of the ex-Peruvian President Alan Garcia. In this case the executive had removed a large number of judges from their positions without following the procedures required by the Peruvian Constitution. The judiciary were also denied protection from external political pressures. As the Commission noted, the dissolution of Congress and the replacement of a number of judges had upset the balance of power established by the 1979 Constitution. [131] Referring to the jurisprudence of the European Court of Human Rights in *Campbell and Fell* [132] the Commission held that 'in determining whether a court is independent of the executive, the manner of appointment of its members and the duration of their terms, the existence of guarantees against outside pressures must all be considered. Moreover, the Commission stated that its own jurisprudence and that of the European Court of Human Rights had found that 'the irremovability of judges ... must ... be considered a necessary corollary of their independence'. [133]   As it further observed: [134]

> That very situation has, for all practical purposes, eliminated the separation of powers and as a consequence has focused many functions in the Executive Branch. That concentration of powers has had the effect of subjecting the Judiciary even more to the dictates of the Executive Branch.

The Commission thus concluded that, by removing the judges, the Government of Peru had seriously compromised the independence and impartiality of the courts and had thereby failed to guarantee due process of law in its jurisdiction. It further observed that the nonexistence of due process within the jurisdiction of a state weakens the efficacy of the remedies provided under domestic law to protect the rights of individuals. [135]

As a final point, it should be noted that the judiciary in certain American states is not only threatened by the violation of the principle of the separation of powers which permits undue political interference in the judicial branches role, but that the very physical integrity of the judiciary is threatened by lawless elements within the state such as drug traffickers or terrorists. In its 1992-93 Annual Report the Commission reported on a study of measures necessary to enhance the autonomy, independence and integrity of the members of the judicial branch. The main focus of the study was on Colombia and Peru, two

American states in which the judiciary had experienced both threatened and actual acts of violence against themselves and members of their families.[136] While the Commission noted some of the measures taken to protect the judiciary in these states, including the establishment of certain secret courts, it nonetheless took the view that the concept of the independence and impartiality of the judiciary was part of a symbiotic whole in the protection of human rights. The Commission said:[137]

> It should be pointed out that the Inter-American Court of Human Rights generically identifies the judicial guarantees essential for protection of non-derogable rights during states of emergency: *habeas corpus* as covered in Article 7(6), *amparo* and any other effective recourse before the courts in accordance with Article 25(1), and all judicial procedures inherent in the democratic form of government and specified in the law of the States Parties to the Convention as set forth in Article 29(c), all of which are to be exercised within the framework and in accordance with the principles of due process of law as set forth in Article 8.

Presumption of Innocence

Article XXVI of the Declaration provides that every accused person is presumed to be innocent until proved guilty, and Article 8(2) of the Convention provides that every person accused of a criminal offence has the right to be presumed innocent so long as his guilt has not been proven according to law. This clearly indicates that the burden of proving guilt lies upon the state. It does not, however, indicate what the standard of proof ought to be. In most cases, however, the standard of proof will be that which requires the state to prove its case beyond reasonable doubt. These issues were considered in *Case 11.084 (Peru)*.[138] In this case a number of Army officers were arrested following a meeting at which they discussed the possibility of restoring democratic rule to Peru. They were tried by a military tribunal and given inadequate time or means for preparation of defence.[139] Although the Peruvian constitution placed the onus upon the state to prove any alleged offence beyond reasonable doubt, in accordance with the principle of *in dubio pro reo,* this requirement was not followed by the military court. Furthermore, the Commission found that the officers of the military tribunal 'were in no circumstances supposed to make an a priori guilty judgment as they did'.[140]

Another case in which the presumption of innocence was found to be wanting was in the operation of Special Tribunals in Nicaragua by the Sandanista government. These tribunals adopted the view that the fact of membership of the Nicaraguan National Guard or of bodies associated with it amounted to evidence which warranted a presumption of guilt. The Commission observed in this case that the tribunals began their investigations according to the principle that all Somocistas were guilty until they had proved there innocence. Such an approach is clearly a reversal of the requirement of Article 8(2) and thus violates that provision.

Minimum Guarantees

As indicated above, the minimum guarantees which are contained in Article 8(2) of the Convention are not exclusive. As the Commission observed, other guarantees may be identified by reference to the constitutional law of the States Parties. It should be pointed out, however, that the Article 8(2) guarantees are, the *minimum* guarantees, and therefore any lesser standards will inevitably breach this provision. It should also be noted that the due process requirements must be accorded to individuals on the basis of equality. This means that there must be no discrimination on the grounds established by Article 1(1) of the Convention namely, race, colour, sex language, religion, political or other opinion, national or social origin, economic status, birth or any other social condition.[141] Article 24 further supplements these provisions by providing that all persons are equal before the law and are therefore entitled, without discrimination, to equal protection of the law. The question of discrimination arose in the context of the right to counsel in the case of indigent persons. This will be considered in the appropriate section below.

Right to a Translator

By Article 8(2)(a) accused persons who do not understand or who do not speak the language of the tribunal or court before which they are compelled to appear, must be assisted by a translator or interpreter. The cost of such services is to be borne by the state. To date neither the Commission nor the Court have been required to rule on this matter.

Notification of Charges

By Article 8(2)(b) of the Convention accused persons are entitled to notification in detail of the charges against them. This provision also corresponds to Article 7(4) which states that detained persons must be informed of the reasons for their detention and be promptly notified of the charge or charges against them. These provisions appear to be concerned in the main with pre-trial procedure. Neither the Commission nor the Court have been called upon to consider these provisions in detail, but it would prudent to assume that they relate not only to the precise specification of the charges against an individual, but also to details of the prosecution's case against the accused person. Since by Article 8(2)(f) an accused person is accorded the right to examine prosecution witnesses or experts in court, it must be assumed that the accused is entitled to know in advance the identity of these witnesses or experts.

Adequate Time and Means for Defence

Article 8(2)(c) of the Convention provides that accused person must be given adequate time and means for the preparation of their defence. What is 'adequate time and means' in any situation will inevitably depend upon the particularities and complexities of the case. The more complex a case, the more time will be necessary for its preparation. Similarly, in complex cases an accused person will necessarily require greater access to the lawyer or lawyers preparing his or her case. It might also be inferred that since accused persons are also given the right to defend themselves personally by Article 8(2)(g) of the Convention, then they must be given access to the necessary resources to accomplish this task, including, presumably, access to the appropriate legal texts. Whether the period of time allowed for an accused person to prepare his or her defence is adequate may also arise as a matter of inference. In *Case 10.198 (Nicaragua)*[142] a former National Guardsman was arrested and charged with espionage. He was held in prison incommunicado for 30 days and compelled to make self-incriminating statements. He was granted no legal assistance in the preparation of his defence and was ultimately sentenced to 30 years in prison after a trial which was completed within six weeks of his arrest. The Commission held that it could be deduced that given the shortness of the period in which he was detained, tried and sentence it was proper to conclude that he had not been accorded adequate time and means for the preparation of his defence as stipulated in Article 8(2)(c) of the Convention.[143]

In the Commission's follow-up report on Peru in its *1993 Annual Report*,[144] the Commission complained that attorneys who defended individuals accused of terrorism were experiencing serious problems. In particular, attorneys claimed that they were not given sufficient time to acquaint themselves with their client's case nor to confer with their clients prior to trial. In addition to this, attorneys informed the Commission that a number of procedural impediments were placed in their way such as an absence of notification sufficiently in advance of when trials were to take place. The Commission held that these practices were 'detrimental to the most elementary judicial guarantees and due process'.[145]

Right of Self-defence or Assistance by Legal Counsel

Both Articles 8(2)(d) and 8(2)(e) deal with an individual's right to legal representation in criminal proceedings. Article 8(2)(d) provides that accused person have the right to defend themselves personally or to be assisted by legal counsel of their own choosing. In addition to this accused persons are to be able to communicate freely and privately with their chosen counsel. This latter requirement is clearly intimately linked with the preceding provision Article 8(2)(d) the details of which were considered above. In addition to accused persons having the choice of counsel, they also have the right to be assisted by counsel provided by the state if they do not defend themselves personally or engage their own counsel within the time period established by the domestic law of the state concerned. While the state is obligated to provide defence counsel, it does not appear that it is obliged to pay for such counsel. Nonetheless, it seems that these provisions are engaged from the time of the arrest of the accused onwards.[146]

In the Commission's follow-up report on Peru in 1993, it noted that both these provisions were violated. It observed that while in theory those accused of terrorism had the right to defend themselves, in practice the right was so 'seriously shackled' that it was virtually non-existent.[147] Similarly, attorneys in Peru were permitted to defend only one person at a time nationwide if such a person had been accused of terrorism. The Commission held that 'this was a very serious violation of one's right to be assisted by an attorney of one's choosing'.[148] The conditions under which a trial is held may also violate the right of accused persons to defend themselves. In a report on strengthening the autonomy independence and integrity of the judiciary, the Commission noted that secret trials which took place in Colombia in order to protect judges, lawyers and witnesses from violent retribution by terrorists and narco-terrorists violated the right to self-defence. The Commission observed that the fact that the identity of witnesses was not disclosed in such proceedings 'makes it virtually impossible to rebut their testimony and is thus a violation of the accused's right of self-defence'.[149]

The Inter-American Court of Human Rights has also had occasion to rule on the question of the right to counsel in Articles 8(2)(d) and (e). In its

Advisory Opinion OC-11/90 the Court was requested by the Commission to rule, *inter alia*, on whether the requirement to exhaust local remedies was necessary where indigents were unable to avail themselves of legal remedies within a country because of their economic circumstances. In ruling on this question, the Court made a number of observations not only on Articles 8(2)(d) and (e), but also upon the question of non-discrimination in relation to the right to due process.

In answering the questions posed the Court noted that Article 1(1) required states respect the rights and freedoms recognized in the Convention and to ensure to all persons within their jurisdiction the free and full exercise of those rights and freedoms without discrimination on the grounds of, *inter alia*, economic status. Article 24 further required states to ensure that all persons are equal before the law and entitled to equal protection of the law without discrimination. Here the Court ruled that the meaning of discrimination in Article 24 could be determined by reference to the list contained in Article 1(1), thus including equal treatment and equal protection of the law regardless of economic status.[150] Thus the Court held that if persons seeking protection of the law in order to assert rights which the Convention guarantees, found that their economic status prevented them from doing so because they could not afford either the necessary legal counsel or the cost of the proceedings then those persons would be discriminated against by reason of their economic status, and would not therefore be receiving equal protection before the law.[151]

The Court also ruled that the term 'protection of the law' in Article 24 meant that legal remedies for the protection of rights guaranteed by the Convention must also be available. In addition to this Article 1(1) placed a positive obligation on States Parties 'to organize the governmental apparatus and ... all the structures through which public power is exercised, so that they are capable of juridically ensuring the free and full enjoyment of human rights'.[152]

These general obligations established by Articles 1(1) and 24 were, in the Court's view, supplemented by the more specific provisions of Article 8 concerning right to a fair trial. It noted that Article 8 differentiated between criminal proceedings and other proceedings. In criminal proceedings individuals were entitled to 'minimum guarantees' in the enjoyment of a right to a fair hearing, whereas in other proceedings they were entitled to 'due guarantees'.The minimum guarantees to which a defendant is entitled are listed in Article 8(2). Of particular relevance in the instant case were Articles 8(2)(d) and (e).In analysing these provisions the Court noted that they did not require the state to provide legal counsel free of charge. It did take the view, however, that if indigents were in need of counsel and the state did not provide such assistance free of charge, indigents would be discriminated against because of their economic circumstances.[153] Although the Court observed that Article 8 only required provision of counsel when it is necessary for a 'fair hearing', it held that any state which did not provide indigents with counsel free of charge, could not later assert that appropriate remedies existed but were not exhausted.[154]

Furthermore, the Court ruled that if indigents were obliged to defend themselves because they could not afford counsel, Article 8 would still be violated if it could be shown that lack of legal counsel affected the right to a fair trial.[155] In non-criminal proceedings the Court noted that the same principles applied to the concept of 'due guarantees'. Thus indigents were also entitled to a right to a hearing with such guarantees. In determining whether or not a fair hearing in non-criminal cases required the presence of legal counsel depended in Court's view on the circumstances of a particular case or proceedings. This encompassed, for example, the significance, legal character and context of the case within the legal system in question.[156] Here the Court noted that it was not only the right to legal counsel which might affect the fairness of a trial in the case of indigents, but also other factors including the financial ability to cover other legal costs such as filing fees.[157]

The Court also took the view that the principles which underpinned its reasoning in cases of indigence also applied to cases in which lawyers within particular states refused to take cases because they feared that this would lead to reprisals or violence against either themselves or their families. This is a problem which has been evident in a number of American states and which has caused considerable difficulty for persons accused of political or politically related crimes. Relying on the principles enunciated by the Court in *Advisory Opinion OC-11/90: Exceptions to the Exhaustion of Domestic Remedies* it would seem that where the fairness of either criminal or civil proceedings is in question because of the refusal of counsel to act on grounds of fear for themselves or their families, the requirements of Article 8(2)(d) and (e) will be violated.

An issue related to that discussed immediately above are circumstances in which lawyers who take cases with a political complexion are harassed and vilified as a result of this. As the Commission observed in Case *11.084 (Peru),*[158] the 'malicious and unfounded' linking of a defence lawyer to the unlawful activities of which his client has been falsely accused constitutes a threat to the free exercise of the legal profession and 'infringes one of the fundamental guarantees of the administration and of due process, i.e. the right to defense enshrined in Article 8, subparagraph 2 (d) of the American Convention'.[159]

Right to Examine Witnesses and Experts

The right of the defence to examine witnesses present in court and to obtain the appearance of witnesses and experts or other persons 'who may be able to throw light' on a case is guaranteed by Article 8(2)(f) of the American Convention. Although there is little jurisprudence on this point it would seem that this right will be subject to the limitations which exist in most domestic legal systems concerning the presentation of evidence and the materiality of witnesses and experts. Nonetheless, should the court act in an arbitrary manner in excluding witnesses, this would seem to be contrary to the present provision. Similarly, the Commission has held that the testimony of unidentified witnesses is incompatible with the American Convention.[160]

This latter raises the broader question of the secrecy of certain proceedings in order to protect the identity of judges, witnesses and lawyers who may be the objects of violence or intimidation from those involved in or associated with terrorism or narco-terrorism cases. In its report on the measures necessary to enhance the autonomy, independence and integrity of the judiciary, the Commission considered this issue. It noted as preliminary issue that secret proceedings were incompatible with the right of public trial contained in Article 8(5). This, in fact, is not necessarily so, since an exception is made in that provision for cases in which non-public proceedings may be permitted 'insofar as may be necessary to protect the interests of justice'. Nonetheless, the Commission stated that the problems associated with secret proceedings were compounded by the fact that the identity of witnesses were not disclosed, which made it virtually impossible to rebut their testimony.[161]

Self-incrimination

Article 8(2)(g) provides that accused persons have the right not to be compelled to be witnesses against themselves or to plead guilty in criminal proceedings. This provision is further buttressed by Article 8(3) which provides that a confession of guilt by an accused person shall be valid only if it is made without coercion of any kind. While there have been many cases investigated by the Commission in which the use of torture, inhuman and degrading treatment to extract confessions has been evident, it has not explicitly condemned these as violations of Articles 8(2)(g) or (3) but simply as composite violations of Article 8. In *Case 9850 (Argentina)*,[162] for example, the petitioner had been charged with politically motivated offences and a confession was extracted from him by torture. This was then followed by a trial in which certain irregularities occurred. The Commission held that the principles of judicial protection and judicial guarantees contained in Articles 8 and 25 had been violated. Similarly, in *Case 11.084 (Peru)*[163] a number of former army officers had been charged with conspiring to overthrow the government of President Fujimori. Several of the officers had statements taken in the absence of their lawyers and a number claimed that they were subjected to physical and psychological torture to force them to make false self-incriminating statements, which they were made to sign without first reading them. While the Commission held that such actions on the part of the state violated Article 8, it is reasonably clear that these violations were of the particular provisions concerning self-incrimination.

It seems that concrete evidence of ill-treatment short of torture will also violate Article 8(2)(g) and Article 8(3). In *Case 10.198 (Nicaragua)*[164] a former soldier was arrested and charged with espionage. He was held in prison incommunicado for a period of 30 days and compelled to make self-incriminating statements in the absence of any legal representation. He was subsequently sentenced to thirty years in prison. The Commission held that the statements obtained by the prosecution during period in which the petitioner had been held incommunicado invalid in light of Arts 8(2)(g) and 8(3).[165]

It would seem that the net effect of a conviction obtained following a violation of Article 8(2)(g) should be considered invalid and should as a consequence be overturned. Similarly, a confession obtained in violation of Article 8(3) should be excluded by the court. Failure to do so should also result in a successful appeal or the overturning of a conviction obtained on such a basis.

This conclusion is partly supported by *Case 10.006 (Peru)*[166] involving the arrest and trial of the former Peruvian president Alan Garcia. In this case, members of the Peruvian army had entered Garcia's home without a warrant and confiscated a number of documents which they claimed related to alleged offences. The Commission held that this action violated one of the due process rights which was not explicitly mentioned in Article 8(2) of the Convention but which was implicit in Article 8(1):the inviolability of domicile. The Commission said:[167]

> In effect, inviolability of domicile is more than a guarantee of privacy; it is a guarantee of due process inasmuch as it establishes what can be seized, that being incriminating evidence against an individual charged with a crime. When a search of a domicile is conducted without observing the proper constitutional procedures, that guarantee prevents any evidence thus obtained from being used to arrive at a subsequent court decision. Thus in practice it functions as an exclusionary rule, one that eliminates illegally obtained evidence.

While the preceding case is concerned with the exclusion of evidence illegally obtained, it seems clear that illegally obtained confessions should be subject to the same principles. This provision should also be read in conjunction with Article 10 of the Convention which provides for a right of compensation in cases involving a miscarriage of justice.[168]

Right of Appeal

Article 8(2)(h) of the Convention grants convicted persons the right to appeal their convictions to a higher court. In granting this right the Convention is less than explicit about the standards which should be attached to such an appeal. Are, for example, accused persons entitled to representation by counsel? These issues were dealt with by the Commission in *Case 9850 (Argentina)*[169] in which the Argentine Supreme Court had merely denied the petitioners claim without examining or explaining the reasons for dismissing their evidence. The Commission held:[170]

Although it is true that the due process guarantee appears to deal primarily with the stage of judicial lower-court inquiry or investigation of the charges against the defendant, full observance of the principle of due process encompasses all subsequent stages of appeal or review by higher courts, for it is before these that any flaws may be corrected. As zealous custodians of the majesty of justice, the courts that hear an appeal or an application for review must examine not only the grounds for the appeal but also whether or not due process has been observed, even in regard to unreported irregularities.

From this it would seem that all the guarantees concerning due process contained in Article 8 apply to proceedings before an appellate tribunal. This would include the right to counsel where this is necessary for the conduct of a fair trial. At the appellate level, it is inconceivable that a trial could be properly conducted without the benefit of counsel, so it is arguable that there is a stronger right to counsel in the inter-American system during appellate proceedings as opposed to proceedings at first instance.

Another issue raised by Article 8(2)(h) is whether it implies that reasons should be given for all judgments. There is no explicit provision to this effect in the American Convention, but it would seem that an effective appeal may only be executed if there are reasons given for the initial judgment. Support for this view is also derived from the Commission's *1993 Annual Report* on the judiciary in which it states that judgments must cover all points involved in the case.[171]

Non bis in idem

Article 8(4) of the Convention provides that an accused person acquitted by a non-appealable judgment shall not be subjected to a new trial for the same cause. This rule against double jeopardy is evident in the legal systems of most states and may be regarded as a general principle of law. The principle of *non bis in idem* and the concept of a nonappealable judgment was considered in the *Garcia Case* concerning Peru. In this case, Garcia was acquitted on the charge of unlawful enrichment but the same charge was filed against him at a subsequent date. The Commission in considering the matter observed that Article 8(4) of the American Convention upholds the guarantee of non bis in idem and noted that the following elements underlie the principle: first, the accused must have been acquitted; second, the acquittal must be a final judgment; and third, the new trial must be based on the same cause that prompted the original trial.[172] The Commission then went on to examine the meaning of 'accused person acquitted' and held that this 'implies that someone who, having been charged with a crime, has been exonerated from all criminal responsibility, since he has been acquitted because his innocence has been demonstrated, because his guilt has not been proven, or because it has been determined that the acts of which he is accused are not defined as a crime'.[173] Turning to the meaning of 'non-appealable judgment', the Commission stated that this should not be interpreted restrictively, that is, limited to the meaning given to it by the domestic law of the state, rather, in this context, 'judgment' should be interpreted as any procedural act that is fundamentally jurisdictional in nature, and 'non-appealable judgment' as expressing the exercise of jurisdiction that acquires the immutability and incontestability of res judicata'.[174] The Commission then analyzed the applicability of these concepts to both preliminary hearings and hearings which had been reopened. It held that where a court rules on one occasion that an individual cannot be prosecuted by the state because the acts charged are not defined as a crime, another court, citing the same acts, cannot then hold that they constitute a crime. Having exhausted the remedies provided for under the law, this decision must also be uncontestable, that is, it may not be changed during the same proceedings or in later proceedings.[175] In the case of proceedings which had been reopened, the Commission noted that the Convention explicitly refers to the prohibition against instituting a new trial based on the same facts and that from a literal interpretation of its text, it would have to be acknowledged that the violation of the principle of *res judicata* by reopening a proceeding that had already been closed, would not be covered under Art 8(4). It went on to say, however, that it considered that the protection accorded under Art 8(4) 'implicitly includes those cases in which reopening a case has the effect of reviewing questions of fact and law that have come to have the authority of res judicata'.[176] The Commission found that the *Garcia Case* exhibited these characteristics.[177]

Freedom from Ex Post Facto Laws

Article 9 of the Convention provides that 'no one shall be convicted of any act or omission that did not constitute a criminal offence, under the applicable law, at the time it was committed. A heavier penalty shall not be imposed than the one that was applicable at the time the criminal offence was committed. If subsequent to the commission of the offence the law provides for the imposition of a lighter punishment, the guilty person shall benefit therefrom'. While Article 9 clearly comprehends the general principle of law contained in the maxim *nulla poena sine lege*, it also extends further in that it prohibits the retrospective application of heavier penalties, but requires the retroactive application of lighter penalties. The net effect is to grant convicted persons more favourable treatment where lighter sentences are introduced at a subsequent date. This provision clearly links with the provisions of Article 4 concerning the death penalty.[178]

Right to Compensation

As noted above, under the consideration of factors affecting due process, Article 10 of the Convention recognizes every person's right to compensation in accordance with the law in the event that he or she has been sentenced by a final judgment through a miscarriage of justice. The requirement that compensation ought to be 'in accordance with the law' suggests that there must be established criteria for the award of compensation and that such compensation ought not to be available simply on an *ex gratia* basis. It might also be argued that Article 10 impliedly requires that the quantum of compensation should also be established by law.

Right to Privacy

Despite being given the heading of the 'Right to Privacy', Article 11 of the Convention is in fact much broader than this. While Article 11(1) of the Convention protects a person's honour and dignity, Article 11(2) deals with the major issues of privacy concerning interference with a person's private life, family, home or correspondence and from unlawful attacks on a person's honour or reputation. Article 11(3) further provides that everyone has the right to protection of the law against such interference or attacks. As the Commission noted in *Case 10.006 (Peru)*,[179] the rights protected by Article 11 are consistent with those protected by Articles IX (right to the inviolability of the home) and X (right to the inviolability and transmission of correspondence) of the American Declaration[180] and that the underlying rationale of these provision is to prevent arbitrary state interference in the lives of individuals.[181] The Commission has also observed, however, that the right to privacy is not absolute and may be restricted by the domestic laws of state. It has stated that:[182]

> The guarantee of the inviolability of the domicile and of private papers must give way when there is a well-substantiated search warrant issued by a competent judicial authority, spelling out the reasons for the measure being adopted and specifying the place to be searched and the objects that will be seized.

In the case under consideration, however, it was clear that Peru had not carried out the seizures of the petitioner's papers at his home in accordance with its own constitutional requirements and had therefore breached Article 11.

The protection of a person's honour or reputation has not been given much consideration by either the Commission or the Court. It is clear, however, that such protection coupled with Article 11(3) manifests an aspect of freedom of expression which is protected by Article 13. In essence, Article 11 sanctions post hoc controls on that right by requiring state to provide individuals with the right to sue for defamatory statements and other similar acts. It is also connected with Article 14 which grants individuals a right of reply where they have been injured by inaccurate or offensive statements or ideas which have been disseminated by the mass media. It appears, however, that these provisions, including Article 11, will not apply to the so-called desacato laws which aim to protect public officials by criminalizing speech which is critical of such persons. The Commission has analysed these laws and their relationship to the freedom of expression *in extenso* and its findings will be discussed under freedom of thought and expression below.[183]

Although it appears that the main objectives of Article 11(2) is to protect honour and reputation in their intangible aspect by requiring the state to guarantee legal protection, the Commission has taken the view that honour and reputation as understood in Article 11(2) also relates to the physical aspect of the individual. In *Case 10.772 (El Salvador)*,[184] the Commission held that the rape of a seven-year-old girl by a soldier was a violation of this provision.

Furthermore, the Commission has held that Article 11 comprehends the forcible recruitment of an individual into the army since this offends against the dignity of the individual.[185]

Freedom of Conscience and Religion

While Article 12 of the Convention is entitled 'Freedom of Conscience and Religion' its primary emphasis is in fact on rights associated with the holding and exercise of a person's religious beliefs. This is consistent with Article III of the American Declaration which recognizes everyone's right to profess a religious faith and to manifest and practice it in both public and private. Article 12(1) provides that everyone has the right to freedom of conscience and of religion. That right includes the freedom to maintain or change one's religion or beliefs as well as the freedom to profess or disseminate one's religion or beliefs either individually or together with others in public or in private. This provision is thus linked with Articles 13, 15 and 16 of the Convention which deal with the freedom of thought and expression, the right of assembly and freedom of association, observance of which are necessary for the practice and profession of one's faith either individually or in concert with others of like belief. Articles 12(2) and (3) are, however, concerned with the balance which must be maintained between freedom of religion on the one hand and the protection of individuals or society from religious or pseudo-religious practices which may be deemed to be harmful. Thus, while Article 12(2) states that persons shall not be subject to restrictions that might impair their freedom to maintain or to change their religion or beliefs, nonetheless, freedom to manifest these may be subject to limitations prescribed by law which are necessary to protect public safety, order, health or morals or the rights and freedoms of others. States Parties clearly have a margin of discretion in whether they consider a particular religion or pseudo-religion to be an appropriate matter for regulation, but that margin of discretion is subject to oversight and control by the Commission. In a number of cases, the sect known as the Jehovah's Witnesses has been subject to restrictions and its members subject to a number of criminal penalties because of the fact that certain of their beliefs and the practice and manifestation of those beliefs was incompatible with the laws of a number of Latin American states. In particular, the Jehovah's Witnesses' unwillingness to swear oaths of allegiance, to recognize the state and its symbols or to participate in military service on the basis of their religious beliefs led to their prosecution and imprisonment. In the case of Argentina,[186] the Commission took the view that such action was contrary to

Article III of the Declaration, and to a number of other cognate rights protected by the Convention.[187] Of particular concern in this context was the expulsion of the children of Jehovah's Witnesses from state schools on the alleged grounds that they would not salute the national flag. The Commission found that this violated the right to education protected by Article XII of the Declaration. Should such a situation arise today, it would be likely that such action would infringe Article 12(4) which provides that parents or guardians have the right to provide for the religious education of their children or wards that is in accord with their own convictions. Given the context, it is presumed that this latter means their philosophical or religious convictions.

Freedom of Thought and Expression

Of all the rights protected by the American Declaration and the American Convention it is perhaps the right to freedom of thought and expression which has received the most detailed attention by the Commission and the Court. The reason for this is that these institutions have identified this particular right as forming an essential basis for the existence and functioning of a healthy democracy. This rationale has been reiterated on a number of occasions by the Commission and the Court. As the Court said in *Compulsory Membership*:[188]

> Freedom of expression is a cornerstone upon which the very existence of a democratic society rests. It is indispensable for the formation of public opinion ... It represents, in short, the means that enable the community, when exercising its options, to be sufficiently informed. Consequently, it can be said that a society that is not well-informed is not a society that is truly free.

The Commission has also observed that the absence of freedom of thought and expression is a factor which contributes to a state's failure to respect other human rights.[189] It has also stated that freedom of thought and expression has a 'universal character' which contains within it 'the idea of the juridical right which pertains to persons, individually or collectively considered, to express, transmit, and diffuse their thoughts; in a parallel and correlative way, freedom of information is also universal and embodies the collective rights of everyone to receive information without interference or distortion'.[190] The Court has also observed that since this right plays such a crucial and central role in public debate, the Convention places an extremely high value on it and reduces any restrictions to a minimum. It has stated that it is in the interest of the democratic public order inherent in the American Convention' that freedom of expression be 'scrupulously respected'.[191]

Extent of the Right

Freedom of thought and expression is comprehended by Article IV of the Declaration and Article 13 of the Convention. The former, as with other rights protected by the Declaration, is relatively pithy. This provides that 'every person has the right to freedom of investigation, of opinion and of the expression and dissemination of ideas by any medium whatsoever'. After stating that everyone is entitled to the right, Article 13 continues to provide that it includes 'freedom to seek, receive and impart information and ideas of all kinds, regardless of frontiers, either orally or in writing, in print, in the form of art, or through any other medium of one's choice'. It will be noted that Article 13(1) is broad in scope, and the Court has noted that the American Convention is more generous in its guarantee of the freedom of thought and expression than the corresponding provisions of both the European Convention on Human Rights and the International Covenant on Civil and Political Rights. The Inter-American Court has further observed that 'this is particularly significant considering that the ECT has repeatedly asserted that freedom of expression is one of the "essential foundations of a democratic society"'.[192]

Perhaps the first point to note about Article 13(1) is that it possesses a 'special scope and character' since it guarantees not only the freedom to transmit information and ideas of all kinds, but also to seek and receive such information and ideas.[193] The Court has said, 'by simultaneously guaranteeing the right to express and receive such expressions, the Convention enhances the free interchange of ideas needed for effective public debate within the political arena'.[194] It is also of note that the medium of expression is irrelevant. It may be written, oral or pictorial and may be disseminated in print or by electronic means. This latter would now presumably include the various computer based methods of communication, such as the Internet, as well as the more conventional television and radio media. The fact that Article 13(1) presents a non-exhaustive list of potential means of communication by using the term 'this right includes' suggests that future unforeseen and, perhaps, unforeseeable developments in communications technology are comprehended by the provision. It is also noteworthy that transboundary or transnational communication is also protected by Article 13(1). By providing that the right exists 'regardless of frontiers' ensures that all forms of communication ranging from print to satellite telecommunications originating in foreign countries may not be interfered with, save in the circumstances envisaged by Article 13 itself.[195]

Presumption against Prior Censorship and Other Forms of Control

The special scope and character of the right to freedom of thought and expression produces a presumption in favour of the right and a presumption against prior censorship. Given the presumption in favour of the maximum enjoyment of the right, the Court has held, in the context of the licensing of journalists, that the mass media should, in principle, be open to all.[196] Article 13(2), however, specifically articulates the presumption against prior censorship. It states that freedom of expression may not be subject to prior censorship but shall be subject to subsequent imposition of liability which is to be expressly established by law 'to the extent necessary' to ensure, first, respect for the rights or reputations of others or, second, the protection of national security, public order or public health or morals. The rule against prior censorship is also reinforced by Article 14 which provides for a right of reply to anyone injured by inaccurate or offensive statements or ideas disseminated to the general public. Of this the Commission has said:[197]

> The prohibition against prior censorship assures that certain ideas and information will not be automatically excluded from the public arena. Thus, people will not only be free to express their own ideas but will have access to the ideas of others so as to broaden their understanding of the political debate within society. In addition, the right of reply provided for in Art 14 guarantees access to an appropriate medium of communication for those injured by inaccurate or offensive statements.

The nature of post hoc controls on freedom of expression may of course include criminal as well as civil sanctions. Most states possess a concept of criminal libel within their legal systems, but it is more likely that post hoc controls will be exercised by way of civil actions in defamation.

Some consideration should be given to Article 13(3) in this context also. While Article 13(2) deals with direct prior censorship, Article 13(3) makes it clear that the right of expression may not be restricted by indirect methods or means. A non-exhaustive list of indirect methods of restricting freedom of expression includes 'the abuse of government or private controls over newsprint, radio broadcasting frequencies, or equipment used in the dissemination of information, or by any other means tending to impede the communication and circulation of ideas and opinions'. This is clearly very broad and likely to comprehend a wide range of activities other than those mentioned in the list itself, such as controlling access to and use of telephone equipment.

Both the Commission and the Court have been required to rule on forms of prior censorship and indirect control of the mass media. In *Case 9178 (Costa Rica)*[198] Stephen Schmidt, a United States citizen, was working in Costa Rica as a journalist without being a member of the Colegio de Periodistas (Association of Journalists) as required by Costa Rican law. He was charged and convicted with the illegal exercise of the profession of journalist in the absence of membership of the Colegio. Although Schmidt argued that this was a violation of Article 13, the Commission held that freedom of thought and expression was not absolute right and that as long as their was no prior censorship or direct or indirect official control aimed at hindering the free circulation of information or of manipulating it with a specific political purpose, then some restrictions might be acceptable. In this case the Commission believed that the obligatory membership of the Colegio did not restrict the freedom of thought and expression established by Article 13 as long as the Colegio protected the freedom to seek, receive and distribute information without imposing conditions leading to the restriction or curtailment of that right. The Commission stated that 'compulsory membership does not restrict, but rather regulates, freedom of thought and expression'.[199]

Although Dr Bruce McColm dissented from this view, the issue was not remitted to the Court for determination. Costa Rica, which was concerned by the ruling, nonetheless subsequently decided to submit this issue to the Court for an advisory opinion.[200] In this opinion, the Court traversed the area concerning freedom of thought and expression and the legitimate restrictions upon this right in some considerable detail. It has already been noted above that the Court in this opinion considered Article 13 to be of a 'special scope and character' which was derived from the dual character of the freedom to impart and receive information. The Court also noted that this provision made it clear that the means of dissemination of ideas and information included all the communications media.[201] These aspects of freedom of expression emphasize the fact that 'the expression and dissemination of ideas are indivisible concepts'.[202] Given the importance of the interchange of ideas through the medium of free expression, it was the Court's view that, as noted above, the mass media should, in principle, be open to all.[203] This did not mean, however, that all restrictions on the mass media should necessarily be considered violations of Article 13, since the provision itself referred specifically to circumstances in which post hoc control was legitimate.[204] As indicated above, while prior censorship is not permitted by Article 13(2), legal regulation to protect an individual's rights or reputation and the requirements of public policy permit restrictions.[205] Nevertheless, such limitations upon the right are not open-ended and they must meet the requirements of both procedure and form which in turn 'depend upon the legitimacy of the ends that such restrictions are designed to accomplish'.[206] The Court in *Compulsory Membership* specified the requirements which are necessary to invoke restrictions legitimately under Article 13(2). These requirements, which have been adopted by the Commission,[207] are fourfold and must be met in their entirety. There must be:[208]

1) the existence of previously established grounds for liability,
2) the express and precise definition of these grounds by law,
3) the legitimacy of the ends sought to be achieved,
4) a showing that these grounds of liability are 'necessary to ensure' the aforementioned ends.

In analyzing these requirements the Court has placed considerable emphasis on the latter phrase which it has held must be interpreted not only in the light of Articles 29(c) and (d) and Article 32, but also of the Preamble to the Convention, which evinces the States Parties' intention 'to consolidate in this hemisphere, within the framework of democratic institutions, a system of personal liberty and social justice based on respect for the essential rights of man'.[209] Thus the Court has concluded that any restrictions on freedom of expression which were considered 'necessary to ensure' one of the objectives referred to in Article 13(2) must also be judged by reference to the 'legitimate needs of democratic societies and institutions'.[210] In order to assist its understanding of these concepts, the Court has resorted to a comparative analysis of Article 10 of the European Convention on Human Rights and Article 19 of the International Covenant both of which deal with freedom of expression.[211] In *Compulsory Membership* the Court noted that Article 10 of the European Convention was formulated in very general terms which, had it not referred specifically to limitations 'necessary in a democratic society' would have made it extremely difficult to delimit the long list of permissible restrictions.[212] The Covenant on the other hand is more restrictive than the American Convention in that it does not expressly prohibit prior censorship.[213] Nonetheless, the Court was able to derive some guidance from the jurisprudence of the European Court of Human Rights on what is meant by the term 'necessary in a democratic society'. Referring to the *Sunday Times Case*,[214] the Court observed that the European Court had ruled that 'necessary', although not synonymous with 'indispensable' nonetheless implied the existence of a pressing social need. It was not enough to demonstrate that it was simply useful, reasonable or desirable on the part of the state.[215] The

Court also argued that this reasoning was also applicable to the American Convention. Thus, the necessity, and hence the legality, of restrictions imposed under Article 13(2) 'depend upon a showing that the restrictions are required by a compelling governmental interest'.[216] Furthermore, in accordance with the principle of proportionality, the restriction must be 'closely tailored to the accomplishment of the legitimate governmental objective necessitating it'.[217]

Of particular importance in this case, however, was the reference in Article 13(3) prohibiting restrictions on freedom of expression by indirect means which tended to impede the communication and circulation of ideas and opinions. The Court noted that neither the European Convention nor the Covenant contained such a comparable clause.[218] It also noted that it was significant that the provision followed directly upon Article 13(2) which, it felt, suggested a desire on the part of the drafters to ensure that the language of Article 13(2) could not be misinterpreted in a way which would limit the full scope of the right to freedom of expression save to the extent which was strictly necessary.[219]

A further significant difference between the European Convention and the Covenant on the one hand and the American Convention on the other is the fact that the latter prohibits 'private controls' on the freedom of expression.[220] Here the Court was once again forthright in its espousal of the doctrine. Referring to the general obligations imposed on States Parties to the Convention by Article 1(1) it declared:

> Hence, a violation of the Convention in this area can be the product not only of the fact that the state itself imposes restrictions of an indirect character which tend to impede "the communication and circulation of ideas and opinions", but the state also has an obligation to ensure that the violation does not result from the "private controls" referred to in [Article 13(3)].

Some insight into the nature of private controls was given by the Court which indicated that freedom of expression could be affected without the direct intervention of the state by monopolies or oligopolies which tended through their practices to produce such an effect.[221] Although this statement was not subject to further elaboration, it is arguable that it embraces at least two distinct sets of circumstances. First, it may include monopolies or oligopolies in the economic sense in which private individuals obtain control over the news media, and thus control the dissemination of information and ideas. Second, it may include professional bodies, such as the *Colegio* itself, which by the nature of its operations limits the dissemination of ideas by certain classes of person. The former inclusive category might lead to some interesting speculation on the approach which the Court would take should a newspaper owner prevent his journalists from writing about or reporting particular ideas.

In determining whether the requirement of compulsory membership by journalists of the Colegio violated Article 13, the Court indicated that Article 13 could be violated either by a direct denial of the freedom of expressionor, alternatively, by imposing restrictions which were not authorised or legitimate under Article 13(2). In the instant case a number of arguments were put forward in order to suggest that compulsory membership was legitimated by the requirements of Articles 13(2) and 32(2). First, it was argued that compulsory licensing was the normal way to organize professions in order to ensure effective supervision.[222] Indeed, this argument had been accepted by the Inter-American Commission in the *Schmidt Case*.[223] Second, since compulsory membership was a means of ensuring ethical and professional standards, this was useful to the community at large.[224] Third, it was alleged that compulsory membership of the Colegio guaranteed the independence of journalists *vis-à-vis* their employers.[225] The Court found none of these arguments compelling. There was certainly no rational legal argument which suggested that compulsory licensing was necessary for guaranteeing the rights or reputations of others or for the protection of national security or public health or morals within the meaning of Article 13(2)(a).[226] Any justification had to be found within the concepts of public order within the meaning of Article 13(2)(b) or as a just demand of the general welfare in a democratic society as required by Article 32(2).[227] In order to determine whether compulsory membership fell within any of these, it was necessary for the Court to evaluate the concepts. It has already been seen above,[228] that when dealing with restrictions on rights the Court demands that the relevant provisions be interpreted restrictively in order to prevent denial of the rights protected by the Convention. Within these confines, however, the Court declared its understanding of the various concepts. As far as the term 'public order'was concerned, the Court took this to be 'a reference to the conditions that assure the normal and harmonious functioning of institutions based on a coherent system of values and principles'.[229] Within the framework of the Convention, the Court ruled that it was possible to understand the concept of 'social welfare' in Article 13(2) as referring to 'the conditions of social life that allow members of society to reach the highest level of personal development and the optimum achievement of democratic values'.[230] While it was possible to argue that the organization of the profession of journalism into *Colegios* did not *per se* violate the Convention and could indeed be argued to contribute to the Court's understanding of public order through the regulation and supervision of the ethical standards of the profession,[231] the Court also believed that, given the fundamental importance of freedom of expression to democratic life, the very same concept of public order in a democratic society required 'the guarantee of the widest possible circulation of new ideas and opinions as well as the widest access to information by society as a whole'.[232] The Court went on to say:[233]

> Freedom of expression constitutes the primary and basic element of the public order of a democratic society, which is not conceivable without free debate and the possibility that dissenting voices be fully heard.

Given that journalism was the 'primary and principal manifestation of freedom of expression and thought'[234] and therefore differed from other liberal professions whose activities were not specifically guaranteed by the Convention,[235] it was not possible to justify compulsory membership and licensing on grounds of public order under Article 13(2) because it would deprive non-members of the *Colegio* of the right to exercise their freedom.[236] This would be a violation of the 'basic principles of a democratic public order on which the Convention itself is based'.[237] Rejecting the argument that compulsory membership and licensing was a way to enforce a code of ethics and thereby guarantee society objective and truthful information, that is an argument based on social utility, the Court held:[238]

> In principle, it would be a contradiction to invoke a restriction to freedom of expression as a means of guaranteeing it. Such an approach would ignore the primary and fundamental character of that right, which belongs to each and every individual as well as the public at large. A system of control of the right of expression on behalf of a supposed guarantee of the correctness and truthfulness of the information that society receives can be the source of great abuse and, in short, violates the right to information that this same society has.

The Court further declared that no justification for the restriction of the practice of journalism to those who were members of the *Colegio* could be found in Article 29, since it was not 'necessary to ensure' the allegedly legitimate goals claimed by Costa Rica.[239] In order to demonstrate that the restriction was necessary, it had to be shown that the same results could not be achieved by less restrictive measures.[240] Thus the Court held that the law requiring compulsory membership of the *Colegio* for persons who wished to practice the profession of journalism in Costa Rica was a restriction which could not be justified under either Article 13(2) or Article 32(2), and was thus a violation of the Convention.

The criteria enunciated by the Court in *Compulsory Membership* concerning legitimate restrictions to the freedom of thought and expression have been adopted by the Commission in a 1994 in a *Report on the Compatibility of 'Desacato' Laws with the American Convention on Human Rights*. Desacato laws belong to a class of legislation which exists in a number of Latin American states and which criminalizes expression which offends, insults, or threatens a public functionary in the performance of his or her official duties. The rationale for the existence of such laws is allegedly to protect the proper functioning of public administration. In order to test their compatibility with the American Convention, the Commission examined whether they complied with the third and fourth of the American Court's criteria enunciated in *Compulsory Membership*: namely, were the ends sought to be achieved legitimate and were the grounds for liability necessary to ensure the legitimate ends pursued?[241]

In analyzing the first of these criteria, namely, the legitimacy of the ends to be pursued, the Commission observed that the use of desacato laws to protect the honour of public functionaries unjustifiably granted them a right which is not available to other members of society. It said, 'this distinction inverts the fundamental principle in a democratic system that holds the Government subject to controls, such as public scrutiny, in order to preclude or control abuse of its coercive powers'.[242] The Commission noted that it must be the individual's and the public's right to criticize and scrutinize the actions and attitudes of officials in so far as they relate to their exercise of public office. Thus desacato laws restrict freedom of expression because of the threat of imprisonment and fines which attaches to them in cases of breach. Citing the European Court of Human Rights in *Lingens*[243] the Commission noted that 'the fear of criminal sanctions necessarily discourages people from voicing their opinions on issues of public concern particularly when legislation fails to distinguish between facts and value judgments. Political criticism often involves value judgments'.[244] A further difficulty with desacato laws is that where truth is allowed as a defence, the burden of proof is usually placed on the maker of the statement. Such an approach inevitably inhibits the free flow of ideas and opinions by shifting the burden of proof onto the speaker.[245] The Commission argued that this is particularly the case in the political arena where political criticism is based on value judgments rather than on purely fact-based statements. As a consequence of this 'proving the veracity of these statements may be impossible, since value judgments are not susceptible of proof'.[246] Finally, and perhaps most importantly, the Commission noted that the rationale behind desacato laws reverses the principle that a properly functioning democracy is in itself the greatest guarantee of public order. Thus these laws purport to preserve public order precisely 'by restricting a fundamental human right which is recognized internationally as a cornerstone upon which democratic society rests'. The Commission stated that when desacato laws have been applied they have had a direct impact on the open and rigorous debate about public policy that Article 13 guarantees and which is essential to the existence of a democratic society. Thus, in the Commission's view, invoking the concept of 'public order' to justify desacato laws directly inverts the logic underlying the guarantee of the freedom of expression and thought guaranteed in the Convention.[247]

Considering the second question, are the laws necessary legitimately to secure the end pursued, the Commission stated quite emphatically that desacato laws are not necessary to ensure public order in a democratic society. Here the Commission rehearsed the arguments which the Court had advanced in *Compulsory Membership*. It noted that Article 13(2) requires that the restriction of freedom of expression is 'necessary' and that the Court ruled in its advisory opinion that 'necessary' must mean something more than useful, reasonable or desirable. For a restriction to be necessary it must be shown that the legitimate purpose cannot reasonably be achieved through means less restrictive to freedom of expression.[248] Thus, the restrictions must be proportionate and closely directed to the achievement of the government's stated objective.[249] Furthermore, since necessity implies the existence of a 'pressing social need'[250] governments may not invoke one of the lawful restrictions of freedom of expression, such as the maintenance of 'public order' as a means to deny a right guaranteed by the Convention or to impair its true content.[251] Such a restriction would, in the Commission's view, be unlawful.

The Commission concluded that the special protection desacato laws afford public functionaries is not congruent with the objective of a democratic society to foster public debate since a government can defend itself from unjustified attacks by using the media or by recourse to ordinary defamation actions.[252] Thus the Commission noted that:[253]

> Contrary to the rationale underlying desacato laws, in democratic societies political and public figures must be more, not less, open to public scrutiny and criticism. The open and wide-ranging public debate, which as the core of democratic society necessarily involves those persons who are involved in devising and implementing public policy.

The Commission's justification for adopting this approach was that, since these functionaries are at the centre of public debate, 'they knowingly expose themselves to public scrutiny and thus must display a greater degree of tolerance for criticism'.[254]

In a comment on Articles 13(2) and (3) the Commission pointed out that these provisions recognize where the zone of legitimate state intervention begins at the point where the expression of an opinion or idea interferes directly with the rights of others or constitutes a direct and obvious threat to life in society.[255] In the political arena the threshold of state intervention should be higher because of the critical role which dialogue plays in democratic society. The Convention requires that threshold to be raised even higher when the state brings the coercive power of the criminal law to bear in order to curtail expression. Given the effect which criminal sanctions can have on freedom of expression 'criminalization of speech can only apply in those exceptional circumstances when there is an obvious and direct threat of lawless violence'.[256] The Commission concluded that:[257]

> The state's use of its coercive powers to restrict speech lends itself to abuse as a means to silence unpopular ideas and opinion, thereby repressing the debate that is critical to the effective functioning of democratic institutions. Laws that criminalize speech which does not incite lawless violence are incompatible with freedom of expression and thought guaranteed in Article 13, and with the fundamental purpose of the American Convention of allowing and protecting the pluralistic, democratic way of life.

A further example of control of freedom of expression by indirect means occurred in *Case 9726 (Paraguay).*[258] This case concerned a radio station which had been critical of the government of Paraguay. The closure of the station was achieved by agents of the state threatening the station manager and his family, interfering with transmission and causing power cuts. The Commission held this to be a violation of Art IV of the Declaration but Commission also said in its opinion 'the freedom of expression and dissemination of ideas the provisions contained in Article 13 American Convention on Human Rights are in any case definitive, maintaining that the right of expression may not be restricted by indirect methods or means, such as the abuse of Government or private controls over newsprint, radio broadcasting frequencies, or equipment used in the dissemination of information, or by any other means tending to impede the communication and circulation of ideas and opinions'.[259]

While much of the above has concerned direct interference with the right to freedom of expression through the adoption of domestic laws which inhibits communication of information and ideas, the Commission has also encountered a situation in which the removal of an individual from the jurisdiction of the state in question has been employed as a device to silence him. In *Case 9855 (Haiti)*[260] the petitioner left Haiti for the United States where he became US citizen and as a result lost his Haitian citizenship in accordance with Haitian law. Following the demise of the Duvalier dictatorship he returned to Haiti where he attempted to recover his Haitian nationality as permitted by Haitian law. He wished to reacquire his citizenship in order that he might participate in the political process in the post-Duvalier period. An order of expulsion was issued against the petitioner on the ground that he was an alien and because of his undesirable conduct. It was clear that this had been done to silence his criticism of General Namphy, the then President of Haiti.[261] The Commission held that this conduct violated Article 13 of the Convention. In justification of its conduct the Haitian government argued that the petitioner had made statements which were defamatory of political leaders in Haiti. The Commission held, however that 'any abuse of the right of freedom of expression which may be considered to threaten the national security or public order, is subject to vindication by means of a suit pursuant to the libel or defamation laws of the domestic legal system'. In the present case such a remedy not available to the petitioner.[262]

Other Permissible Limitations

Further specific limitations on the right to freedom of thought and expression are contained in Article 13(5). This provides that any propaganda for war and any advocacy of national, racial, or religious hatred that constitute incitements to lawless violence or to any other similar action against any person or group of persons on any grounds including those of race, colour, religion, language, or national origin shall be considered as offences punishable by law. In short, this provision primarily prohibits what is generally termed hate speech or forms of expression which are essentially directed at the destruction of the human rights of others. To date neither the Commission nor the Court have had occasion to pronounce on such matters.

Right of Reply

The American Convention differs from the European Convention and International Covenant on Civil and Political Rights by providing in Article 14 a right of reply for persons injured by inaccurate or offensive statements or ideas[263] disseminated to the public using legally regulated communications media. The existence of this provision would seem to inspired by two related concerns. First, that it is the function of government to create appropriate mechanisms for the resolution of human rights violations occasioned by private actions and, second, as noted above,[264] Article 14 is intimately connected with the fundamental right of freedom of thought and expression which is guaranteed by Article 13,[265] and, in particular, with the limitations which are imposed upon that right by Article 13(2).[266] The Court also noted in its advisory opinion on the *Right to Reply* that other provisions of the Convention also affect directly the   symbiotic relationship between rights and duties in the area of freedom of expression. These are Article 32(2), the application of which was examined in *Compulsory Membership*, and Articles 11(1) and 11(3) of the Convention concerning aspects of the right to privacy.

These obligations to respect the rights of others are, indeed, reinforced by Article 14(1) which provides that injured persons have the right to reply or correction using the same medium 'under such conditions as the law may establish'. This suggests that the right to reply or correction is optional since it is phrased permissively. The Court has, however, rejected this contention. First, it has indicated that states are under an obligation to take the necessary measures under Article 1(1) and Article 2 to ensure the rights guaranteed by the Convention and to give effect to them within their domestic law. Furthermore, the purpose of the Convention 'is to recognize individual rights and freedoms and not simply to empower the state to do so'.[267] Thus, regardless of state action, the right of reply is guaranteed by the Convention.[268] Nonetheless, the question remains as to the precise extent of the right of reply and the degree of discretion granted to States Parties in order to give it full force under its domestic law. Here the Court has noted that the detailed conditions governing the right to reply are not contained in Article 14(1). While, for example, the provision refers to the fact that the right should be exercisable using the same means of communication as that in which the original offending statement was uttered, it does not indicate whether beneficiaries of the right are entitled to the same amount of space, the time within which the right is to be exercised, what language is admissible and so on.[269] The Court has nonetheless ruled that Article 14 requires the 'establishment of the conditions for exercising the right to reply of correction by "law"', but that in guaranteeing the right the contents of the appropriate domestic laws might vary from state to state 'within certain reasonable limits and within the framework of the concepts stated by the Court'.[270]

Despite the permissive nature of the language used in Article 14(1) and the vagueness of the guide-lines established by the Court, it has nonetheless taken the view that this does not impair the duty of States Parties under Article 2 of the Convention to give effect to the obligations contained in Article 14.[271] It is suggested that this is likely to prove problematical for the States Parties which will perhaps be unsure exactly to what extent they must modify their domestic laws to ensure that the conditions of Article 14 are met. The lack of precision in the drafting of Article 14 would certainly not render it self-executing, and it is therefore unreasonable to impose the burden of implementation upon the state without being more specific as to the precise extent of the obligations in question.

It will be noted also that the conditions governing the right of reply or correction must be established by 'law'. The meaning of this particular word had already been considered extensively in the context of Article 30, where the Court noted[272] that it did not necessarily have the same meaning throughout the Convention and had therefore to be determined on a case by case basis.[273] In this case the Court took the view that since the conditions governing the right of reply had to be established by the States Parties in accordance with their obligations under Article 2 of the Convention, it was necessary, in order to comply with that provision 'to adopt ... such legislative or other measures as may be necessary to give effect to [the] rights and freedoms'. This, the Court concluded, included 'all those measures designed to regulate the exercise of the right to reply or correction'.[274] An interpretation of the Court's conclusion would therefore seem to suggest that the right to reply might be guaranteed by measures less than legislation. This would include, for example, any rights derived from common law in States Parties adhering to this system, and, perhaps, executive action short of formal law.[275]

Right of Assembly

The right of peaceful assembly is recognized by Article XXI of the American Declaration and Article 15 of the American Convention. While Article XXI provides that everyone may enjoy the right in concert with others either in a public formal meeting or in an informal gathering 'in connection with matters of common interest of any nature', Article 15 is content simply to recognize the right of peaceful assembly but qualifies it by stating that in order to qualify as such an assembly it must be without arms. Article 15 thus acknowledges that the carrying of arms in an assembly signals an implicit threat of violence which is likely to make the assembly potentially non-peaceful. Furthermore, while the drafting of Article 15 places presumption in favour of freedom of assembly, it also recognizes that the right is subject to potential limitations as long as such limitation are imposed in conformity with the law and are necessary in a democratic society in the interest of national security, public safety or public order, or to protect public health or morals or the rights or freedoms of others.

Given the importance of the right of assembly to the healthy functioning of democracies, it is perhaps surprising that there has been little analysis of this right by either the Commission or the Court. The right to meet to demonstrate solidarity with others, to meet to discuss issues, to demonstrate or to march in protest against government policies are closely linked, if not indivisible from, freedom of expression. Both sets of rights contribute to the democratic welfare of the state and can often be seen as the benchmark for other rights. The Commission has found occasion to mention the right in the context of its country reports and has also found violation of the right in cases involving religious groups, but there has been no substantial investigation of the right similar to that concerning freedom of expression.

Freedom of Association

Articles XXII of the Declaration and Article 16 guarantee the freedom of association. Article XXII provides that every person has the right to associate with others to promote, exercise and protect his legitimate interests of a political, economic, religious, social, cultural, professional, labour union or other nature. Article 16 of the Convention states that everyone has the right to associate freely for ideological religious, political, economic, labour, social, cultural sports, or other purposes. Between the two provisions, especially with their catch-all final provisions, the right to found and participate in most types of association are recognized. Article 16, however, accepts limitations to the right on grounds of public policy[276] and specifically permits states to impose legal restrictions and even deprive members of the armed forces and police from enjoying the right. The reason for this is clearly to allow states to prevent the unionisation of its police and military which, might imply the right to strike for such state servants. The right to strike in such circumstances may, however, be limited by legislative action of the part of the state as permitted by Article 16(2). The right to freedom of association should also be read together with Article 8 of the Protocol of San Salvador which specifically guarantees trade union rights. This provides that States Parties must ensure that workers are able to enjoy the right to organize and join trades unions of their choice for the purpose of protecting and promoting their interests. Furthermore, Article 8(1), as a further manifestation of freedom of association, states that unions themselves are to be permitted to establish or participate in national and international federations or confederations. States Parties are to permit such federations or confederations to function freely. While the right of union members to strike is to be ensured by States Parties to the Protocol,[277] it is once again noticeable that the right of members of the military or the police to unionize may be curtailed or forbidden by the state.[278] As with the broader right to freedom of assembly, limitations on trade union rights may be imposed for reasons of public policy.[279] A further point about Article 8 of the Protocol which should be noted is that while the state is to ensure the right to organize and join trades unions, no one may be compelled to belong to a trade union.[280] Thus, in the absence of an appropriate reservation to Article 8(3) of the Protocol, 'closed shop' or compulsory union bargaining agreements are impermissible in the territory of States Parties. Whether the right to freedom of association in Article 16 of the Convention should be interpreted as comprehending the right not to join a trade union or other association would appear to be a question which the Commission has answered in the negative.[281]

In many American states there exist a variety of professional associations which are established not only to represent their members' interests, but which also perform ethical and disciplinary functions. As the Court observed in *Compulsory Membership,* 'the organization of professions in general by means of professional "*colegios*", is not *per se* contrary to the Convention but it is a method for regulation and control to ensure that they act in good faith and in accordance with the ethical demands of the profession'. This the Court said was compatible with the notion of public order since the existence of professional associations which assured 'the normal and harmonious functioning of the institutions on the basis of a coherent system of values and principles' was entirely consistent with such a notion. In the instant case, however, that Court examined the practice of journalism and took the view that because of its direct relationship with freedom of expression, that is, an activity guaranteed by the Convention, compulsory membership of the Colegio de Periodistas was an impermissible restriction on the exercise of this right.[282] The Court went on to say, however, that certain professions such as the law or medicine, it was permissible to adopt norms of a public character referable to the requirements of Article 32(2) of the Convention in order to secure proper regulation of ethical standards. It further observed that the practice of law and medicine were not activities specifically guaranteed by the Convention. It said

> It is true that certain restrictions on the practice of law would be incompatible with the enjoyment of various rights that the Convention guarantees. For example, a law that prohibited all lawyers from actin as defense counsel in cases involving anti-state activities might be deemed to violate the accused's rights to counsel under Article 8(2)(e) of the Convention and hence be incompatible with it. But no one right guaranteed in the Convention exhaustively embraces or defines the practice of law as does Article 13 when it refers to the exercise of a freedom the encompasses the activity of journalism. The same is true of medicine.

These very issues were raised directly in *Cases 9777 and 9718 (Argentina)*[283] in which the petitioners sought to argue that a law requiring them to register with the Federal Capital Bar Association restricted their right to practise law and thus violated Article 16 of the American Convention. The function of the Association was to regulate ethical behaviour, discipline and other similar matters. The Commission citing its own previous decision in the *Schmidt Case* and the Court's decision in *Compulsory Membership* reaffirmed the position that not all compulsory membership of professional organizations are *per se* violations of the right of freedom of association.[284] Here, relying extensively upon the Court's reasoning in *Compulsory Membership,* the Commission took the view that mandatory regulation of professionals was a matter 'of the proper activity of a public body with the character, rights and obligations of legal persons under public law which is acting in the name and on behalf of the state'.[285] Rejecting the petitioners' argument the Commission stated that this was not something which could be carried out by private lawyers' groups.[286]

Rights of the Family

While Article VI of the American Declaration provides that 'every person has the right to establish a family', Article 17(2) simply provides that men and women of marriageable age have the right to marry and to 'raise a family ... if they meet the conditions required by domestic law'. Article 15 of the Protocol of San Salvador further provides that 'everyone has the right to form a family, which shall be exercised in accordance with the provisions of the pertinent domestic legislation'. The language of the Declaration and Protocol is broader than that of the Convention in this area and may suggest that while the right to single parent or same sex parent families may be guaranteed by the former instruments they are not protected by the latter. Nevertheless, all instruments appear to support the traditional notion of the family by providing in the Declaration that the family is 'the basic element of society' and in the Convention and Protocol that it is the 'natural and fundamental group unit ['element' in the Protocol] of society'.[287] In all cases, the family is entitled to protection by the state and, in the case of the Convention, by society also. The latter requirement suggests that the state must not only create a legislative framework which will allow the family to develop to its maximum potential, but that it must also work actively to create the societal conditions in which families might flourish. The obligations on States Parties in this regard are therefore not simply negative, as has been found to be the case under the European Convention on Human Rights, but connote positive obligations to take measures to maximise the welfare of the family and those whom it serves.[288] Article 15 of the Protocol further provides that the state is also to take measures for the spiritual as well as the material improvement of the family and provides a list of particular matters to which the state must pay attention. First, States Parties are to provide special care and assistance to mothers during a reasonable period before and after childbirth.[289] While this requirement is not evident in the Convention, it is specifically referred to in Article VII of the Declaration which deals with the right to protection for mothers and children in identical terms. Second, states are to guarantee adequate nutrition for children at the nursing stage and during the years of school attendance.[290] Third, States Parties must adopt special measures for the protection of adolescents in order to ensure the full development of their physical, intellectual and moral capacities;[291] and, fourth, states are required to undertake special programmes of family training in order to help create a stable and positive environment in which children will receive and develop the values of 'understanding, solidarity respect and responsibility'.[292] These latter obligations which are established by the Protocol of San Salvador clearly have much more to do with the progressive and promotional activities linked to the availability of a State Party's resources, but they nonetheless provide an insight into the material underpinnings of this particular right. It should also be noted that they have much to do with the rights of the child and should therefore be borne in mind when considering that particular issue.

Whether the difference in the wording of the Declaration concerning the right to 'establish' a family, the wording of the Convention which states that men and women of marriageable age have the right to 'raise' a family and the word used by the Protocol to 'form' a family are crucial is not an issue which has yet been addressed by the inter-American institutions. Certainly none of the instruments appear to give an explicit right to procreate, but it may be arguable that establishing or forming a family is closer to this notion than is the right to raise a family which is the formulation employed by the American Convention.

Article 17 of the Convention goes on to regulate certain aspects of the marital relationship. Article 17(3) requires States Parties to take measures to prevent forced marriages by providing that 'no marriage shall be entered into without the free and full consent of the intending spouses'. Article 17(4) requires states to 'take appropriate steps' to ensure the equality of rights and a balancing of spousal responsibilities within marriage, during marriage and in the case of its dissolution. This provision also makes clear that in the event of the breakdown of a marriage the welfare of any children is to be considered dominant. It provides that 'provision shall be made for the necessary protection of any children solely on the basis of their own best interests'. The American Convention also avoids some of the problems of interpretation which have beset the European Convention on Human Rights by providing that 'the law shall recognize equal rights for children born out of wedlock and those born in wedlock'. This makes clear that children born out of wedlock are to enjoy the same inheritance rights as those born in wedlock in circumstances in which a parent or parents die intestate. The State may not promulgate intestacy laws which discriminate against children born out of wedlock.

Right to a Name

Article 18 provides that every person has a right to a given name and to the surnames of his or her parents or that of one of them. Regulation of the way in which this right is to be ensured 'for all' is to be achieved by the application of domestic law. Persons are also to be granted the right to use assumed names 'if necessary'. The main thrust of Article 18 would seem to be that no one is to be denied the use of a name of their choosing. This should also comprehend the right to change one's name by an appropriate legal method if one so desires. Neither the Commission nor the Court has been presented with an opportunity to rule to any great extent on matters affecting this right, but the Commission has noted that the kidnapping and irregular adoption of children of disappeared persons during Argentina's 'dirty war' of the 1970s constituted a violation of Article 18.[293]

Rights of the Child

The rights of the child are protected by Article VII of the Declaration, Article 19 of the Convention and by Article 16 of the Protocol of San Salvador. Both Article VII and Article 16 of the Protocol are broader than their Convention counterpart. Indeed, as indicated above in the context of rights of the family, Article VII deals not only with the right of children to special protection, care and aid, but the provision also comprehends the right of women in pre- and post-natal situations. Article 16 of the Protocol should also be read together with the later provisions of its Article 15 dealing with the protection of families.[294] While Article 19 of the Convention simply provides that 'every minor child has the right to the measures of protection required by his condition as a minor on the part of his family, society, and the state', Article 16 of the Protocol is more explicit in stating the specific attributes of such a right. The first sentence of this provision is almost identical to its Article 19 Convention counterpart with the word 'status' being substituted for that of 'condition'. It then goes on to provide in addition that every child has the right to grow under the protection and responsibility of its parents. It further states that save in exceptional judicially recognized circumstances children of young age ought not to be separated from their mothers. In addition to this, Article 16 of the Protocol provides that every child has the right to free and compulsory education, at least during the elementary phase of its schooling, and to continue its training at the higher levels of the educational system.

These provisions of the various instruments have not been subject to particularly close scrutiny or analysis by the Commission or the Court. There have been a number of cases where the rights of the child have, however, been mentioned. *Case 10.006 (Peru)*[295] concerned, *inter alia*, the detention of the minor children of the former Peruvian President Alan Garcia by members of the Peruvian army when they broke into the Garcias' house in an attempt to arrest the children's father. Referring to Article 19 the Commission said that it found the measures taken by the Peruvian Armed Forces which deprived the minor children of Dr Garcia of their freedom to be particularly repugnant.[296] In *Case 10.772 (El Salvador)* [297] a seven-year-old girl was raped by a soldier. Following a failure by the state to respond to the allegation, the Commission held that this constituted a violation of Article 19.[298] Article 19 was not referred to, but the Commission considered that the violations of Articles 4 and 7 of the Convention had been aggravated by the fact that victim was a minor.[299] In a number of disappearance cases involving children, while the Commission has not referred specifically to Article 19 it has stated that the fact that the victims were minors aggravates the violation of the other rights concerned.[300]

The Commission has also undertaken a study on the treatment of the children of disappeared persons which has involved a broad analysis of the relevant rights involved. The study on the situation of minor children of disappeared persons who were separated from their parents and were then claimed by members of their legitimate families which was initiated by the General Assembly of the OAS was carried out by Commission in 1988.[301] The focus of the study was to be where children were themselves the direct victims and specific targets of repressive action, even though their kidnapping and theft was meant primarily to punish their parents or grandparents for alleged or suspected involvement in subversive political activities. The cases involved two situations: first, where minors and infants were kidnapped with their parents or, second, where they were born during the captivity of their mothers. The majority of these cases took place in Argentina during the 1976-83 'dirty war', but similar occurrences have taken place elsewhere in the Americas. In most of the cases considered by the Commission, children had been taken from their regular families and given in irregular adoption to other families. In some circumstances the adopting family was one in which the captors of the natural parents were present or they were members of police or armed forces who were cognizant of the origin of the irregularly adopted child.[302] The Commission thus drew a distinction between those who received children without knowing their origin and those who did. The Commission commented that 'the cases in which the new parents are themselves the captors, torturers and executioners of the natural parents, or their immediate accomplices, constitute ... one of the most unusual manifestations of a repressive pathology'.[303] The Commission stated that the norms which were violated by these kidnappings and irregular adoptions were manifold: first, Article 18 of the Convention giving the child the right to identity and name. Second, Article 3 of the Convention and Article XVII of the Declaration recognizing the right to be legally recognized as a person. Third, Article 19 of the Convention and Article VII of the Declaration concerning the right of pregnant women and children to enjoy special measures of protection, and finally, Articles 11 and 17 of the Convention and Articles V and VI concerning the standards of familial protection. As the Commission further observed, 'neither these rights nor those specifically devoted to the child in other international instruments are subject to suspension in situations of emergency envisaged by Art 27(2)'.[304] The Commission commented further that, even assuming a state of internal war existed in Argentina at the time of these occurrences, it would still violated norms of humanitarian law contained in the Geneva Conventions of 1949 and their Additional Protocols 1977.

Right to Nationality

Article 20 of the American Convention and Article XIX of the Declaration guarantee the right to nationality. Article XIX provides that every person has the right to the nationality 'to which he is entitled by law' and to change that nationality if he or she so wishes for the nationality of any other state which is willing to grant it to him or her. Article 20 of the Convention while protecting every person's right to a nationality is rather more specific than the Declaration in providing that all persons are entitled to the nationality of the state in whose territory they are born if they are not entitled to any other nationality. This consequently gives preeminence to the *ius soli* in the absence of nationality based on parentage: the *ius sanguinis*. Article 20(3) of the Convention also provides that no one may be arbitrarily deprived of their nationality or of the right to change it. These aspects of Article 20 were exemplified in *Case 9855 (Haiti)*.[305] In this case the petitioner had left Haiti for the United States where he became a United States citizen, thus losing his Haitian citizenship in accordance with Haitian law. He subsequently returned to Haiti where he attempted to recover his Haitian nationality in conformity with Haitian law in order that he might participate in the political process in the post-Duvalier period. An order of expulsion was issued against the petitioner on the ground of his undesirable conduct as an alien. It was clear, however, that the order of expulsion had been granted in order to silence his criticism of General Namphy, the then President of Haiti.[306] The Commission held that the petitioner had been deprived of a simple and prompt recourse in Haiti to change his nationality and thereby recuperate his Haitian citizenship. This was therefore a violation of Article 22 of the Convention.

The Court has also analysed the right to nationality in some detail. In *Amendments to the Naturalization Provisions of the Constitution of Costa Rica*[307] the Court was requested to rule upon the compatibility of certain proposed amendments to the Costa Rican constitution with Article 20 of the Convention. The proposed amendments sought to make the acquisition of Costa Rican citizenship more restrictive than previously. Not only did the proposed amendments arguably fall *prima facie* within the scope of Article 20, they also raised potential issues concerning discrimination on grounds of nationality and sex.

As a preface to consideration of the specific issues involved in this case, the Court examined the notion of nationality and the attributes which stemmed from it in international law. It observed that nationality was an inherent right of human beings which was necessary for the exercise of political and legal rights *vis-à-vis* the state.[308] While the conferral of nationality remained essentially within the reserved domain of the state granting it, developments in international law placed limits on the power of the state to regulate nationality.[309] Further, the overlay of human rights obligations imposed on states under international law[310] required that states have regard to the conditions established thereby.[311] Under Article 20, two aspects of international human rights obligations were manifest. First, the right gave individuals a minimum measure of legal protection through their link with the state of nationality. Second, it ensured protection against arbitrary deprivation of nationality by the state which might deprive the individual of his civil and political rights.[312] In sum therefore the Court held that:[313]

> Nationality can be deemed to be the political and legal bond that links a person to a given state and binds him to it with ties of loyalty and fidelity, entitling him to diplomatic protection from that state.

This assessment by the Court of the current state of international law concerning nationality would appear to be correct. The traditional view as expressed by the PCIJ in the *Nationality Decrees of Tunis and Morocco Case*[314] that nationality was a matter governed solely by the domestic law of the state in question has undoubtedly been modified by the clear retreat from that position as evinced in the decision of its successor, the ICJ, in the well-known and influential *Nottebohm Case*.[315]

As in *Nottebohm*, however, the instant case was concerned with a change of nationality by the process of naturalization.[316] By this process individuals may seek to change their nationality from the state of their birth to that of another state with whose values and interests they wish to identify themselves. Here, the Court held that since it was individual states which offered persons the opportunity of changing their nationality by naturalization, it was only appropriate that they, the states, should primarily determine the conditions under which it would be granted by the application of their domestic law.[317] Nonetheless, this too was not subject entirely to the discretion of the granting state, since it was again obliged to ensure that its requirements for the conferral of its nationality did not conflict with superior norms of international law.[318] In this regard, while it was primarily for the state to determine whether or not individuals had established the necessary genuine link with the state granting nationality, this too was subject to the overriding conditions of international law.[319] This again is an accurate statement by the Court of the prevailing rules of customary international law which are derived from the ICJ's judgment in the *Nottebohm Case*. While the ICJ was of the opinion that the initial discretion of whether to accord nationality to an applicant for naturalization lay within the jurisdiction of the state, other states were not bound to recognize the granting of nationality unless it could be proved that a genuine link existed between the granting state and the grantee. Such a genuine link could, the ruled, be evidenced by the physical ties and natural affections which the individual could demonstrate. These might include his habitual place of residence and business, the location of members of his family, the place in which his children are educated and so on.

The Inter-American Court, however, recognized that the criteria for the granting of nationality by naturalization, so long as they complied with the primary conditions which it had outlined, were not immutable, and might change to deal with new circumstances. It thus remained open for states to modify their requirements for the grant of nationality from time to time.[320] In the case of Costa Rica, it was clear that the overall purpose of the proposed amendments was to render the conditions for the acquisition of nationality more restrictive. This was clearly within Costa Rica's reserved domain as long as it could be proved that they did not infringe the requirements of international law.[321] Although the Court did not pass directly upon this, it seems by implication that the amendments to the Costa Rican constitution strengthened rather than weakened the requirements of the genuine link principle as enunciated in the *Nottebohm Case*. As regards Article 20 of the Convention, the Court could not identify any potential infringement, since no Costa Rican citizen would be deprived of his or her citizenship by an application of the proposed amendments, nor would they be prevented from acquiring a new nationality should they so desire.[322]

Despite the Court's inability to discern any potential violation of Article 20 by the proposed amendments, it nonetheless felt itself obliged to comment upon other issue of international law which an application of draft Article 14(4) might possibly violate. This the Court did simply to provide some guidance for Costa Rica.[323] The proposed Article 14(4) provided:

> The following are Costa Ricans by naturalization:
> A foreign woman who by marriage to a Costa Rican loses her nationality or who after two years of marriage and the same period of residency in the country, indicates her desire to take on our nationality.

This provision, the Court noted, would result in the effective statelessness for a period of at least two years of a woman who married a Costa Rican.[324] The Court also felt it necessary to draw Costa Rica's attention to two international conventions dealing with the same subject matter as the proposed amendments. This it did without inquiring whether or not Costa Rica had ratified the treaties in question, but even if it had not done so, the Court felt that 'they may reflect current trends in international law'.[325] The treaties and provisions thereof specifically mentioned by the Court were Article 3 of the Convention on the Nationality of Married Women 1957[326] and Article 9 of the Convention on the Elimination of all Forms of Discrimination Against Women 1979.[327]

Right to Property

The right to property is protected by Article XXIII of the Declaration and Article 21 of the Convention. Article XXIII provides that 'every person has a right to own such private property as meets the essential needs of decent living and helps to maintain the dignity of the individual and the home'. Article 21 is more detailed and provides that 'everyone has the right to the use and enjoyment of his property'. Such use and enjoyment may, however, be subordinated to the 'interest of society'. While this latter may seem unduly broad and give scope for the expropriation or confiscation of private property based on *raison d'état* or for purely political purposes, it is clear from Article 21(2) that there are limitations on the application of the societal interest proviso. This provides that 'no one shall be deprived of their property except upon payment of just compensation, for reasons of public utility or social interest, and in the cases and according to the forms established by law'. Article 21(3) also goes further than other international instruments by requiring States Parties to prohibit usury and 'any other form of exploitation of man by man'. What this latter means within the context of the right to property is unclear, but the context seems to suggest that it refers to property based exploitation rather than slavery, forced labour or bondage.[328]

In reviewing these provisions the Commission has said that the right to own property must be regarded as a fundamental and inalienable right, and that no state, group or person must undertake or conduct activities to suppress the rights upheld in those provisions, including the right to own property.[329] It has also said that the international instruments protecting the right to property 'establish universal and regional rules which have become rules of international customary law and, as such, are considered obligatory in the doctrine and practice of international law'.[330] The Commission has also cited with approval the report of the United Nations Commission on Human Rights special rapporteur Luis Valencia Rodriguez on the right to own property. He said:[331]

> The individual incorporated in a state needs a property sphere that is strongly protected in legal terms so that he can live among his fellow citizens as an individual, i.e., freely and bearing responsibility for himself and does not become a mere pawn of an excessively powerful state authority.

The relationship of the right to own property with other human rights is a matter which the Commission has addressed. In its follow-up report on Nicaragua in 1993 it declared that 'the interdependence and indivisibility of all human rights is nowadays unquestionable and, in this context, the importance of property ownership as a contributory factor toward the securing of peace and economic and social development of a state, is assuming growing significance'.[332]

In view of this, the Commission has affirmed that every person's right to individually and commonly owned property is of special importance for fostering the general enjoyment of other fundamental human rights.[333] It will be noted here that the Commission refers not simply to individually owned private property but to commonly owned property also. While neither the Declaration nor the Convention gives a specific right to enjoy property in common, this must be a necessary implication, since nearly all systems of real and personal property provide for forms of joint and several tenure.

It is the Commission's view that the American Convention follows a 'more progressive approach' to the rights of property than similar instruments, while at the same time establishing 'social interest' as a limitation to the enjoyment of such rights.[334] Thus the state may acquire property if three considerations are met: first, the payment of just compensation; second, the confiscation must be for reasons of public utility; and third, there must be observance of the forms established by law.[335] The Commission has also noted that Convention sets guarantees against arbitrary actions by the state in order to prevent expropriation without confiscation or illegal confiscation.[336]

Despite the in-depth analysis of the right to own property and its relationship with other rights, there has been little opportunity for either the Commission or the Court to apply these considerations to concrete cases. In one case cited in the Commission's follow-up report on Nicaragua referred to above, the nationalisation of the petitioner's mine without compensation was held to be violation of Article 21.[337] In other cases the destruction of property and 'creeping expropriation' have been held to violate Article XXIII of the American Declaration. In *Case 10.116 (Suriname)*[338] the spouse of the petitioner was suspected of being a member of a guerrilla group known as the Jungle Commando. He was summarily executed by Surinamese troops and his house was burned down, with loss of his family's belongings. The Commission held this to be a violation of Art XXIII.[339] In a case referred to in a follow-up report on Paraguay in 1986-87 the petitioner complained of the closure of his radio station which had been critical of the then government of Paraguay. The government has achieved the closure of the station both directly and indirectly through threatening the station manager and his family, interfering with transmission and causing power cuts. The Commission held this to be violation of Article XXXIII of the Declaration which, the Commission said, established the 'guarantee and usufruct of the right to property ...'.[340]

Freedom of Movement and Residence

The right to freedom of movement and residence is guaranteed by Article VIII of the Declaration and Article 22 of the American Convention. As with many other of the rights protected by both the Declaration and the Convention, the latter instrument deals with the specific attributes and content of the right in much greater detail than the former. Article VIII thus provides that individuals have the right to fix their residence within the territory of the state of which they are nationals, to move freely within such territory and not to leave it except by their own will. While Article VIII does not expressly specify the right of every person to return to their home country, the Commission considers this right to be implicitly included in the Declaration. It has accordingly maintained that 'the right of every person to live in his own homeland, to leave it and to return to it when he so desires ... is a basic right that is recognized by all international instruments for the protection of human rights'.[341] Thus the allegations of the use of many violent methods to prevent Cuban citizens from leaving Cuba and the absence of a right of return were held by the Commission to violate Article VIII of the Declaration.[342]

    As noted above, Article 22 establishes the right to freedom of movement and residence in some detail. Article 22(1) provides that 'every person lawfully in the territory of a State Party has the right to move about in it, and to reside in it subject to the provisions of the law'. Unlike Article VIII of the Declaration where the right of residence and freedom of movement is restricted to nationals alone, Article 22(1) grants the right to every person who is lawfully within the territory of the state. It is noticeable, however, that this freedom may be restricted by law. Thus it is not unusual for aliens within the territory of a particular state to be required to comply with certain conditions such as reporting to a police station or to reside only at a specific location. Similarly, States Parties must clearly be able to impose conditions of residence upon persons who have allegedly committed criminal offences prior to their trial. The imposition of such conditions would appear to be within the margin of appreciation of the State Party in question and indeed, this is explicitly recognized by Article 22(3) which specifically allows public policy limitations to the right. Furthermore, Article 22(4) permits states to restrict the right of residence in 'designated zones for reasons of public interest'. Thus, restrictions on residence in particularly sensitive military areas or next to prisons would seem to be justifiable under the Convention.

In addition to the right of freedom of movement and residence, Article 22(2) recognizes the right of everyone to leave any country freely, including his or her own. Two points may be made about this provision: first, the right to leave a country is not dependent upon nationality: anyone has the right to leave any state. Indeed, it is because of the denial of this right for which the Commission has consistently criticised Cuba in its reports on that state.[343] Second, while Article 22(2) protects the right to leave a State Party, it does not explicitly give nationals the right of return. This, however, is dealt with by Article 22(5) which states that 'no one can be expelled from the territory of the state of which he is a national or be deprived of the right to enter it'. This provision is unconditional and thus precludes the use of political exile and other similar punishments for political opponents.

The remainder of Article 22 deals with the rights of aliens in the territory of a host state. Article 22(6) requires that an alien who is lawfully within the territory of a host state may only be expelled from it pursuant to a decision reached in accordance with law. This would seem to suggest that an expulsion based on either an executive order properly arrived at or by the decision of an appropriate tribunal will be legitimate. Article 22(6) says nothing about the right to appeal such a decision. It should, however, be remembered that the due process provisions of Article 8 apply to such proceedings and an alien must therefore be afforded 'due guarantees' in any proceedings designed to challenge an expulsion order.[344] Article 22(8) further provides a guarantee of *non-refoulement* by providing that 'in no case may an alien be deported or returned to a country, regardless of whether or not it is his country of origin, if in that country his right to life or personal freedom is in danger of being violated because of his race, nationality, religion, social status or political opinions'. Such a person is by virtue of Article 22(7) of the Convention to be given the right to seek and to be granted asylum in accordance with the legislation of the state in question and in accordance with the appropriate international conventions on the matter if he or she is being pursued for political offences or related common crimes. In addition to this Article 22(9) unconditionally prohibits the collective expulsion of aliens.

Again, the Commission and Court's jurisprudence on this right is not extensive. There have been a number of cases in which involuntary exile and expulsion have been held to violate Article VIII.[345] Refusal to allow a citizen to return home is a violation of Article VII, as is the denial of the right to leave a state.[346] A related matter which has also be adjudged to be a breach of these provisions by the Commission has been the refusal to grant nationals a passport, thereby effectively depriving them of the right to leave.[347] On other occasions Article VIII and Article 22 have been associated with politically motivated kidnappings and disappearances. The very act of unlawful detention and incarceration of victims have been considered a direct impediment to their freedom of movement and residence. In *Case 10.574 (El Salvador),*[348] for example, the petitioner was kidnapped and tortured by members of the armed forces. He was then told that if he returned home he would be disappeared. The Commission held that this action was a violation of Article 22.[349] Indeed, it seems that any wrongful deprivation of an individual's liberty to move at will throughout the territory of his or her state will violated Article 22. In *Case 10.975 (Guatemala)*[350] the petitioner was forcibly recruited into the army. This was held by the Commission to be a violation of Article 22.

The issue of the right to due process in the conduct of deportation and expulsion cases was considered by the Commission in *Case 9855 (Haiti).*[351] In this case, the petitioner had lost his Haitian citizenship after becoming a US citizen. He returned to Haiti where he attempted to recover his Haitian nationality as permitted by Haitian law so he could stand for the presidential elections. An order of expulsion was issued against him on the ground that he was an alien and because of his undesirable conduct. It was clear that this had been done to silence his criticism of the then Haitian President. The Commission held that this action constituted, *inter alia,* a violation of Art 22(6). There had been no hearing at which the petitioner could defend himself and he had thus been deprived of the right to live in Haiti without the due process guarantees inherent in a judicial or administrative procedure. Such procedures would have afforded him the opportunity of being informed of reasons motivating his expulsion prior to issuance of the order, and of having opportunity to defend himself against the alleged charges.[352]

Right to Participate in Government

In a hemisphere in which many states have been noted in the past for their frequent and often violent changes of unrepresentative governments, the right of individuals to participate in government is an attempt to underpin and guarantee the democratic principles upon which the inter-American system is based.[353] The right to participate in government is located in Article XX of the Declaration and Article 23 of the Convention. Article XX provides that 'every person having legal capacity is entitled to participate in the government of his country, directly or through his representatives and to take part in popular elections, which shall be by secret ballot, and shall be honest, periodic and free'. Article 23 similarly provides that every citizen is to enjoy certain 'rights and opportunities'. These include participation in the conduct of public affairs, directly or through freely chosen representative; the right to vote, to be elected in genuine periodic elections which are to be conducted by universal and equal suffrage and by a form of secret ballot which guarantees the free expression of the voters; and, finally, to have access, under general conditions of equality, to the public service of his or her country. It will be noted that both the Declaration and Convention provisions contain limitations on who may exercise the right. In the Declaration it is only person 'having legal capacity' who are entitled to the right, while in Article 23 of the Convention, it is 'citizens' to whom the relevant rights and opportunities are guaranteed. Indeed, Article 23(2) provides explicitly that the law may regulate the exercise of the rights and opportunities contained in that provision, but it may do this solely on the basis of age, nationality, residence, language, education, civil and mental capacity or sentencing by a competent court in criminal proceedings. This list is similar to the restrictions on the right to vote or to participate in public life which are found in most democracies. It will be noted that Article 23(2) is exclusive in the sense that no other grounds may be adduced for restricting rights and opportunities. It is clear, however, that each of the categories provided in the list is capable of broad interpretation which has the potential further to limit the right. It should also be noted that Article 23 is by virtue of Article 27 a right which may not be suspended or derogated from in time of public danger or emergency. Thus declarations of states of emergency or siege may not be adduced as grounds for suspending or limiting the operation of this right. This is in stark contrast to the practice of a number of American states in the recent past. As the Commission has stated, however, 'the exercise of these rights is so essential if societies are to function normally that Article 27 of the Convention prohibits their suspension regardless of the circumstance'.[354]

Application ratione personae

As noted above, individuals are entitled to participate in government at a number of levels, both as candidates for public office and as the electors of those candidates. As the Commission has noted that 'the right to be a candidate in a political election arises from Article 23 of the American Convention on Human Rights, which recognizes the rights of each individual; a) to take part in the conduct of public affairs, directly or through representatives; b) to be elected; and c) to have access under general conditions of equality, to the public service'.[355] The right to participate in government either as a candidate or an elector, however, excludes certain categories of people. While these categories and their associated limitation on the right are those which are usually accepted in most states possessing democratic systems, they nonetheless give rise to questions of interpretation. Such was the situation in *Case 10.804 (Guatemala).*[356] This case involved the exclusion of Rios Montt, the former President of Guatemala, from standing for election because of his previous participation in a *de facto* regime established contrary to the Guatemalan constitution. In analysing this case the Commission stated that it was obliged to take into account Article 32 of the Convention and that it must also have regard to OAS Charter and history of OAS 'in reaffirming the constitutional democratic system as the bases and objectives of the action of the system and its component states'.[357] The Commission observed in this context that the constitutional principle of ineligibility appears in other constitutions of the region and was part of the General Treaty of Peace and Friendship concluded by the Governments of Guatemala, El Salvador, Honduras, Nicaragua and Costa Rica under which these states undertook not to accord recognition to governments established by revolution or coup d'état. This treaty also mutually recognized the principle of ineligibility. The Commission said, 'these principles rejecting the breach of the constitutional order, the disqualification of its leaders for high office, and non-reelection were adopted because they were considered as juridical principles of international relations and common defense of the democratic consolidation of the region'.[358] From these principles the Commission held that the requirement of ineligibility set forth in Article 186 of the Guatemalan Constitution was a customary constitutional rule with a strong tradition in Central America.[359] The Commission then continued to inquire whether ineligibility established a discriminatory principle which was contrary to Article 23 and the general principles of the Convention. In its analysis of other constitutions the Commission found that principle of ineligibility might arise in a number of circumstances, even for democratically elected heads of state who have held office for a certain period of time. Thus ineligibility might be temporally limited or for life. The Commission thus concluded that if it were acceptable under constitutional law for a state to establish a constitutional term for democratically elected heads of state, then it was perfectly conceivable that this same scope could be applied to those who lead a breach of the constitution, as was the case with Rios Montt.[360] The Commission held therefore that the declaration of the former president's ineligibility to stand for election was not contrary to Article 23 of the Convention.

A sequel to the Rios Montt case was that certain candidates for election who appeared on the slate with the former president were also declared ineligible to stand for election. According to Guatemalan law, a slate of candidates which was tainted by an ineligible candidate had to be rejected in its entirety. In *Case 10.804(b) (Guatemala)*[361] the applicant was denied the right to participate in the election as the candidate appeared on the slate with the disqualified Rios Montt. This putative candidate was also denied the opportunity to enforce the right by applying for *amparo* because only political parties were entitled to juridical standing under the constitution of Guatemala. The Commission held that 'the denial based on the lawsuit of one member of that presidential slate can only be interpreted as a violation of the political rights of the other member where the law or the interpretation of it by the electoral organs prohibits or impedes the replacement of the excluded candidate'.

The Commission has also had occasion to point out that regulation of the right to be elected is not incompatible with the Convention. In *Case 10.109 (Argentina)*[362] conditions of membership of a political party were placed on candidates. Denying that this was a violation of Article 23 the Commission said:[363]

> It must be remembered that every electorate comprises thousands or millions of voters, i.e. each elector is a potential candidate with the same right as any other to be elected to public elective office. If democracy is to flourish, that potential makes it necessary for the exercise of this right to be regulated by law.

In reaching this conclusion the Commission pointed out that other democracies of the world contained systems of electoral nomination similar to that of Argentina. The Commission also stated one of the dominant themes of its observations on political rights, namely, that political parties are necessary in a democracy if chaos and anarchy are not to reign.[364]

Criteria Attaching to Elections

The Commission has on many occasions undertaken studies and made a number of pronouncements on the proper conduct of elections. In *Case 10.596 (Mexico)*[365] The Commission restated one of its major assertions that 'any mention of the right to vote and to be elected would be mere rhetoric if unaccompanied by a precisely described set of characteristics that the elections are required to meet'.[366] Thus, in its 1990-91 Annual Report the Commission published a report entitled 'Human Rights, Political Rights and Representative Democracy in the Inter-American System'.[367] In this report the Commission reviewed the various criteria which should attach to the conduct of the electoral process in accordance with the requirements of the inter-American system. It noted that all the major human rights instruments - the Universal Declaration, the American Declaration, the International Covenant on Civil and Political Rights and the American Convention on Human Rights - all agree that elections should have specific properties: they should be authentic or genuine ('honest' in the case of the American Declaration), periodic, by universal suffrage, and conducted in such a way that they preserve the free expression of the will of the electorate.[368] It is proposed to examine each of these requirements in turn. Before doing so, however, it is important to note the clear relationship between democracy and human rights protection identified by the Commission. Reference has already been made to this issue in consideration of restrictions and limitations to the substantive rights guaranteed by the Convention[369] and in the context of freedom of expression,[370] but in a case involving alleged electoral irregularities in Mexico the Commission said:[371]

> The close relationship between representative democracy as a form of government and the exercise of the political rights so defined, also presupposed the exercise of other fundamental rights: The concept of representative democracy is based on the principle that it is the people who are the nominal holders of political sovereignty and that, in the exercise of that sovereignty, elects its representatives - in indirect democracies - so that they may exercise political power. Their representatives, moreover, are elected by the citizens to apply certain political measures, which at the same time implies the prior existence of an ample political debate on the nature of policies to be applied - freedom of expression - between organized political groups - freedom of association - that have had the opportunity to express themselves and meet publicly - freedom of assembly. At the same time, if these rights and freedoms are to be exercised, there must be juridical and institutional systems in which the laws outweigh the will of leaders and in which some institutions exercise control over others for the sake of guaranteeing the integrity of the expression of the people's will - the rule of law.

Authenticity

The Commission has elaborated upon the provisions of Article XX of the Declaration and Article 23 of the Convention by saying that the election of representatives must be 'genuine' means that the will of voters must be reflected in the outcome of elections. It has said that 'put in negative terms, it means there must be no interference that tampers with the will of the ctizenry'.[372] The Commission has also said that election laws and institutions must therefore serve to guarantee that the will of the citizenry will be respected. More important still in the Commission's view is that the 'fundamental currents' of political thought in the country be reflected fully in the drafting of those laws. Given the importance of electoral legislation, it is considered essential that it should be the product of a consensus rather than the outcome of an imposition by parliamentary majorities.[373] There are thus two different components to genuine elections: first, the maintenance of general conditions under which the electoral process unfolds and, second, the legal and institutional systems that establishes the elections and balloting, 'in other words, anything related, either directly or indirectly, to casting the ballot'.[374] In this context the Commission understands 'general conditions' to mean conditions in which there are several political groups participating in the election, all on an equal footing: all the candidates must be able to conduct their campaigns under the same basic conditions. From this it inevitably flows that there must be no direct coercion or undue advantage in favour of any particular candidate. It is also implicit in this that there must be a plurality of candidates and parties.[375] Taken as a whole, therefore, the general political climate must be conducive to the conduct of free and fair elections. Indeed, both the Commission and the Court's jurisprudence make it clear that it is one of the primary obligations of the state to ensure that such conditions exist. The Commission has also stated that another element which should be regarded as essential to the credibility of the electoral process and the genuineness of elections is the exercise of the right to freedom of expression. This view is consonant with the Commission's previous pronouncements on this issue.[376] In the present context, however, it has said that 'this condition presupposes the existence of not only a regulatory structure adequately protecting that right, but also practices that do not entail unfair advantages in the use of the media, particularly the media available to the governing party'.[377]

Universal Suffrage

As the Commission has already noted, the existence of universal suffrage is required by all the major international human rights instruments. While noting that Article 23(2) of the Convention states exceptions to the general concept, the Commission has nonetheless observed that situations occur in which legal impediments are caused by political repression disguised as police action. As it has noted, these measures can be highly effective, because they permit political opponents to use a state's penal code to interfere with their opponents electoral rights. Again, in this context the Commission has highlighted the relationship between the denial of human rights in general and the abrogation of political rights. In the context of the use of the criminal law to curtail political activities the Commission has said:[378]

> Such situations point up the relationship of political rights to other basic rights such as the right to a fair trial and to personal liberty, and their relationship to a system in which the rule of law and an independent judiciary prevail, and the ability of the Judicial Branch to protect members of the political opposition in the exercise of their rights.

An example of the denial of political rights by such means occurred in *Case 9855(Haiti)* in which the petitioner was denied the right to initiate proceedings to recover his Haitian nationality as permitted by Haitian law. Because of the petitioner's inability to recover his nationality his candidature for the presidential election was refused. The Commission held that the inability of the petitioner to initiate proceedings was a breach of Article 25 of the Convention which in turn led to a denial of his political rights under Article 23.

Periodicity

The third requirement identified by the Commission is that elections must be periodic and conducted by secret ballot. The rationale underlying these requirements is that they are necessary conditions to allow the electorate to express its will freely. Since in the Commission's view Article 23 defines political rights, it has once again observed that the 'proper exercise of those rights is related to the observance of other rights and freedoms such as freedom of expression (Article 13), the right to personal liberty (Article 7), the right to a fair trial (Article 8), the right of assembly (Article 15), freedom of association (Article 16), the right to residence and movement (Article 22) and the right to judicial protection (Article 25)'.[379] There has been little specific comment on what constitutes an appropriate interval for the conduct of elections, but the Commission has noted that the postponement of elections for a period of ten years violates Article XX of the Declaration.[380]

Right to Equal Protection

Article 24 of the Convention states quite simply that all persons are equal before the law and that consequently they are entitled, without discrimination, to equal protection of the law. This provision, which constitutes a prohibition of discrimination in legal proceedings, is clearly related to Article II of the Declaration and Article 1(1) of the Convention itself. While Article 24 does not indicate what the prohibited grounds of discrimination might be Article II and Article 1(1) provide a checklist of prohibited grounds of discrimination. Article II states that there must be no discrimination on grounds of race, sex, language, creed 'or any other factor', while Article 1(1) of the Convention adds the grounds of colour, political or other opinion, national or social origin, economic status, birth or any other social condition. As the Court has pointed out in *Amendments to the Constitution*,[381] although Articles 24 and 1(1) of the Convention overlap, their conceptual bases are different. While Article 1(1) seeks to ensure that the rights proclaimed in the Convention are given effect in the domestic law of states Parties without discrimination, Article 24 provides a general proscription against discrimination arising from the application of domestic legal prescriptions.[382] Nonetheless, as the Court has also ruled in *Exceptions to the Exhaustion of Domestic Remedies*, the meaning of discrimination in Article 24 must be interpreted by reference to the list enumerated in Article 1(1).[383]

The philosophical basis underpinning the prohibition of discrimination in the American Convention was stated by the Court to be that 'equality springs directly from the oneness of the human family and is linked to the essential dignity of the individual'.[384] As a consequence of this, no group has a right to superior treatment over another, nor must other groups be treated as inferior. In taking this position, however, the Court did not seek to deny that different forms of treatment of certain groups would on occasion not be discriminatory since, 'not all differences in treatment are in themselves offensive to human dignity'.[385] Citing the judgment of the European Court of Human Rights in the *Belgian Linguistics Case*[386] the Court ruled:[387]

> No discrimination exists if the difference in treatment has a legitimate purpose and if it does not lead to situations which are contrary to justice, to reason or to

the nature of things. It follows that there would be no discrimination in differences in treatment of individuals by a state when the classifications selected are based on substantial factual differences and there exists a reasonable relationship of proportionality between these differences and the aims of the legal rule under review. These aims may not be unjust or unreasonable, that is, they may not be arbitrary, capricious, despotic or in conflict with the essential oneness and dignity of humankind.

It would seem, therefore, that Article 24 prohibits both formal and material discrimination, but that it also preserves the possibility of positive discrimination arising from affirmative action programmes. Such a conclusion would appear to be justified by the paragraph quoted above.

In examining the application of the rule against discrimination in *Proposed Amendments,* the Court also noted that Costa Rica, in determining the requirements for the conferral of its nationality, enjoyed a substantial margin of appreciation.[388] Costa Rica was in the best position to assess the conditions required for conferring its nationality on different categories of applicants.

In applying these principles in the context of a request for an advisory opinion by Costa Rica on the compatibility of certain proposed amendments to the naturalization provisions of the Costa Rican constitution with Article 20 of the Convention, the Court distinguished the different practical circumstances arising from each of the proposals. First, it noted that the proposed amendments required a shorter period of residence for persons of Central American, Ibero-American or Spanish nationality and a longer period of residence for those of other nationality for the acquisition of Costa Rican nationality. The Court considered this difference in treatment justifiable on the grounds that the former shared much closer historical, cultural and spiritual bonds with the people of Costa Rica and were therefore likely to be more easily and rapidly assimilated within the national community.[389]

Not all those with Central American, Ibero-American or Spanish citizenship were, however, to be treated the same in terms of residence qualification within the proposed amendments. The amendments drew a distinction in qualification periods for those who had acquired their citizenship through the *ius soli* and those who had acquired it through the process of naturalization. While the Court felt that this distinction was more difficult to maintain, it nonetheless considered it objectively justifiable on the grounds that Costa Rica might entertain legitimate doubts about the strictness of conditions for the acquisition of nationality by naturalization in some of the other American states.[390] Judge Buergenthal, dissenting on this point, doubted the Court's reasoning. He considered that the distinction was unnecessary because Costa Rica was not obliged in international law to accept the conclusiveness of the grant of nationality to an individual.[391] He further took the view that the requirement was disproportionate, since 'the likelihood that a very small percentage of individuals might act dishonestly is hardly a legitimate reason for punishing the vast majority of honest foreigners'.[392]

Finally, the Court considered the proposed amendment which treated a foreign woman who married a Costa Rican man differently from a foreign man who married a Costa Rican woman.[393] Here the Court noted that the provision was based on outdated notions of paternal authority and conjugal inequality, which was not now a legitimate reason for the different treatment of men and women.[394] The Court further observed that, without noting whether or not Costa Rica was a party,[395] that Article 1 of the Montevideo Convention on the Nationality of Women 1933 declared that 'there shall be no distinction based on sex as regards nationality'. This the Court referred to as a 'decisive impulse' towards equality of treatment on the international plane.[396] To further buttress its argument the Court referred to Article II of the American Declaration,[397] Article 1(3) of the UN Charter,[398] Article 3(k) of the OAS Charter,[399] and Article 17(4) of the Convention which provides:

> The States Parties shall take appropriate steps to ensure the equality of rights and the adequate balancing of responsibilities of the spouse as to marriage, during marriage, and in the event of its dissolution ...

In this case the Court probably identified correctly the trend towards equality of treatment of women in the acquisition and maintenance of a nationality other than that which they originally possessed. The European Court of Human Rights has, however, found itself in difficulty on occasion in correctly identifying social and legal trends. In some cases the Court has been, arguably, premature in identifying that a particular trend has crystallized, whereas in others it has perhaps been tardy in so doing.[400]

While the Commission has not had substantial opportunity to comment on issues of discrimination, it has held that Article II of the Convention is breached when different requirements exist for men and women in cases of divorce. In its *Report on the Situation of Human Rights in El Salvador*[401] the Commission stated that discrimination existed where adultery alone was a sufficient ground for a husband to divorce a wife, but in the case of wife divorcing a husband, adultery had to be accompanied by public scandal or abandonment of the woman. Furthermore, the Commission found that Article II was violated where the law distinguished between legitimate and illegitimate children.

Right to Judicial Protection

Article 25 of the American Convention guarantees the right of all persons to simple and prompt recourse, or any other effective recourse, to a competent court or tribunal for protection against acts that violate their fundamental rights recognized by the constitution or laws of the state concerned or by the Convention, even though such violations may have been committed by persons acting in the course of their official duties. As the Court has said in *Judicial Guarantees in States of Emergency,* Article 25(1) of the Convention 'incorporates the principle recognized in the international law of human rights of the effectiveness of procedural instruments of means to guarantee such rights'.[402] The Commission has further observed:[403]

> This principle generates an obligation for the States Parties to the Convention which is to provide effective judicial means in the event of a violation of human rights of individuals within its jurisdiction. Failure to comply implies a violation of that principle and, therefore, the offending state incurs international responsibility.

As has already been noted above, the overall effect of Article 25 when read in conjunction with other provisions of the Convention, notably Articles 7, 8 and 27, is that the remedies of *habeas corpus* and *amparo* may never be suspended, even during states of emergency or siege.

Article 25(2) further provides that the States Parties to the Convention must undertake to ensure that any person claiming such a remedy as envisaged by Article 25(1) shall have his or her rights determined by the competent authority provided for by the legal system of the state. This requirement clearly links with the right to due process guaranteed by Article 8, and thus the requirements which are present in that provision must also be present in an application of Article 25(2). There is thus a necessity that claims should be adjudicated by an independent judiciary free from the direction of the executive. It has been apparent, however, that in a significant number of disappearance cases the judiciary in a number of American states have been unwilling or unable to take the necessary measures to provide adequate relief to the families of victims. This observation is also pertinent with respect to the other requirements of Article 25(2), namely that States Parties develop the possibilities of judicial remedy and ensure that the competent authorities shall enforce such remedies when granted. The unwillingness or inability of the judicial authorities of States Parties to ensure the effective use of *habeas corpus* and *amparo* in disappearance cases has been evident in very large numbers of individual cases. In these circumstances the Commission has been able to do little more than to recite the almost ritual incantation that the State Party concerned has violated Article 25.

Article 25 may of course be breached in other circumstances. In *Case 10.006 (Peru)* the military exercised judicial jurisdiction in half the country and in the other half a state of emergency existed. Civil guarantees in the form of *habeas corpus* were rendered virtually inoperative. The Commission held that this deprived the Peruvian people 'of a simple and swift recourse before competent courts to protect themselves against acts that violate their fundamental rights' and thus constituted a violation of Article 25.[404] A violation of Article 25 will also occur where an individual is denied the right to recourse to judicial procedures in order to challenge an order of expulsion.[405] The Commission has also held that this provision will be breached in circumstances where a tribunal refuses to review a case where there appear to be sound grounds for so doing. In *Case 9260 (Jamaica)* [406] the petitioner had been arrested and charged with murder. He was convicted and the death sentence was imposed. The petitioner appealed to the Privy Council in London which was the highest court of appeal for Jamaica. During the preparation of the case for the Privy Council certain inconsistencies emerged in the trial record which suggested that there was a substantial probability that the petitioner had not committed the crime. The Privy Council, however, said it would not retry case, review the facts, the weight of evidence or the conflict of evidence, inferences from the evidence or the satisfaction of the burden of proof. As the Privy Council pointed out, its sole concern was with the interpretation of the relevant law. The Commission nonetheless held that this constituted a violation of Article 25.[407]

Another area in which Article 25 has been found to have been breached is in cases where amnesty has been granted to former and current military personnel who have been accused of human rights violations during the tenure of former governments. In a number of cases involving amnesties from criminal prosecution granted to the Argentinian military, the Commission held that this violated Art 25(2) because of the denial of the opportunity to secure a judicial remedy.[408] Further, in a study of Uruguay's so-called Caducity Laws, granting amnesty to military personnel, the Commission once again found that Article 25 had been breached.

Economic, Social and Cultural Rights

The economic, social and cultural rights which are contained in the American Declaration, the American Convention and its Protocol of San Salvador, and the various obligations to which these instruments give rise were discussed in chapter 1 above. While it is not intended to rehearse these issues here, it is nevertheless appropriate to comment upon the Commission's approach to the question of economic, social and cultural rights prior to an examination of the rights to which the various instruments purport to give effect. As early as 1979 the Commission was able to state that:[409]

> In examining the human rights situation in the different countries, the IACHR has sought to establish the organic relationship between the violation of the rights to physical security, on the one hand, and the disregard of economic and social rights and the suppression of political participation, on the other. And this relationship, as has been demonstrated, is largely one of cause and effect. In other words, neglect of economic and social rights, especially when political participation has been suppressed, brings about the sort of social polarization that leads, in turn, to acts of violence by and against the Government.

Indeed, this has been a perennial theme in the Commission's observations on the indivisibility and symbiotic relationship between first and second generation rights. In another context the Commission has stated that any distinctions which are drawn between first and second generation rights are 'categorical formulations that detract from the promotion and guarantees of human rights'.[410] Indeed, it will be apparent from the discussion of some of the civil and political rights above, that certain of the so-called first and second generation rights are hybrid in nature: in other words, they are incapable of rigid or categorical classification in either group of human rights.[411] This conclusion is further supported by the fact that certain second generation rights may be the subject of the Convention's individual petition procedure in Article 44 which seems to suggest that these designated second generation rights have more in common with their first generation analogues.[412] In a number of its country reports the Commission has examined the economic conditions in the states under consideration and has frequently pronounced upon the way in which its understanding of the economic and social conditions impacts upon its understanding of the general human rights situation in those countries. These, analyses and statements are, however, of a general nature and offer little in the way of developing an understanding of the specific content of economic and social rights.

In pursuance of its increasing concern with second generation rights, however, the General Assembly of the OAS directed the Commission to request reports on such rights from the Member States of the Organization.[413] The results of the reports submitted to the Commission have been summarised since 1992 in its Annual Reports. These reports comment on the status of economic, social and cultural rights in the hemisphere and make general recommendations. In its 1992 Report, for example, the Commission regretted the slow progress being made on ratifications to the Protocol of San Salvador with only three states having ratified after a period of five years and stated that 'the ratification by other member states is of extreme importance'.[414] The recommendations accompanying the Commission's *1994 Annual Report* are particularly general and not directed at any particular state. The main recommendations in that report were:

1. Member States should guarantee conditions that enable people to gain access to food, health services and education and should fully enforce minimum wage laws. To this end, Member States should reform basic economic and political structures that inhibit the development of such conditions.
2. When formulating domestic economic policies, Member States should guarantee an economic environment that will enable the poor to participate in the political and economic decision making processes. As an example, Member States should promote respect for labor unions, including their rights to organize, bargain collectively and conduct strikes with the state playing a neutral role.
3. Member States should ensure that socially disadvantaged groups, particularly minorities, do not suffer disproportionately from economic adjustment measures.
4. When formulating the initial study for economic structural adjustment programs and the development and financial institutions with which they work, Member States should avoid programs that exacerbate the conditions of the poor.

Since the Protocol of San Salvador has not yet entered into force, it is difficult to predict how effective it will be in promoting and protecting economic, social and cultural rights in the Western Hemisphere. It might be suggested, however, that the modus operandi of the Commission in this area will emulate the practice of the United Nations Committee on Economic, Social and Cultural Rights in attempting to secure a form of constructive engagement with reporting states.[415] Of course, the inclusion of the right to individual petition in the case of Article 8(a) (trade union rights) and Article 13 (right to education) provides the Commission with a weapon which the United Nations Committee does not yet possess.

Despite the fact that the Protocol of San Salvador's has not yet entered into force, the Commission has had the occasional opportunity to rule on the substantive content of certain economic, social and cultural rights as protected by the American Declaration. Some of these rulings have already been considered above,[416] since, as noted earlier, some of the so-called second generation rights have a hybrid nature, but there are a number of other rights which have attracted comment from the Commission.

Right to Work and Just, Equitable and Satisfactory Conditions of Work

Both Article 6 of the Protocol and Article XIV of the Declaration protect the right to work. The Protocol states that everyone has the right to work. This right includes the opportunity to secure the means for living a dignified and decent existence by performing a freely elected or accepted lawful activity. The Declaration, on the other hand, while recognizing the right to work includes the limitation that this right exists 'in so far as existing conditions of employment permit'. There is no requirement within the Declaration that a Member State must pursue economic policies leading to full employment, but this can be implied from the OAS Charter and the United Nations Charter.[417] Article 6(2) of the Protocol is, however, more explicit in providing that States Parties must undertake to adopt measures that will make the right to work fully effective, 'especially with regard to the achievement of full employment and vocational guidance'. This provision also requires States Parties to develop technical and vocational training projects, particularly for disabled persons. In order to assist women to enjoy real opportunity in the workplace, States Parties also undertake to implement and strengthen programmes which help to ensure suitable family care.

The right of just, equitable and satisfactory conditions of work or 'proper conditions' as they are referred to in Article XIV of the Declaration are elaborated in some length in Article 7 of the Protocol. These include: fair and equal wages; the right to follow one's vocation and to change employment; the right to promotion where appropriate; stability of employment; safety and hygiene at work; the prohibition of night work or unhealthy or dangerous working conditions for persons under 18 years of age; a reasonable limitation of working hours and rest, leisure and paid vacations as well as remuneration for national holidays. While the Commission has not been presented with the opportunity to comment individually on each of these aspects of the right to work, has nonetheless commented on the right to work in general. In the context of employment within Cuba where the government was to all intents and purposes the only employer, the Commission observed:[418]

> The Commission considers that discrimination in employment is a much greater possibility where the state is virtually the sole employer. These features of Cuban constitutional law, when directed against individuals, can result in discrimination

on ideological grounds, which is incompatible with the proclaimed universality of the right to work.

The Commission has also noted the connection of the right to work with other rights within the Declaration, particularly trade union rights. It said:[419]

> It is pertinent to note that the right to work and to the conditions under which it must be exercised is directly connected with the right of association to promote, exercise and protect ... legitimate interests of a labor union nature. (Art XXII ADRDM.)

Trade Union Rights

Trade union rights have largely been dealt with above in the context of freedom of association.[420] It is pertinent to note here, however, that trade unions must be able to function freely and must not be subordinated to the requirements or interests of the state. In Cuba union membership was subordinated to the interests of the Communist Party. The Commission declared:[421]

> The right of association ... cannot be exercised against the existence and purposes of the communist state: the labor unions are not therefore truly autonomous since they are subordinated to the interests of the state and guided by the Party. In addition, the unions' main objectives are connected with production and productivity, but not with defense of the workers' interests.

Right to Social Security

Both Article XVI of the Declaration and Article 9 of the Protocol provide for the right to social security. In similar terms, these provisions state that everyone has the right to social security in order to protect him or her from the consequences of old age and of disability which prevents him or her, either physically or mentally, from securing the means for a dignified and decent existence. Article 9 continues to provide that in the event of the death of a beneficiary, social security benefits must continue to be applied to the deceased's dependents. Article 9(2) also continues to stipulate the kinds of benefits which should be made available by the state. These include medical care and an allowance or retirement benefit in the case of work accidents or occupational disease, and, in the case of women, paid maternity leave before and after childbirth. The extent or quantum attached to these rights is left to the state to determine within its margin of appreciation.

Right to Health

The right to health is included only in the Protocol. This provides that everyone has the right to health which, in the context of the Protocol, is understood to mean the enjoyment of the highest level of physical, mental and social well-being. In order to ensure the exercise of this right States Parties agree to recognize health as a public rather than a private good and to adopt measures in the fields of primary health care, extension of the benefits of healthcare to all person subject to the jurisdiction of the state. This means that all those within the state, either legally or illegally, would be entitled to health care. The States Parties also undertake to carry out programmes of universal immunization against the principal infections diseases and to prevent and treat endemic, occupational and other diseases. In addition to this states are to undertake education programmes for the general population on the prevention and treatment of health problems. Satisfaction of the health needs of the highest risk groups and of those whose poverty makes them the most vulnerable are also to be given attention.

Right to a Healthy Environment

The right to a healthy environment is another right which finds inclusion in the Protocol and not the Declaration. Article 11 of the Protocol, however, is not simply directed at the environment as traditionally understood, since it also provides that in addition to the right to live in a healthy environment, all people should, as a facet of this right, have access to basic public services. While these services are not defined it would seem that they must include at a minimum the right to access to an unpolluted source of water. The extent to which other utilities should be included in such a right is unclear. Certainly, power for forms of heating and perhaps appropriate transport services for those in remote areas might legitimately be included in a broad interpretation of this right.

It is perhaps surprising that given the reference to international cooperation in promoting the right to food, a similar stance was not taken with regard to the environment. Examples of cross border and riparian pollution are evident in the Americas, and it might have been supposed that concerted action in the realization of this right might have been appropriate.

Right to Food

The right to food is recognized by Article 12 of the Protocol. It provides that everyone has the right to adequate nutrition which guarantees the possibility of enjoying the highest level of physical, emotional and intellectual development. At a minimum, this imposes an obligation upon States Parties to eliminate malnutrition. Indeed, the eradication of malnutrition is specifically referred to in Article 12(2) which deals with the mechanics of the promotion of this particular right. Here the States Parties are to undertake improvement of methods of production, supply and distribution of food. In pursuit of this objective they are to promote greater international cooperation in support of relevant national policies. In many respects the need for international cooperation in this field gives some recognition to the right to food not simply as an economic or social right, but also as a species of third generation right.

Right to Education

The right to education is provided for in Article XII of the Declaration and Article 13 of the Protocol. Article XII is phrased in a particularly broad and grandiloquent manner. It provides that every person has the right to an education which should be based on the principles of liberty, morality and human solidarity. It continues in a more pragmatic vein to say that all people the right to an education which will prepare them to attain a decent life, to raise their standard of living and to be a useful member of society. The right is expressed to include equality of opportunity in accordance with their talents to utilize the resources that the state or community is in a position to provide. In any event, all primary education is to be free. It is interesting to note here that the obligation to provide educational resources devolves not only upon the state but also the community. As an intermediate between the individual and the state it is often observed that the community is often best placed to judge local educational needs. It must, however, be the case that it is the state or an emanation of the state such as local authorities as representatives of their communities upon which the obligation is placed to provide adequate resources for education.

As with other rights, the Protocol is much more specific in its elaboration of the content of the right to education. While Articles 14(1) and (2) reproduce the terms of the Declaration, Article 13(3) establishes the measures which States Parties must take in order to achieve the full exercise of this right.

These measures bear a strong a similarity to those contained in Article 13 of the International Covenant on Civil and Political Rights. They include free compulsory primary education; the general availability and accessibility of secondary education in all its forms which should be made progressively free and the accessibility of higher education on the basis of equality for those who have the capacity which should also be made progressively free. As has been obvious with the International Covenant on Economic, Social and Cultural Rights, the need to increase accessibility of tertiary education is often accompanied by increasing cost to the student rather than a gradual diminution of cost. The balancing of these two issues appears to have been at least implicitly accepted by the United Nations Committee on Economic, Social and Cultural Rights.[422] Article 13(3) also requires the encouragement or intensification of the provision for basic education for those person who have not received or completed the entire cycle of primary education. This would seem to require the introduction of adult literacy and numeracy programmes by the state or its agents as education providers. The States Parties are also required to establish programmes of special education for the handicapped and to provide special instruction and training to person with physical or mental disabilities.[423] Significantly, Article 13 maintains the right of parents to have select the type of education to be given to their children provided that it is conformity with the domestic legislation of the State Party and provided it conforms to the principles enunciated in Article 13. This corresponds to the right of parents to have their child educated in conformity with their own religious and philosophical convictions which is specifically provided for in Article 2 of Protocol I to the European Convention on Human Rights. It also interlinks with the freedom of conscience and religion and freedom of thought and expression which are protected by Articles 12 and 13 of the Convention. Article 13(4) of the Protocol also retains the freedom of individuals and entities to establish and direct educational institutions in accordance with the provisions of national legislation. This latter suggests that even in states which have a public school system alone and which forbid the establishment of private schools, that measures must be take to allow persons to establish such schools if they so wish.

Right to the Benefits of Culture

Article XIII of the Declaration and Article 14 of the Protocol both recognize the right to the benefits of culture. Article XIII provides that every person has the right to take part in the cultural life of the community, to enjoy the arts, and to participate in the benefits that result from intellectual progress, especially scientific discoveries. These same elements are present in Article 14 of the Protocol, save that the benefits of technological as well as scientific progress are also to be enjoyed by all. Article 14, however, continues to secure the right of everyone to benefit from the protection of moral and material interests deriving from any scientific, literary or artistic production of which such person is the author. This requires States Parties to put in place legal rules and mechanism for the protection of intellectual property rights. The terms in which this is done is clearly within the state's margin of appreciation. In addition to this States Parties are to respect the freedom which the Protocol says is indispensable for scientific research and creative activity.[424] This right is therefore intimately linked with freedom of thought and expression which are necessarily correlative to proper intellectual pursuits. A further obligation which is placed on states in this area is that they are obliged to take the necessary measures for the conservation, development and dissemination of science, culture and art.[425] The normal methods by which this would be achieved are those which have been set out in a number of reports to the United Nations Committee on Economic, Social and Cultural Rights. They include, *inter alia,* the development of art galleries, museums, national libraries and archival collections. Clearly, such measures may not be appropriate for economically struggling American states, but as a rule there will be some repository for national treasures in most countries. Article 14 finally provides that the States Parties to the Protocol are to recognize the benefits which are to be derived from international collaboration in this field and accordingly they agree to foster appropriate cooperation. In this it mirrors to a considerable extent Article 15 of the International Covenant on Economic, Social and Cultural Rights.

Right to the Formation and the Protection of Families and the Rights of Children

These rights which are recognized by Articles VI and VII of the Declaration and Article 15 of the Protocol respectively have been considered above in connection with the appropriate provisions of the American Convention.[426] As such they are representative of hybrid rights which span the classification of both first and second generation rights.

Protection of the Elderly and the Handicapped

The Protocol of San Salvador contains two novel rights: Article 17 which deals with protection of the elderly and Article 18 which deals with the protection of the handicapped. Article 17 provides that everyone has the right to special protection in old age. This includes the provision of suitable facilities, food and specialized medical care for elderly individuals who are unable to provide for themselves.[427] Elderly persons are also to be provided with the opportunity to engage in productive activities which are suited to their abilities and consistent with their vocations or desires.[428] This suggests that elderly persons must not be required to participate in such work if they do not wish to. In some sense this may be regarded as the right to retire. The state is also required to foster the establishment of social organizations aimed at improving the quality of life for the elderly.[429] Article 18 provides in similar terms for the protection of the handicap. All person who are affected by a diminution of their physical or mental capacities are to be entitled to receive special attention designed to help them achieve the greatest possible development of their personality. In order to achieve this, the States Parties agree to undertake a number of measures. First, to develop programmes aimed at providing handicapped person with the resources and the environment needed for attaining the development of their personality, including work programmes 'consistent with their possibilities' (which presumably means their talents and capacities) and freely accepted by them or their legal representatives.[430] This clearly means that handicapped persons may not be forced to undertake labour which either they or their legal guardians do not consider appropriate. This provision is therefore supported by Article 6(2) which prohibits forced or compulsory labour. States Parties are also required to provide special training for the families of handicapped persons 'in order to help them solve the problems of coexistence and convert them into active agents in the physical, mental and emotional development' of such persons.[431] In a particularly innovative provision, Article 18(c) requires states to consider solutions to specific requirements arising from the needs of handicapped persons as a priority component of their urban development plans. In no other international human right instrument has the interests of the handicapped been so clearly represented. Finally, States Parties are to take appropriate steps to encourage the establishment of social groups in which the handicapped can be helped to enjoy a fuller life.[432]

Notes

1   The use of the term 'marginal' should not be considered pejorative here. It simply serves to demonstrate that the cases considered by the European institutions very often turn upon fine legal analysis which has more in common with the techniques employed by the US Supreme Court than with, say, the UN Human Right Committee.

2   Shelton suggests that this is 'arguably' the case. See D. Shelton, 'Abortion and the Right to Life in the Inter-American System: The Case of "Baby Boy"' (1981) 2 HRLJ 309 at 315.

3   See OAS Doc., OEA/Ser.L/VI.II.66, Doc. 17, 1985, p 150. See also OAS Doc. OEA/Ser. L/V/II.34/Doc. 21, Corr 1 (1974) at 3.

4   UNCHR, Report of independent expert Luis Valencia Rodriguez, E/CN//1993/15, 18.12.92, pp. 26-7. Cited with approval in 1993 Annual Report 442 at 465-6.

5   Inter-American Commission on Human Rights, *1992-1993 Annual Report,* p. 238.

6   Ibid., p. 243.

7   Judgment of 19 January 1995 (1995) HRLJ 403.

8   Ibid., para. 74. Citing its decisions in *Velasquez Rodriguez,* para. 154 and *Godinez Cruz,* para. 162.

9   *Case 2141 (United States of America),* para. 19(b).

10   Ibid., para. 19(h).

11   Ibid., para. 5.

12   Ibid.

13   D. Shelton, 'Abortion and the Right to Life in the Inter-American System', p. 316.

14   Ibid., p 316.

15   See F.G. Jacobs, *European Convention,* p 22.

16   *Velasquez Rodriguez,* para. 155; *Godinez Cruz,* para. 163.

17   *Case 7245 (Nicaragua).* See also *Case 10.563 (Peru),* Inter-American Commission on Human Rights, *1993 Annual Report* 303 at 308.

18   *Velasquez Rodriguez,* para. 157; *Godinez Cruz,* para. 166.

19   *Velasquez Rodriguez,* para. 158; *Godinez Cruz,* para. 198.

20   *Velasquez Rodriguez,* para. 188; *Godinez Cruz,* para. 228.

21   'Draft Declaration on the International Rights and Duties of Man, December 31, 1945' (1946) 40 AJIL Supp. 93. On the drafting history of the death penalty provisions of the American Declaration see W. Schabas, *The Abolition of the Death Penalty in International Law* (1993), pp. 251-4 (hereafter '*Abolition of the Death Penalty*'); J. Colon-Collazo, 'A Legislative History of the Right to Life in the Inter-American System' in B.G. Ramcharan (ed.), *The Right to Life in International Law* (1985), pp. 33-41.

22   *Abolition of the Death Penalty,* p. 254.

23   See *Restrictions to the Death Penalty,* paras. 54-6.

24   Ibid., para. 57.

25   Report on Peru, Inter-American Commission on Human Rights, *1993 Annual Report* 478 at 512.

26   Inter-American Commission on Human Rights, *1986-87 Annual Report* 271 and *Second Report on the Human Rights Situation in Suriname* 17.

27   Supra, pp. 23-5.

28   *Case 9647 (United States)* 147 at 170.

29   Ibid., at 172.

30   Ibid., at 170, para. 53.
31   Ibid., at 172.
32   Ibid., at 171.
33   Ibid.
34   Ibid.
35   Ibid., at 172-3.
36   Ibid., at 173.
37   Inter-American Commission on Human Rights, *1988-89 Annual Report* 158.
38   Inter-American Commission on Human Rights, *1971 Annual Report* 33; *1981-82 Annual Report* 106; *Report on the Situation of Human Rights in Argentina 1980* 29; *Report on the Situation of Human Rights in Chile 1985* 48-50.
39   Inter-American Commission on Human Rights, *1991 Annual Report* 196-7.
40   Supra, pp. 58-61.
41   *Restrictions to the Death Penalty,* para. 10.
42   Ibid., para. 71.
43   Ibid., para. 74.
44   'Report on Peru' in Inter-American Commission on Human Rights, *1993 Annual Report* 478 at 510.
45   Ibid., at 511.
46   Ibid., para. 24.
47   Ibid., at 512.
48   Ibid., at para. 26.
49   Article 27(2) ACHR.
50   Loc. cit., supra, note 7.
51   Ibid., para. 86.
52   See, for example, the majority of individual cases involving Guatemala and Peru reported in Inter-American Commission, *Annual Report 1990-9,* pp. 105-426.
53   *Velasquez Rodriguez,* para. 155; *Godinez Cruz,* para. 162.
54   *Velasquez Rodriguez,* para. 156; *Godinez Cruz,* para. 163.
55   *Velasquez Rodriguez,* para. 187; *Godinez Cruz,* para. 197.
56   *Velasquez Rodriguez,* para. 187; *Godinez Cruz,* para. 197.
57   See, for example, *Case 10.433(Peru),* Inter-American Commission on Human Rights, *1992-93 Annual Report* 110.
58   *Case 10.508 (Guatemala)* Inter-American Commission on Human Rights, *1994 Annual Report* 51 at 54.
59   Inter-American Commission on Human Rights, *1977 Annual Report* 26.
60   On the background to the Torture Convention see supra, chapter 1.
61   *Case 10.574 (El Salvador)* Inter-American Commission on Human Rights, *1993 Annual Report* 174.
62   *Case 7481 (Bolivia).*
63   *Case 7823 (Bolivia).*
64   *Case 7824 (Bolivia).*
65   *Case 7910 (Cuba); Case 5154 (Nicaragua).*
66   *Case 9274 (Uruguay).*
67   *Case 2530 (El Salvador).*
68   'Report on the Situation of Human Rights in Panama' [1989] IAYHR 528 at 560.
69   Ibid., at 616, para. 4.
70   Ibid., at 558.

71 Ibid., at 558.
72 *Case 10.772 (El Salvador)* Inter-American Commission on Human Rights, *1993 Annual Report* 181 at 186.
73 Ibid.
74 Inter-American Commission on Human Rights, *1994 Annual Report* 178.
75 Report on Cuba, ibid., 142 at 161. See also the situation in Panamanian prisons, supra, p. 283.
76 *Case 10.006 v Peru*, Inter-American Commission on Human Rights, 1994 Annual Report (*Garcia Case*), 71 at 102.
77 Ibid.
78 Inter-American Commission on Human Rights, *Second Report on the Situation of Human Rights in Colombia*, OEA/Ser.L/II.84, Doc. 39 rev., October 1993, p. 250.
79 Inter-American Commission on Human Rights, 'Report on Panama', *1990-1991 Annual Report* 479 at 486.
80 Article 1(1).
81 Article 1(2). Note that the definition of slave trade is modified slightly in Article 7(c) of the Supplementary Convention on the Abolition of Slavery, the Slave Trade and Institutions and Practices Similar to Slavery 1956.
82 See supra, p. 280.
83 OAS Doc., OEA/Ser. L/V/II.44, doc. 38, rev. 1, 22 June 1978.
84 At para. 155.
85 Inter-American Commission on Human Rights, *1994 Annual Report* 51.
86 Ibid.
87 *Case 10.975 (Guatemala)*, Inter-American Commission on Human Rights, *1993 Annual Report* 216 at 222.
88 Inter-American Commission on Human Rights, *1992-1993 Annual Report* 207 at 210.
89 *Case 10.006 (Peru)*, loc. cit., supra, note 76.
90 *Winer v UK*, Comm Rep 10.7.86, DR 48, p. 154.
91 *Case 10.006 (Peru)*, loc. cit., supra, note 76.
92 X v FRG, Comm Rep 7.5.81, DR 24 p.103. Cited in *Case 10.006 (Peru)*, loc. cit., supra, note 76 at 99.
93 *Case 10.006 (Peru)*, loc. cit., supra, note 76 at 100.
94 Ibid. Commission citing its own *Report on the Situation of Human Rights in Chile*, 1985, OEA/Ser.L/V/II.66 doc. 17, p. 138.
95 *Case 10.006 (Peru)*, loc. cit., supra, note 76 at 100.
96 Ibid., at 101.
97 Ibid.
98 Inter-American Commission on Human Rights, 'Report on Panama', *1990-1991 Annual Report* 479 at 485.
99 *Case 10.037 (Argentina)* [1989] IAYHR 52 at 90.
100 Eur Ct HR, Series A, No. 9.
101 *Case 10.037 (Argentina)* [1989] IAYHR 52 at 94.
102 Eur Ct HR, Series A, No. 8.
103 *Case 10.037 v Argentina* [1989] IAYHR 52 at 96.
104 Ibid., at 98.
105 Ibid., at 100.
106 'Report on the Situation of Human Rights in Panama' [1989] IAYHR 528 at 564.
107 Advisory Opinion OC-9/87 of October 6, 1987, *Judicial Guarantees in States of Emergency*,

Series A, No. 9, para. 29.

108 *Case 9850 (Argentina)*, Inter-American Commission on Human Rights, *1990-1991 Annual Report* 41.

109 Ibid., at 74, para. 17.

110 Inter-American Commission on Human Rights, *1994 Annual Report* 51.

111 Ibid., p. 54, para. 12.

112 *Cases 10.147, 10.181, 10.240, 10.262, 10.309, 10.311 (Argentina)*, Inter-American Commission on Human Rights, 1992-93 Annual Report 41 at 48 para. 34.

113 Ibid., at para. 37.

114 Ibid., at p. 75, para. 20.

115 Ibid., at para. 22.

116 D. 7987/77 (Aus.) 12/13/79, 18/31.

117 D. 6172/73 (UK) 7/7/75, 3/77.

118 Inter-American Commission on Human Rights, *Seventh Report on the Situation of Human Rights in Cuba*, 1983, OEA/Ser.L/V/II.61 doc. 29 rev. 1, p. 51. Quoted in *Case 10.006 v Peru*, loc. cit., supra, note 76 at 92-3.

119 Inter-American Commission on Human Rights, *1994 Annual Report* 113.

120 Ibid.

121 Inter-American Commission on Human Rights, *1993 Annual Report* 442 at 451.

122 Ibid.

123 Inter-American Commission on Human Rights, 'Report on the Situation of Human Rights in Panama' [1989] IAYHR 528 at 572.

124 Ibid.

125 Inter-American Commission on Human Rights, *1992-1993 Annual Report* 207 at 210.

126 Ibid., at 214. Cited in Inter-American Commission on Human Rights, 'Guatemala Report', *1993 Annual Report* 442 at 456.

127 Inter-American Commission on Human Rights, 'Nicaragua Report', *1993 Annual Report* 442 at 456-7. See for original checklist, Inter-American Commission on Human Rights, *Annual Report 1992-93* 214-215, 'Measures necessary for rendering the autonomy, independence and integrity of the members of the Judicial Branch more effective'.

128 Ibid.

129 Loc. cit., supra, note 127.

130 *Case 10.006 (Peru)*, loc. cit., supra, note 76.

131 Ibid., 95.

132 Ser. A, No. 80, para. 78.

133 *Case 10.006 (Peru)*, loc. cit., supra, note 76 at 93-4.

134 Ibid. Citing the Commission's own *Report on the Situation of Human Rights in Peru*, p. 27.

135 Ibid.

136 Inter-American Commission on Human Rights, *1992-1993 Annual Report* 207.

137 Ibid., at 210.

138 *Case 11.084 (Peru)*, Inter-American Commission on Human Rights, *1994 Annual Report*, 113 at 121.

139 Ibid.

140 Ibid.

141 On the rule against discrimination see supra, pp. 345-7.

142 *Case 10198 (Nicaragua)* [1989] IAYHR 314 at 348, consideranda para. 2.

143 Ibid.

144 Inter-American Commission on Human Rights, *1993 Annual Report* 493.

145 Ibid.
146 Inter-American Commission on Human Rights, *Report on the Situation of Human Rights in El Salvador*, OEA/Ser.L/V/II.85, Doc. 28, rev., February 11, 1994, p. 5.
147 Inter-American Commission on Human Rights, *1993 Annual Report* 493.
148 Ibid.
149 Inter-American Commission on Human Rights, *1992-93 Annual Report* 207 at 210.
150 Ibid.
151 Ibid., para. 22.
152 Ibid., para. 23. Citing its judgment in *Velasquez,* para. 166.
153 Ibid., para. 26.
154 Ibid.
155 Ibid., para. 27.
156 Ibid., para. 28.
157 Ibid., para. 29.
158 Inter-American Commission on Human Rights, *1994 Annual Report* 113.
159 Ibid., 123.
160 Inter-American Commission on Human Rights, *Second Report on the Situation of Human Rights in Colombia*, OEA/Ser.L/V/II.84, Doc. 39, rev., 98.
161 Inter-American Commission on Human Rights, *1992-93 Annual Report* 207 at 210. See also the *Second Report on the Situation of Human Rights in Colombia*, loc. cit., supra, note 160 at p. 249 in which the Commission declared the Colombian secret courts established to try drugs cases to be incompatible with the American Convention.
162 Loc. cit., supra, note 138.
163 Inter-American Commission on Human Rights, *1990-1991 Annual Report* 41.
164 *Case 10.198 (Nicaragua)* [1989] IAYHR 314 at 348, consideranda para. 1.
165 Ibid.
166 *Case 10.006 (Peru)*, loc.cit., supra, note 76 at 103.
167 Ibid.
168 Ibid.
169 *Case 9850 (Argentina)*, Inter-American Commission on Human Rights, *1990-1991 Annual Report* 41 at 75, para. 18.
170 Ibid.
171 Inter-American Commission on Human Rights, *1992-93 Annual Report* 215.
172 *Case 10.006 (Peru)*, loc. cit., supra, note 76 at 105.
173 Ibid.
174 Ibid.
175 Ibid., at 106.
176 Ibid.
177 Ibid., at 107.
178 See infra, pp. 267-74.
179 *Case 10.006 (Peru)*, loc. cit., supra, note 76 at 102.
180 Ibid.
181 Ibid.
182 Ibid.
183 Infra, p. 310.
184 Inter-American Commission on Human Rights, *1993 Annual Report* 181 at 186.
185 *Case 10.975 (Guatemala)*, Inter-American Commission on Human Rights, *1993 Annual Report* 216 at 222.

[186] OEA/Ser. L/V/II.49, doc. 19 corr. 1, 11 April 251.

[187] Article I (right to life, liberty and personal security), Article V (freedom of religion), Article XII (right to education), Article XXI (right of assembly) and Article XXV (right to protection against arbitrary arrest).

[188] *Compulsory Membership*, para. 70.

[189] Inter-American Commission on Human Rights, *1994 Annual Report*, Cuba, 142-3. Citing its *Diez Años de Actividades, 1971-1981*, 326.

[190] Inter-American Commission on Human Rights, *1980-81 Annual Report*, OEA/Ser.L/V/II, p. 122.

[191] *Compulsory Membership*, para. 69.

[192] Inter-American Commission on Human Rights, 'Report on the Compatibility of "Desacato" laws with the American Convention on Human Rights', *1994 Annual Report* 204.

[193] Ibid., para. 31.

[194] *Compulsory Membership*, paras. 30-33.

[195] See infra p. 321.

[196] *Compulsory Membership*, para. 34.

[197] 'Report on Desacato Laws', loc. cit., supra, note 189.

[198] Inter-American Commission on Human Rights, *1984-1985 Annual Report* 51.

[199] Ibid., at 59.

[200] *Compulsory Membership*, para. 30.

[201] Ibid., para. 31.

[202] Ibid.

[203] Ibid., para. 34.

[204] Ibid., para. 35.

[205] Ibid., para. 36.

[206] Ibid., para. 37.

[207] The Commission has said that prior restraint on freedom of expression is absolutely prohibited. The only legitimate restriction to the right is through subsequent liability in cases of abuse. For the imposition of liability four requirements must be met in order for them to be valid under Art 13(2): 1. grounds for liability must be previously established; 2. these grounds must be express and precise within the law; 3. the ends sought to be achieved must be legitimate; and 4. the grounds for liability must be necessary to ensure the legitimate end pursued. Inter-American Commission on Human Rights, 'Report on Desacato Laws', loc. cit., supra, note 189.

[208] *Compulsory Membership*, para. 39.

[209] Ibid., para. 41.

[210] Ibid., para. 42.

[211] Ibid., para. 43.

[212] Ibid., para. 45.

[213] Ibid.

[214] Eur. Ct. H R, Series A, No. 30.

[215] *Compulsory Membership*, para. 46.

[216] Ibid.

[217] Ibid. See also *Sunday Times Case*, para. 62 and *Barthold*, Eur. Ct. HR, Series A, No. 90, para. 59.

[218] *Compulsory Membership*, para. 47.

[219] Ibid.

[220] Article 13(3) ACHR.

221 *Compulsory Membership*, para. 56.

222 Ibid., para. 60.

223 Loc. cit., supra, note 198.

224 *Compulsory Membership,* para. 61.

225 Ibid., para. 62.

226 Ibid., para. 63.

227 Ibid.

228 Supra, pp. 69-71.

229 *Compulsory Membership,* para. 64.

230 Ibid., para. 66.

231 Ibid., para. 68.

232 Ibid., para. 69.

233 Ibid. In support of this contention the Court cited the judgment of the European Court of Human Rights in Austria v Italy in which the latter had said that the purpose of the High Contracting Parties to the European Convention 'was not to concede to each other reciprocal rights and obligations in pursuance of their individual national interests but...to establish a common public order of the free democracies of Europe with the object of safeguarding their common heritage of political traditions, ideals, freedoms and the rule of law'.

234 *Compulsory Membership,* para. 70.

235 Ibid., para. 73. The Court took the view that what doctors and lawyers did, for example, was not guaranteed by the Convention, although regulation of such professions might lead to the violation of the rights of others. The Court here gave the example that a rule preventing lawyers from acting as defence counsel in cases involving anti-state activities would be a violation of the accused's right to counsel under Article 8 of the Convention, but not a violation of the rights of lawyers in pursuit of their profession.

236 Ibid., para. 76.

237 Ibid.

238 Ibid., para. 77.

239 Ibid., para. 79.

240 Ibid.

241 Ibid., para. 59.

242 'Report on the Compatibility of Desacato laws', loc. cit., supra, note 189 at 207.

243 Ser. A, No. 103.

244 'Report on the Compatibility of Desacato laws',   loc. cit., supra, note 189.

245 Ibid., at 208.

246 Ibid., at 209. Citing *Lingens* at para. 46, p. 28.

247 Ibid.

248 *Compulsory Membership,* para. 79.

249 Ibid., para. 46.

250 *Sunday Times Case,* para. 59, pp. 35-6 and *Lingens*, para. 40, p. 25.

251 *Compulsory Membership,* para. 121.

252 See *Castells*, para. 46.

253 *Lingens,* para. 42, p. 26; *Oberschlick*, para. 59, p. 26.

254 'Report on the Compatibility of Desacato laws', loc. cit., supra, note 189 at 211.

255 Ibid.

256 Ibid.

257 Ibid., at 212.

258 *Case 9726 (Paraguay),* Inter-American Commission on Human Rights, *1986-87 Annual*

Report 110.
259 Ibid., at 113.
260 *Case 9855 (Haiti)* [1988] IAYHR 244.
261 Ibid.
262 Ibid., at 252.
263 It should be noted that the word 'ideas' appears only in the English text of the Convention. The Spanish, Portuguese and French texts appear to be concerned primarily with the dissemination of defamatory statements. The texts provide in the material part as follows:
Spanish: '*informaciones inexactas o agraviantes*'.
Portuguese: '*informacoes inexatas ou ofensivas*'.
French: '*données inexactes ou des imputations diffamatoires*'.
264 See supra, p. 312.
265 *Right to Reply*, paras. 23 and 25.
266 Ibid.
267 Ibid., para. 24.
268 Ibid., para. 26.
269 Ibid., para. 27.
270 Ibid.
271 Ibid., para. 29.
272 *The Word 'Laws'*, para. 27.
273 Ibid.
274 *Right to Reply*, para. 33.
275 Cf., however, *The Word 'Laws'* at para. 27 in which the Court declared that restrictions to any of the protected rights could only be effected by legal norms passed in accordance with the appropriate constitutional procedures of each state.
276 Art 16(2) ACHR.
277 Art 8(1)(b) PSS.
278 Art 8(2) PSS.
279 Loc cit.
280 Art 8(3) PSS.
281 See infra, p. 353.
282 See supra, pp. 326-8.
283 *Cases 9777 and 9718 (Argentina)* [1988] IAYHR 60.
284 Ibid., at 134.
285 Ibid., at 132.
286 Ibid., at 134.
287 Article 16(1) ACHR.
288 Cf *Marckx*, Eur Ct HR, Series A, No. 31.
289 Article 15(3)(a) PSS.
290 Article 15(3)(b) PSS.
291 Article 15(3)(b) PSS.
292 Article 15(3)(c) PSS.
293 Inter-American Commission on Human Rights,'A Study about the Situation of Minor Children who were Separated from their Parents and are Claimed by Members of their Legitimate Families' [1988] IAYHR 476 at 480.
294 See infra, p. 357.
295 *Case 10.006 (Peru)*, loc. cit., supra, note 76.
296 Ibid., at 101.

297 *Case 10.772 (El Salvador)*, Inter-American Commission on Human Rights, *1993 Annual Report* 181.

298 Ibid., at 186.

299 Ibid.

300 *Case 9936 (Guatemala)*, Inter-American Commission on Human Rights, *1990-91 Annual Report* 136 at 138; *Case 9948 (Guatemala)*, Inter-American Commission on Human Rights, *1990-91 Annual Report* 142 at 144; *Case 9960 v Guatemala*, Inter-American Commission on Human Rights, *1990-91 Annual Report* 152 at 154.

301 Inter-American Commission on Human Rights,'A Study about the Situation of Minor Children who were Separated from their Parents and are Claimed by Members of their Legitimate Families' [1988] IAYHR 476.

302 Ibid., at 478.

303 Ibid., at 480.

304 Ibid., at 490.

305 *Case 9855 (Haiti)* [1988] IAYHR 244.

306 Ibid.

307 Advisory Opinion OC-4/84 of January 19, 1984. *Proposed Amendments to the Naturalization Provisions of the Political Constitution of Costa Rica* (hereafter '*Proposed Amendments*'), Series A, No. 4 (1984) 5 HRLJ 161.

308 Ibid., para. 32.

309 Ibid.

310 Ibid., para. 33. The Court here cited Article XIX of the American Declaration and Article 15 of the Universal Declaration as evidence for this proposition.

311 Ibid., para. 32.

312 Ibid., para. 34.

313 Ibid., para. 35.

314 (1923) PCIJ, Ser. B, No. 4, p. 27.

315 ICJ Rep. 1955, p. 30.

316 In the *Nottebohm Case*, Nottebohm, who was a resident of, and who had business interests in, Guatemala, had sought to change his nationality from German to that of Liechtenstein in order to avoid the consequences of being a national of a belligerent state in the territory of a neutral state at the outbreak of war. These consequences would have included internment and the confiscation of Nottebohm's property. In the event, Guatemala was not prepared to treat Nottebohm as having validly acquired the nationality of Liechtenstein and interned him for the duration of hostilities. His property was also confiscated. For comment on the *Nottebohm Case* see J. M. Jones, 'The *Nottebohm* Case' (1956) 5 ICLQ 230 and J. L. Kunz, 'The Nottebohm Case (Second Phase)' (1960) 54 AJIL 536.

317 *Proposed Amendments*, para. 36.

318 Ibid.

319 Ibid.

320 Ibid.

321 Ibid., paras. 38 and 39.

322 Ibid., para. 42.

323 Ibid., para. 49.

324 Ibid., para. 46. The Court noted, however, that a draft amendment to this provision proposed by Members of the Special Legislative Committee of the Costa Rican legislature would avoid this particular problem.

325 Ibid., para. 49.

[326]   309 UNTS 65. Costa Rica is not party to this Convention. The material provision referred to by the Court provides:

1. Each Contracting State agrees that the alien wife of one of its nationals may, at her request, acquire the nationality of her husband through specially privileged naturalization procedures; the grant of such nationality may be subject to such limitations as may be imposed in the interests of national security or public policy.

2. Each Contracting State agrees that the present Convention shall not be construed as affecting any legislation or judicial practice by which the alien wife of one of its nationals may, at her request, acquire her husband's nationality as a matter of right.

[327]   (1980) 19 ILM 33. The material part provides:

States Parties shall grant women equal rights with men to acquire, change or retain their nationality. They shall ensure in particular that neither marriage to an alien nor change of nationality by the husband during the marriage shall automatically change the nationality of the wife, render her stateless or force upon her the nationality of the husband.

[328]   See supra, pp. 380-83.

[329]   *Case 10.770 (Nicaragua)*, Inter-American Commission on Human Rights, *1993 Annual Report* 293 at 299, para. 13. See also the Commission's follow-up report on Nicaragua in its *1993 Annual Report* 442 at 465 in which it said that the right to property is 'among the fundamental rights of man'.

[330]   Inter-American Commission on Human Rights, *1993 Annual Report* 442 at 465.

[331]   *Case 10.770 (Nicaragua)*, Inter-American Commission on Human Rights, *1993 Annual Report* 293 at 300, para. 13. Citing ECOSOC E/CN.4/1993/15 pp. 35 and 85.

[332]   Inter-American Commission on Human Rights, *1993 Annual Report* 442 at 465.

[333]   Inter-American Commission on Human Rights, 'Report on Nicaragua', *1993 Annual Report* 442 at 465-66 citing UNCHR Report of independent expert Luis Valencia Rodriguez, E/CN/1993/15, 18.12.92, pp. 26-7.

[334]   Inter-American Commission on Human Rights, 'Report on Nicaragua', *1993 Annual Report* 442 at 465-6.

[335]   Ibid., at 466.

[336]   Ibid.

[337]   Inter-American Commission on Human Rights, *1986-87 Annual Report* 89 at 110.

[338]   *Case 10116 (Suriname)* [1989] IAYHR 190 at 204.

[339]   Ibid.

[340]   Inter-American Commission on Human Rights, *1986-87 Annual Report* 110 at 113.

[341]   Inter-American Commission on Human Rights, 'Report on Cuba', *1994 Annual Report*, 142 at 155-6. Citing its *Diez Años de Actividades, 1971-1981*, 326.

[342]   Ibid.

[343]   See above, p. 336.

[344]   On due process see above, pp. 284-7. See also *Case 9855 (Haiti)* below, p. 338.

[345]   See *Cases 2509 and 2777 (Panama); Case 2719 (Bolivia) ; Case 2794 (Peru)* and *Case 3411 (Chile)* in Buergenthal and Norris, Binder 3, booklet 20, pp. 122, 141, 144 and 149. See also *Case 7378 (Guatemala)* and *Case 4288 (Chile)* in Buergenthal and Norris, Binder 3, booklet 21, pp. 65-79.

[346]   *Case 3411 (Chile)* in Buergenthal and Norris, Binder 3, booklet 20, p. 153.

[347]   *Case 2711 (Uruguay)* in Buergenthal and Norris, Binder 3, booklet 21, p. 41.

[348]   *Case 10.574 (El Salvador)*, Inter-American Commission on Human Rights, *1993 Annual Report* 174 at 179.

[349]   Ibid.

350 Ibid.
351 *Case 9855 (Haiti)* [1988] IAYHR 244 at 254.
352 Ibid.
353 For a review of the instruments relating to democracy and human rights in the inter-American system see D. L. Shelton, 'Representative Democracy and Human Rights in the Western Hemisphere' (1991) 12 HRLJ 353. See also S.J. Schnably, 'The Santiago Commitment as a Call to Democracy in the United States: Evaluating the OAS Role in Haiti, Peru and Guatemala' (1994) 25 *Inter-American Law Review* 393.
354 *Case 10.596 (Mexico)*, Inter-American Commission on Human Rights, *1993 Annual Report* 259 at 269 in which the Commission said, 'The exercise of these rights is so essential if societies are to function normally that Article 27 of the Convention prohibits their suspension regardless of the circumstances'.
355 *Case 10.804 (Guatemala)*, Inter-American Commission on Human Rights, *1993 Annual Report* 206 at 210, para. 19.
356 Ibid., at 211, para. 23.
357 Ibid.
358 Ibid., at 212, para. 28.
359 Ibid., para. 29.
360 Ibid., at 213, para. 35.
361 Inter-American Commission on Human Rights, *1994 Annual Report* 46.
362 *Case 10.109 (Argentina)* [1988] IAYHR 172 at 184.
363 Ibid.
364 Ibid.
365 *Case 10.596 (Mexico)*, Inter-American Commission on Human Rights, *1993 Annual Report* 259 at 270. See also *Cases 9768, 9780 and 9829 (Mexico)*, Inter-American Commission on Human Rights, *1990-91 Annual Report*, Chap. V Section III.
366 *Cases 9768, 9780 9829 and 10.596 (Mexico)*, loc. cit., supra, note 365.
367 Inter-American Commission on Human Rights, 'Report on Panama', *1990-1991 Annual Report* 514.
368 Inter-American Commission on Human Rights, 'Human Rights, Political Rights and Representative Democracy in the Inter-American System', *1990-1991 Annual Report*, 514 at 524. See also a number of cases in which the Commission has said: 'If Art 23 was to be fully respected elections had to be authentic, universal, periodic and by secret ballot or some other means that enabled voters to express their will freely. Laws alone will not suffice; the attitude must be one that encourages proper implementation, and must be consistent with generally recognized principles that govern a representative democracy'. *Case 10.596 (Mexico)*, Inter-American Commission on Human Rights, *1993 Annual Report* 259 at 267 and *Cases 9768, 9780 and 9829 (Mexico)*, Inter-American Commission on Human Rights, *1990-91 Annual Report*, Chap. V Section III.
369 Supra, pp. 49-57.
370 Supra, pp. 310-21.
371 *Case 10.596 (Mexico)*, Inter-American Commission on Human Rights, *1993 Annual Report* 259 at 267. See also *Cases 9768, 9780 and 9829 (Mexico)*, Inter-American Commission on Human Rights, *1990-91 Annual* Report, Chap. V Section III, p. 107.
372 Inter-American Commission on Human Rights, 'Human Rights, Political Rights and Representative Democracy in the Inter-American System', *1990-1991 Annual Report*, 514 at 524.
373 'Report on the Situation of Human Rights in Panama' [1989] IAYHR 528 at 598.

374 'Human Rights, Political Rights and Representative Democracy in the Inter-American System', loc. cit., supra, note 368 at 525.

375 Ibid.

376 See supra, pp. 310-21.

377 'Report on Panama' [1989] IAYHR 314 422 at 432.

378 'Human Rights, Political Rights and Representative Democracy in the Inter-American System', loc. cit., supra, note 368 at 532.

379 Ibid., at 533. See also 'Report on Nicaragua' [1989] IAYHR 423 at 424-6 where the same criteria are referred to in the context of amendments to Nicaragua's electoral laws.

380 Inter-American Commission on Human Rights, *1977 Annual Report* 93.

381 *Proposed Amendments*, para. 54.

382 Ibid.

383 *Exceptions to the Exhaustion of Domestic Remedies*, para. 22.

384 *Proposed Amendments*, para. 55.

385 Ibid., para. 56.

386 Eur. Ct. H R, Series A. No. 24.

387 *Proposed Amendments*, para. 57.

388 Ibid., para. 52. That is, the state had a broad discretion in determining how to implement the Convention rule in terms of its domestic law. On the margin of appreciation doctrine in the European Convention on Human Rights see Merrills, *Development,* Chapter 7.

389 Ibid., para. 60.

390 Ibid., para. 61.

391 Dissent, para. 6.

392 Ibid.

393 *Proposed Amendments*, Article 14(4).

394 Ibid., para. 64.

395 Costa Rica became party to this convention on 17 July 1953.

396 *Proposed Amendments,* para. 65.

397 All persons are equal before the law and have the rights and duties established in this declaration without distinction as to race, sex language, creed or any other factor.

398 The purposes of the United Nations are:
3. To achieve international cooperation in solving international problems of an economic, social, cultural or humanitarian character, and in promoting and encouraging respect for human rights and for fundamental freedoms for all without distinction as to race, sex, language or religion.

399 See supra, pp. 8-10.

400 Compare, for example, *Marckx,* Eur. Ct. H R, Series A, No. 16, in which the European Court was, perhaps, premature in its identification of the acceptance of equal treatment of illegitimate children in all 21 member states of the Council of Europe, and *Ozturk,* Eur. Ct. H R, No. 73 in which the Court was tardy in recognizing legal evolution by holding that since proceedings for traffic violations had been decriminalized, there was no need for an interpreter in such proceedings. See Merrills, *Development,* pp. 72-5 and J.S. Davidson, 'The European Convention on Human Rights and the "Illegitimate" Child', in D. Freestone, *Children and the Law* (Hull: University of Hull Press, 1990), pp. 94-7.

401 At p. 160.

402 *Judicial Guarantees in States of Emergency*, para. 24.

403 *Case 10.006 (Peru),* loc. cit., supra, note 76.

404 Inter-American Commission on Human Rights, *1992-1993 Annual Report* 207 at 211.

405 *Case 9855 (Haiti)* [1988] IAYHR 244.
406 *Case 9260 (Jamaica)* [1988] IAYHR 256 at 270.
407 Ibid.
408 *Cases 10.147, 10.181, 10.240, 10.262, 10.309, 10.311 (Argentina)*, Inter-American Commission on Human Rights, *1992-93 Annual Report* 41 at 48, para. 39.
409 Inter-American Commission on Human Rights, *Annual Report 1979-80,* 143.
410 Inter-American Commission on Human Rights, *1993 Annual Report* 521.
411 See, for example, the discussion on the rights of the family above at pp. 326-8.
412 See above pp. 32-3.
413 See AG/RES. 1044 (XX-O/90), AG/RES. 1112 (XXI-91) and AG/RES. 1169 (XXII-92).
414 Inter-American Commission on Human Rights, *1992-93 Annual Report* 224. This call on other Member States to ratify does not appear to have had any great effect. As of 1994 no further ratifications had been made to the Protocol.
415 See Philip Alston, 'The Committee on Economic, Social and Cultural Rights' in Philip Alston (ed), *The United Nations and Human Rights* (Oxford: Clarendon Press, 1992), p. 475.
416 See supra, p. 33.
417 See Article 55(a) UN Charter.
418 Inter-American Commission on Human Rights, 'Report on Cuba', *1994 Annual Report* 142 at 149-50.
419 Ibid., at 148-9.
420 Supra, pp. 324-6.
421 'Report on Cuba', loc. cit., supra at 152.
422 See 'Concluding Observations' by the Committee on Economic, Social and Cultural Rights on New Zealand's *First Periodic Report under the International Covenant on Economic, Social and Cultural Rights (E/1990/5/Add.5, 1 February 1991)*, E/1990/5/Add.5, 11 and 12, observation B.8.
423 Article 13(2)(e) PSS.
424 Article 14(3) PSS.
425 Article 14(2) PSS.
426 Supra, pp. 326-8.
427 Article 17(a) PSS.
428 Article 17(b) PSS.
429 Article 17(c) PSS.
430 Article 18(a) PSS.
431 Article 17(b) PSS.
432 Article 17(d) PSS.

8 Conclusion

The use of the term 'conclusion' suggests a degree of finality which is unwarranted in a work of this kind. Since the main focus of this book has been the development of the inter-American human rights system and its continuing evolution, it provides only the briefest synopsis of what has been accomplished to date and emerging trends within the system. Rather than being a conclusion therefore, this short chapter constitutes an appraisal of what has been achieved by the system so far, and some speculation on the trajectory which the system might follow in ensuing years.

As indicated in chapter 1, the development of the inter-American human rights system cannot be dissociated from the emergence and evolution of the Inter-American Commission on Human Rights and its powers. The conception and creation of the Commission as an entity without formal legal status within the framework of the OAS signalled a lack of confidence and security by the American states in institutions and instruments of supranational control. Despite this initial lack of confidence, the Commission was able to demonstrate through its promotional and protective activities that it could accomplish useful work and was deserving of the trust of the OAS Member States. The fact that the Commission was subsequently endowed with the capacity to entertain individual petitions alleging violation of certain favoured rights in the American Declaration even before it became an institution of the OAS, bears witness to its fortitude and the culture of respect which it had forged among the majority of the American states at that time. Its eventual transformation into an institution of the OAS by the amendment of the Charter by the Protocol of Buenos Aires in 1967 provided it with the necessary foundation from which to take its promotional and protective activities to a new level. The use of its various mechanisms in both the field of first and second generation rights provide the Commission with a battery of useful weapons with which to pursue its mandate. The country reports and on-site investigations allow the Commission to gather useful and necessary information not only for the purposes of investigating alleged delinquencies by Member States, but also to assist those states in a constructive way. As we saw in chapter 1, the promotion and protection of human rights in all their guises does not necessarily entail a prosecutorial function, but also comprehends constructive engagement of states and the

372

provision of advice and technical support. A salient point to remember about the Commission's competences under the Charter is that they apply to every state in the Western Hemisphere. Even during a period in which the United States of America was unwilling to commit itself to international human rights obligations by way of treaty, it was compelled to respond to the inter-American Commission to answer questions about a variety of human rights issues, including the vexed issues of abortion and capital punishment.

The Commission's role in the operation of other inter-American human rights instruments also deserves comment. As noted in chapter 2, the Commission performs a vital function in the operation of the Inter-American Convention on Human Rights. Not only is the Commission required to assess whether the formal requirements for admissibility have been met, but also whether the petitioner has demonstrated a *prima facie* breach of the Convention. It is also the Commission which performs the central task of conciliation under Article 48(1)(f). In the absence of a final settlement, it is also the Commission which decides whether or not a case should be remitted to the Court where the allegedly delinquent state has accepted the contentious jurisdiction of that institution. While the Commission has had little opportunity to exercise these functions, its practice in remitting cases to the Court has not been free from criticism. It seems reasonably clear that the Commission ought to have sent the *Schmidt Case* to the Court, but failed to do so. The conditions under which the Commission should remit a case to the Court has now been clearly established in the Court's advisory opinions in *Compulsory Membership* and *Certain Attributes*.[1] Once the Commission has decided that a case should be considered by the Court, it is the only body having locus standi to present the case: the individual has no right of appearance. Even here, the Commission's work is not done, since, if the state is found in breach of the Convention, the Commission is then required either to negotiate damages between the parties or to present arguments in the damages phase before the Court. The Commission thus occupies a pivotal position in all aspects of contentious proceedings. It should be remarked that the Commission will also have a role to play under the Protocol of San Salvador when that instrument comes into force. Not only will the Commission be the main destination for periodic reports, but it will also be required to perform the same functions in individual petitions alleging breach of Article 8 and 13 of the Protocol as it does under the Convention. As noted above, the Commission has responsibility under the Inter-American Convention to Prevent and Punish Torture since States Parties are required to report to the Commission on the measures which they have taken in conformity with their obligations under this instrument.[2]

Although the Inter-American Court of Human Rights is still a relatively youthful institution in comparison to the Commission, it has nevertheless already made a decisive impact on the development of the inter-American human rights system. Much of its early work involved the elaboration of principles of inter-American human rights law through the utilization of its advisory jurisdiction by a number of OAS Member States and the Commission. Among its more notable rulings under this jurisdiction have been the finding that the American Declaration represented legally binding norms within the Charter system, thus confirming the Commission's ruling in the '*Baby Boy*' *Case*,[3] the elaboration of rules concerning reservations to human rights treaties and the requirement of exhausting local remedies within the American Convention. The germ of interpretation and elaboration of the substantive rights protected by the Convention can also be found in the Court's advisory rulings. The resolution of questions concerning nationality and freedom of expression, for example, have been subject to extensive analysis. This is in marked contrast to the elaboration of an inter-American human rights jurisprudence under the Court's contentious jurisdiction. Here the Court has been faced with allegations of disappearances, arbitrary killings and excessive use of force against civilians by members of the military. These cases have required the Court to expend much time on dealing with questions of evidence and proof, very often in the face of a recalcitrant respondent state. The *Honduran Disappearance Cases* represent a landmark in the Court's development of its practice and procedure in the area of gathering and weighing evidence. They also stand as another clear signal against the inhuman and barbaric practice of enforced disappearance which has been the scourge of Latin America for too many years. The cases under the Court's contentious jurisdiction have been very much 'fact-driven' and have not therefore allowed it the opportunity to elaborate upon the substance of the rights violated. This, however, may be compared to the way in which the Commission has developed its jurisprudence. Many of the early cases dealt with by the Commission did not, because of their nature, admit of detailed analysis. Again, the Commission was more concerned with garnering information than it was with elaborating the detailed content of the rights violated. The Commission was also faced with Member States which were unwilling to comply with reasonable requests for further and better information, and it was therefore required to employ the use of its presumptive powers under its Regulations more often than not. In recent years, however, there has been a discernible shift in the Commission's approach. There is more explicit analysis of the content of the rights violated and a greater willingness to integrate the jurisprudence of other human rights institutions, particularly that of the European Commission and Court. In addition to this, the Commission has provided a number of very useful reports which were to elaborate the meaning of certain rights. Examples of this are its report on 'desacato' laws and minimum standards for the protection of the judicial branch of government.[4]

It is perhaps also pertinent to mention that both the Commission and the Court have consistently articulated the opinion that the inter-American system is founded upon the precepts of representative democracy, the rule of law, the principle of legality and the separation of powers. Each of these has been elaborated by both institutions, and there seems to be little doubt that these concepts are viewed in a most traditional way. The ideology of the inter-American institutions is therefore heavily and unashamedly formed in the classic Western-liberal tradition. This tradition, as currently articulated and implemented, may have its critics,[5] but it provides the theoretical backdrop against which these institutions measure human rights standards. The future direction of the inter-American human rights system is undoubtedly heavily bound up with the maintenance and progress of representative democracy in the Americas. It may be that the symbiotic relationship between effective protection of human rights and democracy is demonstrable by the fact that democratic regimes are more prepared to respond constructively to the Inter-American Commission when they are the subject of alleged breaches and that such regimes are also more likely to accept the contentious jurisdiction of the Inter-American Court. This is not to say that all the forms of democracy practised in the Western Hemisphere are perfect, but is does suggest that human rights have a better chance of protection within states with such a form of political organization. Stated briefly, there is an organic relationship not only between first and second generation human rights, but also between those human rights and the political system which inspires them. The inter-American human rights system therefore has a substantial and continuing role to play in helping to define and underpin progress in these areas.

Notes

[1] See supra, pp. 185-7.

[2] See supra, pp. 62-5.

[3] See supra, pp. 20-30.

[4] See supra, pp. 295-6 and 318-20.

[5] See S. J. Schnably, 'The Santiago Commitment as a Call to Democracy in the United States: Evaluating the OAS Role in Haiti, Peru and Guatemala' (1994) 25 *Inter-American Law Review* 393.

Bibliography

Alston, P. 'The Committee on Economic, Social and Cultural Rights' in *The United Nations and Human Rights* (Oxford: Clarendon Press, 1992).

Arechega, J. 'The Amendments to the Rules of Procedure by the International Court of Justice' (1973) 6 AJIL 1.

Ball, M. *The Organization of American States in Transition* (Durham NC: Duke University Press, 1969).

Beddard, R. *Human Rights in Europe* (Cambridge: Grotius, 2nd edn., 1993).

Bowett, D.W. *The Law of International Institutions* (London: Sweet and Maxwell, 4th edn., 1982).

Brownlie, I. *Principles of International Law* (Oxford: Oxford University Press, 4th edn., 1990).

Buergenthal, T. 'The American Convention on Human Rights: Illusions and Hopes' (1971) 21 *Buffalo Law Review* 121.

Buergenthal, T. 'The Revised OAS Charter and the Protection of Human Rights' (1975) 69 AJIL 828.

Buergenthal, T. 'The American and European Convention on Human Rights: Similarities and Differences' (1980) 30 AmULR 155.

Buergenthal, T. 'The Inter-American Court of Human Rights' (1982) 76 AJIL 1.

Buergenthal, T. 'The Advisory Practice of the Inter-American Human Rights Court' (1985) 79 AJIL 1.

Buergenthal T. and R. Norris, eds. *Human Rights: the Inter-American System* (Dobbs Ferry, NY: Oceana, 1984).

Buergenthal, T., R. Norris and D. Shelton, eds. *Protecting Human Rights in the Americas: Selected Problems* (Kehl-am-Rhein: NP Engel Verlag, 2nd edn., 1986).

Burr R.N. and R.D. Hussey, eds. *Documents on Inter-American Co-operation 1881-1948: Vol II* (Philadelphia: University of Pennsylvannia Press, 1955).

Cabott, W. *The Western Hemisphere: Its Influence on United States' Policies to the End of Word War II* (Austin, Tx and London: University of Texas Press, 1968).

Camargo, P. 'The American Convention on Human Rights' (1970) 3 HRJ 333.

Carnegie Endowment for International Peace, *The International Conferences for American States: First Supplement 1933-40* (Washington: Carnegie Endowment for International Peace, 1940).

Cerna, C. 'U.S. Death Penalty tested before the Inter-American Commission on Human Rights' (1992) 10 NQHR 155.

Cerna, C. 'The Structure and Functioning of the Inter-American Court of Human Rights (1979-92)' (1993) LXIV BYIL 135.

Cohn, H. 'International Fact-Finding Processes and the Rule of Law' (1977) 18 *The Review of the International Commission of Jurists* 43.

Connell-Smith, G. *The Inter-American System* (London: Oxford University Press, 1966).

Davidson, J.S. 'The European Convention on Human Rights and the "Illegitimate" Child' in D. Freestone, ed. *Children and the Law* (Hull: University of Hull Press, 1990).

Davidson, J.S. *Human Rights* (Buckingham: Open University Press, 1993).

Davidson, J.S. 'Remedies for Violations of the American Convention on Human Rights' (1995) 44 ICLQ 405.

Dijk P. van and G.J.H. van Hoof, *Theory and Practice of the European Convention on Human Rights* (Deventer: Kluwer, 2nd edn., 1991).

Dreier, J. 'New Wine in Old Bottles: The Changing Inter-American System' (1968) 22 *International Organization* 47.

Dunshee de Abranches, C.D. 'Comparative Study of the UN Covenants and the Draft Inter-American Convention on Human Rights' (1968) *Inter-American Yearbook of Human Rights* 169.

Dwyer, A.S. 'The Inter-American Court of Human Rights: Towards Establishing an Effective Regional Contentious Jurisdiction' (1990) *13 Boston College International and Comparative Law Review*.

Ermacora, F. 'Partiality and Impartiality of Human Rights Enquiry Commissions of International Organizations' in *Amicorum Discipulorumque Liber I, René Cassin* (Paris: Pedone, 1969).

Fenwick, C.G. 'The Ninth International Conference of American States' (1948) 4 AJIL 553.

Fenwick, C.G. 'The Charter of the O.A.S. as the "Law of the Land"' (1953) 47 AJIL 281.

Fenwick, C.G. *The Organization of American States* (Washington: 1963).

Fitzmaurice, G. 'The Law and Procedure of the International Court of Justice: Treaty Interpretation and other Treaty Points' (1951) 28 BYIL 1.

Fitzmaurice, G. 'The Law and Procedure of the International Court of Justice: Treaty Interpretation and other Treaty Points' (1957) 33 BYIL 220.

Fox, D. 'Inter-American Commission on Human Rights finds United States in Violation' (1988) 82 AJIL 601.

Franck, T. and H. Fairley, 'Procedural Due Process in Human Rights Fact-Finding by International Agencies' (1980) 74 AJIL 313.

Frowein, J.A. 'The European and American Conventions on Human Rights: A Comparison' (1980) 1 HRLJ 44.

Gilbert, G. *Aspects of Extradition Law* (Dordrecht: Nijhoff, 1991).

Gray, C. 'Remedies for Individuals under the European Convention on Human Rights' (1980) *Human Rights Review* 153.

Gray, C. *Judicial Remedies in International Law* (Oxford: Clarendon Press, 1987).

Haraszti, G. *Some fundamental problems of the Law of Treaties* (Budapest: Akdémia Kiadó, 1973).

Harris, D.J., M. O'Boyle and C. Warbrick, *Law of the European Convention on Human Rights* (London: Butterworths, 1995).

Higgins, R. 'Derogations under Human Rights Treaties' (1979) 48 BYIL 281.

Inter-American Juridical Committee, *Draft Declaration of the Rights and Duties of Man and Accompanying Report* (Washington DC: Pan-American Union, 1948).

Inter-American Juridical Committee, *Report to accompany the Definitive Draft Declaration of the International Rights and Duties of Man and Accompanying Report* (Washington DC: Pan-American Union, 1948).

Inter-American Juridical Committee, *Study of the Juridical Relationship Between Respect for Human Rights and the Exercise of Democracy* (Washington DC: Pan-American Union, 1960).

International Law Commission, *Yearbook of the International Law Commission*, Vol. ii (1966).

Jacobs, F. *The European Convention on Human Rights* (Oxford: Clarendon Press, 1975).

Jones, J. 'The Nottebohm Case' (1956) 5 ICLQ 230.

Kaplan, F. 'Combating Political Torture in Latin America: An Analysis of the Organization of American States' Inter-American Convention to Prevent and Punish Torture' (1989) XV *Brooklyn Journal of International Law* 399.

Kunz, J. 'The Bogota Charter of the Organization of American States' (1948) 22 AJIL 568.

Kunz, J. 'The Nottebohm Case (Second Phase)' (1960) 54 AJIL 335.

Le Blanc, L. J. *The Organization of American States and the Promotion and Protection of Human Rights* (The Hague: Nijhoff, 1977).

Manger, W. 'Reform of the OAS: The 1967 Buenos Aires Protocol of Amendment to the Charter of Bogota: An Appraisal' (1968) 10 *Journal of Inter-American Studies*.

McGoldrick, D. *The Human Rights Committee: Its Role in the Development of the International Covenant on Civil and Political Rights* (Oxford: Clarendon Press, 1991).

McNair, A. *The Law of Treaties* (Cambridge: Cambridge University Press, 1961).

Medina Quiroga, C. *The Battle of Human Rights* (Dordrecht: Nijhoff, 1988).

Merrills, J.G. *The Development of International Law by the European Court of Human Rights* (Manchester: Manchester University Press, 2nd edn., 1993).

Morrison, C. *The Dynamics of Development in the European Human Rights Convention System* (The Hague: Nijhoff, 1981).

Mower, A.G.. *Regional Human Rights: A Comparative Study of the Western European and Inter-American Systems* (New York: Greenwood Press, 1991).

Nolan-Collenzo, J. 'A legislative history of the right to life in the Inter-American System' in B. Ramcharan, ed. *The Right to Life in International Law* (Dordrecht: Nijhoff, 1985).

Parker, M. 'Other Treaties: the Inter-American Court of Human Rights Defines its Advisory Jurisdiction' (1983) 33 AmULR 211.

Robertson, A.H. 'Revision of the Charter of the Organization of American States' (1968) 17 ICLQ 345.

Rosenne, S. *The Law and Practice of the International Court* (Dordrecht: Nijhoff, 1985).

Rosenne, S. *The World Court: What it is and How it Works* (Dordrecht: Kluwer, 4th edn., 1989).

Santoscoy, B. *La Commission interaméricaine des droits de l'homme et le développement de sa compétence par le système des pétitions individuelles* (Paris: Presses Universitaires de France, 1995).

Schabas, W. *The Abolition of the Death Penalty in International Law* (Cambridge: Grotius, 1993).

Schnably, S.J. 'The Santiago Commitment as a call to democracy in the United States: Evaluating the OAS Role in Haiti, Peru and Guatemala' (1994) 25 *Inter-American Law Review* 393.

Schreiber, A. *The Inter-American Commission on Human Rights* (Leyden: Sijthoff, 1970).

Schwelb, E. 'The Law of Treaties and Human Rights' (1975, 16 Archiv des Volkrechts) repr. in W. Reisman and B. Weston, eds. *Toward World Order and Human Dignity* (1976).

Sepúlveda, C. 'Reform of the Charter of the Organization of American States' (1972-III) 137 *Hague Recueil* 83.

Shelton, D. 'Abortion and the Right to Life in the Inter-American System: The Case of "Baby Boy"' (1981) 2 HRLJ 309.

Shelton, D. 'Judicial Review of State Action by International Courts' (1989) 12 *Fordham International Law Journal* 361.

Shelton, D. 'Representative Democracy and Human Rights in the Western Hemisphere' (1991) 12 HRLJ 353.

Sinclair, I. *The Vienna Convention on the Law of Treaties* (Manchester, Manchester University Press, 2nd edn., 1984).

Thomas, A. van W. and A. *The Organization of American States* (Dallas: Southern Methodist University Press, 1963).

Trindade, C. *The Application of the Local Remedies Rule* (Cambridge: Cambridge University Press, 1984).

Trindade, C. 'Co-existence and Co-ordination of Mechanisms of International Protection of Human Rights' (1987-II) 202 *Hague Recueil*.

Vargas, M. 'Individual Access to the Inter-American Court of Human Rights' (1984) *New York University Journal of International Law and Politics* 601.

Vasak, K. 'Human Rights: A Thirty Year Struggle' (1977) *Unesco Courier*.

Index